MORMONISM

A Faith for All Cultures

Mormonism

A Faith for All Cultures

F. LaMond Tullis
General Editor

Arthur Henry King,
Spencer J. Palmer,
Douglas F. Tobler
Associate Editors

Brigham Young University Press

Library of Congress Cataloging in Publication Data
Main entry under title:

Mormonism: a faith for all cultures.

"Edited versions of remarks made at the regional sessions of the Expanding Church Symposium."

1. Mormons and Mormonism—Congresses. I. Tullis, F. LaMond, 1935–
BX8605.M67 230'.9'33 78-7665
ISBN 0-8425-1282-9

Brigham Young University Press, Provo, Utah 84602
Printed in the United States of America
9/78 3M 33023

CONTENTS

Preface, F. LaMond Tullis vii
List of Contributors xiii
Introduction, Martin B. Hickman xxv

CULTURAL DIVERSITY IN THE UNIVERSAL CHURCH
Introduction, Arthur Henry King 3
Essay, Noel B. Reynolds 7
Comments, Hugh B. Nibley 22
Comments, John L. Sorenson 28

THE CHURCH IN ALL THE WORLD
Introduction, F. LaMond Tullis 35
The Church in Europe: Challenges of the Second Century
Introduction, Douglas F. Tobler 37
The Church in French-speaking Europe, Charles A. Didier 44
The Church in Germany, Austria, and Switzerland, F. Enzio Busche 48
The Church in Scandinavia and Finland, Bo G. Wennerlund 51
The Church in England, Peter L. Morley 57
The Church in Italy, Dan Jorgensen 64
Comments, James R. Christianson 65
Questions and Answers 68

Church Development Issues Among Latin Americans
Introduction, F. LaMond Tullis 85
Gospel, Culture, and Leadership Development in Latin America, Harold Brown 106
Mormonism and the Chicano, Orlando Rivera 115
Church Schools in Mexico, Efraín Villalobos Vásquez 126
Building Stakes That Work: Form and Substance in Church Organization, Enrique Rittscher 135
Questions and Answers 141
The Challenges of Church Programs from the Vantage Point of Asian Members
Introduction, Spencer J. Palmer 151
The Church in the Philippines, Augusto Lim 160
The Church in Korea, Rhee Ho Nam 163
The Church in Japan, Seiji Katanuma 169
Comments, R. Lanier Britsch 171
Comments, Spencer J. Palmer 173
Questions and Answers 176
CULTURE AND THE GOSPEL
Introduction, Gordon C. Whiting 181
Mormon Views of Religious Resemblances, Spencer J. Palmer 185
The Role of Religious Symbolism: East and West, Truman G. Madsen 207
Mormon Doctrine and Traditional Japanese Patterns: Suggestions from a Culture of Sight, Seiji Katanuma 226
Teaching Across Dispensations: A Comparative Religion Perspective on the Challenges of Being a Worldwide Church, Gordon C. Thomasson 236
SECULARIZATION AND THE GOSPEL
Introduction, Douglas F. Tobler 279
Mormonism and the Secularization of Religions in the Modern World, Ernst Benz 282
The Political Challenges: Mormons, Governments, and Politics, Robert S. Jordan with Parley W. Newman, Jr. 294
The Church in a Secular World: Freedom, Economic Efficiency, and Equality, J. R. Kearl and Clayne L. Pope 309
Mormonism and the Secular Philosophies: Competing Creeds in the Twentieth Century, Douglas F. Tobler 328
Comments: Elder Neal A. Maxwell 346
Comments: Louis C. Midgley 348
Questions and Answers 354
Epilogue, F. LaMond Tullis 361

PREFACE

F. LaMond Tullis

From among six people in an obscure nineteenth-century village in northeastern America, The Church of Jesus Christ of Latter-day Saints, frequently referred to as The Mormons, has grown and expanded dramatically. Now it includes members in virtually every American city and town, and outside the United States the faith touches the lives of hundreds of thousands of people holding citizenship in more than half the nations of the earth.

Every Mormon knows of the historical travails. The Saints, persecuted for having a prophet who had conversed with God and his heavenly messengers, vilified by writers and politicians, driven from their homes and settlements by mob and bullet, nevertheless survived. In the isolated wilderness of the American West the faithful laid the foundations of a religious and cultural fortress that has flourished to the present day.

With this legacy as both a guide and a challenge, we are attempting in this generation to offer "every nation, kindred, tongue, and people" an opportunity to hear the gospel of Jesus Christ. The scale of this endeavor is new to us, for never before has the Church attempted to take the gospel message across as many boundaries of ancestral customs, languages, nationalities, and races as now. The magnitude of such an attempt—and the drama that it represents—have presented new problems. For one, the diversity of membership we are experiencing in the Church is both blessing and challenging the collective spirit of Mormonism. Change is upon us. And we must try to understand it.

"It has the prospect of being a stimulating experience," was an initial comment to our proposal to hold a series of Brigham Young University Centennial symposia on culture and Mormonism in its new worldwide setting. There was substance to that prospect because on our minds were not only the common religious bonds of our people but also cultural differences among Mormons today and the serious implications some of these have for us.

The subject matter was intriguing. Many people, qualified by experience and commitment to the Church, were prepared to talk about it. These included an apostle, three other General Authorities of the Church, four Regional Representatives of the Quorum of the Twelve, stake and mission presidents, scholars, and administrators. And there was a non-Mormon—Professor Ernst Benz of the University of Marburg in West Germany, a remarkably insightful observer of Mormonism and one of the world's leading scholars on comparative religions.

In all, thirty-eight participants joined us at Brigham Young University for three days of discussions about the relation of secular culture to the gospel of Jesus Christ and to the expanding Church. Among those hosted by BYU's sponsoring College of Social Sciences were citizens of Britain, France, Germany, Guatemala, Japan, Korea, Mexico, the Philippines, Sweden, and the United States of America. The Church had expanded universally. New representatives of its congregations from all over the earth had come to BYU to discuss some of the meaning of that expansion in the lives of Mormons everywhere.

Such a gathering would likely produce both enthusiasm and sobriety among participants and audiences alike. It did. To hear of the growth of the Church, to see the quality of leadership exemplified in the participants, to listen to them speak of the bonds that unite us in the spirit of the gospel, to note their affirmation of the spiritual substance of those bonds, to enjoy their humor and the warmth of their personalities—these were stimulating to all of us. To become more closely aware of the problems that face us, of the tough decisions yet to be made, of the challenges to mind and spirit that a worldwide expansion presents; to face the imminent complexity of policies about the Church's relations with the world—all that was sobering.

This book attempts to convey to a general Church audience the enthusiasm and spiritual uplift of the symposia as well as some of the sobering thoughts. It is done in the spirit of enlightenment, not worry, dissension, or meddling. We have no doubt that in the end the gospel will prevail. We also believe that the contributions of Mormons everywhere will be improved when we better understand the gospel and the diverse peoples who are accepting it. We can thereby profit from Jacob's admonition: Obey the commandments. And learn (see 2 Nephi 9:29).

The essays begin with Noel Reynolds's general discussion of the gospel and culture, in which he draws parallels with some of the difficult cultural decisions confronting the Church a few years after Christ's ascension. Regional sections on Europe, Latin America, and Asia follow. In these sections, leaders of the Church from among its congregations east, west, and south speak with insight, passion, and testimony to the North American Mormon. After these regional presentations come essays on culture and the gospel and on secularization and the gospel. The language of faith and practical insight and the language of faith and scholarship are thereby combined in one volume. The thoughts expressed in all these sections are the authors', and they alone wish to be responsible for them.

We thank Dean Martin Hickman and the College of Social Sciences for financial and administrative help in organizing the symposia and in the preparation of this book. The University Centennial Committee, chaired by Lorin F. Wheelwright, gave its blessing and support to the symposia, as did the University administration, which provided facilities and encouragement. Thanks to the BYU A Cappella Choir under the direction of Ralph Woodward for singing the hymn prepared for the occasion—"Every Kindred, Tongue and People"—with words by Arthur Henry King and music by Robert P. Manookin; to John T. Longhurst for specially arranged carillon sessions; and to Michael Kawasaki for the poster he designed (see front cover).

Neither the symposia nor this book would, of course, have become a reality without the contributions of the participants and discussants. In addition to those mentioned in the "list of contributors" to this volume, we also give special thanks to Elder Gordon B. Hinckley for his BYU devotional address keyed to the theme of the symposia; to Jeffrey R. Holland for chairing the panel on Christ and cultural resemblances and otherwise giving support to the organization of the symposia; to Russell N. Horiuchi for moderating the discussion in the Asian regional panel; and to President Dallin H. Oaks and Vice-president Robert K. Thomas for their remarks, which officially opened and closed the BYU symposia on the expanding Church.

EVERY KINDRED, TONGUE, AND PEOPLE

ARTHUR HENRY KING

ROBERT P. MANOOKIN

right in an - y land; The wrong, by gos - pel truth with-
west - ern church grew strong He bade men stay where they be-
straits to boist-'rous Horn, To sun - set from the gates of
stand; But first we fol - low, voice and
long To add new Zi - on to the
morn, With those long dead and those new
hand, Our Sav - ior, Mas - ter, Lord.
throng And strength - en all the rest.
born, We praise His ho - ly name.

LIST OF CONTRIBUTORS

Ernst Benz

Professor Benz, an internationally known scholar, was born in 1907, the son of a railroad engineer. Following his preparatory studies, he began his university career in 1925 at Tübingen, where he later graduated with a doctorate in philosophy. He then studied in Berlin under prominent theologians such as Van Harnack, Seeberg, and Deissman and subsequently received a second doctorate, this time in theology. Dr. Benz accepted positions at the Martin Luther University of Halle-Wittenberg, next at the Luther Academy in Estonia, and finally at the University of Marburg/Lahn, Germany, where he stayed until his recent retirement. A highly respected religious scholar, Dr. Benz has been a visiting professor in Rome, Paris, Brussels, Stockholm, Vienna, Athens, Cambridge, Tokyo, and at several prominent universities in America. He is a member of many academies of science and has been an extremely productive scholar, authoring over fifty books and four hundred articles and coediting the journal *Zeitschrift für Religions und Geistesgeschichte* for more than twenty-five years. Among his best known and recent works are: *Der Heilige Geist in Amerika* (1968); *Die Vision* (1969); and *Neue Religionen* (1970). Dr. Benz is married to Dr. Brigitte von Boxberger, and they are the parents of three sons.

R. Lanier Britsch

R. Lanier Britsch, associate professor of history, began his teaching career at Brigham Young University in 1966. Earlier he had earned B.A. and M.A. degrees from BYU and a Ph.D. in Asian Studies (History of Asian Religions) from Claremont Graduate School. He is the recipient of several fellowships, including a National Defense Foreign Language Grant, a Fulbright Grant for a summer of study in India, and an LDS Church Historian's Fellowship. He is an active member of the Asian Studies program at BYU and is a member of the Mormon History Association, the American Society of Missiology, and the International Society for Mission Studies. He is the author of a number of articles relating to the history of the LDS Church in Asia and the Pacific and is currently writing a history of the Church in those areas. He is also a counselor in the presidency of the Orem, Utah, Sharon Stake. JoAnn Murphy is his wife. They have six children.

Harold Brown

Harold Brown, originally from the Mormon colonies in Chihuahua, Mexico, and who now makes his home in Mexico City, is Regional Representative of the Twelve to Guatemala and El Salvador. His association with the Church in Latin America has been long and significant—as a special assistant in the Mexican Mission in the 1940s during a difficult period of Church history there, as a mission president in Argentina, as the president of the first stake in Mexico, and now as a Regional Representative. He has studied at Harvard University's Graduate School of Public Administration. At least one of his Harvard seminar papers (which deals with the Church in Argentina) is still on file there.

F. Enzio Busche

Elder Busche was born in 1930 in Dortmund, Germany. During the closing months of the war, when he was fourteen, Elder Busche was inducted into the military, thereby having his studies interrupted for a time. Following a period of imprisonment by the Americans, Elder Busche finished his business studies at Dortmund and then spent three years in specialized technical training with both domestic and foreign printing firms. Thereafter he studied business management for a year at the universities in Bonn and Freiburg. In 1956 he assumed major responsibility for his father's printing establishment, and upon his father's death Elder Busche became a partner and the business manager of the firm. Since that time the firm has expanded and diversified, now employing over five hundred workers. Elder Busche married Jutta Baum in 1955, and they have four children. Joining the Church in 1958, Elder Busche has served as branch clerk, branch president, elder's quorum president, district president, mission counselor, and Regional Representative. Recently he was called as a member of the First Quorum of Seventy.

James R. Christianson

Born in Provo, Utah, in 1932, James R. Christianson served a mission in Switzerland and Austria from 1953 to 1955 and, in 1957, received a bachelor's degree from Brigham Young University. He has worked in the Church's educational system since 1957, having served as principal of the Roosevelt, and Moab (Utah) seminaries, and later as coordinator of Church education in the southern states and in continental Europe. He received a master's degree from BYU in 1962 and a Ph.D. in 1968 from the University of Kansas. Dr. Christianson married Helen Lance, and they are the parents of eight children.

Charles Didier

Elder Didier was born in 1935 in Ixelles, Belgium. Following secondary school preparation in the economics section, he entered the University of Liège (Belgium) and studied in the commercial section, receiving, after two years, the title of Master in Economics. Contacted in 1951 by missionaries tracting in his neighborhood, Elder Didier was baptized six years later. He worked for a machine tool company and a timber company before being asked to assist at the Church's distribution center in Frankfurt, Germany. He returned to Belgium in 1968 to manage the Liège distribution center and remained there until 1970 when he was called to serve as mission president of the France-Switzerland Mission. Elder Didier returned to Frankfurt in 1973 as European area manager of the Church's distribution and translation services. His long experience in the Church has thus combined with his professional concerns. He met his wife in the Church, and they are the parents of two sons. The Church service that preluded Elder Didier's call to serve in the First Quorum of Seventy includes teaching positions in the Sunday School, MIA, and priesthood quorums, branch president, and Regional Representative. He was called to the First Quorum of Seventy in October, 1975.

Martin B. Hickman

Martin B. Hickman is dean of the College of Social Sciences and professor of political science at Brigham Young University. After obtaining his doctorate from the University of Utah in 1954, he served until 1961 with the Department of State, fulfilling assignments in Hamburg, Hong Kong, and Berlin. A member of various professional organizations, he has published two books—*Problems of American Foreign Policy* and *The Military and American Society*—and numerous papers on American foreign policy. He is married to JoAnn Emmett of Logan, and they are the parents of six daughters. He has served as a teacher in many organizations of the Church and as a member of a bishopric.

Robert S. Jordan

Robert S. Jordan was born in 1929 in Los Angeles, California. He received an A.B. degree from UCLA, a M.S. degree from the University of Utah, a Ph.D. degree from Princeton, and a D.Phil. degree from Oxford (St. Antony's College), where he was a Fulbright Scholar. Dr. Jordan has taught at several universities, including SUNY at Binghamton, George Washington University, University of Pittsburgh, BYU, and University of Sierra Leone (West Africa). In addition, he has had a varied consulting background in areas of education, space programs, Western European affairs, and international affairs. He is currently employed as director of research in the United Nations Institute for Training and Research. Dr. Jordan has authored, coauthored, and edited many books, including the Intergovernmental Organizations section of the *Political Handbook of the World,* 1975 edition. He has published in such journals as the *International Studies Quarterly, World Politics,* and *International Organization.* Dr. Jordan is married to Sara Jane Hatch, and they are the parents of four children. Currently, Robert Jordan is Coordinator of the Self-Study Institute for the New York, New York, Stake, having served previously as Sunday School president and ward clerk.

Seiji Katanuma

Seiji Katanuma received his degrees in higher education from Hokkaido National University, Japan. His publications have concentrated upon Japanese modern literature, with special emphasis upon Jugaku and Kokugaku, tracing both native and foreign forms. He has also published on Japanese comparative religion. He has been a visiting lecturer at Brigham Young University on two occasions, and is possibly the only native Japanese member of the Church teaching Japanese language and literature at the university level. Seiji Katanuma's Church activities include service as president, on two occasions, of the Sapporo Branch, counselor in an elders quorum presidency, and member of the education committee of the Japan East Mission. Currently he is first counselor in the Japan Sapporo Mission.

J. R. Kearl

A native of Logan, Utah, Dr. Kearl graduated with a B.A. degree from Utah State University. At the Massachusetts Institute of Technology he earned a Ph.D. in economics (1975), and later did post-doctoral work at Harvard University. Dr. Kearl's professional experience includes teaching at Harvard and at BYU, participating as discussant and instructor at professional meetings, consulting, and reviewing for two publishing firms. Numerous journal articles and other manuscripts are also credited to him. Concerning Church service, Dr. Kearl served in the Philippines as a missionary, as a counselor in a branch presidency, and as a member of the BYU First Stake high council. He and his wife Linda have three children.

Arthur Henry King

Arthur Henry King took his degrees at Cambridge 1928-1931 and Lund, Sweden 1931-1941. He was associate professor of English at Lund from 1941 to 1943 and in Stockholm from 1943 to 1945. He then joined the British Council (an independent organization that looks after British work in cultural and educational contacts overseas and thus specializes in cultural relations between countries), serving in Belgium, Iran, and Pakistan, and afterwards at the headquarters in charge of education. During the course of his career, therefore, Dr. King lived for fourteen years in a Lutheran country and for seven in Islamic countries. During the 1960s he attended many international conferences on education and made inspectorial journeys in Africa, Asia, and the Pacific, also lecturing in American universities. He has published on stylistics and on English as a foreign and second language. He joined the Church in 1966 when he was fifty-six years old, later serving as counselor in the Crawley Branch. On resigning from the British Council and taking up teaching English at Brigham Young University, he served on the Orem, Utah, South Stake high council, then on the BYU Sixth Stake high council. He also served on the Church Hymnbook Committee.

Augusto Alandy Lim

Augusto Alandy Lim has been president of the Manila, Philippines, Stake since 1973. Previously he had served as branch president, district president, and counselor to several mission presidents in the Philippines. He received his LLB from Suleiman University and now teaches law at the University of the East in Manila. President Lim also has a private law practice in Quezon City, the Philippines.

Truman G. Madsen

Truman G. Madsen received his B.S. and M.S. degrees from the University of Utah and his A.M. and Ph.D. degrees from Harvard University. Dr. Madsen is professor of philosophy at BYU and director of the Judeo-Christian area of its Religious Studies Center. He received the Karl G. Maeser Distinguished Teacher award in 1967, and currently occupies the Richard L. Evans Chair of Christian Understanding. A frequent contributor to Church magazines and scholarly journals, Dr. Madsen has also authored several books—among them, *Eternal Man* and *Four Essays on Love.* Forthcoming is an intellectual biography, *B. H. Roberts, His Life and Thought.* Dr. Madsen has served the Church as president of the New England mission and currently as vice-chairman of the adult committee of the Sunday School general board. He and his wife, Ann Nicholls, are the parents of four children.

Neal A. Maxwell

Born in Salt Lake City, Utah, Elder Neal A. Maxwell attended the University of Utah, where he obtained both his B.A. and M.A. degrees in political science. He served in the U.S. Infantry in World War II. For two years he was a legislative assistant to Senator Wallace F. Bennett, later returning to the University of Utah, where he served as assistant professor of political science, dean of students, and executive vice president. He was chairman of the Utah Constitutional Revision Committee, chairman of the United Fund Drive, and the recipient of honorary doctorates from the University of Utah, BYU, and Westminster College. Elder Maxwell had served as a bishop, a member of the YMMIA general board, a Regional Representative, Church commissioner of education, and managing director of the correlation department of the Church before becoming one of the presidents of the First Quorum of Seventy, his current calling. Elder Maxwell has authored several Church-related books. Among his most recent works are *Deposition of a Disciple,* and *That My Family Should Partake.* His speeches and writings have uplifted many hundreds of audiences and thousands of readers. He is married to Colleen Hinckley. They have four children.

Louis C. Midgley

Dr. Midgley received his bachelor's and master's degrees from the University of Utah before earning a Ph.D. from Brown University in 1965. Currently a professor of political science at BYU, Dr. Midgley is the author of several essays in political philosophy and is presently engaged in writing a manuscript on the subject of God in political philosophy. Married to Ireta Troth, Dr. Midgley has three children. He has served as branch president in the BYU Fourth Stake and is now teachers quorum adviser in his home ward.

Peter L. Morley

Peter L. Morley was born in 1924 in Stockport, England. He completed his education at Didsbury School in Manchester and was later employed by a marine insurance company. That employment was broken by a 4½-year service with the Royal Air Force in India. Following World War II, Morley qualified as an associate of the Chartered Insurance Institute and later as an associate of the Institute of Export. He has been employed in administrative positions with a linen hire/laundry firm and with a shipping group doing business in the Pacific region. Currently he is the Church's distribution manager for Great Britain. Morley and his wife, Lilian Rowlands, both joined the Church in 1961. They are the parents of five children. Peter Morley has served the Church in Great Britain as genealogy advisor, YMMIA president, stake and ward Sunday School president, high councilor, bishop, and president of the Manchester, England, Stake and is now Regional Representative of the Twelve.

Hugh W. Nibley

Professor Hugh Nibley was born in Portland, Oregon. An acknowledged scholar, he studied in California, receiving his B.A. from UCLA in 1934 and his Ph.D. from the University of California at Berkeley in 1938. Dr. Nibley joined the BYU faculty in 1946 and is now a professor emeritus. He is a member of Phi Beta Kappa, Pi Gamma Mu, Phi Kappa Phi, and Pi Sigma Alpha and has received the David O. McKay Humanities Award. He has authored several books, among them *Lehi in the Desert and the World of the Jaredites*, *Since Cumorah: New Voices from the Dust*, and his most recent work, *The Message of the Joseph Smith Papyri: An Egyptian Endowment*. Professor Nibley's articles are extensive, spanning both Church publications and professional journals. Also to his credit are a radio series on KSL Radio in Salt Lake City and several pamphlets and booklets. Dr. Nibley has been a much admired and much sought-after teacher and lecturer, inspiring scores of young scholars in many disciplines. He has served the Church in a variety of ways—as Sunday School teacher, elders quorum president, and member of the seventy's quorum. He married Phyllis Draper, and they have eight children.

Spencer J. Palmer

Spencer J. Palmer, professor of history and religion at Brigham Young University, received his higher education from Eastern Arizona College, BYU, and the University of California at Berkeley. In 1976 he was selected to receive the Karl G. Maeser Distinguished Research award. In 1977 he was appointed director of World Religions in the Religious Studies Center, also director of the World Affairs Center at BYU. In Church activities, Dr. Palmer served as president of the Korean Mission, as Regional Representative of the Twelve in Southeast Asia, and for the past three years as a member of the high council in the BYU Twelfth Stake. His publications include nine books and a variety of monographs on history and religion, studies of LDS missionary work in Asia, and a forthcoming volume in the Mormon Heritage Series entitled *Every Nation, Kindred, Tongue and People.* He is now engaged in research dealing with the cult of Confucius, specifically concerning temples and religious rites.

Clayne L. Pope

Born in 1940 in Emmett, Idaho, Dr. Clayne L. Pope received his B.A. degree from BYU, followed by M.A. and Ph.D. degrees in economics from the University of Chicago. His teaching experience includes service at the University of Michigan, the College of William and Mary, and his current position on the economics faculty at BYU. A member of several professional associations, Dr. Pope has also been both a discussant and participant in numerous professional conventions. He coauthored the volume *Economy, Society and Public Policy* and wrote a number of journal articles. Dr. Pope and his wife, Carolyn Moore, have two children. His Church experience includes Sunday School president, elders quorum president, and ward clerk.

Noel B. Reynolds

Dr. Reynolds, currently a member of the Department of Government at BYU, earned degrees at BYU (B.A.) and at Harvard (M.A., Ph.D.) and has been a recipient of many fellowships and awards, including the Harvard Graduate Prize Fellowship, the Richard M. Weaver Fellowship, a National Science Foundation traineeship, a Hinckley scholarship, and the honor of being his undergraduate college's valedictorian. Specializing in jurisprudence, Dr. Reynolds has published on judicial reasoning and has finished a study on the enforcement of morals in a free society. He has been involved in the World Congress of Legal Philosophy as rapporteur of one of four plenary sessions. Dr. Reynolds has also taught in the Department of Philosophy at BYU and has been chairman of that department, as well as having taught in the J. Reuben Clark Law School. He is married to Sydney Smith. They have nine children. Dr. Reynolds served a mission for the Church in South America, was a counselor in the presidency of the BYU Fourth stake, and recently served as bishop of the Orem, Utah, Twenty-Third Ward. Since returning from a sabbatical leave at Harvard University Law School, he has served the Church as his ward's scoutmaster.

Rhee Ho Nam

Rhee Ho Nam, president of the Seoul, Korea, Stake, and recently appointed Regional Representative of the Twelve, was born and educated in Japan. He was baptized into the Church by an LDS serviceman in Korea in 1954 and was influenced in his early Church experience by the presence and teachings of Dr. Kim Ho Jik, the first Korean convert. President Rhee served as branch president, as district president, and as counselor to three mission presidents before becoming Korea's first stake president. By profession, he has been a teacher of language and is especially proficient as an English instructor on the high school and university levels.

Enrique Rittscher

Enrique Rittscher, fluent in Spanish, English, and German, is a Regional Representative of the Twelve. Baptized into the Church in 1966, he has served as a stake president, a counselor to a stake president, and a branch president; and he has held other branch callings. Brother Rittscher, son of German immigrants to Guatemala, was educated in the German school in Guatemala until 1942, then at the New Mexico Military Institute for high school and junior college. Later he studied hotel administration at Cornell University. He is now employed as a marketing executive. Elder Rittscher is married to María Estella Gargollo, and they have six children.

Orlando Rivera

Orlando Rivera is a spiritual leader (having served as bishop of the Lucero Ward in Salt Lake City), a teacher (assistant professor of educational psychology at the University of Utah), an administrator (associate vice-president for academic affairs, University of Utah), and a civic worker (e.g., member of the board of directors of the Utah State Merit Council and the Salt Lake City Civil Service Commission). He is also keenly interested in minority affairs, having served as president of SOCIO from 1969 to 1971, and as a member of numerous committees and organizations seeking ways to improve the educational and employment opportunities of the Latin-American community in Utah.

John L. Sorenson

Currently professor of anthropology and sociology at Brigham Young University, Dr. John L. Sorenson has earned degrees from BYU, the California Institute of Technology, and the University of California, at Los Angeles (Ph.D. in anthropology, 1961). Dr. Sorenson has also been social sciences director for General Research Corporation and president of Bonneville Research Corporation. He has a vital interest in Mormonism and the cultural difficulties of the expanding Church, having authored several Mormon-related articles on this subject and having served as cochairman of the Conferences on the Language of the Mormons.

Gordon C. Thomasson

Gordon C. Thomasson received the A.B. degree from UCLA, majoring in psychology. He did graduate work in religion at BYU and subsequently at the University of California at Santa Barbara, where he was awarded the A.M. degree in religious studies. He is currently a Ph.D. candidate at Cornell University in an interdisciplinary program. He is the author of numerous articles, both in his field and on the culture, religion, and history of the Latter-day Saints. He is coauthor of the article, "Religious Education," in the current (15th) edition of the *Encyclopaedia Britannica*. He filled a mission in North Mexico, has been in several branch presidencies, and currently serves as a Sunday School teacher, a ward welfare project director, and a stake teacher development director.

Douglas F. Tobler

Born in 1936 in Cedar City, Utah, Douglas Tobler began his university studies at Brigham Young University in 1954, receiving his B.A. and M.A. degrees in 1961 and 1962. He subsequently taught at the University of Nebraska, Omaha, for two years (1965-1967) and then received the Ph.D. degree in Modern German and European Intellectual History in 1967 from the University of Kansas. At Kansas, Dr. Tobler was a U.S. Steel and University Fellow. He joined the BYU faculty in 1967 and has published articles and book reviews in American and European journals. In the Church, he served in the Swiss-Austrian Mission from 1956 to 1959 and has served as a bishop and twice as a branch president. He currently teaches the gospel doctrine class in the Orem, Utah, Twenty-sixth Ward Sunday School. Dr. Tobler is married to Carol J. Noble, and they have four children.

F. LaMond Tullis

Professor Tullis has been with the BYU Department of Government since 1969, having taught earlier at Arizona State University as well as lecturing in two universities in Peru. He has combined the practical world with the academic, working for several years as a journeyman electrician, later earning a Ph.D. from Harvard University (1969). Professor Tullis has authored two internationally distributed books—*Lord and Peasant in Peru* and *Politics and Social Change in Third World Countries*—and has published several journal articles and written numerous convention papers and manuscripts, some of which have dealt with the Mormon experience in Latin America. He served a mission in Central America, has been a stake high councilor and branch president in the BYU Fourth Stake, and currently is ward finance chairman in his home ward and scout trainer for the Alpine, Utah, Stake. Professor Tullis and his wife Marta Morrill are the parents of six children.

Efraín Villalobos Vásquez

Efraín Villalobos is general superintendent of the most important and influential private education system in Mexico—the LDS Church school system. Since 1974 Brother Villalobos has had administrative responsibility for thirty-four elementary schools and three secondary schools, with a total enrollment of nearly 10,000 students. He is a third-generation Mormon, and his family, from San Marcos, Hidalgo, comes from one of the oldest branches of the Church in Mexico. He received his higher education at Brigham Young University and the Universidad Autónoma de México.

Bo G. Wennerlund

Bo G. Wennerlund was born in 1926 in Örebro, Sweden. Since 1935, however, he has lived in Stockholm, where he met his wife, Maud, and where they have raised their eight children—four boys and four girls. Brother Wennerlund is currently employed as a purchasing manager of the grain department of one of Sweden's largest flour milling companies. He joined the Church in 1949, and his wife followed four years later. All four of their sons have served missions for the Church. His leadership abilities have been called upon in service to the Church, as he has served in the following positions: mission MIA superintendent, branch president, district president, assistant to the mission president, counselor to five mission presidents, and, since 1975, Regional Representative of the Twelve.

Gordon C. Whiting

Dr. Gordon C. Whiting earned a B.A. at the University of Minnesota, a M.A. at the University of Utah, and a Ph.D. at Michigan State University. He taught for six years at the University of Wisconsin—Madison before coming to the BYU Communications Department in 1974. Dr. Whiting is a member of Phi Beta Kappa, Phi Kappa Phi, the International Communication Association, and the American Association for the Advancement of Science. Besides his teaching duties, Dr. Whiting is director of the Communication Research Center at BYU. He has served the Church as stake clerk and as a member of a bishopric and is currently a counselor in the Oak Hills, Utah, Stake Sunday School.

INTRODUCTION

Martin B. Hickman

As Brigham Young University approached its Centennial in 1976, President Oaks challenged each college to make a significant contribution to that celebration. Only if each college met that challenge, President Oaks said, would the Centennial reflect the intellectual as well as the spiritual growth of the University during its first one hundred years. The College of Social Sciences responded to that challenge with all of the resources at its command. The result was a series of symposia including the following topics: Uncovering Meso-American Civilization; BYU and the History of Higher Education in America; The Mormon Role in the Settlement of the West; Mormons and the U.S. Constitution; The Gospel and Behavioral Science; and The Expanding Church. All of these symposia not only addressed themselves to problems and issues in a scholarly way, but also sought to explore them from the insights provided by gospel principles.

The results of the final symposium, which took as its subject the challenges faced by the Church in its mission to take the gospel to every kindred, tongue, and nation, are reported in this volume. Fortunately, the symposium was held soon after the April general conference of the Church in 1976. It was, therefore, possible to invite Church leaders from Asia, Europe, and Latin America to meet with faculty members from BYU and other LDS scholars in the sessions of the symposium. It was the meeting of East and West, North and South, Church leaders and scholars that gave the symposium a spiritual halo sensed by all who attended. The sessions of the symposium became, for those who attended them, more than scholarly discussions of the transnational and transcultural problems that face any organization extending itself beyond the culture of a single nation. They were spiritual experiences alive with the testimony of the prophetic mission of the Church. Perhaps it is impossible to translate to the printed page the sense of a common fate, a shared destiny that pervaded those sessions; but it is our hope that in some small measure these pages recreate that spirit.

The publication of materials related to that symposium offers a special opportunity for us who have lived our lives in the Church and in the shadow of the temple to catch the spirit of conversion, dedication, and perseverance characterizing the Church in the missions and stakes of Asia, Latin America, and Europe. Those valiant Saints are no less pioneers in building multiple Zions than were the pioneers of 1847 in establishing the House of the Lord in the tops of the mountains. If this volume can help to strengthen gospel ties binding Church members together across the differences that seek to divide us, our efforts will be rewarded and our prayers answered.

This volume could not have been completed without the vigorous efforts of F. LaMond Tullis, who has served as general editor. His tenacity and organizational ability are matched only by his intelligence and sensitivity as an editor. He has been assisted, and very ably so, by Arthur Henry King, Douglas F. Tobler, and Spencer J. Palmer. The Research Division of Brigham Young University and the Centennial committee chaired by Lorin F. Wheelwright provided considerable financial assistance in support of the symposium and the publication of this volume.

CULTURAL DIVERSITY IN THE UNIVERSAL CHURCH

INTRODUCTION

Arthur Henry King

The paper and comments of this section open up the whole series of symposia discussions. The meaning of the term *culture,* the relation of the gospel to worldly cultures; the status of American culture compared with other cultures in the Church; the example of the cultural clash between Jew and gentile in the Primitive Church—these are all matters exemplified during the conference.

It would be well, then, to enter a caveat here. The symposia were largely a series of academic discussions. It was our business to assemble facts, to point out interrelations and interpretations, to analyze and generalize; not to say whether the Church should do this or that, not to state what we think the policy of the Church is, not to arrogate to ourselves the task of judgment that properly belongs to the authorities, not to point at or propound policy; but rather to produce a panorama or kaleidoscope that might prove useful in aiding comprehension.

Two facts stood silently behind the discussion: first, that in the Church there are over three million members from the United States and less than half a million from elsewhere; second, that but for the United States, all the other national units represented in the Church would already have been subjugated by a power inimical to religion. It follows that the relation of each national culture to the gospel may be less important than the relation of all the other cultures to the matrix of the Church: the United States. The very existence of the United States is due to its role as a matrix for the Church. It would therefore seem to lie in the interest of the Church that the matrix should be materially strong (as the law and order of Augustan Rome facilitated the spread of the Christian message in the Meridian of Time). And yet, the culture of the United States, like that of all the Western World and Augustan Rome before it, is in decline: its mass production is derogatory to human dignity; its mass media are subversive of moral standards; its academic learning carefully excludes all matters of faith; and its behavioral sciences foster the arrogance and futility of mechanistic thought. But since everywhere else is worse, it is at least the least unsatisfactory country in the world.

We all know, in the Church, that the gospel is our only true refuge and strength. It follows (as Reynolds points out) that the gospel is subversive of all the worldly aspects of culture. The gospel (as Reynolds and Nibley agree, though Sorenson does not) has its own world view, its own culture, that has been manifested on earth from time to time; yet the Lord has not excluded any culture in the world from his beneficent interest.

We all agree that the gospel comes first; but we are prone to confuse the Lord's commandments with the cultural imperatives of our own culture, and by so doing we make it easier for us to live normal instead of abnormal lives, forgetting that it is not for us to live a culturally normal life, but a gospel life—which may well mean an abnormal and difficult life counter to the surrounding culture. Because the United States is the matrix of the Church, it is particularly easy for American Mormons to make this confusion.

Reynolds considers the tussle in the Primitive Church between Jew and gentile as a means of guidance to our current cross-cultural problems. Consider, as you read him, what would be the modern equivalent to the problem of circumcision. Where is Tarsus—Mexico City? Or is Saul coming to maturity at the lectern of some Lutheran Gamaliel?

Reynolds proceeds to mention intercultural problems in the Church today: administrative style, translation into languages with class dialects (has not English in America and Britain such dialects, as well as Javanese in Indonesia?), secularization (giving pride of place to chance and nature instead of confessing the hand of God in all things), ritual (is not our individual inspiration at moments of spiritual importance better than the establishment of forms? But do not our adolescents of all ages cry out for ritual?)—Reynolds takes them all in his sensible stride. Walk with him.

Hugh Nibley wants to walk with Reynolds, but the walk must be to the temple: Nibley sees the gospel culture as having been, historically, temple-centered. There is, for him, a definite gospel culture that has been embodied on earth from time to time. The city of Enoch is the supreme example, but 4 Nephi gives another (the two hundred years of the united order among the Nephites). Both would include the cultural peaks mentioned by Reynolds (see below p. 10).

John Sorenson would find the discussion above poetical, but naive and unfactual; and he would, of course, be right, in the sense that all discussions of "culture" are naive and unfactual, but not necessarily fruitless. He thinks the word *culture* to be a difficult and perhaps unnecessary one. He sees us all as subject to diverse and conflicting cultural pressures—as men and women, as professionals (whether lawyer or plumber), as coming from various countries, yes, but from varying regions in those countries; as belonging to different generations. He presents us with "tabernacles," with vessels of different shapes that may contain the same gospel. He sees the solution of cultural problems as their disappearance in the light of the gospel; meanwhile, we must struggle to *free* ourselves from our cultures with the help of the gospel, which has no culture. He sees cultures, as the scriptures do and as Reynolds may ultimately do, as "the chains of hell."

In the end, each individual is unique, has his own way to the gospel, his own channel of revelation for his own problems; and it is by his uniqueness, not by his similarity to others, that he shares reality with his Lord and his God. The generalizations of the social sciences may help us by contrast to realize that uniqueness, but in the scriptures that uniqueness is uniquely expressed. The discussion of cultural diversity in the Church will have achieved its end if it sends us back to the scriptures with some fresh scaffolding to give us a new vantage point—or even with some new insights to try out against those everlasting truths of the gospel.

Questions that send us back to the scriptures, new insights that help us to appreciate their complexity—all this and more emerged from the presentations and discussions of this session of the expanding Church symposium. Consider, for example, the following additional points that, as in an outcropping of potentially rich mineral ore, require investigation, thought, examination, sampling. The reader will encounter them in the pages that follow.

1) Is there any cultural form that can leave the content of culture intact? Or is the content partially conditioned by the form? Is it *possible* to separate Mormon culture from American culture, since America is the matrix of the Church?
2) How then can we distinguish between the non-Mormon American values and the Mormon American values of Deseret? Is there a non-gospel Deseret hegemony as well as a Deseret gospel? Granted this should not be a problem at the level of the General Authorities, is it not a problem at the level of the administrator, bishop, teacher, or missionary?
3) Do not Deseret Mormons get the kind of leadership they deserve? For example, if they want to hear that Mormon patriotism and American patriotism are the same thing, is that not what they will hear?
4) Do converts join the Church *because* it is an American church (*the* American Church)? Do people reject the Mormon Church because it is American? Does the Church *have* anti-American members?
5) Are not the cultural problems of non-American Mormons in relation to the gospel more serious than those of American Mormons?
6) Is not every culture lost insofar as it is not Christ-centered? Is not every culture saveable insofar as it becomes Christ-centered?

CULTURAL DIVERSITY IN THE UNIVERSAL CHURCH

Noel B. Reynolds

Since its earliest missionary days the restored Church has faced the problems that come with cultural diversity. The miraculous unity that prevailed in the early Utah period was explained by Parley P. Pratt as the effect of the Holy Spirit upon the minds and hearts of the people and of "the power and keys of the holy Priesthood, and the ordinances and spirit thereof."[1]

Yet, these great achievements have come only after many painful mistakes and unfortunate misunderstandings. Whereas the Church in general seems to be amazingly successful, there is great need for the individual members to become one, as we are commanded. I hope that as we share our experiences and reflections in this symposium, we may be able to help each other develop the kind of understanding that will enable us, as individual members of the Church, to rise above any cultural barriers that prevent us from treating each other as brothers and sisters in Christ. For if we are not one, we are not his.

Cultural problems have long been of interest to academicians in a variety of disciplines, especially history, anthropology, and other social sciences. Although insights have come from academic studies, none has as yet produced a theory adequate either to illuminate fully the problem or to facilitate its resolution. The purpose of this symposium is to search for helpful ways of understanding the cultural complexity of the twentieth-century Church, as well as to develop ideas that may be helpful in reducing the amount of cultural conflict and misunderstanding within the Church. Our resources include not only the insights available from our formal studies, but, more importantly, the experience we and others have had in Church service. It is our hope as organizers of this conference that the Lord will find our purposes pure and our preparation worthy, that we may be protected from error or contention, and that some results of this conference will be of value to the Kingdom of God.

The Concept of Culture

The discussion we are proposing in this conference seems to assume that we know what culture is. But as we go to the anthropologists and other social scientists, we find no general consensus on definitions. The precise meaning of the term varies from one theory of society to another. But the absence of an established definition does not prevent us from raising important issues. I will therefore proceed and assume certain basic notions about culture that seem to be most helpful in understanding our problem from the perspective of the worldwide Church but that avoid the more controversial theoretical issues.

Each man seems to be dependent as an individual on some kind of individual mental world view enabling him to make sense of his experiences. Most men derive their world view from the traditional outlook of their society. In so doing they must master the symbols that communicate that traditional picture of reality within the society. Though there will always be some variation of content in individual world views within a given population, the uniformity displayed by these individual world views is generally recognized as their outstanding characteristic.

Even though individuals seem to build their world views with their own hypotheses for explaining their experience, this construction is ordinarily guided at every turn by symbols that inform the individual of the world view of others in this society.[2] The culture of the individual would then comprise the complete package of symbols and beliefs about reality that gives meaning to all his experience and provides a basis for guiding his life. The culture of a society would be a statistical reflection of the more widely shared elements of the individual cultures of its members.

These group cultures seem to be self-perpetuating, for the individual will always profit from a mastery of the culture in which he is raised as he gains access to the understanding and wisdom of the past, an appreciation for the moral expectations of the community, and general guidelines by which his own affairs can be most successfully conducted. By mastering his culture, he is best able to predict how his society and its members will react to the various behaviors that he might choose in his life.

A great difference exists between mastering a culture and accepting one. A man can learn all the ways of successful social interaction without committing himself to the beliefs of that culture. This capability is exemplified by those individuals who are equally at home in more than one cultural setting and explains why the sons of God are able to survive as pilgrims in a hostile world.

The Gospel Is Subversive of Worldly Cultures

As the gospel comes to men, it presents them with a radical alternative to their previously held world views. The gospel is essentially subversive of the world views perpetuated by the cultures of man; for the gospel does have its own world view, teaching men that everything in this world was created by God, that men themselves are spiritual beings and spirit children of their Father in heaven, and that obedience to his commandments as received through personal revelation takes priority over any requirements of a traditional culture. Thus, as men have fallen and are cut off from the presence of God, their highest objective in life is to exercise their faith unto repentance, following the prescribed ordinances, that they may be reintroduced into his presence.

Every cultural world view is a gospel in the sense that it features some notion of the good life, of human salvation, whether it be in this life or another. Each of these is false to the extent that it does not correctly identify the Savior as the only source of salvation and his priesthood as the human agency through which access to salvation is available. Every worldly culture idealizes some set of moral values by which men are to guide their lives. But the gospel offers a radical and different approach that would be impossible through any worldly culture, that approach being direct individual guidance by God. To the extent that cultural values blind members of a society so that they cannot appreciate the truths of the gospel, these values function as the chains of hell, fastening people to ways of living below the celestial order (Alma 12:10–11). The Prophet recognized that these "creeds of the fathers" are inherited lies that Satan has "strongly riveted upon the hearts of the children of men, . . . filling the world with confusion." These "mainsprings of all corruption" are "an iron yoke, . . . a strong band, . . . the very handcuffs, and chains, and shackles, and fetters of hell."[3] Joseph Smith's deliberate use of such strong language should help us remember the danger of promoting those elements of worldly cultures that conflict with the gospel. All worldly cultures are false gospels in the sense that they perpetuate beliefs and behaviors incompatible with the truths of the gospel of Jesus Christ. Conversely, the gospel will therefore be subversive in the context of any worldly culture.

But having made this point, we must make two important qualifications. First, the Lord himself seems to be responsible for much of what is beneficial in the cultures of the world, providing his children on earth with guidance when the fulness of the gospel is not among them. The law of Moses is only one well-known example of this. Elder Orson F. Whitney once declared in general conference that such wise teachers as Socrates, Confucius, and Buddha "were servants of the Lord in a lesser sense, and were sent to those pagan or heathen nations to give them the measure of truth that a wise Providence has allotted to them."[4]

My other qualification is that the bulk of our cultural paraphernalia may not matter for Latter-day Saints. How a Latter-day Saint expresses love and appreciation to his wife will vary, according to the customs of love and respect in his culture. But all that seems to matter from the Lord's point of view is that he is keeping the commandments *in that cultural setting.* The gospel governs ends, but leaves open the question of cultural means, at least within limits. A missionary in Japan will need to learn that the admonition to treat investigators respectfully will require very different behavior from what he would have guessed as an American, as I will demonstrate in an example later.

As a church, we do not seem fully to appreciate that the gospel of Jesus Christ is subversive of every worldly culture. Ironically, our enemies seem to recognize this better than we do. The accusers of the Savior, Paul, and Joseph Smith instinctively chose to charge them with treason, even though none of them could seriously have been represented as threatening the overthrow of the established governments in their time. Similarly, the persecutions of the Utah Saints under the antipolygamy statutes were at least partially inspired by the sentiment that the practice of polygamy was treasonous.[5]

Although this view may at first seem farfetched, it is based on a very coherent analysis of law and society. For as a leading British judge has persuasively and effectively argued over the last two decades, the essence of a society is its moral fabric and, therefore, practices that threaten to destroy that traditional moral fabric are treasonous.[6] Few Latter-day Saints would fail to recognize that in any conflict between the commandments of God and the revered cultural traditions of their own society, their baptismal covenant entails an obedience to Christ and a rejection of the old cultural norm.

The cultural problems of the Church seem not to stem so much from misunderstandings about the primacy of the Lord's commandments as from failures to distinguish between cultural imperatives and the commandments of God. Such failure invites conflicts within the Church, especially where the membership is drawn from more than one world culture.

Cultural complacency in areas of cultural homogeneity is an even more subtle danger. Perhaps in the long run the cultural conflicts that now come to our attention within the Church will be a means of awakening us all to our unwarranted confidence in cultural norms and remind us that our unity in the gospel must be based on obedience to celestial principles and purity of heart, rather than on cultural compatibility.

The scriptures consistently make it clear that the escape from this darkness and the chains of hell—the traditions of men, as it were—is available only to the penitent: "Yea, he that repenteth and exerciseth faith, and bringeth forth good works, and prayeth continually without ceasing—unto such it is given to know the mysteries of God" (Alma 26:21–22). In this context, we can see the honest in heart as those men who risk the condemnation of their societies by persisting in the search for a world view that gives a consistent account of all their experience: moral, social, and physical. They are not persuaded by offers of gain, power, or praise of men to accept culturally dominant world views when these prove inadequate to explain their own undeniable experiences and spiritual instincts. These men usually recognize their own limitations, especially their inability always to do good and to be a blessing to loved ones. They thirst for something greater. To them is sent the gospel of Jesus Christ. And they are they who receive it with open arms.

The gospel is the "good news" that if men will repent of their sins and call upon the name of Christ, receive baptism and the gift of the Holy Ghost—all through faith in Jesus Christ—and endure to the end, they can return to the presence of God. It is the same for all men in all cultures. It is a mystery to all strangers to the Spirit. It is independent of all world views invented by men, and requires men to be willing to put aside the world view they have had. The new world view it brings can be infinitely extended through revelation *to the individual*, making his knowledge culturally independent and transcendent.

Cultural Problems in the Ancient Church

It is instructive to review how these problems were handled in the primeval Church. The first cultural barrier encountered in the ancient

Church sprang from the Jewish prohibition against associating with gentiles. Apparently, during the life of the Savior this prohibition had for the most part been observed by him and his disciples. When the centurion Cornelius sought the direction of the Lord, it was necessary for the Lord to spend more effort preparing his Jewish messenger than the gentiles to whom he was sent. Peter was thrice shown the vision and commanded to partake of meat that was forbidden in the Jewish law. He was immediately thereafter shown that this vision was given to prepare him to preach the gospel to the gentile (Acts 10:9–35). The response of the Jerusalem saints to this news was predictable, and they accused Peter of going among uncircumcised men and eating with them (Acts 11:2–3). As Peter explained the full story, to the saints at that time came the general recognition that God had "also to the Gentiles granted repentance unto life" (Acts 11:18). Soon after, they also received word that many gentiles had been converted by their brethren who had fled to other cities when the persecution rose during the days of Stephen. They then sent Barnabas as a representative of the Church to these people, "and much people was added unto the Lord" (Acts 11:24).

Once the question of gentile conversion was settled, it was inevitable that further cultural difficulties would arise. The Jewish tradition of circumcision provided an issue whereby the general question of cultural conflicts might be more fully considered. While Paul and Barnabas were in Antioch, some brethren came from Judea teaching that circumcision was necessary for salvation (Acts 15:1). Apparently, a serious dissension developed on this point. Paul and Barnabas, among others, were sent to Jerusalem to lay the question before the apostles and the elders. In the council, it seems that those who had been Pharisees at the time of their conversion—and perhaps still saw themselves as such—argued that it was needful to circumcise new converts that they might keep the law of Moses (Acts 15:5). Peter stood forth at this time to defend the position of the gentiles, observing that these gentiles had received the Holy Ghost as had the Christians of Jewish origins. Recognizing that God had "put no difference between [them]" and had "purif[ied] their hearts by faith," he then challenged the council, "Why tempt ye God, to put a yoke upon the neck of the disciples, which neither our fathers nor we were able to bear?" (Acts 15:8–10). It seems that Peter was arguing that it is not the law of Moses that saves but rather the grace of the Lord Jesus Christ, which was needed by Jews as well as gentiles (Acts 15:11). After Barnabas and Paul had further declared the miracles and wonders that God had wrought among the gentiles, James apparently stood forth to announce a decision on the matter. Recognizing the fact that the gentiles had, in fact, been converted by the power of God and that the scripture prophesied that the gentiles might one day be included, James declared his judgment: "That we trouble not them, which from among the Gentiles are turned to God" (Acts 15:19). Circumcision would not be required. But James did command that an epistle be sent to the gentiles instructing them to refrain from certain cultural practices that would not be acceptable in the Church, that is, eating blood, meats offered to idols—or anything that had been strangled—and committing fornication (Acts 15:29). In other words, the cultural practices of the Jews would not be binding upon the gentiles as they joined the Church, but, on the other hand, certain intolerable practices characterizing the culture of the gentiles would have to be forsaken by those who took Christ as their Savior. We are told that the epistle stating these things was received in Antioch with rejoicing (Acts 15:31).

But the strength of the Jewish religious traditions proved very difficult for the early Jewish Christians to overcome. Paul challenged their mistaken attachment to the law of Moses and taught that the law had been given only as a schoolmaster to an unruly nation—a schoolmaster that in and of itself was not capable of bringing men to righteousness. It could prepare them to receive the gospel, but righteousness itself could come only by faith in Christ (Galatians 3:20–39). For "if ye be led of the Spirit, ye are not under the law";[7] or, as Paul quotes from ancient scripture, "This is the covenant that I will make with them after those days, saith the Lord; I will put my laws into their hearts, and in their minds will I write them (Hebrews 10:16—cf. 8:10).

Teaching on this subject, Paul used Peter's own words: "For there is no respect of persons with God" (Romans 2:11—cf. Acts 10:34). He taught that Jew and gentile will be judged according to their deeds in light of the law given to them. For in the final analysis, it will be only the circumcision of the heart that will be counted righteousness to Jews or gentiles (Romans 2:25–29). Circumcision and uncircumcision in and of themselves are nothing. The circumcision, of course, is only an outward or culturally meaningful sign of a covenant in the heart. Only the keeping of the commandments matters (1 Corinthians 7:19). In the same vein, Paul argues that Greeks with faith will be saved, but Jews without faith will not. They are all the same before the Lord (Romans 9:30 and 10:21).

Not only did Paul attack the traditional distinctions between Jews and gentiles, but he taught that all men must be united in Christ. "By one Spirit are we all baptized into one body, whether we be Jews or Gentiles, whether we be bond or free" (1 Corinthians 12:13). Similarly, Paul taught the gentiles that Christ had abolished the partition between them and the Jews (Ephesians 2:14), concluding, therefore, that all "have access by one Spirit unto the Father" (Ephesians 2:18), being therefore "no more strangers and foreigners, but fellow citizens with the saints, and of the household of God," being "built upon the foundation of the apostles and prophets, Jesus Christ himself being the chief corner stone" (Ephesians 2:19-20). In this spirit he then commanded them that they must grow together as a fitly framed building and become "an holy temple in the Lord" because they are "builded together for an habitation of God through the Spirit" (Ephesians 2:21–22). To the Corinthians, Paul had taught that there should be no division in the Church but that the Saints were to be perfectly joined together, to be "in the same mind" (1 Corinthians 1:10). And thus the Saints were commanded to discard the *old* man, that is, the belief and value systems they had inherited from the world around them, that they might put on the *new* man, that is, the image of Christ in all its purity, and freedom from worldly concern and outlook, for among those who had taken the new covenant upon them "there is neither Greek nor Jew, circumcision nor uncircumcision, Barbarian, Scythian, bond nor free: but Christ is all, and in all" (Colossians 3:11).

This introduces the reconciliation of this problem as it was taught by Paul. He knew and was persuaded by the Lord Jesus Christ "that there is nothing unclean of itself: but to him that esteemeth any thing to be unclean, to him it is unclean" (Romans 14:14—cf. 1 Corinthians 10:23–33). In this and other passages he explains that our eating and drinking should be more governed by considerations of the effect our actions will have on others. "For the kingdom of God is not meat and drink; but righteousness, and peace, and joy in the Holy Ghost" (Romans 14:17). But "it is good neither to eat flesh, nor to drink wine, nor any thing whereby thy brother stumbleth, or is offended, or is made weak," "for he that in these things serveth Christ is acceptable to God, and approved of men" (Romans 14:21, 18). It seems that the members of the Church were admonished to be flexible and to tolerate certain cultural arrangements in the world without compromising their covenants with the Lord. This is further explained in Paul's instructions to Timothy about slaves in which he indicates that master-slave relationships need not be dissolved because of the gospel teachings about equality, but rather they are to be upgraded in order that there be no rebuke against Church teachings, that each might learn to do well in his own position and that vain words and strife might be avoided (1 Timothy 6:1–5).

Lest these teachings be taken to be inventions of Paul, we must remember that they simply extend the recorded teachings of Christ. As we remember the instance where the Pharisees accused the disciples of transgressing the law by not washing their hands when they ate, we find the Savior in his response directly equating the Jewish traditions with the doctrines of men that are taught in place of God's commandments. "Well hath Esaias prophesied of you hypocrites, as it is written, This people honoureth me with their lips, but their heart is far from me" (Mark 7:6). The Savior further explained that they were transgressing the commandments by their traditions (Matthew 15:3), as their traditions made "the word of God of none effect" (Mark 7:13). For men are not defiled by breaking the traditions of their religious culture, but by the evil thoughts and acts that arise out of their hearts (Mark 7:14–23).

Cultural Problems in the Church Today

Value Conflicts

I would now like to consider some of the cultural challenges confronting the Church today. Possibly the most serious problems arise in terms of moral values taught in the Church that have conflicting manifestations in different cultures. One second-hand account reports a Relief Society health and grooming guide distributed in the Central American Mission many years ago instructing the sisters of the Church in ways to apply lipstick and shave their legs. Apparently the responsible authorities did not realize that, in the local Indian culture, a woman did such things only to advertise her availability for prostitution.[8]

A Melchizedek Priesthood manual exhorts a husband to observe the highest standards of modesty and chastity and to treat his wife with love and respect. But when the instruction is elaborated to include kissing his wife as he leaves the house or returns, it raises a serious problem, for example, in a Japanese home where the children protest, demanding to know why he is "biting" their mother.[9]

The Saints in Latin American countries are less enthralled with capitalism than the Americans, who link it with the universal values of personal freedom and work. Capital in these countries is often identified with a protected wealthy upper class and the *absence* of what we would call free markets.[10]

In this conference on the expanding Church, President Rhee Ho Nam of the Seoul, Korea, Stake has reported the serious difficulties the Church faces in fostering LDS marriages. The strong cultural tradition of arranging marriages according to astrological criteria presents almost insurmountable obstacles to bishops who want to promote marriages between Church members but who also want members to retain the good will of their non-LDS parents. Similar cause for offense in part-member families arises in the highly formal annual family gatherings, which everyone is expected to attend and to join in the ritualized worship of their ancestors.[11]

It is possible that as inspired local leaders accept more of the responsibility for formulating programs and courses of instruction, this problem may gradually fade away.

Leadership Style

Another source of difficulty arises when a particular administrative style is promoted throughout the Church, through the formal Church programs, but is effective only within limited cultural boundaries. I have always admired and appreciated the detailed and highly programmed manuals the Church provides for any leadership position. But during my most recent assignment as a bishop I began to suspect that the ability to understand and appreciate such programmatic materials may be very much limited within certain cultural boundaries. These are not the kinds of boundaries that separate nations. Rather, the atmosphere of bureaucratic rationalism that pervades most programmed instructional or administrative materials is most congenial to the educated, white-collar males of Europe and the Americas. But it is hardly intelligible to those who lack this cultural equipment and who, like blue-collar workers and intuitive Indians, usually perceive leadership and its functions in highly personal terms.

As these very carefully written and even inspired program outlines focus the struggling lay leader's attention on a formal program, they may force upon him a very real choice between pouring his every resource into the attempt to master this "foreign" material and compromising the formal program by relying more on the more informal and personal leadership style that his cultural background recommends. His task is further complicated by the fact that the members he serves will very often have expectations that divide along the same lines. Of course, none of these speculations prove that the programmatic approach is not the best general strategy presently available to the Church. They only suggest a possible explanation for some failures. It is certainly worth noting in this context that the marvelous streamlining of the priesthood handbooks and bishop's guide published this past year in new editions seems to betray a heavy editorial hand bent on maximizing both the discretion and the responsibility of priesthood officers at the lowest levels. Certainly, this approach will make it much easier for local leaders throughout the world to develop approaches to church activity that function better in their respective situations.

Communication

One of the major cultural problems concerns communication. We are doing more about this than any other problem. I will not attempt to elaborate on this point, as it has been so well developed by others before,[12] but I do want to recognize that as we set out to translate scriptures, Church directives, and teaching materials, the choices of expression made by translators are crucial. Sometimes an optimum choice is virtually impossible to make. Senator Wallace F. Bennett once reported the interesting experience of joining some Indonesian Saints in the hymn, "We Thank Thee, O Allah, for a Prophet"![13]

Gordon Thomasson uses the very interesting example of Javanese to show the ways in which a choice of language for teaching the gospel and translating Church materials delimits the potential audience, because different levels of language are characteristically used by different social classes and political or religious groups. The language in which the gospel is presented in some countries tends to identify the missionary with a particular cultural or social grouping, thus introducing attitudes and prejudices that should never characterize a presentation of the gospel.[14]

Imposing the American Culture

A very different problem arising from cultural differences—probably the one most discussed in academic circles—concerns the danger of exporting the values of our national cultures in our church work, failing to recognize that they are not gospel values. Non-American members of the Church are best aware of how extensive this problem can be. On the one hand, it may have more or less innocuous results. For example, contrast the following hypothetical descriptions of a new missionary in Japan, one by his new companion, the other by a Japanese native. The companion sees him as "a man with energy and drive, strong, self-confident, friendly, straightforward in manner, a regular Jack Armstrong with the all-American-boy image." But the native will describe this same missionary as "awkward, though well-meaning. He is embarrassingly friendly, and most irritating of all, he is perpetually impatient and possessed of an annoying sense of superiority."[15]

Successful missionaries will soon learn to modify their behavior to suit the culture in which they live. But this phenomenon also has tragic significance when we find good members of the Church being alienated by the imposition of Anglo-American values through Church administration. For example, one brother in Mexico, in reflecting on the high overload of American culture evident in much of the Church administration he has seen, was led to ask, "How much of what has through the years evolved as 'LDS doctrine' is merely the expression of the collective neurosis of that culture to which the gospel was restored?"[16] He went on to explain that he realized that much of what offended him in the Church was in that category and that this thought sent him "scurrying back to the simplicity of the gospel: Christ and Him crucified." His comment concluded with the plea that "this wholesale exportation of cultural/collective neurosis has to be stopped. Let each heal himself of the traditions of his fathers without having to adopt a whole new set of hangups as a prerequisite to discipleship in Christ."[17]

We cannot know what specific experiences over the years produced the pain and anguish that lie behind this brother's comments. Without doubt, the Lord foresaw the consequences of restoring the gospel in the United States of America. The Book of Mormon tells us clearly that he prepared this land and this people for the restoration of his gospel. As we examine American culture, we find it has many virtues that have given strength and have presented worldwide opportunities to the restored Church. But the culture itself is corrupt, and the same scriptures warn of its decline. The challenge that is raised for the dominant cultural group of the Church, the Americans, is to recognize that they have inherited a culture, developed over the last centuries, that is not identical with the gospel. We all need to be more sensitive to the cultural assumptions we might make in teaching the gospel and administering the Church as we are called individually to serve in various capacities.

It is very possible that this problem has an analogue in LDS communities throughout the world as the cultural biases of dominant classes are incorporated into Church practice and become barriers or restrictions to the activity and fellowship of converts with different class origins. Why should lower-class English Mormons expect to *address* their upper-class brethren as "Sir"? Or why should any Saint expect his brethren to address him regularly by worldly titles, such as "Professor" or "Doctor"?

Secularization

Another very different problem concerns not so much misunderstandings between cultures as inherent dangers of most modern cultures *per se* for the members of the Church. Few Latter-day Saints are fully aware of the almost total secularization of most modern cultures and of the pervasive effect of secularization on the cultural values that we have all taken in "with our mother's milk." Secularization generally means stripping our beliefs and cultural symbols of their sacred or divine elements. Instead of seeing the hand of God in all things, secularized people see only chance and nature. This outlook in turn tends to feed the pride of man in his own wisdom, whether based on reason or on science. In short, secularized man must rely on the "arm of flesh." On the positive side, secularization may be of great importance for missionary work as it weakens and even wipes away powerful religious traditions, leaving an open field for the harvest. The danger is that we might succumb to the same disease.

Because of the almost universal secularization of modern cultures, contemporary Latter-day Saints often fail to recognize the many ways in which these cultures lead them to behave very much like atheists, failing to confess God's hand in all things (D&C 59:21). They are tempted to look first to science and government for solutions to the problems of men. They are inclined to trust in their own power, the arm of flesh, in dealing with the world and in providing for their own (2 Nephi 4:34). We encourage each other to become sophisticated in the high culture of the world, accepting its values and standards of evaluation uncritically. Without second thought, we judge our brothers in cultural terms, having regard for the way they dress, for their wealth, for the language they use, for their level of education, and for their racial origins. We frequently take pride in receiving the praise of the world, whether it is directed to the Church generally or to individual members of the Church. In all these things, it would seem we fail to confess the hand of God and our utter dependence on him for all good things.

My reflections further led me to wonder if the antiritualistic bias of American culture may not be depriving us of great blessings. After all, we do not observe the children of pagans, who do have strong life rituals in their cultures, growing up to be atheists; nor do they abandon their family religions. Rather, in primitive cultures, the regular rituals associated with the important events of life serve to define for the child a reality that compels his assent and provides for him an explanation of all his experience.

But such reflections are seriously mistaken. We live in a world different from the primitive cultures studied by anthropologists. Our children will constantly be exposed to alternative secular explanations of their experience. Therefore, we may not be able to guarantee their belief in God by subjecting them to certain formalized and recurrent rituals. Furthermore, we have been consistently warned away from the practices of those Christian churches that have become characterized by their incorporation of elaborate pagan life rituals. Those of us who have witnessed these rituals have recognized their inadequacies as they are compared to the Latter-day Saint ways of handling these occasions. It may be far more significant than we suspect that our ritualistic education is reserved for adults who have proven themselves. The temple ritual addresses us as adults, not children, as the faithful, not as neophytes.

Yet we cannot overlook the importance of providing clear models for the child in his early years that will provide him with an understanding of his parents' faith; for the child's belief and understanding of the divine is shaped in early years, especially as he observes how the divine shapes the important actions of his parents. The farm boy who sees his father dedicate the fields to God every spring has no doubt whence come the rains. But when his father talks about God only on Sunday, as it were, and then conducts his life's business as if Chance ruled the universe, the child may very well learn to farm like an atheist.

Further reflection, however, brought to my mind the law of Moses as an example of the kind of thing I seemed to be grasping at; for, indeed by its extensive formalization of ritual and symbol, heralding the future coming of Christ, the law of Moses did serve the Israelites as a schoolmaster. But it was also for them a stumbling block when it was perceived as an end unto itself, rather than as a means to an end. It was given to them as a lower rather than a higher law.

Thus I was soon convinced that it would be a step backward to seek to build up the ritual content of our funerals, baptisms, and other simple practices. The real answer to secularization seems to lie in the individual inspiration of bishops and fathers who preside on these occasions. They must see that the actual spiritual needs of those present are met without relying on highly formalized symbolic activities to be repeated on each such occasion. By relying on the guidance of the Spirit in the moment, these bishops and fathers can accomplish much greater good, reaping the advantages but not the disadvantages of ritual.

Secularization is indeed a great threat to the members of the Church today. And our modern cultures seem to be its most dangerous agents. But if we can continually maintain the world view of the prophets as reflected in the scriptures and strive to follow the gentle guidance of the Holy Spirit in all things, we will be able to protect ourselves and our children from the subtle erosions of faith that secularization brings. We will always be able to see the hand of God in our lives and in all the world around.

Summary

The problems that arise from cultural diversity in the Church are as old as the commandment to take the glad tidings of salvation to all men. Because the gospel of Jesus Christ invites men to a new way of life and to new views of the real and the possible, it is subversive to all worldly cultures. However, as men embrace the gospel they are rarely freed immediately or completely from their former beliefs. Rather they grow line upon line and precept upon precept.

Since the membership of the Church is drawn from such a variety of cultural backgrounds, it is inevitable that the "cultural baggage" of different groups of Saints will give rise to some misunderstandings and other offenses. We have seen evidence that the ancient Church struggled with such problems and formulated several principles that give us guidance and encouragement today. Not only are we faced with obvious communication barriers and value conflicts, but we are also becoming more aware of other more subtle intercultural conflicts. Like the Christian Jews of the previous dispensation, the naturally dominant United States membership does need to take care to avoid imposing the values of American culture on the worldwide Church, especially where that culture varies significantly from the universal standards reflected in the scriptures. And within national cultures, we need to be aware that certain styles of leadership, teaching, and even informal conversation may be culturally biased so as to discourage cultural subgroups from full participation.

Because of the good will and commitment to the same gospel truths and priesthood authority predominating in the Church, all of these problems can be and are being solved. But the host cultures within which the Saints of today must operate pose one further and possibly much more serious danger to the faith of individuals. The general secularization of modern cultures is an ever-present poison that can be ingested unwittingly with fatal consequences for testimony and faithfulness. Our background cultures constantly interpret our experiences for us in plausible ways that do not admit the reality or importance of God. Only as we individually experience the divine and come to know the reality of that dimension, which cannot be explained in secular terms, are we able to protect ourselves from such cultural poisoning. Intimate and sustained acquaintance with the Holy Spirit is our best antidote.

This lengthy focus on cultural problems in the Church must not obscure for us the fact that as widely scattered and as newly established as the congregations of the Church may be, we see a miraculous unity and progress in the Church today that is due to the preeminence given to the Holy Spirit in the minds and hearts of the people. The true solutions to the problems of worldly culture mentioned in this paper, as Elder Pratt observed over a century ago, still lie squarely in the continued spiritual growth of the membership of the Church.

Footnotes

1. Parley P. Pratt, in *Journal of Discourses*, 26 Vols. (London: Latter-day Saints Book Depot, 1855–86), 4:10.

2. Clifford Geertz, "Religion as a Cultural System," in *Anthropological Approaches to the Study of Religion*, ed. Michael Banton, (New York: Praeger, 1966), 14ff.

3. D&C 123:7–8. Similarly Alma speaks of the chains of hell as ignorance of the mysteries of God (Alma 12:11).

4. *Report of the Ninety-First Annual General Conference of The Church of Jesus Christ of Latter-day Saints*, 3 April 1921, pp. 32–33. See generally Spencer J. Palmer's unpublished manuscript, "Local Cultures and Universal Truth." I am indebted to Brother Palmer for allowing me to read his initial draft.

5. See generally Orma Linford, "The Mormons and the Law: The Polygamy Cases," *Utah Law Review*, vol. 9, no. 2 (Winter 1964): 308–70, which cites statements made by both legislators and courts to the effect that polygamy and the institution which fostered it were inconsistent with and subversive of American society and government.

6. Lord Patrick Devlin, *The Enforcement of Morals* (London: Oxford University Press, 1970), 9–13.

7. Galatians 5:18. See the important confirmation of Paul's teaching in Alma 25:15.

8. This incident was observed by LaMond Tullis when he visited Guatemala in 1957.

9. Seiji Katanuma, "The Relationship Between Culture and the Social Life in Japan and the Church," Paper delivered at the Conference on the Language of the Mormons, sponsored by the Brigham Young University Language and Intercultural Research Center, 31 May 1973, p. 69.

10. F. LaMond Tullis, "Mormonism and Revolution in Latin America," *Brigham Young University Studies* 16, no. 2 (Winter, 1976): 235–49.

11. From Rhee Ho Nam's speech at the expanding Church symposium, April 7, 1976. See pp. 163–69 below.

12. See, for example, the many publications of the Language and Intercultural Research Center, Brigham Young University.

13. An experience reported to me indirectly by John L. Sorenson.

14. Gordon Thomasson, "Choosing our Language after We Choose a Language of the Church," Paper delivered at the Conference of the Language of the Mormons, sponsored by Brigham Young University Language Research Center, 1974, pp. 35–42.

15. Lynn Tyler reported this example to John L. Sorenson. It was apparently formulated by Elizabeth Shattner.

16. From an oral interview of Mario Aranda recorded by F. LaMond Tullis, 1975.

17. Ibid.

Comments, Hugh B. Nibley

Is there a gospel culture? We begin with the idea. Is there a gospel community or society? There clearly is. Zion has always been described as a city, an organized society, set apart from the world. If the community preserves its integrity for any length of time, it is bound to emerge as a separate culture. The earliest reference to the culture I have in mind is Israel as the "peculiar people." Moses and Aaron disengaged the children of Israel from the culture of Egypt, the most distinctive culture of its time. The Lord tells them: "Ye have seen what I did unto the Egyptians, and how I bare you on eagles' wings, and brought you unto myself. Now therefore, if ye will obey my voice indeed, and keep my covenant, then ye shall be a peculiar treasure unto me above all people" (Exodus 19:4–5). The King James Version uses "peculiar treasure" for *segūlah,* a word meaning 'set apart,' 'sealed,' 'removed from the rest of the world.' Exodus continues: "And ye shall be unto me a kingdom of priests, and an holy nation" (v.6). A distinctive culture begins there. The cultural franchise is set down in Deuteronomy. In the light of recent documentary discoveries the true nature of that culture is beginning to appear, presenting ever closer resemblances to the picture Joseph Smith has given us of ancient Israel and early Christianity.

The Mormon basic concept is that we are God's spirit children; that idea separates us from the world: "Ye are the children [of Jehovah Elohim] of the Lord your God." Hence, "Ye shall not cut yourselves, nor make any baldness between your eyes...," etc. (Deuteronomy 14:1–2). Awareness of their heavenly parentage sets Israel apart *culturally* as well as doctrinally.

Their ordinances set them apart too. Every ancient civilization is hierocentric; it is the temple that sets it apart from the rest of the world. And so we read in the 135th Psalm of praises to the Lord, to the name of the Lord and to the servants of the Lord standing "in the house of the Lord [the temple], in the courts of the house of our God" (Psalm 135:2). "Praise the Lord; for the Lord is good: sing praises unto his name; for it is pleasant. For the Lord hath chosen Jacob unto himself, and Israel for his peculiar treasure [for his *segūlah* again]" (Psalm 135:2–4).

In his letter to Titus (2:12–14), Paul translates *segūlah* by a very interesting word that Aristotle uses also: *periousios.* It means a peculiar treasure.

The Saints are to deny "ungodliness and worldly lusts" to become "a peculiar people." The word here rendered "peculiar," *periousios,* designates that part of any wealth that is set aside or reserved in a separate account, not part of the common deposit, a peculiar treasure, something special and set apart to be of value in times of dire need. When the going is bad, this is where we will go for our salvation. Paul continues: "zealous of good works." It is specifically their good works that set the saints apart.

What is the gospel culture composed of? Everything good. Like patriotism, it is more inclusive than exclusive. Its peculiarity, its *segūlah,* is a seal set upon whatever it finds desirable, rendering that thing also peculiar. It is the combination, the structure, that is peculiar, not the separate elements. Our thirteenth Article of Faith sums it up beautifully; we accept everything we put our stamp on. Can anything be more universally appealing, more desirable for the whole human race, than being honest, true, chaste, benevolent, virtuous (that's inner culture acceptable to any society), and in doing good to all men? Moreover, we *seek* after every good thing; we are in the market for everything good. Articles six (dealing with organization, the same organization as the primitive Church), seven (dealing with the spiritual gifts that set the Mormons apart from the rest of the world at this time), and ten, especially (looking forward to another kind of secular environment), all have very strong cultural implications. "We believe in the literal gathering of Israel [the same thing we have already been referring to] and in the restoration of the Ten Tribes; that Zion will be built upon this [the American] continent; that Christ will reign personally upon the earth; and, that the earth will be renewed and receive its paradisiacal glory" (Article of Faith 10). We shall see all these things. These are very special things.

So we believe there is a culture here, a single culture peculiar to Mormons. Brigham Young expressed it well when he said, "We have commenced to organize, I will say partially, in the Holy Order that God has established for his people in all ages of the world when he has had a kingdom on the earth. We may call it the Order of Enoch, the Order of Joseph, or the Order of Peter, or Abraham, or Moses, and then back to Noah, always the same order."[1] It is essentially the same culture, we shall see.

Brigham continues: "We will organize, as far as we have the privilege . . . under the laws of the land . . . ," that is, under its restraining influence, its alien culture. We have to defer to it because we are dependent on it and without those laws we would not even be allowed to exist at all. The gospel would never have emerged. "Many branches of industry have been organized here to help sustain each other, to labor for the good of all and to establish cooperation in the midst of the Church in this place." The concept is of an ongoing culture that had in each dispensation been restored—not the teachings alone, but celestial manners, morals, and environment.

Now, not only is there a single, central celestial culture reserved for the saints, but such a culture has also served as the model for the greatest peaks of human civilization as a whole. Those "Golden Ages," all too few and far between, that have illuminated the long night of history have, I believe, all drawn their nourishment from the memories of lost Zions. Whenever Homer speaks of anything virtuous, lovely, or of good report, he invariably compares it with a heavenly model; whether it is an individual, some godlike hero, a society like the Phaeacians. A dream, or a landscape, it is always compared with some heavenly ideal. Hundreds of graffiti made by the Egyptian pilgrims to holy shrines describe the temples on which they scratch their names as places that make them think they are in heaven. How often the art of the Chinese (flowing robes amid the clouds) refers to its celestial counterparts; the people see themselves as a culture blessed and set apart, frankly styling themselves "the celestials." The brief splendor of Arabic Spain left behind the haunting image of a paradise on earth, just as the Gothic glories of the Middle Ages coming through Byzantium from the court of Persia transmit the heavenly visions of the Asiatics. The Egyptian court was also another heaven on earth, though its real glory was confined to an early dynasty. There have been but few such golden moments in history; their flourishing has been all too brief. But they do seem to follow a common pattern. "We are trying to be the image of those who live in heaven. We are trying to pattern after them, to look like them, to walk and talk like them, to be like them, and build up the kingdom of heaven as they have done," said Brigham Young. Another celestial culture. God has already supplied us with the necessary materials and plans; indeed, the stage has been set for Zion from the beginning. "Heaven," said President Joseph F. Smith, "was the prototype of this beautiful creation when it came from the hand of the creator and was pronounced good." We have a good start.

The clearest evidence that the great cultures of the world were inspired by a common model is their common dependence on one special institution—the temple. Ancient civilizations were what Eric Burrows called "hierocentric" in nature, that is, all their activities and thoughts were centered around the single sacred point, which was marked in every case by the temple and its ordinances.[2] But even apart from that, if we compare the moment of fulfillment of these great cultures such as those of Greece, Persia, China, Arabic Spain, or Egypt, we find the external manifestations are strangely alike. They all sought the heavenly. So it is with us. Brigham Young was the first person to speak in tongues in this dispensation (1832).[3] When he did so in the presence of Joseph Smith, the Prophet declared it to be the pure Adamic Tongue.[4] It was the language of our father Adam, walking in Eden, and the time will come again when the Lord brings again Zion, the likeness of Zion and Enoch; this people will then all speak the language that Brigham Young Spoke. A single language, someday, and a single culture, all based on a heavenly model.

I am going to read from an old book of Adam, a Syriac text[5] discovered in 1819, translated in 1856, and long forgotten, describing an ancient writer's idea of what the civilization of Enoch was like. For him it is a common culture scattered among countless worlds. He tells us what life is like on these worlds. His description is noteworthy because while writers of every age have found the description of hell only too easy, they become lost and unconvincing as soon as they attempt to depict what heaven is really like; that is a task that daunts Dante himself. But this old Christian writer, who has Mandaean connections, tells us that Zion is a place "without discord or dissent," where angels wise and gentle, without malice or deceit, come and go on cheerful assignments. There is a perfect agreement among the worlds, each having its particular glory, and all the inhabitants share their knowledge freely with each other. The worlds averaged one million *parasangs* (a *parasang* is about four miles) apart, and through the people's common knowledge and their common God, the Lord, they share a common glory. They are all incorruptible, without death. They do not grow old or wear out. Their nature is unfailing. They cannot be numbered, and their number is unchanging. Each of the worlds is a Zion, though each is different, for, most delightful of all, there is not monotony; there is a single universal culture which, as described in our own scriptures, "shall come forth out of all the creations which I have made" (Moses 7:64)—the culture of Zion. Yet variety (as Brigham Young often noted) was the very keynote to that culture. But the text describes Zion in negative terms, which are indeed the only terms in which it can be described to people living in another world. Thus in 4 Nephi the only way to tell us benighted people what was going on is to say what was not going on: "there was no contention among all the people, in all the land . . . and there were no envyings, nor strifes, nor tumults, nor whoredoms, nor lyings, nor murders, nor any manner of lasciviousness; and surely there could not be a happier people. . . ." (4 Nephi 13, 16). Not surprisingly, therefore, so we are told in this old Adam text, "each of these worlds is a Zion, having no law courts, no hungry or thirsty, no cold nor heat, no aged or fear, no war, no slavery, no harmful creatures or plants. . . ." How boring it all seems to primitives like us! We already possess the technical know-how to achieve something very near to this, but who wants it? "Magnificent buildings beside tranquil seas, flowing springs of life-giving water, everything vibrates with joy; the wants of the people are few, they move about through the air by the power of flight." They are not overly concerned with technology because their technological knowledge has taken them far beyond our clumsy contraptions. "They are at home with the firmaments, with the 'Jordans' [a special term referring to ordinances], with groves, with kings, with spirits; their beauty is within them and shines out as if they were pure crystal. Force flows through them from the King as they persevere in prayer and song." (It was a demanding thing; the celestial spirits had to work at it—"Force flows through them from the King as they persevere in prayer and song.") "They study and meditate constantly. They exhale a fragrance of divine happiness; each is more remarkable than the other, each more illustrious."

Such a world, we are told, is only congenial "to the spirits of good men; it is a life for the wise and prudent, for the families of Abel, Seth, and Enoch." This state of things is scattered throughout the universe, according to our old Adam text; and the various colonies, in spite of the vast differences between them, are quite aware of each other. In something the same way the fabulous dreamlike cultures of which we have spoken, in spite of their wide spacing in time, were quite aware of each other's existence. Thus Professor Werner Jaeger pointed out that both Plato and Aristotle were devoted followers of Zoroaster.[6] Buddhism, as we know, moved from India to become the religion of distant China. The world of Lehi was one of widely shared cultures. Buddha, Confucius, Lao-Tzu, Mahavira, Zarathustra, Pythagoras, Anthales were all contemporaries of Lehi at that magic moment in history which Karl Jaspers calls the "axial [pivotal] period," that is, the moment when the civilization of the whole world turned on its axis as a new order of the spirit succeeded the old sacral kingship.[7] That was the time when the seven wise men would come together from time to time from the ends of the earth to share their knowledge and wisdom at the Feast of the Seven Sages, knitting all the world together in a common cultural heritage.

Let me conclude with some quotations from the prophets of the Restoration: "The Lord spake unto Enoch [Joseph Smith, Jun.], saying: Hearken unto me, saith the Lord your God, . . . who have assembled yourselves together; . . . it must needs be that there be an organization of my people . . . in the land of Zion—Or in other words, the city of Enoch [Joseph], for a permanent and everlasting establishment and order unto my church, . . . that you may be equal in the bonds of heavenly things, yea, and earthly things also, for the obtaining of heavenly things" (D&C 78:1–5). Such passages plainly look to the distinctive culture being "of one heart and one mind" (Moses 7:18), setting them apart from all the others. "We are following," said Brigham Young, "the customs of Enoch and the holy fathers, and for this we are looked upon as not being fit for society. We are not adapted to the society of the wicked. . . ."[8] The strong word that Brother Reynolds has used here today is that we are subversive to certain cultures. Brigham says much the same thing: ". . . we are looked upon as not being fit for society. We are not adapted to the society of the wicked and do not wish to mingle with them."[9]

What I wish to indicate, very briefly then, is that behind all this there is a culture of Zion, a culture that has the virtue of being an eternal one, yet never boring, never monotonous. It is something toward which we should be striving. There are cultural images here, and there is a cultural reality, and we move into it by faith and prayer. It is not a pure figment of the imagination, because every time human cultures have reached a real peak they have been infatuated with this idea, and have been convinced that they were imitating the heavenly model and doing the best they could. There *is* a gospel culture.

Footnotes

1. *Journal of Discourses*, 26 volumes (London: Latter-day Saints Book Depot, 1855–86), 17:113f.

2. Article by Eric Burrows in S. H. Hokke (ed.), *The Labyrinth* (London: SPCK, 1935). See also Hugh Nibley, "The Hierocentric State," *Western Political Quarterly* 4 (June 1951):226–53.

3. Joseph Smith, *History of The Church of Jesus Christ of Latter-day Saints*, ed. B.H. Roberts, 7 vols. (Salt Lake City: The Church of Jesus Christ of Latter-day Saints, 1932–51), 1: 279.

4. Ibid.

5. The text is in J. P. Migne, *Dictionnaire des Apocryphes* (Paris: 1856), 1:26–27. All subsequent references to the Syriac text are referenced to this volume.

6. Werner Jaeger, *Aristotle* (London: Oxford University Press, 1948), pp. 132–36.

7. Karl Jaspers, *The Origin and Goal of History* (New Haven, Conn.: Yale University Press, 1953), pp. 1–21.

8. *Journal of Discourses*, 10:306.

9. Ibid.

Comments, John L. Sorenson

Although I have to be painfully abbreviated, I have a number of things I would like to say: many of the things that Brother Reynolds and Brother Nibley have said I find insightful and good; a number of other things I do not understand; some others I do not believe at all. I will probably dwell on the latter, because the purpose of discussion is not just to share praise. However, we come out in the end in rather similar positions even though we may get there by different routes.

I find an illustration in this symposium session of the observation by Janet Dolgin, a non-Mormon student of Mormonism, who recently commented on the difficulty of language use among the Mormons.[1] It appears that, as we have grown in size and become more varied and diverse in our backgrounds, we have, in a sense, counteracted our variety by trying to construct a common language. But what has really happened is that we use the same words with such different meanings that we talk past each other. That is part of the problem with the word *culture*. There are probably at least ten different meanings of culture that have been used so far this morning. I will add a few more. The result: I do not think culture is a very useful word for expressing a concept; I am not sure what we are talking about; and I do not think when we get done we will know much better.

I cannot let Brother Reynolds get away with saying that he wants to avoid the more controversial theoretical issues in the hope that we can then focus on more fruitful discussions. This seems to me something like telling a group of nineteenth-century physicists or chemists, "I don't want to argue about ether; I just want to find out what significance it has." I think we had better think carefully about the significance of the theoretical issues if we are going to use language involving them. Language provides tools, and I do not know how we can think in an orderly or systematic or fruitful manner unless we control our tools. It makes a lot of difference, if you are going to manufacture a cabinet, whether you pick up an axe or a plane.

The term *culture* as Brother Reynolds has used it bears only one of a substantial number of meanings. He has taken one that depends heavily on Clifford Geertz, an anthropologist, and has offered several metaphors (and indeed most meanings of culture turn out to be metaphors, not true definitions). For example, Geertz has spoken about culture as being not in the heads of individuals but having its own existence, like a Beethoven quartet. That is not a very clear position. Elsewhere, Geertz speaks of culture as like an old city "which one learns to know only slowly and very completely. The experience is not to be learned as such." Well, those metaphors are picturesque, but they do not provide a definition of culture that is useful to me.

Other people use images of culture as a map of behavior. But it would make a great difference whether the "map" is handed to you or whether it is self-made inside your head. Others would say that culture is like a radar, by which the cultural participant assesses his surroundings all the time to find out what is going on. Some others would say it was like a gyroscope or guidance device installed by one's parents.

I think it makes a considerable difference which of the meanings of culture we use. Is culture something that is strongly definitive, something society imposes upon the individual and that the individual has great difficulty escaping from so that his view of the world or universe is handed to him, as it were? Or, alternatively, might it be that culture is a set or structure of hypotheses which the person keeps trying out and refining to see if they will actually help him to deal with the world in which he is living?

I just do not find culture to be a very useful term. Unfortunately, it has come into common usage, and we all suppose we know what it means. We have heard it so many times that we are no longer curious about what it might mean, so we use the term without understanding it. I do not understand it, and I have been studying "culture" for a long time. I try to learn how people conduct their lives. I try to see how they view the world around them, how they view themselves, how they are guided toward what is desirable or essential or unavoidable in life. But those things do not all fit together consistently in a single definition of culture.

Another difficulty is that people have multiple cultures. No one can possibly belong to only one culture, however you define it. Could we suppose there to be a culture of females? To some degree that could be so. Do physicians have a culture? Are there local or regional cultures? At least in a very general sense similarities in behavior, thought, and world view uniting such groups can be considered cultural similarities. All of us are subject to a number of these patterns or sets of regularities, and we may pick and choose among them according to the circumstances in which we find ourselves from time to time.

I am not sure, therefore, what cultural patterns the gospel confronts, on the one hand, or is expressed through, on the other. Female culture, or the local culture, or a family culture, for that matter, as much as the American culture, may impinge on the gospel, or vice versa. I am just pointing out the difficulties in the use of our language.

Now I would like to take a slightly different tack and show that Brother Reynolds and I do end up on somewhat similar grounds. I offer a picture of the regularities in human behavior and thought of the following sort. Human existence, at least in mortality (that is all I can say much about), is dependent upon what the Lord in one place calls "tabernacles" (D&C 93:35). I am speaking here of "natural man." We all are in that category. These tabernacles are concrete forms through which feeling, thought, meaning, intention, and so on are manifest. The material body is a tabernacle for spirit. The nervous system is a tabernacle for perception, if you will. Language is a tabernacle for conceptions. Texts and monuments are tabernacles for history. Social institutions are tabernacles for cooperative action or conflict.

Tabernacles are essential. There is no life, there is no meaning, there is no substance without tabernacles. Tabernacles are like containers for fluids. Most fluids have to be confined in vessels in order to be useful. The tabernacles we have for the gospel are symbols—verbal, ritual, or esthetic. I cannot understand how the gospel could be expressed except through the tabernacles of symbols, and these symbols are, if you will, culturally set by different people. I cannot imagine any language in which the gospel cannot be expressed with total adequacy. Every functional set of biological features found among mankind is adequate to tabernacle a spirit of man. Any functioning set of social institutions is adequate for the Church or gospel actions to act through (see 2 Nephi 29:7).

I am reminded of the containers in a chemistry laboratory. There are beakers and test tubes of all sizes and shapes, and then there are all those kinds of containers that I don't even have names for. They all have their functions and different benefits. In one place one container serves better than another. But none of them is of much value without content. To me the gospel is a content. Culture is a kind of vessel, as biology is a kind of vessel. Therefore, I see that the gospel can act through the culture of any people on the earth, just as it can be expressed through any language.

The gospel may also be kept out by culture features in any culture, including our own here in "Deseret." Any beaker in the laboratory may have a hole in it, or the reverse—an obstruction blocking its mouth. Or it may be dirty or melted out of shape. So the cultural or linguistic vessels that serve mankind may be only more or less adequate, including "Deseret" culture.

Clearly there are some cultures that are preferable, just as a tempered glass test tube is inherently superior to one of clay for heating fluids in the chemistry lab. Some human materials are apparently superior. Some social forms are too. I suppose that is the case as far as culture is concerned too. I think some of the things that Brother Nibley was talking about, some of the cultural and social forms that have existed, are substantially preferable to other forms. Yet, I think we can find a way to work through any of the cultures of which we are aware, to cause the gospel to be expressed in them adequately. Wherever there is a human being who desires "greater light and knowledge," we have ways to help him. The gospel is, in one sense, then, subversive in the same sense that acid may be subversive of certain containers. It is not necessarily so—it depends on the quality of the container.

Finally, I do not think that culture, as that term is used by most social scientists, is the same thing as the gospel. I do not think there is a gospel culture as such. Ultimately, I believe culture will be transcended when men have the spirit of truth in its fullness. For natural man, culture is a guide written in shorthand; for spiritual man, there will be no need for culture. Meanwhile, in the transitional stage, we have to struggle with the realities of human life as we see them, but our struggle ought to be to find a way to escape the influences of culture through accepting clarities of the spirit.

Footnotes

1. Janet L. Dolgin, "Latter-day Sense and Substance," in Irving I. Zaretsky and Mark P. Leone, *Religious Movements in Contemporary America* (Princeton, N.J.: Princeton University Press, 1974), pp. 722–66.

THE CHURCH IN ALL THE WORLD

INTRODUCTION

F. LaMond Tullis

Within two decades after the restoration of the gospel of Jesus Christ and the organization of his Church in 1830, the Mormons had begun to send missionaries to all parts of the world in search of the honest in heart ready to receive the gospel. The Church established missions in Great Britain and in various countries of Europe and the islands of the Pacific. With equal courage and daring the first Mormons also attempted, but failed, to establish the work in Latin America, India, Italy, and elsewhere.

While failure to establish an early foothold in some areas dampened the spirit of many a missionary who had borne incredible sacrifice and hardship in his service to the Lord, the successes experienced elsewhere, notably in Great Britain and the Pacific Islands, and even in Germany and Scandinavia, helped to compensate. But eventually even in the areas of early failure the kingdom began to grow—in some places at an unbelievable speed—and it became customary among our people to speak of an "expanding, worldwide Church." Something of the experience of that expansion in Europe, Latin America, and Asia is reported in this, the regional section of the monograph.

Australia, Canada, New Zealand, Samoa, Tonga, Africa, and other places where the Church has prospered are not included here because the problems of organization, unavailability of participants, and menace of time and financial constraints combined to exclude them. Hence the discussions here are meant to illustrate and exemplify the Church's experience as it has expanded into the world, not to be inclusive either geographically or in terms of themes that could usefully be treated.

In this section Church members from Great Britain, France, Germany, Sweden, Mexico, Guatemala, Japan, Korea, and the Philippines speak to us, and in particular to their North American brothers and sisters. We receive their testimonies, their witness of the gospel, their troubles, and their counsel as they discuss the meaning of the expanding Church in their lives. Themes of emigration and secularization in Europe, rapid conversions and ethnic tensions in Latin America, economic travail and the challenge of tradition in Asia, and, above all, the unifying pull of the gospel—all this and more we find in these pages.

We find strength in the leaders represented here. We also find candor and honesty. We will do well to listen to that candor and honesty, to emulate it, and to learn, for our individual lives, the implications of the messages expressed.

Presented here are edited versions of remarks made at the regional sessions of the expanding Church symposium. What may be lacking in polish is compensated for by a spontaneity and a freedom of expression that are refreshing and stimulating. These are words from men of experience, who, by virtue of testimony and conviction, lay legitimate claim to our considered attention.

THE CHURCH IN EUROPE: CHALLENGES OF THE SECOND CENTURY

INTRODUCTION*

Douglas F. Tobler

When young Jakob Tobler first encountered Mormon missionaries in his native Switzerland in 1857, he could hardly have dreamed how this event would affect him. Yet we now know that his subsequent decision to cast his lot with the peculiar "American" sect not only completely changed his life but also affected the lives of his descendants into the fourth and fifth generations.

After their baptism in a nearby lake, Jakob and his wife Catherine labored diligently during the next three years to help build their fledgling branch in Herisau in the eastern part of Switzerland. Though both were to be disappointed by the responses of their own families to the gospel,

*The introduction to this section, by Douglas F. Tobler, is a revision of an article published in the August 1976 issue of the *Ensign*. The editors express appreciation to Church publications for permission to adapt from it here. The essays following the introduction are, for the most part, edited transcripts of prepared speeches presented at the expanding Church symposium. Peter Morley was unable to deliver his address at the symposium because of illness; his written report is included here. The focus is on the changes that have taken place in the last ten years in Europe.

Jakob was nonetheless instrumental in baptizing sixteen neighbors; and he confirmed another sixteen. Like all the other new Mormons, they worked earnestly to build the kingdom in their part of the world.

Yet the tasks were difficult. Persecutions soon arose. Some of the stalwarts emigrated. And the young Tobler couple, as Jakob later recalled in a sacrament meeting in Santa Clara, Utah, heeded their own desires and the urging of the Spirit "to gather with the Saints" in the tops of the mountains. There they could practice their new faith in freedom, meet and enjoy the company of apostles—a cherished childhood longing—and raise their family in the atmosphere of Zion. So, that May in 1861, they bid their families farewell, made their way to England, and there joined over nine hundred other Saints from all over Europe who were also embarking on a new life in America. That new life promised them and the thousands who followed during the next century and a quarter not only a religious haven but economic prosperity and social recognition and educational opportunities surpassing their most optimistic expectations.

In the lives of Jakob and Catherine Tobler we can discern some of the elements of a pattern that characterized the Church in Europe during the century and a quarter prior to 1960:

1) *The homogeneous economic and social background of most of the Saints*

Most Europeans who joined the Church in that age were industrious, God-fearing people from the lower socioeconomic strata of their societies—artisans, peasant farmers, factory workers, miners—who commanded little wealth and less status in their traditional cultures. Only a rare soul, like Karl G. Maeser, had the formal education necessary to give him some social mobility in European society.

2) *The preeminence of the "Gathering"*

The emigration of the Saints to the Great Basin Kingdom (and later to the United States generally) was essential for the establishment of the foundation of Zion in America. But it placed a heavy burden on those who remained in Europe. It was difficult to develop a nucleus of enough two- and three-generation Latter-day Saint families to provide the permanence and stability needed to sustain the membership and help the kingdom in Europe grow. Most Saints were torn between going and staying, and those who stayed literally started their branches over again and again. Sometimes an entire branch emigrated; but more often, couples and individuals who had been the most active and dependable were the first to leave.

3) *Reliance upon American mission presidents and missionaries*

The heavy dependence on foreigners to bear most of the administrative and some of the teaching responsibilities is also noted. European members were often dependent on them for their own understanding of the gospel principles and practices and did not always develop the sense of full responsibility for the progress and well-being of the Church in Europe. In an age of strong nationalism, members and nonmembers therefore tended to see the Church as a foreign Church primarily recruiting Europeans for its kingdom in America.

4) *Hostility of European society*

During most of the nineteenth and the first part of the twentieth century, Europe was generally hostile to and contemptuous of the Mormons, their church, and their doctrines. At first, under the influence of traditional Christian churches, Mormonism was considered an aberrant, immoral, polygamy-practicing "sect," a word with dire connotations in most European languages. Later, as the secularization of European culture progressed, Mormons were rejected either for their unsophisticated fundamentalism and fanaticism, or ignored because of their numerical and doctrinal insignificance. In any case, the European cultural, religious, and intellectual leaders did not see any reason to take Mormonism seriously.

5) *Protestants become Mormons*

The Church found most of its converts in the countries of northern and central Europe, primarily where Protestantism had been dominant since the time of the Reformation; governments and people in Catholic countries were less open to a message different from the ones they had grown up with.

Today there is ample evidence that this pattern of early Church experience in Europe is changing. In 1974 I interviewed over forty Mormon leaders and members living in wards and branches ranging from Oslo to Milan and from Helsinki to Edinburgh. The picture that emerged from my research was different from the conventional one held by both the native members and the missionaries. What I saw happening among Mormons in Europe was something similar to what I had observed, as a young boy, happening in America during the 1930s and 40s. I call it a process of internal consolidation and emerging respectability which, in America, helped create the foundation for the tremendous growth of the Church since the 1950s.

That foundation is now also being laid in Europe. This is not to say that all is well in the European Zions, but the process has begun and the "multiple Zions"[1] spoken of by President Harold B. Lee are likely to become as much a haven for the Saints in Europe as the Great Basin Kingdom in America was for those of another era.

Some of the changes taking place in Europe are well known and significant: the general increase of Church membership in Europe from 34,000 in 1950 to 129,000 in 1974; the calling of native brethren as General Authorities, Regional Representatives, and mission presidents; the recent creation of new missions in Belgium, Italy, and France and of new stakes in Denmark, Sweden, and France; the holding of regional conferences that provide necessary spiritual, psychological, and social support to members whose daily struggles in smaller wards and branches sometimes make it difficult to perceive the real parameters of the expanding Church; the perfecting of programs for intercultural communications where manuals, handbooks, and instructions of all kinds are written in a language sensitive to local culture and therefore conducive to understanding and implementation; and the building of chapels during the past decade and a half that bear both material and psychological witness of permanence and stability in the community. All of these, and many other equally publicized changes, are contributing their share to the important consolidation by which the Church gradually and naturally works out its universal destiny.

But there are also quiet changes taking place beneath the surface and away from the lights where, as Elder Richard L. Evans has said, common people and common Saints bring about uncommon results. For example, though often burdened with heavy day-to-day cares of Church administration, the new generation of European Church leaders has long-range perspectives, and they exude a quiet optimistic confidence in the future of the Church in their countries now that the age of emigration is over. Where in times past new Mormons would be won, be assimilated into the branch, and then leave for America, and where Mormon children would mature and then emigrate to find marriage partners of their own faith—now they remain, if not in the home ward or branch, at least within an enlarging and more mobile European Church population. More importantly, local Church units are now beginning to enjoy the blessings not only of numerous complete families—father, mother, and children—but of a network of two- and three-generation families who provide stability and leadership within the branches. These kinds of Mormons have also become a more effective leavening agent in their communities for changing the image of the Church, thus planting seeds with neighbors and friends that later missionaries will harvest.

Recent studies in America and Canada have confirmed the decisive influence Latter-day Saint families who are happy, practicing Christians have upon their non-Mormon neighbors.[2] We may even predict that to the extent European Mormon families are able to provide this example in societies where family disarray has become epidemic, many friends will be moved to inquire about the Church. One can hardly overstate the central role strong nuclear families can have for the total well-being of the Church.

Equally important in the long run is the trend for more young European members to serve missions. While I do not have the statistics to show how many are presently serving, the example of the Salzburg Branch, which had six missionaries in the field in 1974, is becoming more common. Moreover, in 1974 most European mission presidents were setting goals of twenty-five or more native missionaries for each mission.

The example of Elder Wolfgang Pils from Darmstadt, Germany, serving in 1974 as a mission assistant in the London, England, Mission, provides not only a prototype that many European brethren have and will follow, but is also reminiscent of the impact of returned missionaries on the Church in America after World War II. During his mission, Elder Pils experienced the usual spiritual rebirth, learned the gospel through study and faith, and was able to discuss it in considerable depth with members and nonmembers alike. He also gained valuable experience in the spirit and practice of church administration under the guidance of a master teacher. He formulated a resolve to return to his home to share in the work there. But, in addition, Elder Pils also made plans for university training in medicine, which will prepare him for an influential role in community affairs wherever he may choose to settle. Parenthetically, the growing interest Latter-day Saints show in participating in higher education and in community and national affairs is also an encouraging sign of the times.

In several stakes and districts, members with mission experience or its equivalent are already providing a changed spirit of Church leadership. The influences of the postwar democratic age, together with the breakdown of traditional authoritarian family and social customs, have helped produce a leadership that has become more aware of better ways to exercise priesthood authority as counseled in Section 121 of the Doctrine and Covenants. In addition, instruction and example by native brethren are developing a leadership practice based on unfeigned love and service without vanity. Some results have already been dramatic. Interviews conducted in this spirit with youth and with adults desiring to attend the temple have new powers of teaching and motivation that had previously only partially been used. In the years to come the benefits of this type of leadership, well-known to a generation of American Saints, will become increasingly apparent in Europe.

Other recent institutional changes in the Church in Europe can only be mentioned here. These include the establishment of the seminary and institute programs with their systematic study of the gospel and the resultant strengthening of testimonies. Earlier European Saints had often desired more Church literature in order to become gospel scholars. Now more young Latter-day Saints have mastered English, a few native European Church authors are emerging, and there is an improved transcultural translation of a broader range of Church literature. All of this bodes well for producing a generation that not only believes the gospel but knows what it believes.

The changes also include the temples and temple worship. It is difficult to measure the impact of temple worship, but conversations with European Saints often turn to expressions of gratitude for new insights into life and new motivation from the instruction and spirit coming from the temple. Moreover, as already noted, more careful interviewing by local authorities for temple visits has also done its part in strengthening the Saints.

Besides the several ways we have considered in which the Church in Europe is gradually consolidating itself as an institution and the broadened membership developing a firmer self-identity, certain changes taking place in European society in general are creating a more favorable climate for the Church. Consider, for example, the important experience gained by the European peoples in the practice of democracy and how this has helped break down many traditional prejudices that historically kept them from considering a "new" religion. This democratic upswing is especially important for the younger generation, who have a greater yearning for a whole philosophy of life or ideology than their parents' generation, spiritually scarred as it has been by wars, depression, and false "gods that failed." One Latter-day Saint university professor in Berlin, Dieter Berndt, sees the recent European student demonstrations as expressions of the young people's desire to free themselves from the values of the past and find something substantial to believe in. Berndt believes that many of these youth will come into the Church if we can successfully communicate our message to them.[3] With such talent and ambition, he believes the prospects of the Church are bright.

Other Europeans are approaching the Church favorably from another perspective. Professor Ernst Benz [whose essay on Mormonism is included in this volume], the noted scholar of religious history from the University of Marburg (W. Germany) is one of them. He told me that European scholar-intellectuals can no longer condescendingly consider Mormonism a sect. After two visits to Utah, Benz taught seminars to theology students at the University of Marburg, pointing out not only the unusual vitality in Mormonism as compared to traditional Christianity, but the uniqueness of Mormonism's cosmology. He also emphasized the similarity of the Mormon doctrine of God-man relationships to that preached in the early Christian church and by several European mystics.[4] Against this backdrop, Benz has argued that attempts to dispatch the Mormons through the old polygamy diatribes or, in a more modern setting, as a monolithic bastion of finance capitalism, fall short of the mark and will not do.

The long-range psychological significance of Mormonism losing its disparaging "sect" appellation, plus the willingness of educated Europeans to examine Mormonism for ideas that may help them in fashioning a happy, meaningful life in today's world should not, in my opinion, be underestimated—particularly considering that ten times more European students are presently attending universities and colleges than there were in the 1920s and 1930s. It is conceivable that as confidence in traditional Christianity continues to decline, those seeking a new creed to believe in will more seriously consider the Church and its doctrine.

Another environmental change affecting the Church is the economic recovery and prosperity that has come to Europe since the end of World War II. Mormons in Europe, as in America, now more than ever before enjoy a new affluence and also reflect a broader spectrum of social classes. These conditions, plus the training and hard work of common working-class parents, have made it possible for second- and third-generation Mormons to have educational and other opportunities for professional careers and community recognition and to bring sophisticated leadership skills to Church assignments. Significantly, these Mormons are able to interest like-minded friends with similar expectations to consider membership in the Church.

Finally, the changing climate in Europe will undoubtedly be affected positively by events such as Elder Charles Didier's forthright 1973 explication of the Church's doctrines and mission over French national television, by the invitation of the publisher of *The Times* of London to a mission president in England to publish news and features on the Church, by the life and work of a successful but humble government officer in Sweden, and by the thousands of optimistic Saints in both free and restricted parts of Europe who foresee a future built upon but not determined by the past.

As a consequence of all these changes, the Church not only has developed stability and permanence in countries where Mormons have lived for nearly a century and a half, but also has gained a strong foothold elsewhere in the traditionally Catholic countries of France, Italy,

Spain, and Portugal, and is preparing to carry its message to Greece, Yugoslavia, and other parts of Eastern Europe.[5]

This evaluation may seem to some euphoric. I am aware of the problems that beset the Church in Europe; they are not to be taken lightly. Temptations are as great in Europe as elsewhere, and the Saints there are as human as anywhere in the world. But there are, as I have tried to point out, numerous similarities and parallels with the condition of the Church in the United States a decade or two ago. Thus European Saints and leaders need not be discouraged. In the preconsolidating days in America many sacrament meeting attendances hovered around ten and fifteen percent, and the number of missionaries in the field or young people being married in the temple was not nearly so high as it is today. Nevertheless, a foundation was being laid for the expansion of the Church, first in the rest of the United States and then in the world. Europe will not lag behind; the harvest there is by no means over. What is presently happening to the families of Hans Malzl, Jean-Albert Babin, Thomas Hill, and Bo Wennerlund in contemporary Europe could have happened to Jakob Tobler and his generation in the nineteenth century only in America.

THE CHURCH IN FRENCH-SPEAKING EUROPE

Charles A. Didier

My dear brothers and sisters, I am pleased to be among you and to share with you information about some of the developments of the Church during the last ten years in Europe, particularly in the French-speaking areas. I have selected ten facts that, in my opinion, have helped in this development and have put the Church where it now belongs.

Going back to 1966, I think one major event took place that year which subsequently really helped the development of the Church. This was the establishment of the distribution center in Belgium. For the first time, members in the French-language area had a ready supply of Church literature: all the handbooks; all the lesson manuals for the Relief Society, Sunday School, and Priesthood; and publications dealing with programs and conferences.

Just to let you know what this means, when I joined the Church, all we had were the Book of Mormon and about twenty sections of the Doctrine and Covenants. There was no Pearl of Great Price, and no priesthood or Sunday School manuals. I remember very well the typical priesthood lesson in those days: there we were, a maximum of four to six members sitting with the missionaries, sharing a sheet of paper with some text that the mission had published. Each member would read from the same sheet of paper and then pass it to the next person. That was the priesthood lesson. The Sunday School manual was not much of an improvement—something the mission had printed—and it was the same manual year after year. So you can imagine what it was like when in 1966 we received the first home evening manual in our own language, and when we started to have priesthood and Sunday School manuals, not only for the adult class but also for the children. Different Primary manuals also became available for the different classes. Thereafter, we started to receive the Doctrine and Covenants; not just twenty sections, but all the sections. This was followed by the Pearl of Great Price. Then we were able to read in our own language *A Marvelous Work and a Wonder,* and to receive many other hardbound books recently translated into French. And so, suddenly, we received the essence of the Church; in fact, all these materials—that lack of which had held Church development back—were now literally within our grasp. And for me, this became one of the most important events to help transform the Church in Europe in the following years. This fact—the expansion of translation services in all of Europe, the translation of valuable reading materials into eight major European languages, and the ready availability of the translated works through the distribution center—have all combined to serve the Church well.

The second fact I want to mention is also an important one. Right after the publication of all the new materials, local priesthood leaders were called to take the place of the missionaries in branch and district presidencies. Up until then, missionaries were spending much of their time serving in local priesthood positions. Gradually, local members began to occupy all the branch presidencies.

A third fact followed in good order: the division of the different missions and districts into smaller units, thus providing the mission president with better control, not only of the missionaries but also of the local leadership. I remember when only one mission existed in France. The missionaries saw the mission president once or twice a year. Today the missionaries have the pleasure (I don't know if they call it a pleasure) of seeing their mission president every six or eight weeks; and, besides being able to have better control over the missionary work, the presidents can help the missionaries more effectively in their proselyting work. These developments—the division into smaller units for better control and more effective proselyting, improved language abilities acquired through the language training mission, and improved preparations and the discussions—have now combined to give missionaries something systematic to follow. I remember the first two missionaries that came to my home. All they had was the Book of Mormon, some pictures of Indians, and a few other things. That is how they had to teach the people, so to speak. They did a good job. I am here today, and that is one result of the system; but I think it took years to convert some people. I remember it took eight months to convert my mother. Now, thanks to the discussions, we can convert investigators faster and in a much better way because there is an organized system. So, to summarize the third fact, we now have better training, smaller units, better control, and better language abilities on the part of the missionaries.

The fourth fact is the building of "real" chapels. I say real chapels because before 1966 members met in what we call meeting halls, but which were, in fact, apartments, or sometimes not even that. On occasion it was very difficult to bring people into those places because they were not at all adequate. So around 1966 a real construction program was begun. Soon we saw chapels blossoming everywhere—in Belgium (three chapels in three years), in France, and in Switzerland. Of course, this attracted people; members were no longer afraid to bring their friends and converts to the Church, and it really helped to build up the image of the Church.

I turn now to the fifth fact. When the building boom started and after we had more members, people began to be impressed with the improved quality of the Church in our own lands. The members did not want to emigrate to the States any more. They started to stay in their own cities. It means that we saw more and more marriages among our young people. Earlier, it had been a real problem for young girls to find a husband in the Church, and so most of them flew to America to find a husband. All this was a good sign of activity. Our members were marrying among themselves, and at the same time we saw the activity in the temple increase by more than 150 percent in just a few years.

The sixth fact is that thanks to those marriages and because of the new conversions we are now starting to see in all of Europe a second Mormon generation. Right now the second Mormon generation is between fourteen and fifteen years of age; these are the future leaders of the Church. Before too long we will see them in action as local missionaries. I remember that when I was mission president in 1970—there were three French-speaking missions at that time—we had a total of fifteen local missionaries for a population of ten thousand members. Three or four years later there were forty-five local missionaries. I know that within one or two years from now we will have more than a hundred. So we see a real increase in the number of local missionaries, thanks, of course, to an inspired Prophet who constantly encourages us to call every young man on a mission. I think the Prophet's call to us will be followed.

The seventh fact is, I think, very important in the development of the Church; it deals with the supervision provided by the program of the Regional Representatives. For the first time there was a real decentralization of the Church, and the quality of communication between Church headquarters and the missions in Europe greatly improved. During the first ten years I knew the Church, I saw one General Authority. That was all. Absolutely no contact, no realization of what the Church could become in Europe and was here in Salt Lake City. The supervising program of the Regional Representatives has helped local leaders both to become acquainted with the programs of the Church and to become much better leaders.

At the same time the Regional Representatives were called, a reorganization of the departments of the Church was begun—financial, real estate, legal, and building. All the departments established their representatives in certain cities. For us, this meant the development of a regional office representing those departments in Frankfurt. Again, better control meant better help could be provided to the mission presidents and to the local leaders.

The eighth fact aiding the development of the Church in Europe is the program of seminaries and institutes implemented there recently. I am very pleased to see here Brother [James R.] Christianson, whom I knew, and who was, so to speak, the founder of this program in Europe. I am very pleased to report to him that, thanks to his efforts, today there is a new spirit among the youth. There is a new knowledge about the Church; and thanks also to a great program, we shall have not only better missionaries from our youth but improved leaders in the future. They will know the history and doctrine of the Church better and will be better examples, thus bringing about the conversion of many other people.

Another fact, the ninth, that also helped was the creation of area conferences. We had our first area conference in Munich in 1973. For the first time in the history of the Church in Europe, we had a gathering of more than thirteen thousand members of six or seven different nationalities together in one place, to see or listen to the prophet of the Lord there in our midst, and to listen to the messages of the other General Authorities. I think that was a unifying factor for the Saints in Europe. It gave them a better idea, again, of the reality of the Church and the reality of the leaders. They had heard about the leaders; they had read about them; but they had never seen them. The area conferences have really helped.

Finally, the tenth fact is Church growth and the creation of stakes. The first French-speaking stake was created in Paris, France, in November 1975. But this is only the beginning. Our goal, now, is to have a new stake created in what I call the Latin area of Europe every two years. It will require a lot of effort and a lot of sacrifice from the members. But I know the things I am trying to explain to you are true, that the Church in our area will grow, as it grows elsewhere in the world. I leave that testimony with you in the name of Jesus Christ. Amen.

THE CHURCH IN GERMANY, SWITZERLAND, AND AUSTRIA

F. Enzio Busche

My dear brothers and sisters, it is with humility that I have accepted the call to take part in this symposium, "The Church in Europe: Challenges of the Second Century."

As a convert to the Church from Germany, I would like, at the beginning of my remarks, to say a word of thanks—thanks for an all-encompassing and unpretentious love and devotion that thousands of young men and their families have shown my family, my brothers and sisters in the Church, and countless numbers of my countrymen. Most of those young people have come from this western part of the United States and have had a close personal relationship with this great and unique university [BYU]. It is my hope that the day is not far when masses of people from the nations in Europe and from the world will understand the light that radiates from this part of the earth.

In accordance with my assignment, I will make an attempt today to report on the development of the Church during the last ten years in the German-speaking areas of Europe. This report is, of course, only the subjective observations of one individual—an individual who is a native German, who was converted to the gospel of Jesus Christ eighteen years ago, and who has been a Regional Representative of the Council of the Twelve, assigned to Germany for the last 5½ years. Let me preface my observations by saying I am firmly convinced that the development of all aspects of the Church during the last ten years will aid the growth of the Church in the future more than previously would have been thought possible. Growth and development, according to my experience, are dependent on the faithfulness, the obedience, the willingness to sacrifice, and the devotion and love of the local leadership. We have had visible success in all areas.

The German-speaking area presently [1976] includes six missions and seven stakes. The youngest of these is the Düsseldorf Stake, formed just three years ago. Even though the Church had four German-speaking stakes ten years ago, it is apparent that the understanding of the Church's worldwide mission of salvation, with its accompanying organizational, educational, and logistical responsibilities, was still in its beginning. There were practically no local missionaries, and the mission presidents of those days were all sent from America. Only a few newly completed chapels and buildings representative of the Church were available.

Looking at numbers, one sees that the Church in the German-speaking areas has grown only about 10 percent in the last ten years. However, one can find some areas with tremendously good growth and others with stagnating or shrinking membership. In analyzing this situation, I must conclude that where the local leaders have failed to recognize either the extent of their responsibility in Christ's plan of salvation or the devoted activity it requires, no growth can be expected.

Milestones for the development of the Church in Germany were the regular visits by General Authorities as well as the visits by priesthood leaders and leaders of various committees of the Church to regional meetings. Along with these visits and the work of thousands of industrious missionaries and exemplary mission presidents and their families, more and more local members began to catch the vision of their personal responsibility in the Church; actual church life acquired real content and purpose. Today nearly everywhere within the German-language area are local branches with responsible leadership functioning in harmony with both the letter and the spirit of the gospel.

An especially visible sign of growth in our area is the building program of the Church. Between 1960 and 1965 twenty-two chapels were built. Between 1966 and 1970 an additional twelve were constructed, and between 1971 and 1975 twelve more came into existence. Today every mission district and stake has several meetinghouses designed and built to Church standards, thereby allowing members to enjoy the full gospel programs of human and spiritual development. Applications for building construction presently being processed indicate that in the years to come the building program of the Church will continue to grow.

The growth and development of the missionary program among the German-speaking youth is especially notable. Ten years ago few young people went on missions; those who did were sometimes admired but more often derided. Today there are approximately seventy missionaries in the field from German-speaking countries, and bishops and branch presidents have accepted the goal to view each young man as a prospective missionary. I do not hesitate to say that a large portion of this success is a direct result of the seminary program of the Church. This program was initiated about four years ago in Germany and has grown and expanded consistently in this time. The leadership of the seminary and institute program has gradually been put into the hands of qualified local members. I am certain that in the future the influence of this program will grow even stronger. For instance, in March of this year a special education week was held in Hanover for students of high schools and universities. Approximately forty young people attended this outstanding gathering and were thrilled by many spiritual experiences.

The calling of Brother Hans-Jürgen Saager as president of the German-Düsseldorf Mission marks the first time that a German member was called From Germany as mission president. It may well be that one day other residents of Europe will be able to receive such important callings as that of mission president.

I feel that I should also mention the exceptionally important role mission presidents have played in the German-speaking areas in the past and in the present. They and their families have given examples of happy family life, obedience to the laws and commandments of the Lord, and service under difficult conditions. These examples have been of importance to the development of the Church in our countries. It will be a special challenge to the local leadership of the Church to emulate the example of the great mission presidents of the past.

A blessing for the members of the Church in Europe was the area conference held in the summer of 1973. Here we felt the love and closeness of the prophet and the other General Authorities of the Church. We are looking forward with great pleasure to the area conference, which was announced for the summer of this year in Germany, [1976] in my home town of Dortmund. The leadership of the local stake is shouldering the preparations for this conference.

Perhaps the most important improvement in the Church in Germany is that since the fall of 1975 a General Authority has been assigned to our area. He has been in constant contact with the local leadership and has instilled in the missionaries a new drive and enthusiasm by giving a new dimension to missionary work. The members in Central Europe are thankful for the calling of such a dedicated leader as Elder [Joseph B.] Wirthlin. In the short time he has been among us, the members of the Church have grown to love him, and we are already seeing the first fruits of his labors.

We have also found the teacher development and meetinghouse library programs of the Church to be especially valuable. The high quality of the training materials for the auxiliary organizations and the priesthood has made a lasting impression upon the members.

The growing faithfulness of Church members is documented by temple statistics. Many of the brothers and sisters sacrifice a week of their vacation to spend this time in the temple to dedicate themselves to the work of salvation. The temple facilities are being used 300 percent more now than ten years ago, though the growth of membership shows only an increase of 10 percent. We see also in the Swiss temple in Zollikofen, in the person of Brother Immo Luschin von Ebengreuth, the first local German resident to be called with his family as a temple president.

We are also thankful for the television films of the Tabernacle Choir, which have received wide airing in the German-state owned television system. Since the Church is in its initial stages of public relations work in Europe, such films help us overcome an abundance of false information about the Church that has been spread through newspapers, radio, television, and literature. It seems almost as if other churches and politically motivated individuals have made a methodical attempt to spread false information about the Church. This causes many people in the German-speaking areas to see the Church in an unfavorable light.

Members and missionaries will be challenged more and more to make the Church known through their lives and testimonies to the public. In spite of images both positive and negative, the Church in many circles is still practically unknown. The continued growth of the public-relations work of the Church in Europe will have the goal of bringing the Church to its justified position in the public eye. This way, men of goodwill will have the opportunity to see the fruits of The Church of Jesus Christ of Latter-day Saints and understand the message of the restoration of the gospel of Jesus Christ in our day.

Though much has been done, we recognize, by seeing the masses of people following materialistic and ungodly philosophies and suffering from the results of these teachings, that we are still in the beginning. We notice that we will have to sacrifice more, to work harder, to listen more prayerfully to the words of the prophet in order to bring the fulness of the gospel with its fruit to the hearts of millions of people in the countries of Central Europe. It must be done. It will be done.

THE CHURCH IN SCANDINAVIA AND FINLAND

Bo G. Wennerlund

It is a stimulating experience for me to be here in this place I have heard about for so many years. This is my first time in the United States, and as I have been a member of the Church for twenty-five years, you will understand how much I have heard about BYU, the Tabernacle Choir, the templegrounds, everything. And this is the first time I have seen them. It is a dream come true.

It will not be possible to comment on all the factors I think should be mentioned here as a part of the development of the Church in the Nordic area.[6] So I will save time and words by a couple of transparencies I have prepared [reproduced here as a data table]. I hope they will help you to follow me.

You have already heard that I am a native Swede. I have been working in and serving the Church in Sweden since 1949, and just recently in November I was called as a Regional Representative of the Twelve to the stakes in the Swedish and Danish regions. My experiences and observations will, of course, be based very much upon my observations in Sweden. But as I have also traveled in Norway, Finland, and Denmark, I have consulted priesthood leaders there, and they endorse what I will now present as valid for their areas, too. So I think this report can fairly be considered as a report on the Church in all of the Nordic countries.

By way of background, table one shows some figures I think will be of interest to you. In the first column you will see the number of inhabitants in each nation. In the second, you find the area of land covered by each nation, expressed in square kilometers. The third shows the population density. Here you will notice that the Nordic area and the United States are not very different, while the people in West Germany and Great Britain, in the eyes of a Scandinavian at least, seem to live almost on top of each other. (I hope you don't mind, Brother Busche, when I say that!) It is quite different with us. There are, in other words, large unpopulated areas in the four countries.

Table 1
GEOGRAPHIC AND POPULATION COMPARISONS

Country/ Area	Number of Inhabitants	Km^2	Inhab/ Km^2	LDS Members	LDS Members per 100,000 Inhabitants
Denmark	5.1 mil.	43,000	118.6	4,245	83.2
Finland	4.9 "	337,000	14.5	3,226	65.8
Norway	4.0 "	324,000	12.3	3,050	76.3
Sweden	8.2 "	450,000	18.2	5,451	66.5
Nordic Area	2.2 "	1,154,000	19.2	15,972	71.9
USA	22.2 "	9,363,000	23.5	2,267,850	1,030.8
West Germany	67.2 "	249,000	269.9	22,979	34.2
Great Britain	57.0 "	244,000	233.6	73,006	128.1

The next column indicates the number of LDS members. Here you see a great difference—16,000 in our area; 2.3 million in the United States; 23,000 in West Germany; and 73,000 in Great Britain [1974 figures]. More interesting, however, is the last column where the number of LDS members per 100,000 inhabitants is seen. Later I shall make a comment on that. Yet these figures do represent milestones in the development of the Church. If you look back a few years to consider the development of the Church in the Nordic area since World War II, some of these milestones are easily detected.

Now, I would like to present my choice of factors that have had the greatest influence on the development of the Church and on the growth of its members. Before the war and immediately thereafter, church meetings and activities in the Nordic countries took place, with a few exceptions, in rented premises. From 1948 to 1954 mission presidents were authorized for the first time to purchase meetinghouses for the branches in these missions. For example, in Sweden alone, twenty-four buildings were bought and remodeled to suit the needs of the membership. This meant, to members and nonmembers alike, that the Church had come to stay. No one any longer had the feeling that the Church, together with the missionaries, would suddenly move from his town.

This feeling of permanency was of great importance to the Church and its members. During 1948 and 1949, hundreds of faithful, experienced members had emigrated, thus emptying strong branches and leaving behind them branches that had to start from the very beginning again. In the wake of this a special call came again from the First Presidency of the Church in the beginning of the fifties for the Saints to stay in their own lands to build the kingdom there. My family had planned to leave Sweden in 1953. Yet we stopped those plans immediately when this call came to our attention. A few members have emigrated since then, but not so many that the Church has suffered.

Then, another factor of importance to us occurred during the Korean War, 1950 to 1953, when the number of missionaries was greatly reduced. This was a sad thing; but as is often the case when bad things happen, something good comes of it. In our missions, it meant that missionaries could no longer be bound to assignments as branch presidents, district presidents, auxiliary superintendents, and so forth. Local leaders had to be called. This was the beginning of the training of local leadership.

Not long after the call to the members to stay in their lands, the First Presidency announced plans for the construction of a temple in Switzerland. With this announcement, an important motivation to emigrate was done away with. But this was not the only result of having a house of the Lord in Europe. In a few years, most of the leaders in the missions had been to the temple with their families. Gradually, the results could be seen. In Sweden, for example, we used to say to each other, "We have stopped playing around in the Church now." In other words, we wanted to say that we had learned to take our lives, our callings, and our membership in the Lord's Church more seriously. And we were blessed in our homes and in our Church work.

During the years 1959 to 1966 we had General Authorities residing in Europe, specifically Elder Alvin R. Dyer and President Ezra Taft Benson. At the same time, we had strong mission presidents who particularly stressed the law of sacrifice. Some members in Sweden, I remember, grumbled that these mission presidents were a little too tough. Today, I am glad. I met one of those mission presidents at a reunion last week in Salt Lake. I said, "We will always be grateful that you had the courage to demand sacrifice from our hands." And I particularly recall his saying to me, "Brother Wennerlund, I want you to know one thing. I never hesitate to ask a member to make a sacrifice, because I know he will be blessed; and I know he needs the blessings." That was the kind of theme stressed heavily in those years. Before that time we did not know of any ward budget to be paid; we did not know of building funds. We had never been asked to pay for the maintenance of our meetinghouses.

Here is another development. Our Sunday evening meetings had previously been called public meetings, with no sacrament administered. Even though President Spencer W. Kimball in his visit to our area in 1955 had organized the first elders quorums in Sweden and elsewhere, these did not begin to function as such until Elder Dyer and President Benson came. Thereafter local brethren were called as councilors in the larger districts. Many changes were made, and the main body of the Priesthood was united in its support of the mission presidents, giving as much as demanded. And the membership followed. When I look back on those days, I do not think we would have been ready to accept it all if it had not been for the prior construction of the temple in Europe.

Around 1960, the present Translation Services Program began to take form, at least as we saw it in our missions. Handbooks of instruction, lesson manuals, leadership materials, and church literature became available in our own languages. I remember the joy we felt when the first priesthood handbook for district and branch presidents came from Elder Alvin R. Dyer's office in Frankfurt. As the translation program developed during the years that followed, it played an important role in the growth of the Church in northern Europe. Influenced by the correlation program, the new home teaching program, and the home evening program,

Church leaders placed emphasis on more advanced leadership training. The effect could be felt in what I like to call the "one-church, one-program program," indicated a few years ago by President N. Eldon Tanner of the First Presidency.[7] The result of this development was shown by the organization of the Copenhagen, Denmark, Stake in June 1974, and the Stockholm, Sweden, Stake in April 1975. The formation of these stakes was not a change in organizational form only. We felt the strength of our stakes in the wards and the branches.

A spirit of maturity has come to our lands. We have seen leaders grow as never before. We now see bishops assuming their responsibilities in ways unknown to the branch presidents of old. There is a spirit of growing faith, of devotion, of willingness to magnify priesthood callings.

Now that is what I have written down. But I would like to make some additional comments about the present and future situation for the Church in the Nordic area, thereby reinforcing my contention that things are improving. The member-missionary program, for example, is beginning to come of age. President McKay's call—every member a missionary—is starting to take hold. As an illustration of its increasing effectiveness, two months ago in the Stockholm area there were forty-four member referrals that the missionaries had not yet had time to visit! That had never happened before. Contrary to what missionaries had always done, they are now spending more time teaching than searching. That does not mean we have reached the goal yet, for we members are not yet involved in supporting the missionaries as we should be. The importance of the home evening teaching program, for example, is not yet completely understood. But we are working on it. Stake presidents are working on it. Mission presidents are working on it.

Aside from the member-missionary program, the leadership training has been improved through the flow of advanced materials. And the seminary and institute programs have helped to prepare a new generation of leaders more qualified and enthusiastic than ever before. I will tell you my personal experience with this. I had five children at home studying seminary the first year it began. We would get up early in the morning and there, sitting in different places in our house, our young people would study the gospel. This was a wonderful experience. Other families have experienced it, too. The work is going forward very well with seminaries and institutes, and they have had a great influence on the young people. Thus I agree completely with Elder Busche that this is a major reason for the missionaries going out from our own wards and branches. At the present time, for example, more than 10 percent of all full-time missionaries in the Nordic area are our own local missionaries. Last week there were fifty-eight local missionaries out in the field, and more are going out every month. For example, in my own ward, five more local missionaries will be called before the end of this year.

So I would say that while the development of the Church may not show the number of converts and baptisms we see in Latin America, the Church has nevertheless been growing rapidly in quality in our area; and with the quality will also come results in growth and expansion. I said to one of the stake presidents not long ago when I was visiting them: "With these men that you have available, the good leadership you have, the result must come. It must come and it will come. I know it will." So I believe the future is bright for these areas.

Let me illustrate our potential for expansion in another way. I do not know how much you know about this area, but on the map you can easily find Denmark, Norway, Sweden, and Finland. At present we have a stake organized in Copenhagen, the capital of Denmark. We have another stake organized in Stockholm. But let's look at the future. In Oslo, President [John] Langeland recently reorganized the Oslo and the Drammen districts (which are close to each other) into one district in the south of Norway with 1,700 members and a fully organized district council. It is now functioning as a stake, working for stakehood. I don't know how long it will take; I can't prophesy about that. It's up to the General Authorities to do that.

Let me cite another example. I was over in Finland recently and met with President [Stephen] Mahoney. He showed me on a map that he had submitted a recommendation for the Helsinki District with 1,400 members and the Turku District (or Abo District, as we say in Sweden), with close to 1,000 members. He had recommended a combination of those two districts to make it strong and ready for stakehood. It was turned down, however, because some of the northern branches in the Turku District were too far away from Helsinki. But he said, "Next time I make the recommendation, I want to take those northern branches and put them into the Tampere District; that will make it a district with a little more than 2,000 or 2,200 members." He added, "We are not ready yet for stakehood, but we soon shall be."

May I conclude by mentioning something I believe is really interesting. A quite new spirit is coming into our schools, and they are showing interest in us. This certainly is a new development. Just six years ago I was assigned by the mission president to write the statement about the Church to be sent to all the publishers of encyclopedias and information books of that kind destined for the schools; we knew that a new edition was forthcoming. Yet at the time they showed little interest in us. "We thank you very much for the help you are offering," they wrote back, "but we have already asked divinity scholars to write about the several churches, among them also the Mormon Church."

The publishers then came out with materials that are not completely true. They forgot to include things that are important, while mentioning things that are less important. But changes have now come.

I had the privilege of working closely with a doctor of divinity in Stockholm who is influential in the schools. This man, Dr. Persson, is a member of the Association of Teachers of Religion in Sweden's public schools. He is also working with similar organizations in Norway and Denmark. Through him, new books on religions are being printed. He has discarded the old books because they are not factual. "These old books," he said, "will not be used any longer." Interestingly, I was asked to provide material, which was presented to Dr. Persson last week to be printed in a new book for junior high school students (ages thirteen through fifteen in Sweden). At last Sweden's students will get the story straight.

There are other interesting developments in the schools. The Church Educational System has produced a teaching kit. A thousand copies are now available to the public schools, and new orders are coming in. In addition, Church literature is now being spread among the libraries. We have just received an order for 275 copies of the Book of Mormon to be placed in school libraries, and in public, university, and private libraries.

I will conclude now by saying that I am grateful for all the support we have received in the past and still do receive from the Saints in America. But I am happy also that the Church leadership has been wise enough, and that the mission presidents that have come have been wise enough, to place more and more responsibility on local leaders. And we are proud in Sweden also that a new General Authority has been called from among the native Europeans. The Swedes said, "Isn't that great? We've got a General Authority." I do not think we ever said "we" about France or Belgium before. But now we do. I leave my testimony, brothers and sisters, that the work is going forward everywhere, and we know that it will go forward also in the Nordic area. I leave this testimony with you in the name of Jesus Christ. Amen.

THE CHURCH IN ENGLAND

Peter L. Morley

In May 1840, in the premiere issue of the *Latter-Day Saints' Millennial Star,* the editor, Parley P. Pratt, formally announced a general conference of the Church to be held in Manchester the following July 6.[8] That same edition carried a report of another Church conference that had met in the Temperance Hall in Preston, Lancashire, the previous April 15. Thirty-three branches with a membership of 1,671 were represented. Included were thirty-four elders, fifty-two priests, thirty-eight teachers, and eight deacons of the priesthood.[9]

In addition to this report, Brother Pratt added a brief observation of a phase of English life of the time, vividly corroborated in the works of Charles Dickens: "Landing in a certain Town in England, from a distant country, not long since," he lamented, "I felt my heart pained for the multitude of beggars, and of other persons apparently in distress, who almost thronged the streets."[10] During the next century and a quarter, many like these became Saints and left Britain's shores for the kingdom centered then in Nauvoo and later in the Great Basin. Their descendants, in vastly improved economic conditions, are at present dotted about in a majority of the stakes in America.

Because the new era of Mormonism in Britain is so recent, the pattern of the early period is still vividly etched in the memories of older British Saints. In private correspondence Brother J. Wiles of Ipswich Stake recalled how "at one time members . . . had to meet in a chicken coop to avoid the gangs who were out to tar and feather the Mormon missionaries. [Even] in 1950 a church member was viewed with . . . hostility and suspicion."

By 1976, however, the Mormon scene in Britain has, indeed, changed dramatically. The emigration stream of yesteryear has dwindled to a trickle while the membership for Great Britain and Ireland now pushes beyond eighty thousand. Full 40 percent of the active have joined the Church within the past five years. Where only a few years ago there was the one traditional British Mission, today there are twenty-three stakes, nine missions, and 285 wards and branches. When President Harold B. Lee announced to the 10,000 Saints assembled at the historic Manchester conference in 1971 that in Great Britain the "Church has come of age,"[11] only the most visionary and optimistic could have forseen the 20,000 who, five years later, would throng to each of the separate conferences in London, Glasgow, and Manchester.

Perhaps even more significantly, British Saints have assumed and now provide the permanent leadership for the Church in Great Britain. All four Regional Representatives, all stake presidents, the London Temple president, and the Scotland Edinburgh Mission president, as well as an increasing number of full-time missionaries, are now coming "on stream." The foundation for this growth of the past ten years was laid during the rebuilding years following World War II. Then, an energetic building program, the benefits of which were not immediately felt, plus the construction of and blessings that derived from the London Temple, all combined to increase the level of understanding, spirituality, and commitment to the faith of the members.

More significantly, if less visible, there has emerged an LDS society or culture among the members, so different in its daily and weekly structure from that of the world. British Saints have become self-conscious as a "peculiar people," a group set off from the rest of society, trying to influence it while living within it. The result has been a common striving toward righteous lives, improved leadership, and a strengthening of the membership. President Michael R. Otteson of the Liverpool, England, Stake tried verbally to capture a part of this transformation:

In the summer of 1976 a prominent Church figure on assignment to the British area conferences was heard to comment in the most glorious terms on the growth of The Church of Jesus Christ of Latter-day Saints in the past few decades. A missionary in England some forty years ago, he could not get over the total transformation of the Church in Britain since those early days. Certainly, from the time when the Church was directed from a single mission in Liverpool to the creation of twenty-three stakes, the local membership had seen dramatic growth. But the progress of the Church in Britain today is more than just in numbers. Astute observers have noted a change in the atmosphere within the Church itself.

It would be difficult to determine whether the "type" of convert to the Church in 1976 is substantially different from that in 1946; probably the background both professionally and educationally is not strikingly different when looking at the whole picture. The difference is not in the people themselves, but in their attitude both to the Church and to nonmembers. The newly baptized Latter-day Saint of the nineteenth century invariably had to face disapproval and often the hostility of family members as well as friends. The alternative to being virtually an outcast in an English community where "Mormons" were always strange was usually to emigrate. Many did; and the pride and the kinship which they felt for the Church was taken to the Salt Lake Valley, never properly developing in the British church.

Today, it is by no means uncommon to hear the words "I'm proud to be a Mormon." While the traditionally British reserve still curbs this outward expression to friends and neighbours, the pride is still there and it is growing. It is not difficult to see why. Mass communications, hand-in-hand with growing membership, have eradicated much of the old-fashioned prejudice and superstition about the Church. While this is still there, there is no doubt that it is much diminished. Twenty years ago it was unusual to hear favourable comments passed about the Church by nonmembers. Today people write letters to newspapers commenting on the manners of our missionaries, the work ethic of our members, and the morals of our teenagers. This kind of thing is always difficult to quantify—what we are evaluating is a mood, a feeling that the Church is now strong enough and well enough known to make us feel more ready to openly declare our allegiance. With people much better informed about the Church than they once were, this trend can only further develop.

The outward sign of the Church growth is the creation of stakes. That has confirmed to the membership that the Church is here to stay. It is not a temporary way-station while we pack our bags for the United States. The number of emigrants has now dwindled to insignificant proportion compared with the number of local baptisms. And as each stake is created the local membership respond with a commitment to build and work even harder.

This renewed confidence is a remarkable force if it can be tapped. Certainly we are seeing men and women work harder and make greater sacrifices more readily.

What is particularly relevant today is that many of the people have already acquired leadership ability and positions of prominence in the community. Businessmen, educators, professional men are joining the Church and quickly assuming leadership positions. We have more bishops, stake presidents and Regional Representatives than ever before per head of population, and it is showing in the development of our church programmes which, despite the smaller number of Saints in the wider community, are remarkably well advanced and often the equal of those in the longer established stakes of the Church.

Another expression of the changing Church in Great Britain, with an emphasis upon the development of two-generation Latter-day Saint families, came from Gordon Williams, stake president in Huddersfield. Recalling a conversation with President Harold B. Lee, Brother Williams remembered the prophet's words: "Before a stake can say it is mature there has to be an effective seventies quorum, a welfare project, and a patriarch." President Williams continues:

We have to understand that to become really expansive we have to learn these two lessons—to change our attitudes when and where necessary, and to sacrifice.

There are families who are beginning to support their young men on paid missions; there are chapels built which are being paid for on completion; there are welfare programmes and home storage that are beginning to take root. As we grow in these areas of correct attitudes and sacrifice we also see our children learning these precepts and in a few years they will be performing, as only they have known how from childhood, for as Christ said, he did those things which he had seen his father do.

We are thankful that the Saints have taken heed of the promptings of our leaders and have stayed to build the Church within our own lands—and I use the plural to acknowledge the contribution the Saints have made in their own lands in Scotland, Ireland, Wales, and England.

Other milestones have been the development of and increased services given from our Church offices in Lichfield, the Church Distribution and Garment Production units in Manchester, and now, after extensive microfilming of genealogical records of the British Records Office and records of other churches, the genealogical libraries in four stakes with the main centre at Hyde Park Chapel, London.

Progress has also been achieved through the introduction of the seminary and institute programs. As a result of special conditions, we could not feasibly organize seminary and institute on a released-time basis. It was similarly impractical to organize them on an early morning basis. Consequently, the Home Study programme was developed in Great Britain in 1968/69. We started with 200 students, but by 1976/77 we had enrolled 2,350 in the seminaries and 2,300 in the institutes.

Another illustration of the process of transformation has been the acceptance of the Church by the media, now in a complimentary manner, and by friends in higher places who can do much to enhance our image. This is also coming from the Saints as they increase in perception of the work in which they are involved and add to their spiritual awareness. All this combines to change not only the Church but the face of the British landscape. Consider, for example, that Mormonism has achieved greater respect and visibility while traditional churches wage a war for mere survival. Brother Arnold Matthews of Leicester, England, Stake observed that to thinking people, the traditional Christian churches no longer

bore any resemblance to the original concept presented by Jesus Christ. Like a creeping paralysis, the apostasy had strangled the living Church, leaving in its place an organization that 'Praised God with its lips, but whose heart was far from Him.'

We are an island nation that rose to heights imposed upon it by world conditions, and the experience of our past history is ingrained into our people. These experiences have produced traits of perseverance and tenacity within the membership of the Church, a people who will not be deterred, and who, having laid a sure foundation for growth during the past decades, look forward with assurance to the future.

As a people we have endured much of any earthly refiner's fire. When the world tells us that we are "down," it is more than likely that another "finest hour," when we "fight alone" is at the door. Destiny has had us stand alone in the face of mighty opposition, a David amongst Goliaths: in the face of the Spanish Armada; during the Napoleonic Wars where great strength was set against us; all of this followed, a century later, by two World Wars. Even when we were standing alone and all seemed lost, the Lord has seen fit to preserve our Isles with help from other nations. These experiences and historical memory have developed within the Saints a heritage of courage. This is apparent in the Church in Great Britain in our determination to build the kingdom and, following our natural heritage, to endure to the end, for only the final victory is that which counts.

One observer metaphorically summarized this transformation in this manner:

It seems from history and experience that whenever a battle rages it is very often a thin line of ardent fighters, loyal and heroic, who turn the tide of battle and win the oscars from those for whom they fight—although few of them ever fight to gain those oscars. And so it seems that in the Church we have a similar situation, where we have a thin crust of priesthood with their wives and families who, with zeal and diligence, together with sacrifice and testimonies, keep the other two-thirds of the membership alive and growing and expanding. The thin crust, however, seems to be thickening, and heroes are being made from the other two-thirds—to the surprise of many! Thus tremendous growth of the individual has been brought forth, although we do not forget those who laboured many years before and created the foundation on which to build, but nevertheless a thin line of priesthood is now moving away from the wall—having been up against it—with a confidence heretofore unknown, for no longer are we defending ourselves; there is no longer the embarrassment that may have once been felt, only a strength of character and a desire to be known. There is no longer the feeling of inadequacy, but rather strength and a fear of no one; for the people are learning that when fear knocks on the door, faith answers it, and fear no longer is there.

As we remember the American Bicentennial, we join with you in recognizing that the establishment of the only true Church had to be in your land. Nevertheless, in modesty and humility we remember not only the tens of thousands who left Britain's shores in the founding years, but also those who are at present contributing to a similar growth of the universal Church in our lands.

The scene beheld by Parley P. Pratt when first "landing in a certain town" has in other ways long since vanished. British Saints now enjoy many benefits from an enlightened generation and have perhaps through their repentance not only helped save the land from becoming another Sodom and Gomorrah but have helped bring the Lord's blessings of prosperity into all their lives. Today's Latter-day Saints have the prosperity to sustain both the Church and their families. Educational opportunities, as never before, have become available to the Saints, especially to the youth. These have not been provided by the Lord for worldly profit but for the spiritual growth and establishment of the kingdom. In addition, unlike the "beggars" of the nineteenth century of whom Parley P. Pratt made note, the British Saints have health sufficient to fill our callings and magnify our membership and the attainments of the Church. Saints have registered substantial progress in acquiring positions of influence in local and national affairs. They thereby contribute to a changing climate in the country, calling favourable attention to the Church, its members, and their accomplishments. Thus in the midst of today's plenty, it has become possible for the Saints, for the larger part, to be adequately clothed and fed, to own their own homes, and to develop the leadership ability and quality that knows how to use its time wisely for the building of the kingdom.

With these improved external conditions and a new spirit of example, the Saints are better prepared to exploit a growing trend in Great Britain for the people to question the religious practices and traditions of the past. In Britain there is a demonstrable decline in the activity of other churches and growing skepticism about their doctrines. Conventional churches and religion have little impact upon society, and are especially inadequate for people who at critical times in their lives want answers and cannot find satisfaction. The LDS Church, on the other hand, shows an increasing retention of its members as well as a pronounced tendency for whole families to be baptized.

Retaining our membership within our shores must surely continue to build strength in the Church, though there will always be those who will depart to other lands. Yet the economy of the Westernized world is not so markedly changed from one area to another as to create emigration in large numbers. As we build in our own countries there will surely be a cross-fertilization of LDS society, but there is also a feeling of "being ourselves." The Irish remark about "the English trying to teach us their ways, . . . but they might as well go chase . . ." raises a valid consideration for British Saints, for whilst we are keenly desirous of learning the Lord's ways, there is a strong feeling against becoming "Americanized." Even though we may ultimately adopt the same type of society, we still have need to feel that it is we ourselves who are doing it. Even so, within the units of the Church, we see those wards and stakes in America as a target to which we must aspire so that as a Church we may provide the same facilities throughout. Guidance and direction are surely needed from those who have the relative experience, but the doing of the work must be local, or how are we to grow? We certainly have the leadership potential within our ranks.

In sum, there is a new spirit for the Church in Britain, both among the members and abroad in the land. We are thrilled by the development of the Saints and the Church in our own land and have pride in our membership and a confidence in the future. But we also gain strength and additional desire to "be about our Father's business" when we see the growth of the Church in other lands. Thus tremendous growth of the individual has been brought forth, although we do not forget those who laboured many years before and created the foundation on which to build. I return to paraphrase an earlier thought: a thin line of priesthood is now moving away from the wall with a confidence heretofore unknown, for no longer are we simply defending ourselves.

President Albert S. Green of Nottingham gave poignant expression to this new spirit:

It really is inspiring and makes one proud to be a member of such a living and virile Church when we see all around us other denominations closing their buildings for lack of support. Why they can't see the truth shining from the LDS Church I don't know. Why they can't see and accept the wonderful doctrines and how they conform to the scriptures, I can't understand. Still, I see great years ahead for the Church here and abroad.

The Saints in the British Isles are now truly, "Saints for all seasons." Having established themselves, they will take their part in seeing the work of the Lord fulfilled, particularly as the units of the Church multiply and divide to multiply again in one "eternal round."

THE CHURCH IN ITALY*

Dan C. Jorgensen

The first missionaries to Italy—among them President Lorenzo Snow—arrived around 1850 and, after encountering great difficulties, made some converts among the Waldensian people in the valleys of the Alps. Subsequently, in the 1850s and 1860s, all of these members left Italy for Zion. They established their homes and lived out their lives in America.

*Dan Jorgensen, formerly president of the Italy Milano Mission, 1971–74, was in attendance at the conference and was invited to present, spontaneously, some insights on the Church in Italy.

The Church did not come back to Italy again until the 1960s, when four or five converts among Italian "guest workers" in Germany—we call them *Gastarbeiter* in Germany—returned to their homes and thereafter helped to get the Italian branches established. The brethren then felt the time was right to send missionaries once again into Italy. They sent missionaries from Switzerland and Germany into the northern parts of Italy to test the waters. Inspired by the Lord, the First Presidency then directed that missionaries from Switzerland and Germany be sent into Italy on a full-time basis. Finally, a mission was established in 1966 with headquarters in Florence. The work had begun.

In addition to the handful of Italian converts who returned from Germany to Italy, bringing the gospel with them, there were also some American military personnel serving in Naples at the naval bases in Sicily and along the Adriatic coast. There were others, too. For example, in 1967 my wife and I came to Italy—to Milan—for my company. There we found two members of the Church. We thus doubled the membership of the Church in the city. Interestingly, the other two members were also recent arrivals. One sister had been converted in Austria, the other in Brazil. The Brazilian sister had also come to Italy to work.

So I was in Italy from almost the beginning of formal missionary work, at least in this century. Since then—1967—we have seen the spirit of the Lord come upon that land and touch the people who have waited so faithfully and so long for the gospel to come. When I left Milan in 1974, there were nearly four hundred members in that one city. The three branches were all staffed entirely by local brethren and sisters. The same was true for the districts.

I would estimate that there must now in Italy be close to four or five thousand members of the Church. At conference [April 1976 general conference] I heard mention of ninety to one hundred baptisms a month in Italy. So the work continues to move forward rapidly. We have seen many blessings come to that land. I leave with you my testimony that the work will continue there and throughout Europe among this great people.

Comments, James R. Christianson

Brothers and sisters, I am grateful for this opportunity and am especially honored to be on a panel with these brethren. I knew them in Europe and had an opportunity to work with them. They are the great men you know them to be. They are typical of many leaders we now have in Europe—men who have joined the Church or who have been in the Church for years and who are second- and third-generation Latter-day Saints. They are prepared now to take over and direct the affairs of the Church throughout Europe. Much of what has needed to be said has been said. I would like to add just a few comments in several areas.

Mention was made of the organization of the stakes. This is one of the most important things that has happened in Europe in the last ten years. When I was a missionary in Switzerland and Austria in 1953 to 1955, we had one high priest in the Swiss Mission. He was a genealogist who had come back from the United States to work there—an old Swiss brother. We had no high priests in Austria. The organization of stakes has now made it possible to have high priests where before there were none. And with the ordaining of high priests, of course, we have bishops and stake presidents. Recently I was called to be a stake president, and I had my first opportunity to ordain a bishop. I gained a new appreciation of what it means for a person to be a bishop, and to have bishops among us. Setting this man apart was a deeply religious, spiritual experience for me. I realized anew that this is a great calling bringing with it tremendous responsibilities and powers. And so to have bishops called throughout continental Europe, along with stake presidents and others who are called to preside as high priests, has had a deep and significant impact upon the Church in those countries.

Another thing I would like to mention is the translation program for Europe to which Brother Didier referred. This was organized and was functioning before 1970. But in 1971 a decision was made to have the actual translation take place in Europe, as also the reviewing and the correcting, without it being sent back to the United States for approval. This was important. It may seem like a small thing, and yet it made possible the production of materials in a much shorter time than was previously possible. They used to take about eighteen months from the time an item was approved for translation until it was produced. With the new arrangements we found that when we first started producing seminary materials in early 1971, we could receive an item and in three months have it translated, corrected, produced, and ready to distribute to the members. This happened with all the seminary materials we produced that year. So this was important when you consider the volume of material that was suddenly available for translation—thousands upon thousands of pages for both seminaries and institutes. It was not just important, but absolutely necessary. In the seminary program you cannot have materials arriving a month, two months, or six months late. Either they have to be there on time or the program does not function. So this was a significant step.

As has been indicated, the organization of the seminaries and institutes began when the first teaching materials were made available in

1971. I had the privilege of being in Europe to work with this program. I can say that mine was a very simple task. As soon as we started talking to the brethren, each of these here and others, it was just a matter of handing them the ball, and they carried it all the way. There was never a time when anyone in Europe objected to having the seminary program instituted. The stake presidents, the mission presidents, the Regional Representatives, and the bishops were all excited and in favor of it. And so in a very short time—the first year, in fact—the program spread throughout Germany, Switzerland, and Austria. The following year it was introduced to the rest of continental Europe. Starting with some 1,500 participants, we now serve nearly 5,000. I think it is difficult for us to predict or to appreciate what kind of impact these developments are going to have not only on the lives of those who are participating but upon future generations.

It is true that teaching materials were produced for Europe prior to 1971. But most things available were for the older members of the Church. So there was a vacuum that needed to be filled. Thus it seems that the right materials, the right program, the right people, and the right time all came together to fill a critical void. Here were materials produced for young people and made available to them—and written purposely for them. The youth responded in an amazing fashion. For example, we have the experience in the United States (and I have worked with the seminary program for many years) of having maybe 40, 50, or 60 percent of our students in areas not served by released-time programs who participate in home study seminary. In Europe it was not unusual for whole countries to have 70 percent of their numerous youth participating in the home study programs. The first year in Sweden, for example, we had 231 participants, and of those 96 percent completed the course, almost all of them studying on a daily basis. If you know anything about home study seminary and the problems involved in that, you will realize that this accomplishment is remarkable.

This experience with home study seminary was repeated year after year, in country after country. The young people, their parents, and their leaders were ready because they responded in such an amazing way. It is too early to assess adequately the impact of this program. It has been functioning now, as Brother Busche said, for almost five years. In spite of such a short time, however, we do know that the number of local missionaries is increasing, in some cases almost fourfold. We believe the seminary program is partly responsible. I remember an instance in one stake in which we wanted to exchange the seminary for the institute program. But the stake president put up some resistance and finally told us he would rather we did not make the changes because, pointing to some sixteen young people who had been called on missions, he felt the seminary program was greatly helping him. With that kind of success he did not feel the need to make any changes. Of course, there are many factors that we can attribute to this success. We do, however, feel that seminary and institute have played a significant role.

There are other indicators as well. One we can point to is the decline in the number of young people who previously left the Church or who became inactive. Most of those participating in the seminary and institute programs are staying in the Church; this was not true in years before 1970. In 1970 and 1971, as I introduced the program, I talked to these people throughout the area, telling them that the time would come when we would write the history of the Church in Europe and we would find that these years, these early years beyond 1970 when the program was introduced, would be considered a turning point for the Church in Europe. I still believe this to be true. I think that the statistics in years to come will bear this out—that the knowledge of the gospel is a tremendous motivating power. It makes all the difference in the world in how a person responds to a call and then how long he stays in that call. Or, for that matter, when discouragements come and defeats and pressures from the outside arise, it will make a difference whether he even stays in the Church. We will find that these young people who are taking part (and many older ones as they come into the Church and immediately take part in this learning process) will stay in the Church and will become the leaders and the parents of future generations of Mormons. They will, in turn, have a tremendous impact on the growth and the development of the Church. It's good to be with you. I bear you my testimony that the gospel is true and that this work and all the things that these brethren have talked about are a valuable part of it. And I say it in the name of Jesus Christ. Amen.

Questions and Answers*

Question

What happens to the members in the transition from missions to stakes?

Charles Didier

The most important fact is that in the missions it is a little like thinking about the celestial kingdom. It's a dream. A stake is a dream for

* The presentations on the Church in Europe evoked a lively response from the audience. Some of the questions sparked extended commentaries from the visiting authorities and gave them an opportunity to expand and, in some cases, to clarify their ideas. Some of the exchange is presented here.

many missions. Yet when the opportunity is presented, the members certainly realize they can do it; and it means that the full load of responsibilities is upon local leaders. No longer do they depend upon the mission president (who in 90 percent of the cases has been an American). So the most important point is that the leaders realize they have to do it. And they do.

The members themselves realize they are now able to receive the complete program of the Church, to participate in it, and really to start to understand what sacrifice means. As one of the brethren mentioned here—and I know very well because I had the same experience—ten years ago we didn't know about building funds or missionary funds. For some members, it was a real problem to accept that they had to sacrifice more. Many came to me (I was then a branch president) saying, "President, you're asking us to participate in the budget. What is that? When the missionaries came, they only asked us to pay tithing, and that's it. Now you're asking more and more and more. When is there going to be an end of it?" I said, "Never."

That's the idea of the stake.

F. Enzio Busche

I hope that I am able, with my limited knowledge of the English language, to explain my feelings correctly. I think there is a special danger for people living for generations, or even years, far away from the central stakes of Zion, because they tend not to develop the feeling of responsibility that an individual member should have. I was baptized and converted to the Church while living in the mission field, and I must say that the mission president was far, far away; the image of the Church was just the image of the weak local branch. Today, eighteen years later, I see that what we had was really not the full Church of Jesus Christ of Latter-day Saints, but rather a local organization with the Book of Mormon and some words of the gospel.

The true knowledge of what it meant to bring to pass the salvation and eternal life of every human being was much too high for us to reach. Thus, when you live for years in such a branch, you need to get a new conversion, new rhythms, new push, and new challenges. These new challenges come when a stake comes. Then you have no excuse. You can't say, "The mission president didn't tell me," or "The mission president is too far away." The members themselves bear the responsibility. When they have questions, they go on their knees and ask the Lord how to do it, when to do it, and where to do it.

This experience brings the members closer together, but it also creates a division. Some Saints grow up very rapidly, as, for example, in

Germany in one of the recently established German stakes, the Düsseldorf Stake, where we have had a tremendous growing experience. Its excellent leadership and baptisms seem unbelievable. On the other hand, some others have not similarly taken up the challenge. They stay in their own ways, and the Lord will have to do something about it. So with this challenge of stakehood, if it is taken correctly, the local leadership comes closer to the Lord and the Church and the members make more progress.

Bo G. Wennerlund

It is, I think, a difficult question to answer. But I think the best answer can be given in one phrase: the spirit of maturity. I remember when one of my boys was growing up. We had a discussion about something; I do not now remember what the subject was. I do remember, however, that I stated my opinion and then he said, "Yes, that is your opinion; but that is not mine, Daddy." That was the first time I'd ever heard those words from him. I looked at him; he seemed like a grown-up person, with his own opinion, not just his father's. After that I did not look upon him the same way. How can you tell when your son has grown into manhood, when he is no longer a boy? It is hard to tell exactly what happens, and when it happens. That is exactly what happens when a stake comes into being. As was indicated here, they have to make their own decisions, not ask somebody else. I would say that is the spirit of maturity.

Arthur H. King

There are two points from my background in Britain that I would like to make in confirmation of what the brethren have had to say. I preface these by noting that I spent my first five years in the Church in a branch. There was only one high priest in that branch. The seminary program was introduced there in 1968, and I taught it for three years. Now my points: First, the enormous differences that I at once noticed, when I went to the north of Britain, between the atmosphere there, where there were stakes, and the atmosphere in the south where there were just branches. I am convinced you cannot lead a full life in the Church until you have stakehood. You do not even know that you are not living a full life because you do not know what a full life is. But the difference is tremendous, and it can be pointed to with one simple word: *responsibility.* The sense of dependence in a mission branch district is very great. You do not realize how dependent you are until you prepare the way for a stake.

The second thing I should like to endorse from personal experience and knowledge is the close connection between attending seminary and going on a mission. Seminary is where young people are prepared for missions, and, above all, it is where they are inspired to go. At least it inspired my seminary students, and paramount in that inspiration was the material about the history of the Church. Students found a great deal of the seminary material challenging, because, of course, it was the same as you have here.

In addition, there is a different standard of knowledge in Europe—an earlier intellectual development—than you have here. Conversely, here you have greater social responsibilities, but there they are not part of a person's development until he or she gets much older.

Question

What effect do the extensive social welfare policies and the political conditions have upon the European Saints?

Bo G. Wennerlund

I think we should take into consideration that in Europe we have, for centuries, had a tradition of a state religion that does not, basically speaking, require anything from its members. You are saved without your own work. In addition, European countries now have a social security program that is extensive; it even solicits people to come and get help. Just a year ago I got a pamphlet informing me of my rights to receive help. "Do you know that you have a right to have help?" it said. Then you could check to see if you fulfilled the income and other requirements. In other words, the government is going out, telling people they have a right to ask for social security help.

In Sweden, at least, there is a growing feeling among many people that all this has gone too far, and Swedes are dividing up more and more into two camps over the issue. Some are for socialized services and some are against them. Yet, while many people realize that the government has gone too far, they also realize that some people really do need this help. We are concerned about it in the branches and the wards. In general, we can see that it weakens people if they lean too much on these things, but at the same time the welfare principles of the Church are now being taught more strongly in leadership and Church meetings. Saints in the northern European area are just now learning to understand the true welfare principles. Yet I do not know the effect all this may have upon the proselyting program. It is hard to determine.

One of the questions I asked in a recent seminar for regional representatives was: "Should we refer people (that means half of our membership) to the social security program or not?" The answer given was that in principle we believe in being independent in all ways. I home teach two families who are very recent converts to the Church. I do not know much about their previous stand in these questions, but they have accepted the Church's position completely because it is a gospel principle. Unfortunately, though, I believe the tradition of inactive religion, together with the social security programs, are getting into the people's blood. It is something we will have to keep an eye on because the people are leaning more and more on it.

Charles Didier

I think there is a double aspect to this question. The first is the political: so far, we have had no problems with the members and the political conditions. The first signs I have seen were three weeks ago in Italy. The technique of minority left-wing groups is to create fear among the people. I was in Milan the day they broke into several shops, creating disturbances among the people. The members are now asking, "What should we do? Should we vote for this or that party?" The policy of the Church is not to interfere, not to tell the members how to vote. They know what they have to do. That is only a small matter, and I do not consider it very important. We have no other problems in the other countries in what I would call the Latin area.

On the question of social security, we know this is quite developed in our countries. Again I do not see any interference with the Church programs, with the exception that sometimes members of the Church get the idea they may require the same help from the Church that they receive from the government without working. It creates the idea, "I have the right to receive." And sometimes members come to the bishop and say, "I paid my tithing; I have the right to be helped without working or without donating." Of course, this is contrary to the principles given during the last conference and all the conferences of the Church.

F. Enzio Busche

It is a very interesting question. In my opinion it is the most important challenge for Europeans today. I want to add a note about the social situation to what has already been mentioned. My wife and I have four children. They are all teenagers. My oldest son is now nineteen and is preparing to go on a mission in about two months. For Christmas he gave me a personal gift, an eight-page letter. In this letter was the most valuable gift a son can give his father, the expression of his feelings. I was able to look into the heart of a nineteen-year-old boy being raised in contemporary Germany. I can say that I was somewhat shocked. I have always thought I was very close to my children, but I had the same experience as Brother Wennerlund, an encounter with an independent personality. What I found there in that letter was a great cry for help.

In Germany today things are being taught in the schools that would be unbelievable here in America. When my boy was sixteen, he was challenged by his teacher to practice free love. Such diabolical requests have just one purpose: to destroy the possibilities of developing feelings of true love and self-respect. Here we must surely see the whole plan of the adversary to destroy mankind. This is the kind of challenge we are faced with in Europe. I see the situation in America, but unfortunately we in Europe are about five or six years "ahead" of you. You must face the problem now while you, here, have time to prepare.

My oldest boy also told me about his two closest friends, the best ones he could find, both of whom are not members of the Church. One is living with a married woman and feels no shame about it; the other is living with a sixteen-year-old girl. He lives at home, but most of the week he's staying with her, and he also feels no shame about it.

In order for my son to remain faithful under these conditions he has to spend a lot of time thinking, praying, and studying. Therefore, I can tell you we appreciate the organizations of the Church very much, especially the institute and seminary program that gives our young people the possibility of gaining a testimony on their own. I can just say that it is a miracle for me (this is not just one case; it's my son), but I know that all the young people that are growing up in Germany have to make just as important decisions very early. Even when they are deacons they must decide what direction they will go. Already, at that age, they are learning to stay clean. And then they will become really strong, and you will see marvelous local missionaries coming out of this people.

They have met the challenges and have become tremendous people. You see how pleased they are, how devoted they are, and how much they know that the Church is true. They frequently have more success in missionary work than their American missionary companions because they know exactly what they are teaching and why they are teaching it.

Our challenge in Europe now is to expose the wicked strategic plans of Satan to destroy the people. You must admit he has been very successful. These social conditions may be only in the background of people's thinking to make them desire everything without giving anything. This is Satan's plan. The Germans, you know, are the inventors of socialism. Karl Marx was a German; Hegel was a German. At a recent meeting Elder [Thomas] Monson quoted the German philosopher Arthur Schopenhauer's pessimistic life philosophy; people believe it today, so that the message of the restored gospel is a real challenge. We have to go through many, many walls and layers to get to the hearts of the people, to let them feel the spirit, and to convert them. We have to do this, and we will. There are millions of good people who are not members of the Church; they are children of our Heavenly Father. We have to find ways and means to convert them; otherwise they are lost. It takes real sacrifice, example, and another strategic plan that the Lord has revealed through his prophet to overcome this and to bring to pass eternal life and the salvation of mankind in Europe.

Bo G. Wennerlund

Of course it is a moral situation, too. I would like to add this experience to what has been said. In the schools they are showing movie films of explicit instruction in sexual education, as they call it. We were concerned about this, not wanting our children to see these films. There is an organization called the Home and School Organization where parents and teachers are organized together like your PTA, and there the question of sex education came up. The teacher explained the nature and purpose of the films that were going to be shown. Nobody said anything. So I spoke up, saying that, quite frankly, I did not want my children to see any film that I have not approved. I recommended the same policy to the Association. All parents in the group agreed with me. Before I spoke up, nobody had said anything, but when I expressed myself, all agreed definitely that no film was to be shown without parental approval.

Another example of the anxiety about the deteriorating moral climate is that, although a large number of unmarried couples live together without shame, hundreds of people do not like it. But they dare not speak against it. That is why I think we have stressed in leadership meetings and in district conferences the importance of parents being active, of taking an active part in these home and school organizations. I think we can do a lot of good here. People have been brainwashed. They say, "Well, everyone seems to agree with this, so I had better do it too." But in their hearts I am sure they are not so convinced. That is my conviction and my experience. Saints need to be taught to speak up in society for what they believe in.

Dan C. Jorgensen

Perhaps just one comment with regard to the question asked about crime in Italy. Italy has always been known for a certain amount of crime. The Mafia has its origin in Italy. But I would not want anyone to have the impression here that this is in any way a serious problem for the Church or even for Italian people. In Italy one learns to live with the situations that exist. Personally, I call New York City my second home and have lived there several of the past fifteen years; I feel much more secure anywhere in Italy than I ever do in New York City. I just wanted to put that on the record and let you know that crime is not a serious problem, and in no way does it impinge on our activity or hurt our members there.

Question

Are we seeing, or shall we see in Europe, members of the Church becoming politically active, taking a greater political role? As the Church matured in America, we saw that happening here. Is it desirable for the Saints to become involved in social and political organizations?

Charles Didier

What I think is desirable is the need for a voice to speak for our beliefs and for the doctrine of the Church. But even though desirable, I have not yet seen members becoming politically active. For example—and I will speak for France and Belgium where we have about 12,000 members—I know of only one member who is seriously involved in politics. I think I know how the other brethren think politically, but with all the things we are involved in with respect to the Church, our members think becoming politically active is not the right thing to do. They are therefore afraid to accept political positions. They think it will demand too much time or they will have to sacrifice certain things in the Church. This is why they are not interested.

F. Enzio Busche

I would say it takes a lot of maturity to really understand the principles of salvation of the gospel of Jesus Christ, and at the same time, become politically involved in Europe. When you get to this degree of gospel understanding, you suddenly have so many church responsibilities that you hardly find time for the political arena. In the German area, I know personally of only one man who is politically involved, but I doubt he will do much good because he is so misunderstood. I think the best situation is to speak up, locally, where you are. As Brother Wennerlund has said, the Mormon people need to take advantage of the opportunity to speak up and express the principles of the gospel in their neighborhoods, their social organizations, and in their communities. Political organizations never resolve the problems that bring to pass the eternal life of human beings.

Question

I would like to add one thing, though, about this business of being politically disinterested. I know the Church in Germany and in Western Europe is in its beginning state; I cannot, therefore, expect too much. I have, however, the audacity to believe that Mormonism must begin to lead out, certainly in the political arena. In Germany the situation has been such that it was impossible for members to identify with the left. On the other hand, the right has been identified so strictly with the Catholic Church and, in addition, bears the historic burden of having been associated with Nazism. The members fall between stools. Do you believe that this is a problem? I am wondering, therefore, what political possibilities remain for the members in Europe? In other words, on the assumption that the Doctrine and Covenants's injunction that "when the wicked rule, the people mourn" is still valid, I am wondering what we should expect to see in the future without lamenting what might have been if conditions had been more settled. I believe it would, indeed, be lamentable if we were to sit back and say, "Well, we can't really say much in the political sphere because we are too busy with our church activities." Over the long run such an attitude would be regrettable, both for Europe and for the United States as well. Would any of you like to respond to the Doctrine and Covenants's challenge that we become involved and choose good, wise, and honest men and make sure that good and wise laws are passed rather than simply sit back and regret that unwise and unjust men are ruling?

Bo G. Wennerlund

I do not know of any Church member in Scandinavia who has been politically active or elected to public office. But in the younger generation, this is coming. Today many strong young men in Sweden, for example, are becoming politically aware and interested. They will have an influence on our political life in the future. I also know of young men in Denmark, too, who are involved. It is coming, and I think it is very desirable.

Also, women are now encouraged to become involved in politics. The encouragement is such that voters sometimes vote a person into office simply because she is a woman, not because she is qualified. Please do not misunderstand that statement. I believe there are women who can qualify to get into the government.

We also have some outstanding women in the Church. In the Stockholm area we recently had open houses to which we personally invited all the top Stockholm government leaders. I personally was assigned by the bishop to invite the mayor of the city. He came, and was very appreciative for the invitation. At the open house were two of our outstanding LDS women speaking on the situation of women in the whole man-viewed society. I wish those speakers had been broadcast all over Sweden. I said to the stake president, "Isn't that your future Relief Society president?" That is the kind of women we need, women who can speak out, because today when women speak, the radio, TV, and the mass media pick up what they say. In this respect I think we will soon see women do a lot of good in political life.

At the same time, the Church and the priesthood are always told never to interfere in the political business by giving advice to members on how to vote. I believe, and we believe, that we teach people true principles and let them govern themselves. I think that is the line we have to follow.

Charles Didier

I think it is important to be involved in politics, so to speak, but not to defend the Church position in a political manner. Don't misunderstand me. We need our leaders to defend our rights and to defend our constitutions. That's one thing. But if we involve the Church in day-to-day political affairs we will go in the same direction the Catholic Church went many, many years ago.

Having established those provisos, I still hold that the Church in Europe is not ready to take political stands. We are struggling so much just to establish ourselves that our people are not ready to be involved in political situations. When our members in the stakes and missions labor with one, two, three, four, or even five positions in the Church, they cannot devote their time to anything else. When we have many more stakes, the time will come when we will see our people become involved in political situations and start to defend themselves. But right now I am afraid it is much too soon. When you study the history of the Church, you will, I believe, see exactly the same pattern.

Question

I have been impressed with one aspect of a question raised by Dr. Reynolds in his keynote address yesterday. It is that the gospel somehow overcomes social barriers. I understand that the political history of Europe has been one of considerable animosity among the nations of Europe. I noticed earlier that Brother Wennerlund said that the people in Sweden have taken Brother Didier [a Belgian] to be their own representative among the General Authorities. Is this statement symptomatic of the attitudes of Church members in Europe, that they transcend traditional national prejudices and identify with each other and with the other members of the Church community? If so, what are the major causes of this?

F. Enzio Busche

I can say from the German point of view that, after the Second World War, Germans were forced to overcome nationalistic feelings. It is absolutely no problem for Germans living today in West Germany—not just Church members—to feel completely united with people in all other countries. So it is very easy for a German Saint to be a brother to a Swede, or to a Dane, or even to a Frenchman. Moreover, they could have the same closeness with Americans, with Japanese, or with anybody else in the world. I would say that maybe the German has learned the hard way that we are all children of our Heavenly Father.

Charles Didier

There is one way, one Church, and one Lord. I believe this is the identifying factor among the members in Europe. Aside from that, all national borders are open and there is a freer flow of communication among people than ever before. But among the members, I think that this is really the uniting factor—one way, one Church, one Lord—and especially one prophet, leading all the members.

Bo G. Wennerlund

I would like to mention an example that might answer the question. In 1956, the first time my wife and I went to the temple in Switzerland, we arrived late one night. In the morning we went to the chapel for Sunday School. When we heard the hymns of the Church sung in German, we both started crying. The same spirit was in the song; that same feeling was among the people. Then a man stood up and gave a talk. He closed with his testimony, and when he bore his testimony in German, the thought came to me that the spirit that gave him his testimony had given me mine. There is no doubt that the spirit of the gospel is a bridge between people. It is a great experience to travel across continents and hear your own songs, the ones you learned by heart in Swedish, being sung by other people in their language. I regularly receive Church supplies from the United States. Recently, in planning for the Helsinki area conference, I got, by mistake, a shipment of materials printed in Japanese. There were a couple of songs in the package; I could see from the music that one was "Come, Come Ye Saints," although I could not read the words. So in a home evening I said, "Okay, children, now we are going to sing this song." I showed them the song and they said, "This looks great. This really is an international Church." That is the feeling. This is also why this Church is the only power on earth that can create peace. There is no feeling of nationalism among the members of the Church—not when they gain a testimony.

Question

I have two questions. There has been a strong feeling among the members of the Church in other countries that everything in the Church is Americanized. Is this true in Europe? Earlier, we barely touched some of the points about the youth who are crying for help. Hence my second question: What is the Church doing for the youth, both in and out of the Church? What about the success of the evangelical crusades among the youth around the world?

Charles Didier

I will try to answer your questions. Do we still have the American influence in our programs? I'll be very frank with you, and I will say yes, in a way. However, the Church programs are adapted more and more, not, I would say, to our culture, but to the one true culture, the culture of Christ. Of course, we have our own habits, customs, and so on; it is well to retain and use them, although we recognize there is an American influence in the Church programs because they are prepared here.

Secondly, you mentioned the youth gatherings of Billy Graham and other evangelists. I would like to see their results. We have had such gatherings in Europe now for many, many years. Do we see a change in the youth? No. Youth are attracted by evangelists talking about Christ's principles. But there are no results. The crusades to European cities come for one, two, or three days, and then they go and leave the people abandoned, really abandoned. Now look at the Church and what we do with our youth. We are training them. We are giving them seminary and institute classes, and we see the results in the growth of local missionaries and of local leaders. We have a power to produce the future leadership for the Church in our area. When young women or young men really want to put into practice the Church programs, they become true disciples of Christ. That is what we are trying to do with them.

James R. Christianson

Recently, in Sweden, the Ministry of Education introduced a program into the schools where students were asked which churches they would like to learn about. An overwhelming majority of these young people wanted to learn about Mormonism. The Minister of Education contacted us and asked if we would provide them with some material. As a result we prepared an outstanding kit, and it is now being used in many of the schools. It tells the history of the Church in four filmstrips while providing students with worksheets. The results so far have been impressive.

When social studies teachers received the kits, many had questions about how to use them. They were invited to contact the Church to receive instructions. I was told yesterday that in one area ninety-three public school teachers came together to be instructed by our missionaries and our seminary and institute men. In another area there were seventy-five. This is a way of contacting young people we have not had before, of teaching them about the Church in a very unbiased and clear way. One noted newspaper in Stockholm received so many calls from young people wanting to know where to locate the Mormon Church in order to join it that they contacted the Church and asked if we could not give them some information for these young people. We are now planning to reproduce the kits for schools in all the countries of Europe.

Question

Considerable mention has been made of the seminary and institute programs. I have several questions dealing with the institute program, and also with European Mormon university students who might be involved with it. Could you tell us how many of our young people are going to universities in Europe? In the past, we have seen many come here to Brigham Young University. Are they returning to your countries or remaining in America? How large are your institute programs in Germany or in France? Are they really connected with some of the universities there, and can we expect to see more of our young people educated in their homelands?

James R. Christianson

All of our institute programs are self-instructed, so they are not tied to a university. Earlier, we failed to mention a big change that has taken place in Europe in the last ten years—the far greater number of LDS young people attending universities. In Germany alone, just before I left [1975], we counted 120. That does not sound like many, but just a few years before there were no more than ten or fifteen. In Italy a large number of young people coming into the Church are university trained.

When we set up the seminary and institute program throughout Europe, the mission presidents called sixteen young men to direct the program in their respective countries. Each of these men, with the exception of two, had graduated from a European university, and each has done a marvelous job.

All students are being influenced by the political ideologies circulating in the universities of their respective homelands. Thus we will find our Mormon university-trained youth more politically active than other generations have been. Inasmuch as more of our people are attending the universities, we might see, in the years to come, increasing numbers of members who will be involved politically. This will be a positive thing.

Question

For a long time one of the considerations for the slow growth of the Church in Europe was the opposition of the established churches. Is that situation any different today? Are the churches so weak, apathetic, and secularized that they make little difference any more?

F. Enzio Busche

I think there has been a complete change in attitude as far as I can see. It is a fact that when we were converted about eighteen years ago, the churches on the local basis were trying to attack the Church. Now it is completely changed. In the past years I personally have had visits from priests and ministers from the two major churches in Germany—the Catholics and Protestants. They came to our chapel to see me to ask how we do it and to see what they can learn from us. They admire our situation; they admire the progress that the Church has made; and they feel they can learn a lot from us. As a matter of fact, a group of eight Catholic and Protestant clergymen invited my wife and me to a meeting for just one purpose: to tell them how they can improve their youth program. We were shocked that Protestant and Catholic ministers from our hometown, people who know us and who were our personal enemies ten years ago, should ask us such a question.

Just the other week we had a visit from a Catholic organization in our hometown to see the fruits of the Mormon Church. Our major enemies, if we can call them that, are no longer the churches, but the philosophies of [Herbert] Marcuse, [Theodor] Adorno, and their followers. They are the real contemporary opponents of the Church.

Bo G. Wennerlund

I would like to mention two items in answer to this question. One of the families that I home teach, for example, had been contacting different churches in search of the truth. At last the missionaries came to their home, and they joined the Church. On the very first home teaching visit I made, just two weeks after they had been baptized, the family had invited a minister from what we call the Swedish State Church. He was participating in the home evening. The wife called me before I came, "Is it all right to have invited him?" "Oh, yes, of course, he is welcome," I said. And it was a very positive experience. To make a long story short, he began by introducing himself. He said he just "happened" to be in this [state] church. First, he had been converted to God, then had educated himself and had become a minister of this particular church. But, he said, he could just as well have gone into another church. Then he said, "Do you really mean that this is the way you work? You go to the homes and visit your members like this?" I said, "Yes. I have four families that my companion and I see every month." He said, "This alone is reason enough to join your church. This is what churches need." What I want to indicate with this account is that a new generation—he was between twenty-five and thirty years old—is coming to the fore in the other churches. This is my first point.

The other is the prevailing opinion that religious people are a little screwy. (What word do you use?) That is true; that is how people feel. I think this is something that is a disadvantage to the Church. Other churches have made the teachings of Christ unpopular. "If he's religious," they say, "don't pay any attention to him." That is the kind of statement you often hear. But there is a change coming, however slowly. I have noticed that among businessmen I meet everywhere; at least one hundred times, I have heard men say to me, "Do you want to have something to drink?" "No, thank you." "Do you want a cigarette?" "No, thank you." Then they say, "Why don't you drink?" And so on. I explain why, and after a while, they come back with other questions: "What does that really mean? What does your church teach?" Then, I have a few points that I tell them each time. I begin with the apostasy from the church that Christ organized; that it was prophesied that the Church would be restored; and that it has been restored with prophets today. That is about what I say. We do not go into it more deeply than that. When they ask further questions on what we believe on this and that aspect of religious life, then almost always, I hear this statement: "Well, if I ever would be religious, I think this is the church I would like to join." So, the Church is coming. The missionaries are working, going through cities over and over again. People are changing their opinions. Hence, I believe the more positive public opinion is coming about not because of the other churches but because the gospel is becoming known, and the true image of the Church is being planted in the minds of people.

Footnotes

1. President Lee explored this idea in his address at general conference, as reported in *Report of the One Hundred Forty-third Annual General Conference of The Church of Jesus Christ of Latter-day Saints,* April 6–8, 1973 (Salt Lake City: The Church of Jesus Christ of Latter-day Saints, 1973), pp. 4–10.

2. Unpublished research done for the First Council of the Seventy.

3. Interview in 1974 with Dieter Berndt, University Professor, in Berlin.

4. Ernst Benz, "Der Mensch als Imago Dei," *Eranos-Jahrbuch,* 38 (1969):297–329.

5. *Deseret News 1976 Church Almanac* (Salt Lake City: Deseret News, 1976), pp. E14–21.

6. Scandinavia (Denmark, Norway, and Sweden) and Finland.

7. President N. Eldon Tanner explored this idea in the area conference in Stockholm, Sweden, in 1974. His address is reported in *Report of the First Denmark, Finland, Norway, and Sweden Area General Conference of The Church of Jesus Christ of Latter-day Saints,* Stockholm, Sweden, August 16–18, 1974 (Salt Lake City: The Church of Jesus Christ of Latter-day Saints, 1975), pp. 107–11.

8. Parley P. Pratt, "Conference Notice," *The Latter-Day Saints' Millennial Star* 1 (May 1840):24.

9. Parley P. Pratt, "At a General Conference," *The Latter-Day Saints' Millennial Star* 1 (May 1840):20–21.

10. Parley P. Pratt, "Temperance," *The Latter-Day Saints' Millennial Star* 1 (May 1840):21.

11. Harold B. Lee, address in *Report of the First British Area General Conference of The Church of Jesus Christ of Latter-day Saints,* Manchester, England, August 27–29, 1971 (Salt Lake City: The Church of Jesus Christ of Latter-day Saints, 1972) pp. 131–42.

CHURCH DEVELOPMENT ISSUES AMONG LATIN AMERICANS*

INTRODUCTION

F. LaMond Tullis

The airport, some seven miles long, was both the highest and longest in the world. Yet as we taxied up to the new international terminal near La Paz, Bolivia, the air did not seem any lighter or less useful because of the altitude. But the evidence soon struck home: first, as the cockpit crew emerged, each man with an oxygen bottle strapped to his waist and a breathing harness attached; second, as we hurried from the plane to the terminal complex to escape the inclement weather. Accustomed as we were to other climes and seasons, our breathing quickened and pulse rates rose as we struggled to adapt to an atmosphere that was both rare and sparklingly clean. Altitude: 14,500 feet. That is 10,000 feet higher than the valley of the Great Salt Lake (which generations of Mor-

*(This section on the Church in Latin America includes an introduction by LaMond Tullis, essays by Harold Brown, Orlando Rivera, Efraín Villalobos Vásquez, and Enrique Rittscher, and a question-answer exchange with the audience. Issues dealt with, within the context of the rapid and successful expansion of the faith in Latin America, include language and communication, translations, leadership, temporal well-being, membership growth and institutional development, and ethnic and national pride.)

mons have looked upon as their Rocky Mountain homeland), and a good 2,000 feet above Mount Timpanogos, a treeless ensign that, with both austerity and majesty, dominates the southern valleys of Utah's Wasatch front.

More than 6,000 Mormons live in Bolivia, some of them in the *altiplano* (high mountain plateaus) less than a day's walk from the daily routine at the international airport with its scream of jets and rush of people. Two of those Mormons are Marcelino Alvarado and his wife María.

"Wouldn't you like to meet them?" asked a missionary from Salt Lake City who had learned both Spanish and Aymara, a prominent pre-Columbian language still spoken in parts of Bolivia and Peru and the mother tongue of some 800,000 people. It is the only language that Marcelino and María know. Mormon missionaries have learned that language and have taught the gospel to many of those who speak it.

"I'll be your interpreter," missionary Craig Stevens added. "I can promise that your interview will be among the most memorable you will have." So it was.

For the interview, we rode by bus over roads that were initially serpentine until we had climbed some 1,500 feet from the pit into which the Spaniards had thrown the capital city of Bolivia. Then, once on the altiplano, we traveled straight as a rifle shot for fifteen miles to Viacha, a small town where Aymara is still spoken right along with Spanish, Bolivia's national language.

From Viacha it was either by foot or bicycle. I elected bicycles, which we rode for some thirty minutes along a dirt path that lay in an immense valley floor ringed on one side by the white-capped Cordillera Real and on the other by rough, eroded breaks. My senses were struck by the crashing presence of silence, boundless austere beauty of landscape and horizon, and adobe huts with thatched roofs and dirt floors that irregularly peppered the valley for as far as we could see. The homes, each with a small acreage of meadow and cultivated land, conveyed an image, perhaps a false one, of security and serenity. Eventually we came to the home of Marcelino and María, one no different in kind or quality from the others we had observed.

My attention was immediately drawn to a small potato crop undergoing a unique dehydration process, a sow with her litter of piglets, a cow and her calf, a dozen head of miniature sheep, and nearly as many lambs. These were Marcelino's and his wife's. In a good year they might make as much as $200 (U.S.) in cash income. Thus they had lived, earning sufficient means to raise and educate their four sons and pay the doctor for the two or three visits they had made in their some seventy-three years of life.

That was how Marcelino and María wanted it. The peace and quiet of the country was for them. "No city life for us," they said. It was fine that their children should live in the city, but the elder Alvarados were a generation attached by sentiment and preference to the land.

Yet, contrary to many other people living in the altiplano, Marcelino and María had stimulated their children to get an education in the local public schools in Viacha (to which they walked every day). There the children had learned Spanish and obtained marketable skills, which they later used to good advantage in acquiring relatively well-paying jobs in Bolivia's larger cities.

Marcelino and María were, in a sense, already "different." And when they heard the gospel in their native language, their hearts were filled and their spirits quickened. Not only in the cities was it possible to find a satisfying religion, but also in the relatively remote countryside. And in their own language, too. So six years ago Marcelino and María joined the Church; and they advanced in office, experience, and responsibility.

Marcelino and María. Mormons. He is a bearer of the Melchizedek Priesthood. They are your brothers and sisters. And mine.

Earlier in May of 1976 I had visited southern Brazil, an enormous land of fertile plains, lakes, and rolling hills, with a population as un-Indian as that of Salt Lake City. Portuguese, Germans, Slavs, Spaniards, English, even Americans fleeing the chaos of the South during and following the U.S. Civil War—all had established major colonies in the Brazilian South. Subsequently the Japanese came. Over a million of them now live in São Paulo alone. In spite of such heavy immigration of diverse nationalities, however, and even though a little German and larger amounts of Japanese are still spoken in the land, all immigrant groups now speak Portuguese, Brazil's national language.

Mormons live in Brazil—over fifty thousand of them. And in Curitiba, a city lying as far south of the equator as Brownsville, Texas, does to the north of it, a stake conference was being held. There, in a city bustling with commerce, industry, and 400,000 people, not every taxi driver knows where the Mormon stake center is. But once seen, it cannot be mistaken. The building obviously meets all the Church Building Department's architectural and construction standards. A certain amount of Utah's Wasatch Front goes to the world even in architectural style, much of it dictated by the functional needs the buildings are intended to meet. So there it was, on an attractive knoll in an equally attractive middle-class neighborhood. And numerous members could be seen driving their own cars to the meeting, an experience that is rare in Bolivia where Marcelino lives.

The choir sang with a precision and excellence that would make any director anywhere proud. The speeches were all good to excellent; some were even eloquent. I noted the presence also of a Brazilian Mormon youth group that had toured the country as musical ambassadors for the Church. Thousands of Brazilians had looked upon those Mormon youngsters with respect, perhaps even envy.

"Meet my son, Moroni," said the proud father of a tall and well-proportioned teenager of seventeen years. "He will be a great missionary one day." The son seemed inclined by both spirit and dedication very likely to fulfill that prophecy.

Other fathers introduced me to their sons—Nephi, Joseph, Samuel. They, as were many others, were already serving the Church as part-time junior missionary partners while also studying architecture, science, journalism, medicine, law, and technical trades in commerce and the automotive industry. Literate, urbane, confident. Southern Brazil has several thousand young Mormons like that: Nephi, Moroni, Joseph, Samuel, and all the rest—Jasón, José, Aldo, Oscar, Saúl, Antonio, Thomas, Wilson—Maria, Flavia, Sara, Elizabet—and scores more of my Latter-day Saint brothers and sisters—many of whose forefathers pioneered a wilderness no less challenging than the vast expanse of Deseret, which the first Mormons turned into prospering communities.

The foregoing vignettes present two glimpses of the extremes in real-life conditions among Mormons in Latin America, where the growth in Church membership is among the most rapid in the world. As if North-American members of the Church sensed this, several years ago they said that "by 1980 the first language of the Church will be Spanish, not English." When the membership figures for 1980 are known, there is every reason to believe this statement will prove *not* to be correct. But the currency of the projection is nevertheless reflective of the common members' awareness that, by any standards, the Church's growth in Latin America seems incredible. Sons and daughters who have served in Latin American missions, where it is not uncommon for a missionary pair to baptize a dozen or more people into the Church every month, come home and "make their report." Church members conclude that something big is happening in Latin America—and it is.

Actually, as recently as 1960 all Spanish- and Portuguese-speaking members of the Church combined in Latin America accounted for only 1½ percent of the Church's total membership. Yet by 1971 that total had risen to 7 percent, and by 1975 to over 9 percent. The best projections for 1980 show it rising to 11 percent of the total membership, and by 1990 to nearly 17 percent, or one out of every six members. Inasmuch as the Church's membership is growing rapidly among many language groups throughout much of the world, this progressive Latin American gain is quite remarkable. In absolute terms, the growth is even more dramatic, as shown in Figure 1.

The statistical increase in the number of Mormons in Latin America is striking; but more so is the story of the actual propagation of the faith, for herein lies the drama of men's hearts and minds as they struggle with commitment and change, triumph and misfortune. The historical highlights below offer a fleeting glimpse of an experience that has now affected the lives of hundreds of thousands of Latin Americans, not to mention the thousands of missionaries from many lands who have taught them.

The Beginnings

The same generation of Mormons so instrumental in the Church from the very beginning was also the first to take the restored gospel to Latin America. In 1851, only four years after the arrival of the Saints in the Great Salt Lake Valley, Parley P. Pratt, his wife Phoebe Soper, and Rufus Allen set sail for Chile to open the South American mission of the Church. Pratt had long dreamed of such an undertaking and had invested prodigious energies to bring it about.

As far as we know, the Pratts and Rufus Allen were the first to attempt to take the gospel message across the Spanish-language barrier. In preparation, they studied Spanish grammar before leaving the United States. They crammed for more than six weeks (between bouts of seasickness) while in voyage to Chile. And they subsequently made a systematic effort in Chile to perfect their language skills. But the first people to whom Elder Pratt explained the Mormon mode of baptism nearly laughed themselves sick as they tumbled out into the street in mirth. Once recovered, they returned to apologize; but the lesson upon Elder Pratt was indelible: communication was more than grammar and words.

Other problems besides language and communication—cultural isolation and shock, personal tragedies (including the death of the Pratts' infant son in Chile), lack of correspondence with loved ones in Utah, political turmoil in the land, and the grip of tradition on its inhabitants—all combined to motivate the missionary party to withdraw. The first missionary efforts in Chile were therefore short-lived, lasting only a few months. More than a quarter of a century passed before Mormons once again seriously thought about preaching the gospel in Spanish, and

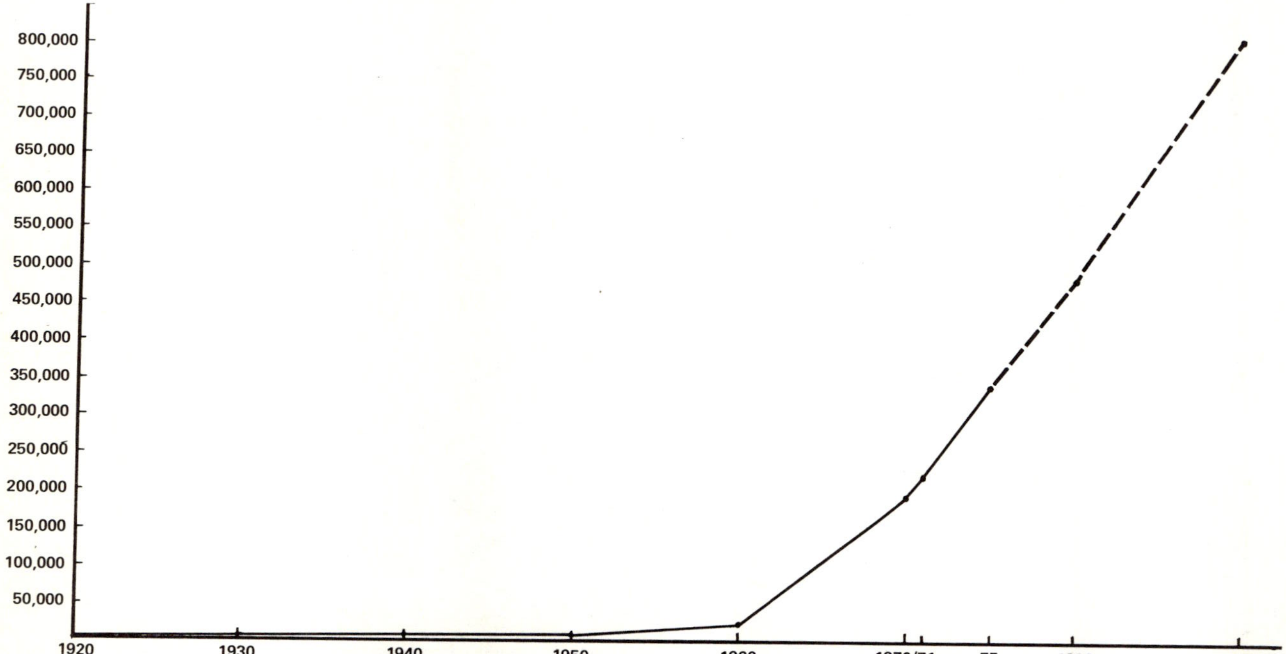

	1920	1930	1940	1950	1960	1970/71	75	1980	1990
Mexico	2,314	3,773	4,196	5,915	12,695	67,965/75,000	160,596	161,000	300,000
Central America					3,097	28,805/34,214	141,211	68,000	133,000
South America		73	751	1,936	9,750	93,875/108,348	40,483	250,000	640,000
TOTAL	2,314	3,846	4,947	7,851	25,542	190,645/217,562	342,290	479,000	803,000

FIGURE 1. CHURCH MEMBERSHIP, SOUTH AMERICA, CENTRAL AMERICA, AND MEXICO, 1920-1975

SOURCE: Howard Nielsen & Gordon Irving

nearly three-quarters of a century passed before the Church reopened a mission in South America (in 1925 in Buenos Aires, Argentina).

In the meantime, however, primarily between the late 1870s and 1890, Mormonism went to Mexico, literally *en masse*. During that time hundreds of North American Mormons settled in Mexico's northern state of Chihuahua after yet another mass exodus in pursuit of the religious freedom they thought the American constitution should provide but obviously was not guaranteeing them. Fleeing U.S. marshals over the issue of polygamy, they hoped for a more tolerant political spirit in a Mexican homeland. Their settlements grew and, many said, flourished.[1]

These English-speaking Mormon colonists in northern Mexico ultimately provided the Church with the expertise it needed to cross the Spanish-language barrier with the gospel message. Having resettled in order to practice their faith in safety and peace, they also found it both convenient and necessary to learn Spanish in order to conduct business and to generally relate to the Mexican socio-political environment. Some of the colonists thus learned Spanish; many of their children learned it very well.

As early as 1879 the colonists began to send out missionaries to the Mexican nationals in whose country they lived. Indeed, in the early years, they and their children provided nearly all the leadership and early missionary service for the Church's operations in Mexico. Later it was the same way in South America after the mission was reopened there. Rey L. Pratt, for example, a grandson of Parley P. Pratt and himself a colonies Mormon, was the first Spanish-speaking missionary to return (in 1925) to the South American continent that his grandfather had abandoned three-quarters of a century before. Like Rey Pratt, a long succession of mission presidents and missionaries who have served in Mexico and in Central and South America learned their Spanish in the schools, playgrounds, and orchards of Colonia Dublán and Colonia Juárez. The colonies thus proved to be the wedge for the permanent establishment of the gospel in Mexico and, for that matter, in all of Latin America.

When in 1925 the Church asked Rey L. Pratt to take leave of absence from his position of president of the Mexican Mission in order to accompany Elder Melvin J. Ballard, an apostle, to South America to reopen the mission there, he went, not to Chile, where his grandfather had landed seventy-three years before, but to Argentina. Ironically, it was thought that Pratt's eloquent Spanish-language skills were required more for dealing with government politicians and bureaucrats in Argentina than for preaching the gospel. The actual missionary work was to be pursued among the hordes of German-speaking immigrants, not the Spanish-speaking natural residents. For this purpose German-speaking Elder Rulon S. Wells was included in the missionary party to facilitate crossing the gospel language barrier.

With only marginal success among the German immigrants, however, the missionaries soon embraced wholeheartedly other nationalities in Argentina—Italians, Spaniards, and, of course, the old Argentinian stock itself. Many of these were baptized. Thus the national population as well as many immigrant nationalities have contributed strong and faithful members to the Church. This outcome was never in doubt, for even as events developed in the early years, Pratt spoke more Spanish as a missionary than he ever did as an ambassador to Argentinian government bureaucrats.

Within ten years after the Ballard-Pratt-Wells party had landed in Argentina, the gospel had also taken root in Brazil. As in Argentina, it had gone first to the Germans, then to many other immigrant nationalities and old-line population stocks. The harvest has been particularly striking in Brazil, a land where the national language, and now also the language of the Church there, is Portuguese.

From these humble, tenuous, and often chaotic beginnings, the restored gospel has expanded to include nearly every country in the western hemisphere and to embrace hundreds of thousands of members in a religion that is more and more respected and encompassing. Members, temples, chapels, schools, leadership development, and improved quality of life and spirit—these are some of the hallmarks of the Church in Latin America. People are taking notice.

Latin Americans in Mexico, Central America, and South America have embraced the gospel. So have Latin Americans who live in the United States of America. In the United States live some twelve million people whose ancestral customs, mother tongue, and race are partly rooted to the soil that was once Mexico's and to the heartbeat of Latin-American lands. Mexican-Americans, Chicanos, Hispanos—the names vary; yet whatever they choose to call themselves, they are in some way part of the fourth largest Latin-American community in the world, preceded only by the countries of Brazil, Argentina, and Mexico. These Americans of Latin-American ancestry have also produced generations of Mormons whose strength and fidelity are seen in the records and whose sons and daughters are now represented throughout much of the Church.

Whether in Mexico, Central America, South America, or the United States, the accomplishments of the Latin-American Saints have been significant. These accomplishments have not been achieved without problems, misunderstandings, or heartaches. Indeed, now we see that the very magnitude of the Church's contemporary growth increasingly obliges us to take note of the paradoxical sentiments of hope and despair, motivation and frustration, and love and distrust that accompany the expansion of the gospel message today. That is part of the challenge our people face as we approach the twenty-first century.

The issues associated with these sentiments are as important as they are interesting. We might call them the "enduring issues," because in one form or another they become the subjects of the serious conversation and thinking of many Latin Americans and North-American members of the Church. All this is a natural consequence of the efforts of good men and women to recognize and then attempt to solve difficult problems. Thus, just as difficulties arise to occasion despair, frustration, and distrust, so also do Church members seek to resolve the ensuing dilemmas in favor of hope and love. If there are failures—and there are—one should nevertheless not fail to notice the preponderant successes.

Foremost among the issues that have brought both pleasure and pain to Latin-American and North-American Mormons in their experience with the expanding Church are those dealing with language and communication, translations, leadership, temporal well-being, membership growth and institutional development, and ethnic and national pride or, in some cases, cultural insensitivity. As the essays in this section deal in one way or another with all these issues, it will be helpful to look at them here so that subsequent comments by our Latin-American participants will be better understood.

Some Enduring Issues

Language and Communication

Whose language should be spoken here? What kinds of communication skills are required for preaching the gospel across the boundaries of language, ancestral customs, race, and nationality? These are two of the main "enduring issues" among Mormons in the area of language and communication. A brief background will illustrate.

As the Church expanded, it became apparent that the need for missionaries for Spanish-speaking lands would exceed the capacity of the Mormon colonies in Mexico to produce them. Soon other young men and women with no proven language ability were called on thirty-month missions (twenty-four for sisters) with the anticipation that six of those months would be used for learning the language (while working in the field) and the balance spent in preaching the gospel. There were no specialized helps to speak of, and the missionaries prided themselves in "being able to do it without going to a language school as the Protestants did."

But eventually we got our missionary language school, too, largely through the pioneering efforts of Ernest J. Wilkins. Now there is a full-fledged Language Training Mission in operation near the Brigham Young University campus where the most sophisticated language-training methods known are employed. Before receiving their mission calls, young men and women are even given language aptitude tests to screen out those whose language learning capabilities may be low.

Somehow the new training in foreign languages, while enhancing the missionaries' speaking capabilities, did not completely produce the communication expertise desired. Evidence trickled in. Missionary mannerisms idiosyncratic to North-American culture continued to offend many Latin Americans. The North-American missionaries, on the other hand, were often puzzled and perplexed by their own new experiences. Indeed, landing in a place strange not only for its language but for its customs, food, and dress traumatized many missionaries. It reduced their effectiveness and sometimes turned them into crass "cultural imperialists." And that was offensive to the Latin Americans.

Seeking to reduce the magnitude of that problem, the Church began to integrate "cultural packages" into the training programs of its missionaries who were destined to serve in an other-than-English-speaking mission. With these packages the young missionaries began to acquire some pragmatic sensitivity to comparative culture and "cultural language." The institutionalization of this combined language-training and cultural-training approach is witnessed by the Church's recent construction on the BYU campus of a huge complex for its Language Training Mission. And Brigham Young University's Language and Intercultural Research Center continues to provide "cultural awareness" materials for the missionaries in this foreign-language learning program.

Thus, several "negatives" associated with large numbers of people crossing language barriers are being dealt with by better preparation, not only in language, but also through increased cross-cultural awareness. This preparation has not, nor will it, eliminate all the issues of language and communication in the Church; but in some areas it has certainly reduced their intensity.

The second important language issue relates to cultural pride and cultural insensitivity. We see it in two ways. The first is with North-American Mormons living temporarily or permanently in a Latin-American country who nevertheless want to keep their own language and cultural traditions alive, both in and out of the Church. Latin Americans criticize them for "keeping yourselves apart and aloof," for failing to integrate into the local social fabric of the Church.

On the other hand, Latin-American Mormons residing either temporarily or permanently in the United States who want to preserve the dignity of their ancestral tongue and culture and hold their religious meetings in Spanish are criticized for "not assimilating and speaking the language of the country you live in." English-speaking members living in Latin America insist on their language rights. Latin-American members in the United States wonder why their Spanish-speaking branches and wards are closed down. Mexican and Central- and South-American Mormon leaders are told to learn English. In turn they wonder why so many Americans who spoke Spanish or Portuguese as missionaries can so easily forget their skills. Can there be nothing done to make us all bilingual, they ask? (Some have even suggested that elders quorums be organized on the basis of language ability, not geographic convenience, as a means of helping the ex-missionary to retain his skills and be better able both to inspire and teach successive new generations of Mormons to cross language and communication boundaries with some ease, elegance, and pride.) Whose language should be spoken here? What is the language of the Church? A membership that is more and more heterogeneous will increasingly ask those questions.

Translations

A second enduring issue, inexorably tied to the issue of communication, deals with translations and encompasses both the quality and the availability of religious and organizational materials translated into Spanish and Portuguese.

As to the availability, we note that Parley P. Pratt prepared the first Spanish translation of parts of the Book of Mormon as an adjunct effort to his attempting to preach the gospel in South America. While Elder Pratt's translation is no longer in use in the Church, he did employ it in the Spanish classes he taught in Salt Lake City after his return from Chile. But not until around the turn of the century did copies of the Book of Mormon in the Spanish language actually gain circulation. Moreover, the Book of Mormon, for a long time, was the only Church literature available in Spanish. There was none in Portuguese.

Along with the Book of Mormon, a few Spanish-language pamphlets used in proselyting were prepared, several by Rey L. Pratt who, around 1925, also prepared a hymnal for Spanish speakers. But preparation of other materials was slow, and much of it resulted from "bootstrapping" in the field. In this manner the Portuguese edition of the Book of Mormon was eventually prepared, as also were missionary proselyting helps, study guides, and sundry other materials.

Even as late as 1936 only thirty sections of the Doctrine and Covenants had been translated into Spanish (by Antoine R. Ivins), and none of the Pearl of Great Price. As the clamor for literature increased, the Church responded by hiring Eduardo Balderas to handle Spanish translations. But Portuguese-speaking members of the Church were left to fend for themselves. For a long time Latin-American members thought of themselves as stepchildren in the Church. Where was the literature, they asked? In desperation, even as early as 1936 in Mexico, some Mormons were learning English in order to read of the doctrines and principles of the Church.

Improvements have now been made. Today, literally thousands of pages of materials are translated each year by Church translation teams working in the United States, Mexico, Argentina, and Brazil. Yet the materials relate primarily to the program needs of the Church (e.g., seminaries, institutes, Sunday Schools, youth programs) or are conference addresses or administrative manuals. They do not, generally, include very many Church books. Second-, third-, and fourth-generation Latin-American Mormons wonder when they will get anything new, when they will be able to read more than lesson manuals and the fundamentals, when they will be able to expand their study of the gospel using the same printed materials available to North-American Mormons.

Many Latin-American members continue to learn English in order to better grasp the literature of the Church. But there is "defensive pride" in this, it is said, for the member's efforts in English are not always made with a warm heart. Moreover, many who could profit by an expanded translation list simply will not, or cannot, learn English solely for the purpose of reading "American" materials.

On the other hand, the Church says the translation problem is a matter of priorities. "We are doing what we can." There is little question that the efforts are prodigious; and they are increasing. Aside from that, not a few have noted that some materials published in English are better left untranslated.

As the educational level of the members of the Church in Latin America rises, the intensity of the issue of availability of translations will probably increase. After one has read everything in translation two or three times, where does one go? The question may sound purely academic; but it is one that the Latin-American Saints ask more and more.

If the quantity of translations has been an issue, so also has their quality. In those early days (which, in some areas, extended to the late 1950s) where in desperation missionaries made translations in the field, the quality was fair to poor, as one might imagine. Yet even when professional translators took over, the regional dialects presented problems, especially in the Spanish language. Translations made by Spanish-speakers native to Mexico frequently offended members of the Church in Uruguay and Argentina, and vice versa. Many of these problems are now in the background, however, because the Church has made impressive progress in moving from "translation" to "transculturalization" in the materials it authorizes for languages other than English. As such, professional translators in the United States, Mexico, and Argentina all have a look at the materials and attempt as best they can to weed out expressions and illustrations idiomatic to a single country or region.

With respect to the *adequacy* or *quality* of the current translations, we have a great deal now of which to be proud. On the other hand, the *quantity* issue will be with us for some time.

Leadership

Leadership, a perennial issue in the Church, but one made more pronounced by taking the gospel to other cultures, has been of substantial and, in a certain sense, enduring concern for Mormons in Latin America. In its orientation to this issue, the Church has gone through several distinct phases. In the initial period of the expansion of the faith (up to about 1924 in Mexico and to 1942 in Argentina and Brazil), missionaries foreign to the lands in which they worked held virtually all leadership positions in the branches and the missions (there were no stakes until 1961). Exceptions to this general pattern were rare. This condition prevailed even though much of the missionary work in Argentina and Brazil until 1942 was done among German immigrants, in their own language, and with the support of several Germans who had been converted in Europe.

In the second phase of the leadership issue (from approximately 1925 to 1936 in Mexico and 1942 to 1946 in Brazil and Argentina) the Church turned substantial local leadership responsibility over to local members. This phase was initiated more out of necessity than design, but it worked. The necessity in Mexico derived from the *Cristero* rebellion, which obliged the Mexican government to expel all foreign missionaries—Catholic, Protestant, and Mormon. In Brazil and Argentina the World War II draft stopped all missionary work by North Americans. Local leaders rose to the challenge and carried on. Some people were surprised that the local brethren did so well in their new responsibilities.

The Church entered a third leadership phase (after 1936 in Mexico and 1946 in the rest of Latin America), at which time North-American missionaries once again assumed most of the leadership positions in the branches and districts of the missions. That condition prevailed until the late 1950s in some areas and early 1960s in others. Many Latin-American Mormons suffered personal traumas over this turn of events, which, in Mexico, contributed directly to a schism that for ten years ruptured the harmony of the Church.

But now the Church has entered the present phase, which calls for maximum leadership development among local members. Contrary to what happened in the past, it is rare today for a foreign missionary to have substantial administrative duties in wards, stakes, or branches, although he may still do so in activities directly related to the proselyting functions of the missions. If the missionaries do get involved in leadership positions in the wards, stakes, and branches, it is to help develop local leaders, not to replace them.

This new emphasis on leadership development and training coincided with the remarkable growth of the Church that initiated the decade of the sixties (see Figure 1). Within a very short time a majority of the Church's members in Latin America could count their years of membership on the fingers of one hand. That was hardly time to acquire appropriate leadership skills and commitment to take on the most challenging local positions in the Church unless a tremendous amount of concentrated help was given. In any event, local leaders were scant, and people became more and more aware that the Church had no adequate vessel into which it could receive so many that were so new.

This time the authorities decided not to fall back on the missionaries for administrative help. For their part, the missionaries were heavily extended in new proselyting programs and, in any event, were themselves ill-prepared to take on traditional leadership responsibilities. Things were now too complex. Thus, once again men and women who had been Mormons for only a scant few years were thrust into substantial positions of responsibility.

New traumas arose from all this newness, both in the lives of individuals as well as in local organizations. Yet few now doubt that in large part the leadership development effort has been relatively successful. Nevertheless, new experiments for leadership improvement are being carried out, one of the most notable being in Chile, where enormous resources and commitment are being invested in the development of an autochthonous Church leadership.

Leadership development among Mormons in Latin America has also been greatly enhanced by the increasing numbers of young Latin-American men and women returning home from missions. For generations wards and stakes in the United States have benefited by this continuous influx of young people who are both relatively experienced and dedicated to the Church. Now, with rapidly increasing numbers of local missionaries being called in Latin America, the wards, branches, and stakes are, and will continue to be, blessed by their own young members who have served successful and honorable missions.

If the historical issues relating to Church leadership dealt primarily with *if* or *when* local Latin-American members would be given responsible leadership positions, the issues today are decidedly different. Now many wonder if people raised in a culture that emphasizes paternal, authoritarian, and sometimes dictatorial authority patterns can produce leaders capable of exercising leadership according to gospel principles of stewardship and consent. On balance there have been both notable failures and successes on this count. In his essay, Harold Brown discusses some hopeful portents for the future.

Temporal Well-being

The majority of members of the Church in Latin America come from the lower middle to lower social classes. Most are relatively poor, some are illiterate, others suffer from malnutrition and disease that they, of themselves, are unable to cope with at the present time. Of course, there are among our Latin-American members many educators, lawyers, trained technicians, skilled workers, and a few medical doctors. One usually finds them in the large cities—Rio, São Paulo, Curitiba, Pôrto Alegre, Montevideo, Buenos Aires, Santiago, Lima, La Paz, Quito, Bogotá, Caracas, and Mexico City. Educated, urbane, relatively well-to-do, we have them. But they are the exception, not the rule. Therefore, it is not to them but rather to the majority that we now direct our attention.

Until the mid-1960s the general practice of the Church in Latin America was not to involve itself institutionally in temporal matters: education, health, economic well-being, or other opportunity-sustaining or opportunity-creating enterprises. Many people in the field—mission presidents, missionaries, and visiting authorities—both assumed and said: "Preach the gospel to the people of Latin America, and all else will follow." It did not, just as President Joseph F. Smith had reminded us years ago when he said that a religion which cannot save a man temporally cannot hope to save him spiritually.[2] As thousands of Latin-American members hit intolerable dead ends in their temporal lives, it became apparent that the Church would, after all, need to reconsider the relevance of Brigham Young's example for the modern day. The colonizer of the Mountain West, it was noted, had set up schools, universities, hospitals, farms, factories, banks, cooperatives, and credit unions right along with chapels, tabernacles, and temples. And within two or three generations the effect on the social and economic level of the Saints in Utah was remarkable.

Some people began to wonder if the same would not be appropriate for our people in some areas of Latin America. Otherwise it might be difficult if not impossible for members and their children in some places to become the kind of Mormons both the Church and they knew they should. It was hard, President Harold B. Lee had said, for an illiterate member to follow the admonition to read the scriptures.

The anxieties continued to percolate in many quarters. But it was the Church Educational System that first put them on the front burner when it began to found school systems in Mexico, Chile, and Bolivia. Its efforts have continued to the present day, even after it became apparent (certainly by 1970) that a policy of founding schools in the whole of Latin America (and Asia) would bankrupt the Church. Thus while no more schools are currently being built, promising young members are given grants to further their education in governmental and private institutions in their respective countries as well as in the United States. The Church also sponsors literacy programs and other educational activities in areas of human nutrition, business enterprise, agricultural development, and public health. Suddenly a new brand of missionary has become important for specialized functions in the field. Health missionaries and agricultural missionaries now take their place right alongside those called for regular proselyting missions.

For a long time prior to the founding of these new programs of temporal concern, numerous ex-missionaries had spoken of the limitations that adverse temporal conditions place on a new member's capability fully to participate in the gospel. Many who said, "What can we do?" in fact did nothing. Others contributed to scholarship, missionary, and building funds. But one, in particular, dedicated his life. That was Cordell Andersen who, in 1964 and in the company of his wife and family, left for Guatemala to do what he could for the temporal well-being of his brothers and sisters there.[3] In the last thirteen years he and his family, in spite of much opposition and calloused faultfinding by some North-American Mormons, have made a significant contribution to both the spiritual and temporal welfare of dozens of Mormon families. Members of the Church now read who were not able to before; many now have occupational skills they did not have before; numerous are in better health than otherwise would be expected. Truthfully, the hope that Andersen's Indian Development Foundation in Guatemala will not fail is now widely shared.

The development of the Church's programs designed to enhance the temporal well-being of its members in Latin America has followed a pattern similar to that of developing local leadership. Fifteen years ago, for example, there were no temporal-development programs. Some people dreamed about having them; others argued they were not part of the Church's mission. But today we do have them. What some once saw as being "not part of the gospel," today we see as a fully integrated and correlated part of it. There are problems with implementation, with coverage, with personnel. Yes, we know that. But problems have not invalidated a good idea and some notable successes, in both the development of leadership and temporal well-being.

While development programs help to solve old problems, they also create new ones. Similarly, old issues have bequeathed new ones and in turn have produced their own new problems with which the Church must deal. For example, the LDS schools in Mexico and Chile can no longer accept all member children who would like to attend. The resources and physical facilities simply do not exist to accommodate the current and projected demand. That problem will become more acute as more and more people join the Church, then seek to send their children to its schools. As one might imagine, such a bind in a world of high expectations creates a considerable amount of anxiety among the members. It is no different, perhaps, for the American stake president whose daughter is refused admittance to BYU. "Whose tithing is used for what?" he says.

Another contemporary issue deals with highly motivated and talented young members who are falling away from the Church. The Church's encouragement in educational areas has now got a whole new generation into preparatory and advanced studies, either in Latin America or at BYU. But many of those with the most talent and best preparation drop out of the Church. Why? And many of those who go to BYU do not return to their homelands to help their own people begin the process of generational transfer of skills and insights, leadership and development. Why? How are we to preserve the cream from souring? How are we best to use the talents and developed capacity of a new generation? A lot of people are thinking about these issues right now.

Membership Growth and Institutional Development

It was not the halting and often discouraging *early* missionary work in Mexico, Argentina, and Brazil that raised the main issues of membership growth. To some extent slowness and discouragement were both expected. The long civil war in Mexico and its even longer aftermath had greatly disrupted Church activities in that country. Everyone knew that. And schismatic movements such as the Third Convention, the Church of the Firstborn, and Margarito Bautista's New Jerusalem also took their intermittent tolls. Growth that was slow, halting, and problematic was considered to be more or less normal in Mexico. Such expectations also applied to Argentina, where a hoped-for harvest of German immigrants was largely frustrated. As if to dramatize that frustration, in 1925 an apostle of the Church, Elder Melvin J. Ballard, could be seen days on end passing out Church literature on the street corners of Buenos Aires. Everything else he had tried in Argentina had failed. No, it was not the slowness of growth in the early part of this century that raised the most important growth issues. Those were reserved to accompany the spectacular membership increase of the early 1960s.

What lay behind these rapid transformations? A new missionary administrative structure with better-trained missionaries, a new breed of mission presidents trained in the fields of hard advertising and product sales, a new eschatological commitment on the part of the Church, hundreds of thousands of Latin Americans ready for a new value commitment, an increased presence of the Holy Spirit, all these combined in the 1960s to produce spectacular consequences for the Church. A critical threshold of some sort seemed to have been reached, a catalyst found.

Who were the new members? For the most part they were young, single, and female, or else they were from split families, with mothers and children becoming the new Mormons. All this derived not so much from selective proselyting as from those norms and values in Latin-American culture that relegate religion to women and children, and "more important things" to men. Men simply were not so prone to pay attention to a religious message, Mormon or any other. They never had been.

At the same time the phenomenal new baptismal rate was occurring during the 1960s, the Church, preparatory to its eventually forming stakes and wards in numerous Latin-American countries, was also rapidly transferring leadership obligations and opportunities to local members. This we have seen. But there were relatively few men in the Church at the time, and fewer still who were qualified for major administrative assignments. Thus in those days a very few local members carried burdens nearly without precedent in the modern period of the Church's existence. Truly these men and women were pioneers in our own lifetime.

It was a curious administrative arrangement under which all this occurred. The North-American mission president was operating for a maximum number of conversions to the faith. But he assumed little or no responsibility for what happened to the new members. The established local members—and the new leaders—were expected to do the fellowshipping, the integrating, the shepherding, and the caring. Yet the new leaders were hardly prepared to handle a magnitude of growth that would perplex even the most experienced Church leaders.

The new local leaders needed new members with at least minimum leadership capability. What the mission presidents delivered was a tremendous quantity of members who were mostly inexperienced by any relevant leadership standard. The enterprise simply broke down, with relations between local ecclesiastical authorities and some North-American mission presidents becoming strained indeed.

This impressive increase in the number of Mormons in Latin America had exceeded the Church's institutional base for receiving them. It is not surprising, therefore, that for a while in the 1960s the dropout rate in the Church was nearly as great as the baptismal rate. Some observers were inclined to believe that was to be expected. Had it not happened in the early days of the Church in the United States too? Others were alarmed. What could be done?

In the early 1970s a general administrative reassessment of the state of Church growth in Latin America produced a new orientation. The Church wanted members, lots of them. But it needed them attached to member families. Not only does the Mormon faith emphasize the role of families in its doctrines of salvation; it also, from long experience, knows that from member families the strongest new generations of Mormons emerge. Rather than working with individuals in a socially isolated context, the missionaries began to work with families. The missionaries found ways to contact and influence men. Encouragement from wives and children, whose own baptisms frequently hinged on the decisions of their husbands and fathers themselves to be baptized, motivated the men to consider baptism seriously. Husbands with wives and parents with children: that was the new thrust. Aside from that, young people were not directly proselyted with the same intensity as before.

All this began to have a dramatic impact on the membership profile of the Church. One of the consequences today in Latin America is a better leadership base and a better institutional vessel to receive the new members. There is greater family strength in the gospel. And out of that strength a new generation of youth born into the Church is receiving the teachings. Harold Brown, the first stake president of the first Spanish-speaking stake in the world, has remarked that the leadership in the weakest of the new stakes organized in Mexico in 1975 was considerably stronger, better prepared, and more adapted to the needs of the Church than was the leadership of the first one over which he presided in 1961. The prospects for quality continue to improve.

The "quantity problem" of the 1960s, particularly in the demographic thrust in which it came—young, female, split families—probably did produce a "critical presence," a threshold effect as it were, that provided an ultimate breakthrough for the Church in Latin America. If pursued to its logical end, however, the early trend would have been suicidal. But now, helped in part by the family and leadership reinforcement that the seminary and institute systems give, our prospects look good. To be sure, problems remain, as they always will and as they do everywhere. But we are looking at the balance of things here.

Ethnic and National Pride

North Americans, in general, have a great deal of pride in their national heritage, ancestry, and way of life. Currently, English-speaking Mormons in the United States find these sentiments of pride and justification considerably reinforced by an official Church posture that emphasizes patriotism to America and respect for its officials, its political and economic system, its foreign policies, and the freedoms of conscience and liberty of choice that, for Americans, have historically accompanied them. The crumbling of such freedoms and liberties elsewhere in the world lends a certain poignancy to the Church's current emphasis. In this regard, the destiny of America and the destiny of the Church throughout the world are seen to be heavily intertwined. Thus, in the minds of some, as the Church is revered, so also should America be revered.

Mormons in other lands recognize the key role America has played in the restoration of the gospel and in the evolution of the Church to a position of importance and strength. But in varying degrees of amusement, anxiety, and anger they find offensive the conclusion of many English-speaking members that middle-class American culture, politics, economics, and language are the Lord's ideal way. And they voice their sentiments.

Quite understandably, such sentiments, let alone their expression, come as a shock to many old-line Church families in the United States who find it difficult to understand how a Guatemalan could have pride in his native land and heritage, or how a Mexican or Chicano could swell with more emotion over Cahuatémoc and the Niños Héroes than "Deseret" Mormons can over George Washington and Abraham Lincoln. A kind of defensive pride thereafter produces a misunderstanding of one another's ethnic and national sentiments. Tears and recriminations sometimes follow.

The amusement, anxiety, and anger are played out most vividly between Deseret Mormons and other Mormons who historically had adverse political and economic relations with dominant institutions and social groups in the United States. Currently, these "other Mormons" are to be found, for the most part and insofar as they relate to Latin America, among Mexican Mormons and Chicano Mormons (Mexican-American Mormons). "Please listen to us," they say.

Few North-American Mormons do listen, however, for they frequently consider the ethnic pride and national sentiments of others to be childish and ill-taken. The Mexican and Chicano Mormons, in despair, respond: "We love you as brothers. But how can we keep you from destroying what we hold dear—our heritage, our ancestral customs, the human sentiments of our people that also have a collective memory in history, that also were born in conflict, nurtured in sacrifice, preserved in dignity?"

The Church has attempted to heighten the ethnic and cross-cultural empathy of its transcultural membership through its Relief Society organization. For several years the Cultural Refinement lessons received by thousands of sisters throughout the world have concentrated on understanding members in diverse countries wherever the gospel has been accepted. Yet there is a long way to go. Ethnic diversity within a single faith poses some very special challenges for a brotherhood in Christ. We have the challenge. It will take an expanded awareness and sensibility among members everywhere, and a conscious desire to develop a capacity for cross-cultural empathy and sensitivity, to bring about a harmonious brotherhood. A great many Latin-American Mormons hope their American brothers will be as successful in this pursuit as the Lord would have them be. Increasing numbers of North-American Mormons share those sentiments. Perhaps in that we can look optimistically to the future.

How do Latin-American Mormons feel about these and related issues? What do they perceive their experience as having been as they have attempted to receive the gospel across a cultural frontier? What prospects does the future hold for our relationship one with another? What new insights and new sense of brotherhood should Mormons everywhere attempt to acquire in order not only to enhance the expansion of a faith but to develop a universal brotherhood in Christ among those who embrace it? There are many challenges that face us—all of us—as we attempt to weld diverse peoples and nationalities into a brotherhood that is one as much in heart, mind, and spirit as in numbers and doctrinal fidelity. The Latin-American contributors to this section of the book deal with some of those challenges. As we grapple with their ideas, our specific challenge as readers is to try to understand, to comprehend, to struggle responsibly with our own biases and preconceptions, to reflect on our strengths and, finally, to rejoice in having difficult opportunities yet to encounter.

GOSPEL, CULTURE, AND LEADERSHIP DEVELOPMENT IN LATIN AMERICA

Harold Brown

It is fitting that "growth issues" be the general focus of this Latin-American section of the essays on the expanding Church. In less than two decades since 1960 the present membership of the Church in Latin America has increased fifteen times; and half the present members have been in the Church less than five years. As with the increase in members, the institutional development of the Church, slow in the beginning, has also dramatically advanced in recent years. Mexico and Central America offer good examples. In 1961 the first Latin-American stake was established in Mexico City. The Church now has thirty-one stakes in Mexico and an additional five in Central America. Moreover, by April 1977 another dozen stakes will likely be created. This sixteen-year development is comparable to what happened in the first seventy-five years of existence of the entire Church—one-half its total life span. But the contrast is even more striking. In South America, the other great region inhabited by Latin-American peoples, the Church is also growing rapidly in membership and in the development of wards and stakes. Indeed, so substantial has the record been that a temple is now under construction in São Paulo, Brazil.

Interesting questions are arising from this rapid increase in members and in the development of wards and stakes to administer Church programs among them. The issue of leadership looms large, of course, because stakes must be self-sufficient in leaders. In particular, and in keeping with the general orienting theme of these symposia on the Church's relationship to culture and secular society, what bearing do the cultures of Latin American peoples have on meeting the Church's new leadership needs? Indeed, how well equipped are the converts to enter into the pattern of life prescribed by the gospel and to achieve real Latter-day Saint homes, thereby creating a climate for the development of successive new generations of leaders? Do their cultural patterns facilitate this or do their mores represent barriers too difficult to surmount? Can the members and new leaders handle the conceptual problems of the doctrines and the administrative and organizational demands of the programs? What has our experience been on these basic leadership-related questions?

I would like to approach a discussion of these questions by first examining the qualifications leaders in the Church should have—especially stake leaders. I will then suggest that most problems of leadership are not unique to any region or culture, and that, knowing this, the Church has now created leadership programs currently of substantial assistance among new converts everywhere. Nevertheless, cultural diversity does bring both benefits and problems for the development of new leaders, and each region of the Church has its own experiences in such development. Thus, I will also reflect on cultural patterns in Latin America that specifically affect three key leadership skills: 1) *authority righteously exercised,* 2) *general program administration within the framework of gospel stewardship,* and 3) *human motivation.*

What should leaders in the Church be like, especially stake leaders? I will develop this theme (in order later to contrast it with actual accomplishments in Latin America) by referring to eight of nineteen principles that President Spencer W. Kimball specified in a recent talk, entitled "The Image of the Stake," delivered to the Regional Representatives of the Twelve. The focus is upon the stake president, but the observations pertain to other key leaders as well.

1. A stake president should administer programs that have spiritual substance in every aspect of their activities. In order to do this he will study the gospel and rely upon the Lord.
2. A stake president must see and understand the basic vision, goals, and objectives of the gospel as the Lord defines them. He must recognize that the development of fathers in his stake capable of enhancing the spiritual welfare and individual conversion of members of their respective families is his primary concern and the focal point of all that he does. Fathers have an eternal responsibility and need to be taught the doctrines and duties of the kingdom.
3. A stake president needs to know the gospel, live its precepts, and be guided by the Lord to be a light for all to follow.
4. A stake president needs to understand his stewardship, learn how effectively to administer the Lord's will, and train others to do likewise.
5. A stake president should foster unity, Christian brotherhood, peace, and tranquility among members under his jurisdiction and thus cause Zion to increase in beauty for all to see.
6. A stake president keeps his stake well organized and fully functioning, and thus is mindful of the needs, problems, and challenges facing bishops and other leaders and members in his stake.
7. A stake president consults counselors for counsel, but in the final sweep of things will make the primary decisions himself and then submit those decisions to his counselors for their judgment. In like manner the stake president consults his high councilors in matters of stake concern. Neither counselors nor high councilors make the major decisions, but they may counsel and vote to sustain or ob-

ject to the president's proposal. A wise stake president will not intimidate those who voice objection, but rather will listen and weigh carefully the reasons for their objections. They may prove to be compelling.

8. A stake president knows that practically all Church activities within the stake come under his jurisdiction, including the work of the wards through the bishoprics. He will thus work to provide adequate leadership for those activities. This involves bringing around him other members with special talents, gifts, and inspiration to help guide special facets of the work.

President Kimball then summarized what is expected of a stake president in these words:

> *A stake president's success will depend largely on his reliance upon the Lord; on how much inspiration he can receive to perform his responsibilities. . . . This kind of leader must have a strong feeling of responsibility, moral courage, and a will to complete his responsibilities against all odds. He will need to develop good judgment and effective administration, always as guided by the spirit.*
>
> *He recognizes and acknowledges the work and worth of others. He has a warm personal relationship with people and he commands their respect by his treatment of them. He exerts influence with, rather than power over, his people. He listens attentively and sympathetically. He encourages and motivates others to be excited and responsive to their responsibilities. He encourages self-responsibility in others. He organizes his meetings well and keeps his people posted on their work and responsibilities.*
>
> *He carefully and prayerfully calls and initiates people in their responsibilities so that they may understand what the Lord expects of them in their calling. He has a systematic review of every system of the stake so that all facets and all programs are receiving the benefit of his stewardship and his guidance. He recognizes that the stake presidency is to guard the people's morals and to look after their welfare and teach them in the way of eternal life. He recognizes that a stake will be far from perfect whose leaders exercise unrighteous dominion.*

As you might imagine, not all stake presidents and leaders, either in the United States or in Latin America, meet the ideal criteria set forth by President Kimball. In that regard we can say that the problems respecting the development of leaders in newly expanding areas of the Church know no cultural boundaries. It is a universal problem, perennially illustrated by the gap in leadership talent and capacity that has always existed between the mature stake and the mission district.

In the past the training of new members has often been inadequate. Too much was expected of mission presidents who were frequently loaded with the work of several stake presidents in addition to their proselyting activities. Compounding this have been the large numbers of new converts who have not had a history of experience in a church that requires action and involvement rather than the passivity of simply listening to a priest or a minister. All new members have had to learn, as part of their conversion, that this Church is like a beehive, that activity earns the rewards of heaven, and that just believing will not take one far in his quest for exaltation. The leadership development problem, then, is universal, and is not peculiar to a Latin-American heritage.

In dealing with general leadership development challenges, the Church has moved to create conditions under which new stakes, new stake presidents, and other leaders, many of whom have been in the Church less than five years, can rise to the standards set by the Lord and enjoy success in participating in programs to that end. In Latin America this has been facilitated by the assigning of Regional and Area Representatives to both stakes *and* missions.

With this background—that ideal stake leadership is based on sound gospel principles, that problems in developing leadership are not unique to any given culture, that the Church has placed heavy emphasis on and given considerable assistance through the Regional and Area Representatives to developing leadership throughout the Church—we can now ask the two central questions that deal with culture and leadership:

1. What aspects of national or regional cultures in Latin America need to be overcome in order that Latin-American Saints may develop an LDS culture and thereby enjoy the full blessings of the gospel and the Church's programs in their personal lives?
2. Conversely, what strengths inherent in the cultures of Latin America facilitate the required transition so that members may enjoy the leaders they need and also be able to participate fully in the Church and the gospel?

The questions, in their most fundamental aspect, are these: Do Latin-American cultural patterns facilitate or impede the accepting and living of the gospel message? After a decade and a half of direct involvement in the process of developing new stakes from parent stakes and mission districts, I can say that I know of no aspect of culture in Latin America that cannot be turned to an advantage for the Church. This can be done either by capitalizing on an inherent strength within the culture or by transforming a misguided or misused cultural trait into a Latter-day Saint pattern of conduct.

Such an apparently radical statement calls for a comment on cultural transformation or cultural change. Change from what to what? Is it our objective to substitute the cultural traits of one country or region for those of another? What a wealth of cultural diversity would be lost to the Church and to the world should such a misguided effort be undertaken and achieved! No, the question of cultural change or transformation deals, not with making all Mormons cultural carbon copies of one another, but rather in teaching them the principles of the gospel which, when lived, do produce a basic common denominator in the diverse cultural fabric of the Church. That common denominator is what we call the LDS or Mormon culture.

This LDS culture is very real. It is shared by Church members of all cultural backgrounds. It has arisen from a universal practice within the Church of a type of socioeconomic life based on principles of the gospel. The beliefs, attitudes, and practices growing out of the living of the gospel and of the pursuit of the objectives of the priesthood and of the Church have developed the patterns of living that are appropriately called a Latter-day Saint or Mormon culture. When we speak of cultural change, then, this is our point of reference. We take new members from their respective cultures and help them to adopt a Mormon or LDS culture. All the remaining cultural diversity stands and grows as one of the great beauties of the worldwide Church.

Now let me say again, I know of no cultural element in Latin America that is not or cannot be made into an asset to Latter-day Saint or Mormon culture. Yet the process of adopting the LDS culture is a challenging one, especially when President Kimball's image of a stake and the qualifications of its leaders, as reviewed above, are accepted as the ends to be met. Especially is the task difficult for a stake president and his quorum of leaders and for a bishop and his total team who must exercise authority, stewardship, administrative skills, the art of human motivation, righteous dominion, good judgment, compassion, and correlation, or in other words, total spiritual leadership in their effort to bring their members into the LDS culture.

Let us look at three of the above—authority, administration, and human motivation—in relation to cultural traits in Latin America that pose interesting questions as they are made into assets for the LDS culture.

Authority and Culture in Latin America

Authority as understood by most of our Latin-American converts is experienced on three levels: authority exercised by the head of the family; authority exercised by the boss at work or the teacher at school; and authority exercised by governmental, political, administrative, and regulatory agencies.

Authority and the family

Paternal or maternal authority as exercised in Latin America ranges from tender understanding to despotic paternalism. However, one general characteristic stands out; it is that the wife and children recognize the father as the head of the family. In other words, Papa is Papa. The training starts early. A male child frequently is given a position of deference and privilege within the family relative to his sisters. Indeed, he often grows up "spoiled." Thus begins the attitude of male dominance, rather widespread in Latin America, popularly called *machismo.* In its traditional packaging, this element of self-esteem is incompatible with the gospel and the LDS culture because it relates more to privilege than to responsibility, more to self-assertion than to cooperative action.

Authority and employers

Authority exercised by the boss at work traditionally has been paternalistic, authoritarian, and, at times, despotic. In contemporary Latin America, labor laws more and more favorable to workers' rights are tending to make the boss more temperate in his exercise of authority and the laborer more demanding of his rights. However, this does not necessarily make the laborer act more responsibly. Frequently, the more authority he gets the less productive he becomes in his work. It is a curious paradox. In the traditional setting authority was exercised either in an abusive or paternalistic way. Now it is frequently exercised in an irresponsible way. Then, and now, authority brought privilege, not cooperation or responsibility. Thus, in general, the experiences that Latin American converts have had in an authoritarian hierarchy do not exactly coincide with the expectations of "authority righteously exercised" in the Church. Authority that abuses, patronizes, or acts irresponsibly is not an authority that forms part of the LDS culture. It is a corruption.

Authority and government

Authority exercised by governmental officials—be they politicians, political appointees, or civil servants—is often excessively self-serving and arbitrary. One of the general results among those citizens who in one way or another are required to deal with government is their use of influence to transact business and to gain desired ends. In a word, authority exercised in this manner fosters corruption. Rewards come to those who can corrupt the most effectively and efficiently. In the LDS culture such behavior cannot exist, for it makes a mockery of brotherhood and equality, service and integrity, honesty and "anxious engagement" in worthy causes.

As already asserted, the traditional exercise of authority at these three levels is incompatible with a Church culture based on stewardship, effective administration, human motivation, righteous dominion, judgment, and compassion. How then can we also assert that traditional norms and practices relating to authority can be an asset to Latter-day Saint culture?

Well, Papa being Papa is actually a good starting point for the father's being the patriarch in his home and actively and enterprisingly seeking the resources available to him through the Church, the community, and the nation for the benefit of his family. Even the custom of gaining desired ends through influence develops a highly beneficial resourcefulness that does not disappear when repentance and understanding bring about a change of objectives and of methods. Enterprise, self-esteem, and the exercise of priesthood authority for righteous leadership can and do replace a misguided *machismo* once the leadership concept of Latter-day Saint culture is understood and becomes operative.

Administrative Skills and the Church

As with the exercise of authority, the development of administrative skills adequate for the functioning of the Church also has some roots in culture as well as in experience and education. The cultural conditions that influence the way administrative skills are exercised are well known and sometimes substantially aid or impede leadership development within the Church. Culture, as well as educational and other experiences, frequently affects people's ability or capacity to understand and communicate concepts, to organize personal time and effort, to orchestrate a complexity of programs and projects with a sense of correlation, to use human and material resources effectively, and to employ the art of human motivation.

In analyzing the administrative capabilities of our converts in Latin America, we note that education, experience, and culture have created some obstacles to the development of administrative skills appropriate to the Church's functioning. Again, however, I emphasize that the obstacles themselves can, in many instances, be turned to advantages for the Church, as I will later show.

In the area of experience and education, we must begin by noting that relatively few of our converts have been administrators at a level that would give them any significant transferable experience. Opportunities to lead groups or communities are limited in Latin American social organization; and leadership opportunities in religions outside the

LDS culture are practically nonexistent. The same is true of opportunities for education. Most of the converts do not have a level of education that equips them to deal with organizational procedures that presume a high degree of written word and number sophistication.

But, I must emphasize, this is changing. Leaders trained within the Church are now sharing the gospel with others of their own cultural level and inspiring them to develop and progress in their abilities. At the same time we have seen a gradual accumulation of professionally trained converts who have expanded horizontally into their own cultural levels with the gospel message. Ten years ago, at the time of the division of the first stake in Mexico City, not enough university-level students in the Church could be found to form an institute group. At the present time approximately 1,400 such students are in Mexico City alone. This provides a corps of leaders well prepared to handle gospel concepts and program administration. And it might surprise some of you to know that Latin-American students tend to be more conceptually apt than do Western Americans. Having taught seminary classes in the United States and religion classes at Brigham Young University, I was delighted at the relative facility of my seminary and institute students in Mexico to grasp and vocalize gospel and philosophical concepts. The Spanish language lends itself to expressiveness, and Latin Americans are generally an expressive people—both artistically and verbally.

Administrative discipline was noticeably absent in the early beginnings of stakehood in Mexico. But the leadership training programs of the Church, expanded administrative experience in Church organizations, and ever-increasing levels of formal education have produced people possessing administrative skills that dispel all apprehensions about an administrative capability to meet the demands of the rapidly expanding Church. Administrative skills have become prominent values in the Latter-day Saint culture of our area.

Once our people are taught and given an opportunity, it is their very lack of education and experience that makes many of them invest prodigious efforts to improve themselves. With enthusiasm they impress others who may have inadequate education and experience, and especially their children, that for them it is also possible. Thus a lack of educational and other experiences, when coupled with opportunity and the Latin American's generally advanced ability to grasp abstract concepts, combine to offer a positive note to the development of administrative skills among the Latin-American Saints. This development is enhanced by the increasing number of converts who come into the Church already equipped with many leadership skills and educational achievements.

Human Motivation and Culture in Latin America

Let us consider the art of human motivation, the third category we deal with in relation to culture, within the concepts of righteous dominion, loyalty, honesty, and judgment.

One of the greatest challenges to the Church in any culture is to move its leaders from practices of unrighteous dominion to the human relations practices of the Latter-day Saint culture. The Lord forewarned us of this problem when he revealed to the Prophet of the Restoration that "we have learned by sad experience that it is the nature and dispositon of almost all men, as soon as they get a little authority, as they suppose, they will immediately begin to exercise unrighteous dominion" (D&C 121:39).

What are some of the problems inherent in the culture in our area in Mexico that portray this challenge? One is the problem of paternalism (discussed in the section above on authority). A dramatic illustration of its ineffectiveness in the Church is driven home in the comparison of the behavior of bishops who are older and have not grown up in the LDS culture and younger bishops who have. The older bishops tended to tell the youth in their wards what to do; they laid down the law and expected it to be obeyed. The need for personal interviews and the development of a relationship of warmth and understanding was not comprehended. These bishops experienced many frustrations as they saw their authority diminish and their ability to lead impaired. On the other hand, the younger bishops, to a greater extent the product of Latter-day Saint culture, interviewed their members formally and informally, and their relations with both adult leaders and the youths themselves grew warm and goal-oriented.

Under the old traditional ethic that understandably influenced many older bishops, authority meant privilege; and "confidence" (*confianza*), so important to traditional authority, required unconditional support from followers and cohorts. Followers who had *confianza* were the loyal ones; and when the man in authority meted out judgment, this loyalty brought special privileges and also exemption from penalties. Thus honesty meant one thing among those inside the circle of *confianza* and another in relations with those outside it.

Honesty or the use of truth has two meanings in the non-Mormon Latin-American culture, one moral and the other tactical. In commerce and conflicts, the tactical use of the truth prevails; and little, if any, remorse is felt or shown when a misrepresentation is discovered or withheld facts come out. This tactical use spills over into the area of personal honesty and manifests itself at times in the form of gross deception.

But more often it is a reason for not facing up to responsibility, or it becomes a device for removing pressure. In Spanish we say *para salirse del paso*.

In the Mormon culture there is, of course, a single honesty. A new convert does not always achieve a change to this standard at the moment of his conversion or baptism. The same is true of some of the leaders who have been reared outside the LDS culture and who are still struggling to adapt themselves to new norms and values within it. Many of them constantly struggle to divest themselves of the old custom of developing *confianza* with supporters and cohorts.

In the LDS culture, Church leaders bring into their circle of concern and love every young man and woman, not because he or she is a supporter in the right or in the wrong but because he or she is a child of God. When the leader makes judgments, he makes the same corrective demands for one as for another. He learns that correction and salvation are goals and not rewards for misguided loyalties to or punishments for opposing a leader.

These Latter-day Saint cultural values are being achieved in Mexico and elsewhere in Latin America. We could talk of other cultural elements such as punctuality, compassion, and concern for the inactive or misguided as they relate to the successful transition into stakehood and to the approximation of what President Kimball holds out as the ideal for leaders in the Church everywhere—strong feelings of responsibility, moral courage, and a will to complete responsibilities against all odds. But the discussion here has at least illustrated my thesis that cultural characteristics in our area, when channeled and transformed into Latter-day Saint cultural patterns, represent sources of strength and creativity more than barriers to the effective development of the Church.

MORMONISM AND THE CHICANO

Orlando A. Rivera

The experience of Mormonism among Spanish-speaking people in the United States dramatically illustrates the challenge of moving across tradition, cultures, and ancestral norms with a single faith. Perhaps more so among my people than among others does the expansion of the LDS faith portray, as LaMond Tullis has said, "a story of hope and despair, motivation and frustration, success and failure." This paradox needs to be better understood. I hope my statement will contribute to that understanding.

The Latin-American population in the United States about which I speak is significant. It is larger than the entire population of many countries, constituting the fourth largest Latin-American community in the world—exceeded only by the huge nation of Brazil (itself nearly as large as the United States) and Mexico and Argentina.

There is a problem of exact numbers, however. We do not really know how many people we have here. One of the reasons for this is that the 1970 United States census failed to enumerate the Spanish-speaking population. The census takers recorded native Alaskans, Hawaiians, Koreans, and many other ethnic groups, but they did not enumerate the Spanish-speaking as a distinct group even though we pressed them to do so. As a consequence, the figures we receive are without doubt conservative because they underestimate our numbers. (And we have numerous people who are here illegally; it is hard to enumerate them regardless of the census categories!)

Except for immigrants from Brazil, almost all of my people speak Spanish. Some have lived in this country for many generations; others have come only recently. Our people now reside in every state—from New Mexico where over 30 percent of the population is of Spanish-speaking descent, to California, where they comprise between 11 and 12 percent of the entire population, to Texas with 17 percent, to Illinois and Michigan, where each probably has nearly a hundred thousand Spanish-speaking people residing within its borders. Interestingly, the Spanish-speaking population of Los Angeles is larger than most urban populations in Latin America except for the very largest cities there. Aside from that, one-third of all Puerto Ricans now live in New York City. This gives you some indication of the large numbers of Spanish-speaking people residing in the United States. We have concluded that the official estimate of 11.5 million is conservative and that a more accurate figure would place this number closer to 15 million.

In the Church, people refer to us as Lamanites. Some have thought this to be offensive. But for most of us it is not, especially those of us who identify ourselves as Americans of Mexican descent. We call ourselves Chicanos, and all Chicanos think of themselves as having an Indo-Hispanic background, of having ancestral roots native to America as well as to Europe. Thus, your considering us Lamanites is in no way offensive, but rather acceptable to our people. We are proud of our native American progenitors.

The Central Question

So much for some of the basic aspects of our people. Now let us focus upon one central question that illustrates the challenge of taking the gospel across frontiers of ancestral customs, language, and traditions. Why is it that in the borderlands of the United States and Mexico the expansion of the LDS faith is so much more rapid and impressive in Mexico than in the United States? In the Mexico Hermosillo Mission, for example, a handfull of missionaries baptized more than a thousand people in one month. Why does not such a remarkable occurrence happen in the United States among the 15 million or more people who in some way participate in a Latin-American heritage? I do not have exact data to back me up, but I would venture to say that we do not have a thousand baptisms in the entire nation among Spanish-speaking people.

Why is this so? Are the people that different on each side of the border? No, I do not think our differences are that great. We identify very closely with our brothers across the border. I think we understand each other in cultural terms very well. Yet the difference in baptisms has to be explained in some manner. Surely there is an explanation as to why missionary work is so effective in Mexico and yet ineffective with the same people in the United States.

I would like to speculate with you on an answer. I will do so by focusing upon the twin concepts of cultural pride and cultural breakdown as applied to my own people, and cultural imperialism as applied to the larger Anglo-American majority among whom we live.

Noel Reynolds, in his paper on "Culture and the Gospel" given at the first session of this symposium, suggests that we should not waste too much time on the definition of culture. Yet I think we have to give some consideration to culture if we are to identify those differences that exist between our peoples and that help to explain the differential success in the missionary activity. I will not get into an argument over what definition is best, but I simply wish to say that, for most of us, culture refers to the life-style that people adopt and to the norms and values associated with it that give order to their society or to their group. It helps them cope with the environment in which they live by distilling bits of collective wisdom that have proven useful in enabling a people to survive. This life-style, with its codes for living, coping, and surviving, is somehow transmitted from parent to child, generation after generation.

When we consider that the cultural characteristics of my people in the United States had their roots in the traditions of my people in Mexico or in other parts of Latin America, we can see why, culturally, we are more alike than we are different. Our mothers saw to that. Yet, obviously, the environment in which we live does have an impact on us, and it does influence our culture and our values. Consider, therefore, that people with similar cultural roots residing in the United States and in Mexico are living in quite different environments. Perhaps herein lies the foundation for an answer to the question of why missionary work is so much more successful among Spanish-speaking people in Mexico than among those same people in the United States. Is it the environment, one generally dominated economically, politically, and socially by other than our people, that holds the answer?

To be able to explore adequately this facet of the question, it is necessary to understand the *mode of entry* of a people into whatever environment or society in which they find themselves. With this need in mind, I want briefly to review certain elements of the history of our people in the United States with the hope that this will shed more light on the relationship of a people's environment to their adoption of the gospel message.

As you know, the early sixteenth-century Spanish exploration of the New World brought Cortés to Mexico and others to Central and South America with the motive, generally, to exploit the land for its gold or other exportable treasures. Spanish explorers with the same intent also came to North America. Among these were Ponce De León, Pánfilo de Narváez, Cabeza de Vaca, Coronado, and de Soto. Their explorations failed to find gold for Spain, but the Spanish kings did seem to see some value in the lands the explorers had claimed for them. Thus in the late part of the sixteenth century a Spanish colony, San Gabriel, was established in what is now northern New Mexico.

That colony, and after 1598 many others, grew and flourished in areas not far from present-day Utah. The colonists' culture was influenced both by their residence in Mexico and also their heritage from sixteenth-century Spain; but being isolated from both Mexico and Spain, they developed their own unique life-style. Paramount in that life-style was the establishment of family villages along the tributaries of various rivers. As such, we might describe those early pioneers as having had a cooperative society, agrarian in nature, and with sixteenth-century Iberian cultural characteristics and language.

When you live in a cooperative society, especially one made up of family villages, you probably do not compete too much with one another; rather, you help one another to survive. One of the products is an almost classless society. As such, there is opportunity for all members of the group to enjoy human dignity and respect, for it is not so necessary for some people to have more than others and for some people to look down upon others as a way of elevating their own statuses. On the contrary, everyone is treasured—including the elderly and the children—because people are treasured. This life-style must have existed for nearly 2½ centuries. But then something happened to our people who had resided for this long time in what is now the United States of America. It was the coming of the Anglo-American.

The first significant wave of Anglo-Americans into Mexican territory occurred in what is present-day Texas. The Americans agreed to abide by Mexican laws, but did not. When they found that Mexico was serious and that my forefathers' country would not tolerate human slavery within its borders, the Americans sought to have their own republic. They rebelled, primarily over the question of slavery. Then Santa Anna, poorly equipped with muskets and indigenous soldiers, was unable to recruit the kind of force that could put an end to the rebellion. Mexico therefore lost. The independent Republic of Texas was thus born in 1836 in slavery and intrigue. Later, in 1845, the Republic was admitted to the Union as a state.

But American expansion did not stop there. Under the presidency of Polk, we heard of Manifest Destiny, a doctrine declaring that this country was destined by God to span the entire continent of North America. To make this point, in 1846 the United States declared war on Mexico. The coveted Mexican lands were the entire southwest of the present-day United States of America. My people were in their villages then, living the quiet life of a cooperative society.

Some people opposed the United States' going to war with Mexico, including even Abraham Lincoln. But in those days Congress decided whether the United States should wage war, and by a one-vote majority the advocates for war won. A United States military expedition invaded Santa Fe at about the same time the Mormon pioneers were coming west to settle in the Great Salt Lake Valley. (I always say that for a while the Mormons were Mexicans, because they resided in territory within the borders of Mexico.) The Mormon Battalion participated in the Mexican War, though it did not engage in any hostilities. Under Phillip A. George Cook it did, however, take Tucson, and later San Diego.

The Americans came; our world, our environment, suddenly changed. Abruptly we were thrust into the nineteenth century while still living a sixteenth-century culture of cooperativism. We were invaded by many people coming West—the adventurers, the gold rushers, and the settlers.

All this threatened our people. So in 1849 they rebelled. The main rebellion occurred in New Mexico and gained sufficient proportions to take the lives of many people, including the governor of the state. But United States troops eventually suppressed the rebellion. Because of this, our people probably experienced greater oppression than they ever had before.

How was one to get out of the mess? Why not join up? Why not be a part of the new America? Thus, in 1850 New Mexico, predominantly peopled by former citizens of Mexico, applied for statehood. The Congress of the United States refused the application, however, and in fact did not permit statehood for New Mexico until 1911.

For whatever reason statehood was refused, the economic, social, and political consequences of the "dependency status" the refusal fostered are best described by the term "colonialism." Colonialism is a condition wherein the people have no power, where external control rules over their affairs, where their culture and life-style and values are deprecated, and where they therefore experience what in the present day is called "institutionalized racism."

I think the condition of colonialism still exists because, while millions of people from other Latin-American countries have come to swell our ranks, we Spanish-speaking people in the United States are still largely disfranchised. It is rare that we obtain positions of responsibility or leadership in policy-making positions that allow us to exercise self-determination. Those of us who do get such positions often find ourselves compromised to the extent that if we express ourselves in our own way, from our own perception, we come under intense pressure to "conform."

I bring these things out to emphasize that if "internal colonialism" is a good description of present-day Spanish-speaking people in the United States, we have a good environmental explanation of why the Mexican-Americans have never fitted into the mainstream of this country. They tried—particularly our parents. They played what we call today the assimilation game. But they found so many barriers to assimilation they finally gave up. One of the consequences among their frustrated children was the Chicano movement, a kind of cultural retrenchment. We tried to leave our culture behind and adopt the culture of the dominant society, but that society avoided an accommodation by raising barriers to the kinds of opportunities that would encourage a new acculturation. As a consequence of this and the new cultural retrenchment, we now experience a certain suspicion of anything that is not from our own people. We accept anything "alien" very reluctantly.

Our people in Mexico experience similar feelings, particularly toward the Spaniards. They recognize that Spain colonized them and forced upon them certain ways of life. In an analogous way, our people in the United States were invaded, captured, and oppressed. So we perceive anything "American" with some suspicion, I suppose. Consequently, when something as American as Mormonism is presented to us, my people do not find in it anything to embrace very readily. That is part of the explanation why Mexican-Americans in the United States do not embrace Mormonism with much enthusiasm.

Aside from that, however, and because of the colonial experience we have suffered, I think we lack a certain self-confidence and self-assurance that allows us to be assertive enough to leave our culture or our traditions and to find out what being a convert to Mormonism really means. Thus, as our people look upon Mormonism as an "American" institution, they do so from the twin vantage of suspicion and insecurity.

Not surprisingly, under these conditions, the American Mormon missionary finds it difficult to cross such barriers, which for him have as much psychological impact as they do upon the Mexican-Americans themselves. There are barriers that inhibit such a bridging, and they are as inherent in the Anglo-American as they are in the Chicano. I observed this once to my chagrin with some missionaries who had a brown paper bag on the wall. I said, "What is that for?" The missionary told me, "When that bag begins to look white, then it is time for me to go home." That was offensive to me. But I think it illustrates that before a missionary can let go his traditions he must also develop self-confidence and internal strengths. Perhaps that is not too unlike the condition in which my people find themselves in our inability to leave some of our traditions behind.

On the other hand, our people in Mexico do not live under the kind of environmentally induced suspicion against Americans that my people in the United States do. Moreover, they frequently do not have the lack of self-confidence and personal identity that we experience here. Thus it is quite possible for an American missionary to go to Mexico, learn the language, grow to understand, love, and respect the people, and teach them very effectively. The only barriers to his success are his own cultural hangups. In general, those hangups have not been sufficient to undermine the missionary work in Mexico. However, when the Anglo-American hangups are coupled with the inherent environmentally induced suspicion and cultural retrenchment that exists among Mexican-Americans in the United States, it is nearly impossible to bridge the barriers. Thus we see considerably greater missionary success in Mexico among the Spanish-speaking peoples than we do among those same people in the United States.

People say, "Well, while you are in this country, why don't you leave your traditions behind, drop your suspicion, and become a true American? Why do you qualify your citizenship by calling yourself Mexican-American?" As is our answer to the question of differential missionary success, our answer to this one is related to the environment, to the mode of entry, or to the history of our people. We did not come here with the same motives or ambitions as other immigrant groups. Others came to the United States with the aspiration of leaving behind their old ways and traditions, even their languages, and adopting the American culture and lifestyle to participate in the American dream. But you see, to the Indian, America came to him, not he to America. The same holds true for us. America came to us, not only because of our Spanish heritage but also because of our Indian heritage. With that, and recognizing the barriers to assimilation, it is difficult for us to leave behind whatever it is that we are and accept that which we cannot be accepted into. Some of the perceptions that exist, then, among minorities, are that the policies and practices of Mormonism as a representative practicing American institution must certainly be of a colonial or racist nature. Thus it is not unusual for people to be shocked to find that I, a Chicano, am also a Mormon. I ask them why it is such a shock to think that I am a Mormon. Their typical response: "How can any minority ever be a Mormon when Mormons are so racist?" It is a circular argument. But it is almost beyond the comprehension of minorities that maybe Mormons are not racists. It is particularly difficult when we do nothing to try to dispel that image of ourselves.

The LDS Culture: All Alike or Different?

Brother Harold Brown said in his presentation that there seems to be a Mormon culture. And Dr. Reynolds tried to explain this in his paper. I think they must be right, because Mormon Americans are certainly different from non-Mormon Americans. And those of us who are Mormon Chicanos seem to be different from the Chicanos who are not Mormons. So our faith does influence our culture and our values. It causes them to change, and perhaps to converge. Presumably that convergence, that adapting of central aspects of the Mormon way of life, brings us together a little better into a brotherhood that partially bridges the cultural gap between us.

But even on the bridge we encounter cultural tension and misunderstanding. In the Church we are always told that we are no longer of a particular nationality or ethnic group but are rather united in the LDS faith. It is as if to say that "LDS" is a sufficient and complete culture independent of anything else, and that we should all be able to leave behind whatever other traditions or characteristics of our life-style we may have and adopt it. This, in its simplistic description, is impossible. We converge culturally upon the central aspects of our religion and adopt the central norms and values associated with the ordinances and doctrines, but we still have those old traditions and certain cultural characteristics that we simply cannot and do not want to leave behind. This raises conflicts within the Church between us and some Mormon Americans who perceive their own total cultural package as somehow being synonymous with the "LDS culture." This uncritical assumption prescribes that we "foreigners" should change culturally but that no such requirement is imposed upon those of the "central Mormon culture."

Let me explain. In other parts of the country where I have held positions in the Church, say in Georgia, I found myself to be very comfortable with LDS members who were not Chicano. But here in Utah things happen that are perhaps unique but that clearly call attention to the more secular cultural characteristics of our members. For instance, you are really "in" if you are a Mormon with a pioneer heritage. That heritage may have nothing to do with your qualifications for the kingdom, but you are in. Anyone who does not have that heritage seems almost by definition to be a foreigner. This is an ironic stance when you consider that my people had lived here for 250 years before the Mormons came. Pioneer vintage, then, doesn't make very much of an impression on us. Indeed, when the Mormons were asked to settle my valley, the San Luis Valley in Colorado, they arrived there in the middle of the winter and would certainly have starved or frozen to death if my people had not taken them into their homes. Interestingly, that is why I am a Mormon today. My great-grandfather took some Mormon families into his home to save them and in the process was converted.

In attempting to bridge the cultural gap that separates your people and mine in the United States, the Church has tried different strategies. One of the early ones—begun, I think, by Rey L. Pratt—was to establish branches among the Spanish-speaking people in what was then called the Spanish-American mission. That was a time when many of my people joined the Church. Somehow, we were able to relate to one another. We were able to be Mormons, and we were able to participate fully in the Church. Somewhere along the line, that strategy changed. Some people began to say that if we were going to be Americans, we ought to *be* Americans. Since English is the language spoken here, we ought to speak English. That being the case, all people should go to their neighborhood wards, including the Spanish-speaking people. Starting in California, Arizona, Texas, and other places, many of our Spanish-speaking branches and wards were therefore closed down. (Part of the motivation may also have been that if they were not the Church could have been subjected to criticism for practicing segregation. Or perhaps people were suspicious of Chicano activities.) But members who were observant of these closures recognized that many of my people became inactive in the Church. Those of us who were more acculturated to American ways were able to participate in the wards and continue in the Church. Others—many, many others—dropped out.

When we begin to say that "English is the language spoken here," we really are expressing a strategy of cultural assimilation that smacks of cultural imperialism. Today, most Chicanos will not accept that strategy. What it really means to us is that our history, our heritage, our culture, our language, all that we really are as a result of our historical memory is somehow deficient or even pathological.

Because of the environmental factors I have noted—conquest and colonialism and their impact upon our people, suspicion, initial lack of self-confidence but now a cultural assertiveness and retrenchment—some of our people have opted for living within this country but separately from the rest of the society. Thus when we have a ward such as the Lucero Ward in Salt Lake City, this is exactly what we want. We feel very comfortable in the Lucero Ward, and we are effective there. In other cases, too, whether in education, business, or the professions, we have found that when we are in a position of self-determination we can and do succeed with our own people. But this means that we must have an opportunity to plan for and administer and do things in our own way, for our own selves, completely independently.

Yet it is difficult to have this kind of independence and self-determination in a country like America. And truthfully, we are not sure that so much ethnic independence is what we want in the long run. For the present time, however, the strategy most Chicanos prefer the Church and the nation to take is one of mutual respect, allowing us to be ourselves, to appreciate and understand and learn of our own history and culture. Hopefully, others will appreciate what we have, and a mutual understanding and respect for one another will ensue.

We have models of success in intercultural acceptance and appreciation. In Utah, for instance, there used to be two small towns in Bingham Canyon—Butterfield and Copperfield. These towns were cosmopolitan in a cultural sense, having people from many nationalities and several religions. But somehow the people learned to get along with one another and acquire a certain mutual respect. Almost everyone who ever lived in either of the towns recalls with nostalgia how pleasant it was. They did not have social problems arising from cultural differences until the towns were dissolved and the people began to move into the cities. Today, they do have these problems.

We Chicanos feel that unless we can maintain some of our cultural heritage we will disintegrate and ultimately be destroyed. The disaster is already in front of our eyes. I take, as an example, a point raised by Harold Brown in his paper. Cultural characteristics of our people include family solidarity and a family-oriented life-style, he says. Also, as he emphasized, our tradition is for the father to be the head of the house. *El hombre es la cabeza de la familia.* (We are quick to add that the *mujer,* or the woman, is the neck, and that anywhere she turns the head goes!) While the man has the strong responsibility in his role to look after the family and to provide for it, to discipline the children and make the decisions, it is really the mother who sets the tone for her children. It is she who is the *ama de casa.* While she indulges the children and gives them tremendous physical affection, she also gives them responsibilities. And she teaches them to respect their parents and their elders. Why give up these cultural characteristics? I think they are beautiful ones, and they are iminently compatible with Mormon values.

You no doubt would agree. But when you are in a disadvantaged socioeconomic situation, as are our people in this country, the father frequently cannot obtain the kind of work that permits him to support his family as his traditions suggest he should. He begins to lose face and turns to anomic behavior such as alcoholism or drugs, or perhaps he even leaves the family. The family starts to break down. The children leave it disoriented and misfitted, either to their own culture or to that of the dominant society.

By the same token these disastrous changes affect the mother's role in the family too. For one thing, she has to go outside the home to find work. With all this happening, the children have a hard time maintaining a respect for either father or mother that they culturally, traditionally, would have. A devastating cultural gap separates the generations. So we are teaching our people to have pride in self and to preserve the dignity of the family in something of a traditional way.

The many lines of discussion I have laid out in this essay illustrate some of the reasons why we preserve and strengthen our own culture as an island in a vast sea. And it is interesting to me to see that some of the best of our own youth who are in college are some of the first to go back and learn about their own traditions and their own culture and their own heritage. I wonder if we have the capacity in this country—or the capacity within this Church in this country—to have the mutual respect for one another that does not require us all to be alike, that permits us to enjoy one another's association despite our diverse backgrounds.

Success in the lines I have laid out will take a lot of thought—even changes in what we are doing. I talked to a sister who came to general conference; she says that in her area they no longer have a Spanish-speaking branch. They go to church with the rest of the people but sit in the corner and put earphones on in order to receive a translation of the proceedings. I do not know if that reflects full participation in the Church. It may be the best we can do. I hope not.

It seems to me that, if we can face up to these issues, there is no reason why the Church missionary effort cannot be as successful in the United States among my people—the Lamanites—as it is among them in other parts of the world.

CHURCH SCHOOLS IN MEXICO

Efraín Villalobos Vásquez

My general topic is "Educating Mormons in Latin America," but I want specifically to deal with some of the problems and prospects of the Church Educational System in Mexico. In order to do this it will be helpful to present some general facts about the Church in Mexico so that you may better understand the social foundation of our schools and the environment in which they have developed.

During the last twenty-five years the expansion of the Mormon faith in Mexico has been remarkable. From a membership of only 5,646 in 1950, the Church has since grown to include in 1976 more than 150,000 people. As you can see from figure two, most of them have joined the Church within the last five years.

Alongside this growth in members, the Church's organizational and institutional base has also expanded. Consider, for example, the increase in the number of stakes. The first one in Mexico was organized in 1895 in the Mormon colonies in Chihuahua; the second (in Mexico City) in 1961. Between 1961 and 1974, however, 1.44 new stakes, on the average, were organized annually. Then in only one year, 1975, 17 additional stakes were created. Figure three dramatically illustrates the development.

When we consider Church schools, we see a similar pattern. While Mormons have had schools in Mexico virtually from the beginning of the Church in my country (for example, in 1887 the first schools were established in the Mormon colonies in Chihuahua, and in 1944 another one was started in San Marcos, Hidalgo, about fifty miles north of Mexico City), it was not until 1960 that rapid growth got underway. Since then the Church has founded thirty-seven new schools, the last one in 1974. All combined, our schools now include thirty-four elementary, three junior high, one preparatory, one normal, and one high school (Academia Juárez). As shown in figure four, they are located in fifteen states and in the Federal district.

As you might imagine, with such changes in both the membership of the Church and in the growth of our schools in the last fifteen years,

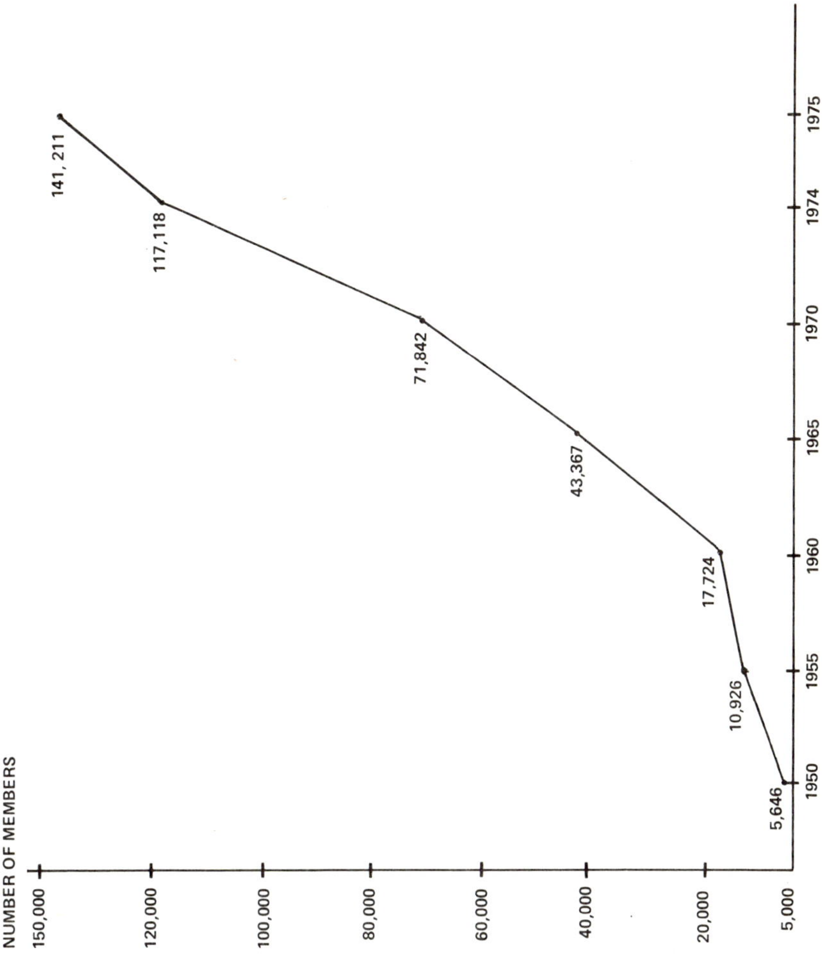

FIGURE 2. CHURCH GROWTH IN MEXICO FROM 1950 TO 1975

classroom enrollment has also increased substantially. In 1960 we had 1,114 students enrolled. Today our schools serve more than 9,653. Of these, 74 percent range from six to twelve years of age, 24 percent from twelve to seventeen, and 2 percent are eighteen or older.

Why do we have Church schools in Mexico? The reasons are multiple, not the least of which is the lack of adequate educational facilities in my country for our people. For many of our children no Church school

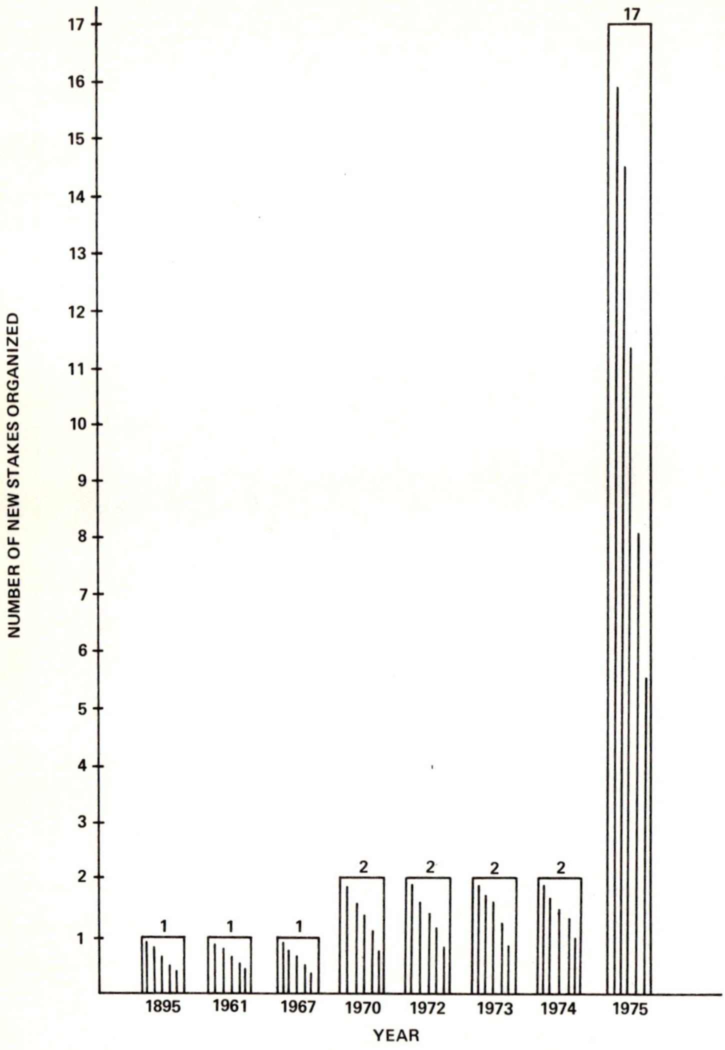

FIGURE 3. STAKES ORGANIZED IN MEXICO FROM 1895 TO 1975

would mean no school at all or, at best, schooling of a kind that would be grossly inadequate.

A second reason we have Church schools relates to the kind of education one receives in the public schools in Mexico when such education is available. It is atheistic, and it does not foster moral principles. Due to the enormous expansion of the Church, with so many new members we

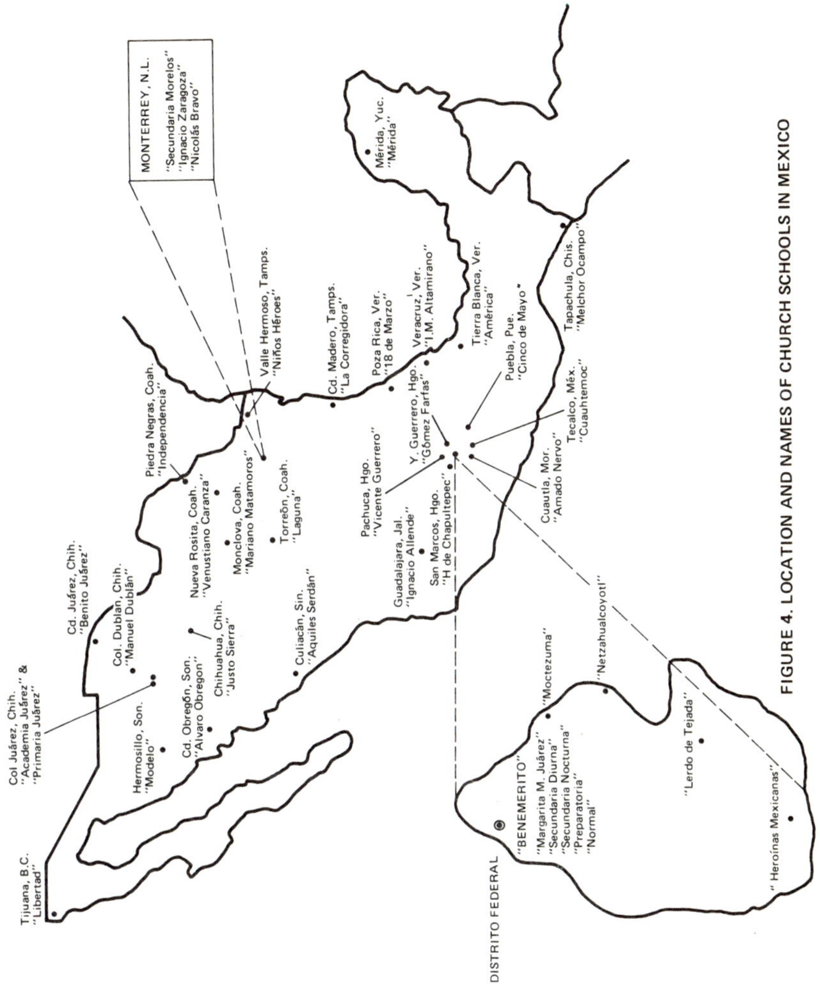

FIGURE 4. LOCATION AND NAMES OF CHURCH SCHOOLS IN MEXICO

need to prepare leaders for the Church with testimonies and experience who can become an ensign to our people. The Church schools greatly contribute to this end.

A third reason relates to the custom in my country of conducting government on a very personalistic basis. With their combination of excellent training and ethical foundation, our school graduates are taking

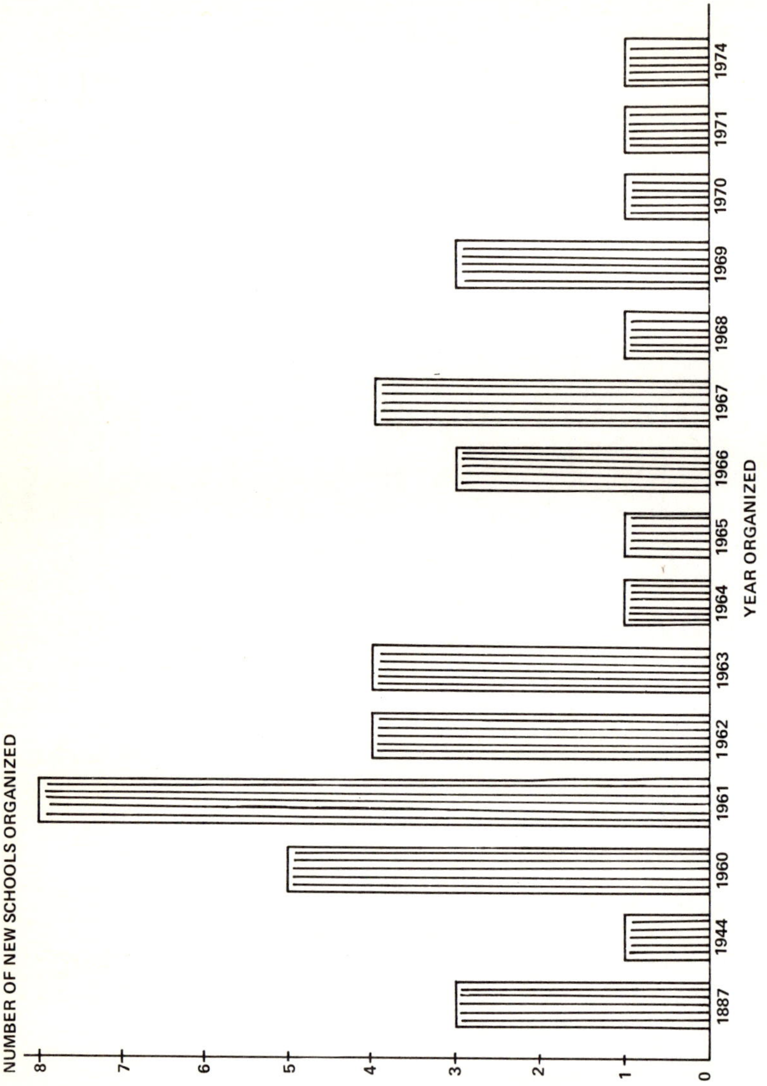

FIGURE 5. MEXICO CHURCH SCHOOLS GROWTH FROM 1887 TO 1974

their places in government circles, are improving government services, and are improving the image of the Church in Mexico. Finally, the Church, through its schools, is able to help a greater number of its members pursue their training beyond what would otherwise be possible.

The adequate realization of these functions and goals is a great challenge, not only because of the inherent difficulties always found in

Name of School	Year Org'd	1961	1962	1963	1964	1965	1966	1967	1968	68-69	69-70	70-71	71-72	72-73	73-74	74-75	75-76
Juarez Academy	1887	260	270	267	296	279	282	243	263	282	216	221	156	262	272	236	220
Manuel Dublan	1887	184	199	187	194	163	172	157	149	140	124	186	260	250	235	280	297
Juarez Elementary	1887	115	168	158	158	150	155	128	128	128	127	129	130	117	118	129	125
Heroes de Chapultepec	1944	167	167	127	117	133	131	130	127	125	125	153	144	143	155	177	204
Benito Juarez	1960	83	106	114	148	142	152	152	164	170	161	166	150	197	131	210	175
Justo Sierra	1960	72	105	108	112	113	127	156	193	171	201	185	215	158	145	174	211
Ignacio Zaragoza	1960	73	147	129	89	99	119	106	116	106	142	196	169	160	130	184	163
Nicolas Bravo	1960	81	44	60	97	100	139	153	183	190	132	108	190	177	154	139	139
Niños Heroes	1960	51	84	72	79	53	87	86	92	127	134	139	148	142	130	153	155
Laguna	1961	107	98	135	151	121	125	119	168	167	123	218	255	218	250	268	263
Margarita M. Juarez	1961	121	144	156	182	212	210	274	274	310	318	427	475	650	695	725	719
Moctezuma Xocoyotzin	1961	79	66	99	104	118	139	153	153	162	176	184	224	296	234	251	280
Heroinas Mexicanas	1961	53	72	60	82	123	133	131	131	128	129	164	163	178	175	174	185
Cuauhtemoc	1961	119	151	212	160	138	132	161	161	160	172	183	210	216	209	194	204
Amado Nervo	1961	71	96	124	140	159	166	200	200	162	163	199	203	181	167	193	194
Cinco de Mayo	1961	74	127	140	151	168	176	139	139	152	107	192	187	194	192	239	243
Ignacio M. Altamirano	1961	93	99	110	150	207	223	202	202	265	222	281	311	311	280	375	330
Venustiano Carranza	1962	–	65	63	43	63	81	98	89	118	114	142	140	146	110	115	143
Alvaro Obregon	1962	–	76	87	105	123	118	128	127	106	107	105	147	128	110	164	159
Vicente Guerrero	1962	–	60	53	72	86	114	117	117	109	78	73	68	67	89	116	129
America	1962	–	58	88	95	105	99	116	116	88	97	70	93	93	109	121	147
O.E.A.	1963	–	–	67	85	117	96	109	109	107	109	112	111	97	128	137	139
Valentin Gomez Farias	1963	–	–	64	75	97	97	103	103	99	105	87	90	93	89	102	88
Independencia	1963	–	–	65	66	71	119	95	104	107	128	178	210	185	143	184	160
Modelo	1963	–	–	89	91	86	96	135	115	78	95	89	83	79	110	127	102
Benemerito Sec. Day	1964	–	–	–	125	295	498	531	582	636	850	775	887	944	1106	1084	1166
Lerdo de Tejada	1965	–	–	–	–	133	147	143	143	137	155	133	113	154	204	214	240
18 de Marzo	1966	–	–	–	–	–	123	193	193	189	175	200	254	295	306	404	415
Melchor Ocampo	1966	–	–	–	–	–	83	94	94	111	98	99	108	112	137	172	161
Libertad	1966	–	–	–	–	–	75	86	88	88	86	86	96	103	116	195	142
La Corregidora	1967	–	–	–	–	–	–	129	109	164	204	235	317	287	262	278	270
Ignacio Allende	1967	–	–	–	–	–	–	109	109	198	190	214	207	229	202	218	209
Benemerito Normal	1967	–	–	–	–	–	–	61	61	103	125	109	98	119	111	113	137
Benemerito Preparatory	1967	–	–	–	–	–	–	88	88	164	226	278	450	560	601	612	577
Benemerito Sec. Night	1968	–	–	–	–	–	–	–	–	30	52	105	128	146	155	176	192
Merida	1969	–	–	–	–	–	–	–	–	–	107	160	158	181	179	222	209
Morelos Primary	1969	–	–	–	–	–	–	–	–	–	77	98	125	–	–	–	–
Morelos Secondary	1969	–	–	–	–	–	–	–	–	–	50	110	187	176	161	225	220
Aquiles Serdan	1970	–	–	–	–	–	–	–	–	–	–	114	138	141	180	163	177
Mariano Matamoros	1971	–	–	–	–	–	–	–	–	–	–	–	161	151	119	165	142
Netzahualcoyotl	1974	–	–	–	–	–	–	–	–	–	–	–	–	–	109	173	222
TOTAL		1803	2302	2834	3167	3654	4414	4904	5190	5577	6000	6903	8059	8245	8408	9531	9653
Increase over previous year			499	532	333	487	760	490	286	387	423	903	1156	186	163	1123	122
% of increase			27.67	23.11	11.75	15.37	20.79	11.10	5.83	7.45	7.58	15.05	16.74	2.30	1.97	13.35	1.28
Number of additional schools			4	4	1	1	3	3	1	1	3	1	1	0	1	0	0

FIGURE 6. STUDENT ENROLLMENT IN LDS SCHOOLS IN MEXICO, 1961-1976

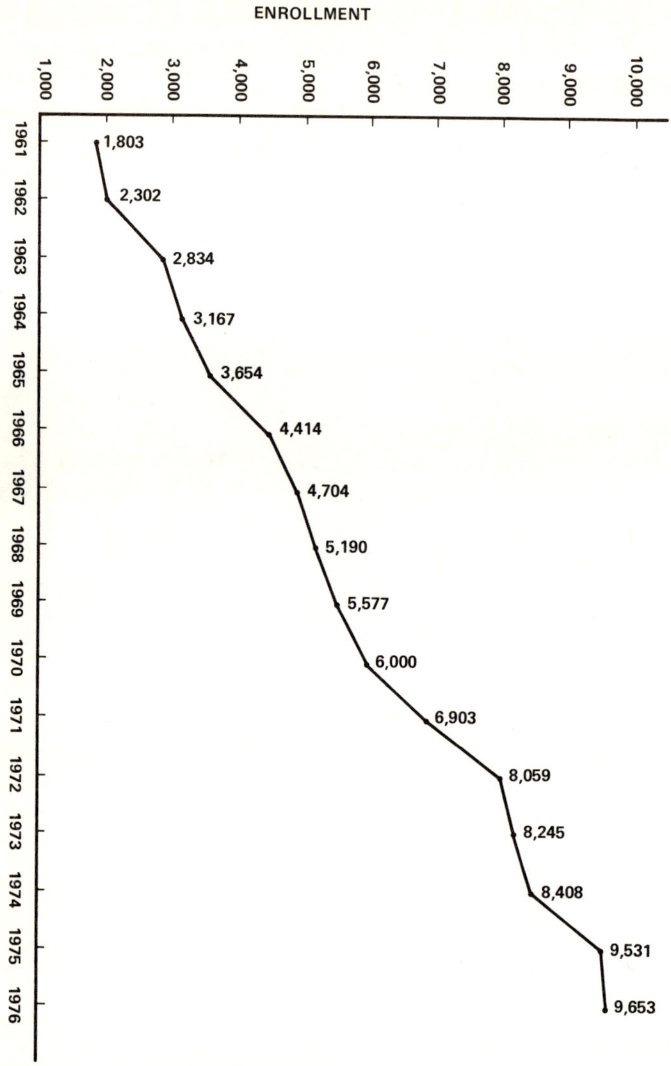

FIGURE 7. GROWTH IN SCHOOL ENROLLMENT IN LDS SCHOOLS IN MEXICO, 1961 TO 1976.

educational programs but because of the unique political environment in which we live. Let me illustrate. Article three in our national constitution, dealing with education, states that all education in Mexico shall be maintained completely free of any religious doctrine. The constitution further states that churches, ministers or priests, and any other group that propagates a religious creed shall not interfere in any way with the education of the children of Mexico. Otherwise, the state may selectively withdraw its official recognition of the schools in question, and the students therein are left—in terms of their records and prospects for going on to advanced schooling—as if they had never attended a school at all.

This is why each year the government investigates all private schools, ours included, in order to insure that the educational programs are officially valid. If the programs meet the official criteria, the schools are certified for another year. One of the mechanisms of control is the requirement that each teacher sign a document declaring that he or she is not a minister of any religious creed.

The limitations the government has placed on the influence of religion in the schools of Mexico have their origin historically in the great power and dominion of the Catholic Church. Because of the overbearing pressure of that church and because of its undermining the development of my country, a long line of political authorities has considered it necessary to weaken that power and dominion and thereby to purge one of the cruelest and strongest enemies to our freedom. That is why there is a constitutional law against religious schools in Mexico.

The twelfth Article of Faith in our Church states that we, as members of the Church, should be subject to the law and to those who rule over us, and that we should be obedient. This makes our work exceptionally complicated in Mexico, for how can we fulfill the law and also meet the educational and spiritual needs of our people? Surely the Church cannot justify tithing expenditures strictly for secular educational pursuits alone.

One way we fulfill the law and also meet our own need to inculcate moral principles is through example. We ask each employee to be, above all else, an example of the principles of our faith, and to abide by those recommendations that make possible the creation of an LDS environment in the classroom. To help us, bishops give appropriate ecclesiastical interviews at least once a year. (They also are required to sign recommendations for any student desiring entrance to the school. If the bishop will not sign, we will not admit.)

But there are other ways as well that help us in the creation of a proper environment in our schools. In teaching the secular philosophies the government requires, our teachers do so by comparing them with the ethical philosophy of the Church. They are thereby able to draw appropriate conclusions for righteous living. Students rarely fail to see the striking difference.

We have additional helps, too. A large percentage of our students at the huge Benemérito campus in Mexico City board and room at the school. In our student housing the dorm parents use the family home evening manual and other appropriate literature to teach the principles of gospel living. At Benemérito, and in all our other schools in Mexico, we also have the help of the seminaries and institutes. By law these institutions must be rigorously separated physically and administratively from the schools. And they are. But wherever LDS schools exist, so also, in close proximity, do the seminaries and institutes. They help a great deal in developing a proper moral foundation for life.

On account of all these factors—our superior educational programs, our moral teachings, the examples of our staff and faculty—we continually receive entrance applications from the children, relatives, and friends of officials of Mexico's Department of Public Education and also of senators, governors, and other public officials. So we manage to log some accomplishments. We strive to do our best academically. This is precisely what generates so much demand from nonmembers to enter their children in our schools, for they are the best in Mexico.

The academic record we have achieved in our schools is legitimately contrasted with that of other Mexican schools. This derives from a standardized curriculum in all schools the government certifies. The Ministry of Education also reviews the tests each school gives to assure that the entire curriculum is covered. That our students learn more and perform better academically is now widely recognized.

In his election campaign, the president-to-be of Mexico, José López Portillo, visited the Benemérito campus because he considers it to be the best in Mexico and an example for the whole country to follow. Not surprisingly, four of the eight leaders in the president's campaign speechmaking class were young Mormon men. One of them attends our preparatory school on campus, and two are graduates from the same school.

But this good academic record, of itself, would be of insufficient value to justify the expenditure of Church funds unless the schools also played an important role in the building of the Church. Our efforts in this direction have brought some successes. Many of our school graduates are now serving as Church leaders—stake presidents, bishops, high councilors—in the respective areas in which they have established their homes. In addition, 114 graduates have completed successful missions, and fifty-three students are presently serving missions. We do not have hard data on some of these accomplishments because we have just started our alumni follow-up program. But Church leaders throughout the land see the schools making a great contribution to the building of the Kingdom. I note a recent survey made of stake and mission presidents in Mexico (November 1975). Their feelings are that where Church schools exist the general activity of the members, their attitude, their development as leaders, their unity and brotherhood, and the Church's growth and image are better than in areas where we do not have schools.

In the Church's schools in Mexico, students receive superior scholastic training. Aside from that, through example and comparison, they receive a moral and ethical foundation for living. Then, in the seminaries and institutes, they also participate in experiences designed to improve the quality of their spiritual well-being and their knowledge about the Church. Truthfully, we look forward to a good future.

BUILDING STAKES THAT WORK: FORM AND SUBSTANCE IN CHURCH ORGANIZATION

G. Enrique Rittscher

We had a devastating earthquake in Guatemala a few weeks ago. As you can well imagine, it has been foremost in my mind ever since. As I reviewed my original notes on the subject of building stakes that work, and as I prayed for inspiration to improve those notes, the thought came to me that it would be more significant to relate our recent earthquake experience to my subject rather than try to develop it abstractly. I say this because the earthquake had a profound effect on our lives and caused many of us to realize what a great blessing it is to be counted among the Latter-day Saints.

The earthquake, or better said, the social impact of the earthquake, may in the long run affect us more than the initial physical force that in a matter of seconds tumbled more than a million homes and killed over twenty thousand people. The social dislocations following that tremendous unleashing of geological forces will affect the lives of millions for years to come, both adversely and beneficially.

Some of us who suddenly found ourselves in key positions that demanded special coordinating and directive action began to realize how very valuable the previous week-by-week and month-by-month building of our stake organization turned out to be. It also showed how much further we yet have to go. The shock and tragedy initiated by the quake dramatically demonstrated that we could have profited from much better organization; but it also showed that we did have an advantage as we moved to help many of our brethren in need.

Many of our Mormon families continued for days to live in danger because of the severe aftershocks, many of which were as destructive as "normal" earthquakes elsewhere. Many members had no place to sleep or eat because of the destruction of their homes. There was no milk, no bread, no water. The streets were full of rubble and dirt—hot, dusty, and dry during the day; cold and windy at night. People spoke of typhus and other fearful diseases. Reports of more and worse earthquakes to come rapidly circulated throughout the city. Scavengers and hoodlums were a constant threat and danger. This was the situation that fell upon us at 3:03 a.m., 4 February 1976.

Imagine yourself comfortably asleep when you are awakened by a dull, thumping sound that grows to a strange eerie roar as it shakes your house with a unimaginable intensity. You suddenly come to the realization that you, your wife, your children, your home, all that you have and hold dear, are being most disrespectfully tossed about without your being able to control or do anything about the situation. The crashing and banging and violent heaving continue. The house is left in total darkness because the electrical service lines throughout the city have been ruptured. My wife nervously exclaims, and quite understandably so: "*Los hijos—rápido.*" ("The children—quick.")

We get the children, who are understandably frightened, and yank them downstairs through the disorder of fallen books, flowerpots, bottles, and jumbled furniture. Piling everyone into the old faithful Volkswagen microbus, we nervously drive out from the garage below our home to the opposite side of the street where there are no high walls that can tumble upon us. Our own seven-foot-high adobe garden wall had been tossed over into the street. Then we look about, and flashlights start blinking. The ground has calmed down. Neighbors are in the street talking excitedly. Miraculously, our home, except for the garden wall, is intact, although some dishes, books, and flowerpots lie about in a most disorderly fashion. The ground starts shaking again, but then calms down. It was still shaking a few days ago when I left home. We have had over 1,500 tremors, some of them major, since the original quake.

After nervously investigating what damage to life and property we and our neighbors had suffered, we realized, as we watched the sun rise on a new day, that we all had been very lucky. The radio already had begun to speak of thousands of dead and uncountable homes destroyed. The telephones in our area were working, except for long-distance lines, and so we called our relatives to inquire of their condition. We then spoke with the mission president and decided to meet and lay out a plan of action for our people.

We visited the chapels in my stake where some of the more afflicted members had gathered and there verified the priorities: shelter, water, food, medicines, typhoid vaccines. I contacted the bishops and other leaders, and they got the plastic sheets the mission office had purchased from a factory to distribute for temporary makeshift shelters. We met with some of the bishops and members of the stake high council and decided to buy basic foodstuffs—beans, rice, powdered milk—to distribute to the wards, and from there to the afflicted members. The money came, at the moment, from nonexistent fast offering funds. We assumed that the Lord would send help, which he soon did. Saints from all over, including the United States, came to our aid.

Some of our bishops and high councilors proved themselves worthy of medals. They worked relentlessly and got others to help them, even inactive members. In the wake of this disaster, the Church organization automatically started to work, and it was heartwarming to see how the leaders started to help each one of the afflicted members of their groups, and how the members themselves helped each other. We only had to give some guidelines, some suggestions, some congratulations, some money, and the organization worked. Thus, the stake organization, even though quite incomplete, was sufficiently well developed to permit it to mobilize resources for the more obvious needs of our people.

The blessings of the Church came to the members in many ways. Some were visible, like the plastic, the food, the medicines. But perhaps the more worthwhile ones were the blessings of many of our leaders and members having a chance to prove themselves—of doing their part, of helping their fellowmen, of having a worthwhile cause, of being useful. Executive committees started to work. The Relief Society began to measure up to its name. A member who is a baker made bread, and the elders quorum in his ward delivered it to the homes, the makeshift plastic huts, the improvised tents of afflicted members. One brother with a pickup truck transported water in big jugs to be distributed to the members in need. Very few of our members have cars or pickups.

In a few days we sent out messages over the national radio asking our members to have a special fast and prayer for the needy, requesting that the savings derived from the fast be brought to their bishop so that he could help those most in need. We received responses that were substantial, in fast offerings and in comments by nonmembers who listened to our messages.

We held sacrament services on Sundays—our only general meetings during the crisis—out on the basketball courts next to the chapels. The government had issued orders that no public meetings be held inside any of the buildings. Then, right after the meetings, we gave typhoid immunizations to those who wanted them and to some of the children who didn't quite want them.

At the start we had coordination meetings three times a week with bishops and elders quorum and Relief Society presidencies. As we began to get things under control, we were able to reduce the frequency of meetings to Friday and Sunday evenings, and then only to Sunday. True, our reports got behind—some more! In addition, some problems continually confronting us took a lower-than-usual priority, and we postponed discussion on them.

But a new sense of unity, purpose, and achievement has come into our stake. Attendance at our meetings has increased; tithing and fast offering donations have increased. We all realize more fully that we have many great blessings and that among them is being able to work with such fine brethren and sisters in an organization that we know can be made to work, to know that we are in the Church of our Savior and have a chance of becoming like him—which is, after all, the main substance of all our endeavors.

That was a four-page preamble. I decided to include an account of the earthquake because the emergency it created brought out the need in a most clear and dramatic way of getting ourselves better organized in form and in substance. Elder [Harold] Brown (the Regional Representative of the Twelve for Guatemala) has been telling us this without the need of an earthquake.

We in the Guatemala City Stake are probably one of the least organized stakes. In fact, I heard it said some time ago, I do not know whether in jest, that we were a sort of pilot stake. If we could get going under our conditions, no doubt the programs of the Church would work in any other place, too. Therefore, any observations we make on the theme of building stakes into organs of substance as well as form have to be considered in that light.

If we have made some headway in the building of a stake that works, it has been through the help of many of our good brethren who have more experience than ourselves. Through a lot of trial and error—mostly error—we now are coming back to find that, had we followed more closely the instructions set forth in the manuals, we would have worked less and done more. This, then, has been one of the important lessons we hope to have learned—to use the manuals more effectively.

To help explain to ourselves the need of having substance as well as form in our stake organization, we have found it useful to look at the forms and functions of a simple object, such as a table or a chair. Objects have different forms according to their intended use. Dining tables, kitchen tables, writing tables, though all basically similar, vary in form because of their expected use. This use, in a way, can be termed the function or the substance of the existence of the form, or the reasons for its existence or form. Clearly then, form limits or facilitates the effective functioning of an organ, depending on the substance it is intended to deliver.

Our stake, because of its form, though incomplete, gave good service and is giving good service to its members as shown during the earthquake emergency. The substance would have been much more effectively provided, however, had the form of our stake organization been more complete or better designed to meet the emergency, especially in the perfecting of the Saints.

Religious organizations, such as our stakes, that have as their objective the perfecting of their members have to take on the needed form for such an objective. The Apostle Paul in his epistle to the Ephesians states it thus: 'He gave some, apostles; and some, prophets; and some, evangelists; and some, pastors and teachers; for the perfecting of the saints, for the work of the ministry, for the edifying of the body of Christ" (Ephesians 4:11–12). At this time the edifying of the body of Christ in our area—the Church membership, if you please—needs construction workers to reconstruct homes. The form of our organization, therefore, has had to be adapted to this end, to more adequately deal with the temporal needs of our people.

The Apostle Paul continues: "Till we all come in the unity of the faith, and of the knowledge of the Son of God, unto a perfect man, unto the measure of the stature of the fulness of Christ" (Ephesians 4:13). Sacrament services, Sunday School classes, seminaries, home evenings—these constitute the structure or form that facilitates the communication of the substance that will help the Saints and qualify them for salvation and exaltation.

Paul continues, "That we henceforth be no more children, tossed to and fro, and carried about with every wind of doctrine, by the sleight of men, and cunning craftiness, whereby they lie in wait to deceive" (Ephesians 4:14). We have to make both form and substance attractive for our young and old so that they will prefer our meetings to those of others—and to movies also. We, especially the leaders, have to set examples of warm and kind but firm and efficient behavior. That is where we continually must grow if we are going to be able not only to meet emergencies like earthquakes but the general emergency of helping people become Christlike in their thoughts and actions.

The form of our stake is basically preset in the manuals and by the rhythm of our meeting and program schedule. This, combined with the physical facilities we enjoy, supplies the form or framework within which the substance of our religion is continually developed. The substance, which should never be confused for the form, is the result, in the lives of the men, women, and children, of the combined effect of buildings, organizations, meetings, schedules, manuals, and so forth, and of the ways leaders, teachers, and others use all these facilities or forms.

More and more we see that our leaders learn to speak the truth in love, as Paul instructs, being no more like children but doing according to the effective working in the measure of every part. They learn to improve the form in its self-generating dynamic strengths so as to improve the substance. This all has to be taught to our people, most of whom are recent converts to the Church. The good example and effective instructions we receive from the visiting authorities help greatly toward this end. Temple excursions and reading the scriptures and other Church publications also help to give substance to the form.

But spirituality gives the greatest substance, and any forms not contributing to it are certainly less desirable than those that do. Thus, besides making better use of the manuals, bulletins, and guidelines, the other one main ingredient we have found to give proper substance to the possible perfection of our stake is the degree of spirituality injected into the proceedings and shown by the participants—especially the leaders. By spirituality, we mean the kind of humility, grace, evidence of conversion to the faith, and love that permits leaders, teachers, and members to express this spirituality through kind words and efficient acts. In this way, the substance of Church work improves even though the structures or forms that house it may be deficient—incomplete organizations, improper meeting places, disorganized meeting agenda, lack of punctuality. If a sufficient amount of spirituality is present, many other, if not all other, deficiencies become secondary, and the purpose of the Lord is nevertheless accomplished. That is, the substance of the organization is still achieved, the perfecting of the Saints goes on.

In the earthquake we saw that despite our deficiencies in form and organization the stake nevertheless facilitated the extending of more help, love, and concern in an organized way than would ever have been possible in its absence. A deficient form is better than no form, because when people care enough to become spiritual, they can. Now we see that increased spirituality in our stake is blessing us to strengthen our organization and its procedures and to help us get along with our task more efficiently.

A word on buildings and their contribution to substance. New facilities, though needed, do not necessarily or always contribute to the substance of the gospel as expected. An example derives from our Sixth Ward before the division of our stake. Originally housed in a rather humble and perhaps ugly rented building, the Sixth Ward had very good Sacrament service attendance and good attendance also at ward activities. Everyone seemed to have a lot of fun. When the ward changed to a new shiny chapel about three blocks away, however, attendance dropped to about half. What had happened? The best we could figure out from interviews was that the absentees belonged to a type of personality and economic level unaccustomed to such surroundings; they thus felt uncomfortable and out of place in this new chapel. (Also, of course, not all had participated, or participated enough, in the construction of the chapel.) They had been used not only to the old chapel but to the level of discomfort, or relative lack of comfort, in which they considered themselves to be at home. They found themselves too far out of their accustomed frame of reference. We see this phenomenon in marketing when in some neighborhoods a new shiny supermarket has a rough time taking away the clientele from a nearby older grocery store or rebuilding its old clientele after moving to a newer, larger, and less homey place. Therefore, it might be interesting to consider that, although better chapels are desirable from most points of view, sometimes the design and the architecture and the amount of luxury and comfort ought to be related to the degree of acceptance by the people of that locality.

And now just a few last words on humble spirits. How wonderful it is to see, in spite of the most adverse and disorganized forms of meetings, the spiritual growth of some of our members. These are the spirits who were no doubt preordained long before receiving their earthly bodies and callings. They are truly the backbone of our Church no matter what the obstacles, no matter how poor the form or show of substance. I am sure that there are several in every ward and stake. One in our ward who comes to mind has little if any schooling, is very poor, earns his living as a badly paid carpenter, and has four little children and no wife by his side. His wife deserted him; his relatives, who are not members, will not help him because he is a Mormon. He has not remarried because he lives with the hope that his wife will return to him someday. He always arrives at meetings punctually, and so do his children. He has a ready smile and is willing to stay even to late hours if he is needed; and he lives very far away. He never criticizes anyone. He finds a good word to say about even those who might have caused him grief. Should I go on? Yes, he pays a full tithing, contributes to the fast offering fund, helps the missionaries, sings in the choir, you name it. He is one of our very best members.

Questions and Answers

Question

This afternoon I spoke to a man about this symposium who said he was a former branch president in a Spanish-American branch. As we began to talk about the problems that Spanish-speaking people in the

United States face today, he said: "Wait twenty years until the nonassimilated ones die off, and then you will not have the problem." He seemed not to recognize that there is a constant influx of Mexicans into the United States, or that his definition of assimilation was cultural genocide for my people.

Another returned missionary from Texas claimed that his mission president had asked him not to proselyte Mexicans anymore because they were, for the most part, wetbacks and illiterates, and thus unqualified for leadership positions. My question: Do our people realize, or are they aware, of the impact that such statements have on the Chicano community in the United States and upon its general willingness to listen to the gospel message? Do they realize that for every Mexican integrating into the American society, whatever that is, there are two more crossing the border with the same cultural problems and the same language handicaps? Do they realize that, while Church membership in Mexico grows with leaps and bounds, there is only a trickle of converts from among the twelve million Chicanos in the United States? And while we do comprise the fourth largest Spanish-speaking community in the world, I doubt that we can find among us the fourth largest Spanish-speaking community in the Church. ¿Qué pasó? (What happened?)

Harold Brown

Orlando [Rivera] has already addressed himself to that question and has done it very ably. So I do not know what can be added. Among the panelists it is he who has lived this situation, and I think he has analyzed it well.

Orlando Rivera

I would like to respond some more, however. I will just have to say that the man raised some good questions for which I do not have answers. But I do think that if we can begin to find answers to those kinds of questions we will then begin to resolve the question as to why more Chicanos are not entering the Church. I think the real challenge to us here, inasmuch as our Church is crossing many frontiers throughout the world, is to learn to cross them in America, too. I wonder if we have the capacity to do so within this country. I wonder if we can recognize cultural pluralism within the United States itself.

Comment

Mr. Rivera gave an example of the use of translation headsets clustered in a back corner of a chapel. But in Miami they have spread the headsets throughout the chapel in such a way as not to have the Cubans sitting in one place and the Americans in another. This has done a lot of good, and the Latin people are really becoming Americans. They have assimilated well. We had some problems in the beginning just after the Spanish-speaking branch was closed down. But now, as in the investigator's class, there is one American; all the rest are Latins.

Orlando Rivera

I am really happy to hear that, but I would like to comment on your comment. Dade County, Florida, is made up mostly of Cubans who came to the United States fleeing Castro's regime. Most of them are not disadvantaged. They came with their skills, their professions, and their middle-class background. With these assets they have been able to acculturate to a new life more easily and do so without so much loss of dignity and self-respect. But I wonder if the Miami case is really a multilingual approach. It seems to me it is still a monolingual approach to the Church and the gospel, with understanding facilitated through headphones.

Harold Brown

I find it interesting that the comment from the floor on Florida was made in such a way as to distinguish Spanish-speaking people from Americans. Which side of the language barrier does this bias come from? Is it primarily the Spanish-speaking or the English-speaking people of the Miami area who promote it? Or is it both? I would find it hard to believe that the bias was being promoted by the Latins because they are, in a sense, more American than the Scandinavians who came here about three hundred years later. Maybe, inadvertently, by our choice of words and biases we are contributing to making a mild problem an acute one.

Enrique Rittscher

About ten years ago in Guatemala when I first joined the Church, I noticed there was a minority group that was in a way isolating itself. That minority was North Americans. When I became branch president, I had a serious talk with them about the advantage of being able to speak both the language of their own culture and the language of the country in which they resided. That way they could fit into both cultures easily. I reminded them that it is a worldwide Church, that there should be no barriers or frontiers among us. And I insisted that everyone meet together and associate together at branch socials. From there on, in our branch, we just went ahead. I do not think we have that problem now, at least not to that degree.

Now consider the application of this example to the Spanish language here. You are living on the equivalent of a linguistic fault line. And just as with an earthquake, it is not a matter of if you are going to have one when you reside on a fault, but when. The same thing will happen with Spanish. It is not if you are going to have more Spanish-speaking people in the Church, it is simply when. Integration and our mutual understanding would be facilitated both north and south if we all became bilingual while at the same time not becoming clannish and isolating ourselves.

Question

In the area general conference in Munich [24–26 August 1973], the members of the Church were asked to learn English so that the General Authorities would not have to try to communicate with them in multitudinous languages. I have wondered if in the opinion of any one of the panel members it really would be feasible to ask the same thing of the Latin-American Saints—that they offer some kind of acquiescence to the dominant language of the Church here, just like the American members are being asked to do with respect to Spanish in Guatemala. And would that not be a valuable thing to do?

Orlando Rivera

I cannot speak for Latin Americans [people of Latin-American ancestry who are not living in the United States] because I do not know how they feel about this. Let me tell you, however, what happens to us Chicanos here. In the Lucero Ward [in Salt Lake City] most of our sacrament meeting talks are given in Spanish. And for any stake leader who comes to our ward, we go out of our way to provide him with an interpreter. When those same leaders speak in our ward meetings, however, they make no effort to provide an interpreter for our people who do not speak English. Nor is this done in our stake conferences. So the issue gets to be a sensitive one. I wonder if this is not the reason why many of our people do not attend stake conferences.

As an aside, I found it interesting that you say the *dominant* language of the Church is English. I suppose you mean because it is used the most. But will that always be the case?

Comment

I come from the most class-conscious society still in the world—Britain. The Church in Britain is made up mostly of lower middle-class and some working-class members. When the missionaries come to Britain they find, probably quite instinctively, what their social level in British society is. They then willingly go to the houses of that social level but resist going to houses above it. They know they will get the social brush-off. Now, after that crude example, let me come back to the Chicanos. It seems to me that what we have been told tonight shows clearly that the class situation has ameliorated in Mexico (because there is a considerable variety of social classes now in the Church there) but that, with respect to the Chicanos, it has not done so in America.

We have been talking about Chicanos within the context of race and language. But far more important than race or language is the question of a society's assessment of what that particular body's social class, on the whole, is. We, in Britain, being a class conscious society, normally see crime problems, race problems, and language problems as fundamentally exacerbated class problems. If that is the case here, the Chicano's problems in the Church are primarily social class problems.

Harold Brown

I would like to give you a little history and perhaps a little understanding of why we do not have a class problem in the Church in Mexico, although class consciousness in the society as a whole certainly continues to exist to some extent.

Many years ago, going back to 1857, a political leadership began to develop in Mexico based on certain liberal propositions that expressed themselves, in part, with a movement to dignify a downtrodden segment of Mexican society—the Indian. These political leaders determined that the most viable solution to a severe racial and ethnic problem in Mexico was to glorify the origins and ancestry of the Indian population. (In the process some anti-Spanish rhetoric and policies emerged, too.) But this dignification of the Indian population—which, by the large, because it was isolated, remote, and not incorporated into the national life economically and culturally, was the poorest in Mexico—had positive results in breaking down class barriers.

The whole process of dignification began in the Mexican school system. As a youth I remember the emergence of this concept in the textbooks—that on the Indian side Mexico had a very glorious, praiseworthy historical background. And so the names of Indian leaders—Indian patriots—of the early empires and kingdoms began to emerge in this literature. This process of dignification has now gone to the point that people generally make no attempt to evade identification with their Indian origin.

So we now have a situation favorable to the passage of people from the lower to the very highest economic levels in the country. They break through whatever barriers may exist by education and by integration into the mainstream of national culture and society. Hence there is no social class problem coterminal with racial or ethnic origins.

Now when I say there is no problem with barriers, I am speaking about the official posture of the country and about the sentiments of the general population. There are still people of an aristocratic tradition who are frightened by this emergence of dignity.

All that is, of course, a very different matter from the Chicano problem in the United States. Here you are dealing with a minority, with a language problem, and with a diversity of understanding of what is best for the national life. (And I am not going to get into an expression on that because my situation is related with Mexico and with Central America. Besides, I can get into deep water very fast by identifying with the Chicano problem—although I have my own feelings about it—and I think it would not be too hard to guess what they are. In my talk I expressed my view that the diversity of culture was part of the great beauty of the worldwide Church; by saying that, I think I have said enough.) But this matter of class consciousness, of class barriers, of moving from one level to another in economic life, education, and in all these other things—we simply do not have to live with them in Mexico as significant problems.

Comment

It seems to me that Brother Rivera hit on an important reason for the difficulties the Chicano is having in the Church today. It does not come only from language, although that is a problem. It does not come only from differences in culture, although culture is a problem. It seems to me that a good deal of the problem, probably even more important than these factors, is economic class, as the previous brothers mentioned. Even in the United States the middle-class members of the Church have difficulty relating to people of the working class. And a much higher degree of inactivity exists among working-class members than among white-collar or professional class members. So I think it is as much a problem of economic class as it is of culture or language.

Question

I have a question for Brother Rittscher. Referring to Brother Rivera's discourse, would the condition of the Chicano in the United States's culture compare with that of the Indian within the Latin-American culture of Mexico and Guatemala? On this level the Church there faces similar problems in integration as it does here (Does it not?) because it proselytes people from both the European and the Indian cultures.

Enrique Rittscher

Within our stake boundaries we have very few Indians, if by that term we mean people who dress, eat, and live in a traditionally indigenous manner. We do have a few who dress in Western-style clothes. They integrate very well. So there is no problem there. When they come to meetings with their Indian dress, they are treated just the same as everyone else. However, I do not know if they feel as much a part of things as does everyone else.

Question

Is their native language respected?

Enrique Rittscher

Well, the ones who do come into the city have all learned Spanish because they are a little scared to come in if they have not.[4]

Question

I was really surprised to see the remarkable result of the missionary work in Mexico. Do you think there is any connection between the establishment of the Church schools and the success of the missionary work? The reason I ask is that in my country—Japan—most of the Buddhist sects have schools, as also does the Catholic church. They also have a large number of members. Could you please respond?

Efraín Villalobos

I believe there is a direct relationship in Mexico between the growth of the Church and the establishment of the schools. Let me illustrate by a personal example. As a youth I used to be subjected to severe questioning about my membership in the Church. In school I was told that only illiterate and unschooled people would join the Mormon Church. In large part I think that was true then because when I was in preparatory school in Mexico there was not, as far as I knew, one engineer or physician or any other professional man in the Church. Thus, it was hard to find anyone in the Church from whom you could seek advice on professional or educational matters. But now that we have a great learning center in Mexico City, the Mormon people feel proud of being Mormons, and they have pushed to improve their education and qualifications. This has helped to improve the image of the Church in Mexico, and more and better prepared people are therefore interested in looking into it. Thus, I think the schools in Mexico have really helped the Church grow.

Harold Brown

I would like to respond to that question also. The existence of the school and seminary system in Mexico—all of it a part of the Church Education System—has had significant impact in two respects. First, it has given us a positive identity, as Brother Villalobos has pointed out, which we otherwise would have achieved only after perhaps a much longer time. However, even more significant than the identity is the relationship of the schools to the development of leadership among our people in Mexico.

Because of the rapid growth of the Church we were headed into a leadership crisis in the 1960s. The cultural and educational levels of the people who were coming into the Church in that earlier stage, as Brother Villalobos has indicated, were very low. Consider that with the creation of the first stake we had only a very thin veneer of priesthood leadership. We did not have the depth we needed. When the stake was divided, we still did not have the depth. There was a paucity of tried and tested leadership.

That problem has been solved by two elements. One is by internal education, the other by the professional and educated people who have come into the Church who turn around and share the gospel with people of their own cultural level. Accordingly, at the present time we do not have a leadership crisis. Recently, the Church organized fifteen new stakes in one day. I made the remark to the General Authority who had come to preside over that reorganization that the weakest stake in leadership of those fifteen was stronger than the stake over which I presided, which was the first Spanish-speaking stake in the world. That is quite a transformation. The schools and seminaries have had a very significant role in the development of that leadership capacity.

Question

I am wondering why we have schools only in Chile and Mexico. Is the need not just as great in Guatemala, and if so, why don't we have them there? Or, *when* will we have them? Indeed, what brought about the establishment of schools in the first place?

Harold Brown

If you want a historical response to it, I can give you one very quickly. The schools are in Mexico because we needed them, and we started them before the big influx of new members. The schools are in Chile because Delbert Palmer, the first president of the Chilean Mission, could see the need for them and he pushed for them.

But for all the good the schools have done, we also now know that they are voracious in their economic demands, growing quickly beyond the capacity of their beneficiaries to respond economically. The Church made a projection of the financial implications of establishing schools around the world in areas that had the same basic needs existing in Mexico and Chile. It was found we would be heading into a problem we could not handle. We simply did not have, nor do we have, the required resources. The matter is that simple.

There was no discrimination between Mexico and Chile and other parts of the world. It was simply that the schools there were the basis of experimentation that resulted in a later analysis showing the advantages of putting the tithing money budgeted for education into the seminary and institute program. This program does not tend to create the economic demands the schools have created.

It is true that as late as 1974 one more school was added to the system in Mexico, dictated by the needs to round the system out. But there are no projections for more schools in Mexico. It is done, finished, and we will have to live with what we have.

Question

I would like to direct my question to Brother Rittscher, but also to Brother Brown. The administrative policies for many of the auxiliaries of the Church have grown and changed primarily in relation to changes in the economic and social structure of the central or Rocky Mountain West. They are appropriate and inspired for this particular point of social-economic development. However, when the manuals are translated and sent, for example, to Guatemala to be handled in, say, the Quetzaltenango or Mazatenango districts or the stakes in Guatemala City, one might suppose that some of the administrative mechanisms may not make the transfer. We might therefore assume that you as local representatives can use your inspiration to decipher which policies to implement and how to adjust them to fit the local needs. Now the question: Brother Rittscher, how do you arrange with your Regional Representative [Harold Brown] to qualify and justify what is local inspiration in relation to the inspiration of the administrative manuals?

Enrique Rittscher

It really depends on how inspired and sharp-sighted our Regional Representative is in catching us in our inspired moments. We have a very sharp-sighted Regional Representative!

Question Continued

It seems to be a serious problem. How do you relate the manual that is inspiration for the majority to the local inspiration in the changed cultural context? And how do you make sure you both agree on what it is that works well?

Harold Brown

I would be happy to respond to that. There is a misconception—I mentioned it in my talk—about the conceptual acumen of Latin Americans. Latin Americans handle concepts with greater facility than do Western Americans; and, according to my observation, I have found no problem of understanding. But there is a problem of implementation. We have had so much thrown at us over a period of time that to re-channel to get these programs going really takes some time.

The difficulty is not because the programs are not adaptable or because they do not fit our needs. In the last ten years, and especially in the last five years as correlation has come into focus, any cultural adaptation of materials has become less and less necessary because the programs are based on the basic concepts of the gospel.

Footnotes

1. Of the original colonies the Mormons founded in Mexico, two even survived (though greatly crippled for a time) the seven-year Mexican civil war of 1910–17. Today they are flourishing bicultural and bilingual communities in northern Mexico (Dublán and Juárez).

2. Joseph F. Smith's statement is quoted in William E. Barrett and Alma P. Burton, eds., *Readings in LDS Church History,* 3 vols. (Salt Lake City: Deseret Book Co., 1958), 3:364.

3. Elizabeth Shaw gives some personal insights from her visit with the Andersens, in "Alone in a Valley: Cordell Andersen's Private Peace Corps," *Sunstone* 1 (Spring 1976):45–52.

4. In the countryside away from Guatemala City, the gospel has been preached in the Quiché, Kekchi, and Cakchikel languages.

THE CHALLENGES OF CHURCH PROGRAMS FROM THE VANTAGE POINT OF ASIAN MEMBERS*

INTRODUCTION

Spencer J. Palmer

Preceded by Western commercial and political expansion into the world, Mormon missionaries first reached the coast of southern and eastern Asia in the mid-nineteenth century. Initial interest was centered on India, Burma, and Siam, arising naturally from British colonial involvements in those areas. British members of the Church serving in the armed forces of their country in these areas of Asia sent repeated requests to LDS headquarters in Liverpool for literature and missionary assistance in meeting the proselyting opportunities as they saw them. In 1851, an East India Mission was officially established, and although it never really enjoyed the benefits of a mission home or mission organization in the conventional sense, eventually more than a dozen mis-

*(This section is introduced by Spencer J. Palmer. Following his essay are statements by Augusto Lim, Rhee Ho Nam, and Seiji Katanuma. Comments by R. Lanier Britsch and Spencer J. Palmer follow, along with a question-answer exchange with the audience. Grateful acknowledgment is given Russell N. Horiuchi for his stimulating introduction of the panelists and for moderating the discussion.)

sionaries, led by Nathaniel V. Jones as president, worked there on assignment from Salt Lake City to carry out random and itinerant tracting and preaching. During the early 1850s these brethren traveled widely throughout southern and southeastern Asia in search of converts.[1]

Referring to their work, B. H. Roberts observed: "There is nothing more heroic in our church annals than the labors . . . of these brethren of the mission to India."[2] They labored most effectively among Europeans. But because they were not prepared to speak, write, nor read the native languages, nor to understand local customs and religious beliefs, and in part because they were so far removed from the established Church and its leadership, these young elders soon became discouraged. By the fall of 1854 most of them were yearning to return home. Elder Robert Skelton, the last to do so, reported that there were only sixty-one members, preponderantly British, in India and Burma at the time of his departure in 1856. Eleven additional converts had emigrated to Utah.[3] And the work among the natives, promising at first, had greatly diminished, and in part backfired. Although one branch in India of about three hundred members—comprised mainly of natives—had at one time been established, it quickly declined when the new converts learned that, unlike the practice apparently common among other Christian groups in India, the Mormons had no intention of giving them cash rewards for accepting baptism into the Church. Thus, the East India Mission was a great test of faith for the missionaries. Moreover, aside from a few steadfast European converts who later figured prominently in Utah affairs, it was an abortive exercise.

In a special conference of the Church held in the Salt Lake Tabernacle in August of 1852, President Brigham Young reemphasized the worldwide mission of the Church by calling nearly a hundred new missionaries to serve in all parts of the globe. Three of these reached Hong Kong in April of 1853 and, under the leadership of Elder Hosea Stout, began to labor among the Chinese. But the Chinese were in the throes of the Taiping revolution at the time,[4] and the elders were entirely confined to the safety of Hong Kong, whose foreign inhabitants were protected by British gunboats. There, without funds and friends, the elders had little opportunity to reach the natives of the country.

Yet the situation was more complicated even than that, for the elders could neither read, write, nor speak any of the Chinese dialects or languages. For Elder Stout the scene was bleak and pitiful. After less than a year of frustration and disappointment, he and his companion returned to the United States. In a letter from San Francisco to Church headquarters in Salt Lake, Stout explained the missionaries' inability to leave any lasting impression on the people of the Chinese empire:

*We found about 250 Europeans, or the would-be-*Nabobs *of the world, merchants, officers of the civil government (no common class which are found in English colonies in other parts of the world). This class we found almost unapproachable, on account of their wealth and popularity, and look with contempt upon all who are not of the same grade with themselves; also a few lawyers, doctors, and a* small sprinkling *of missionaries also of the upper circles, luxuriating upon the proceeds of the cent societies at home, and the miseries of the people in that region.*

There are about one thousand soldiers, and most of whom are Irish and Scotch, some English, some blacks from Ceylon. . . . they are as corrupt as vicious habits can make them. The balance of the population is made up of four or five grades of Chinese, ranging from the merchants to the coolies, who are the carriers of burdens; also Malays, Lăscars, Parsees, Portuguese, Negroes, Tartars, etc., a heterogeneous mass of tongues, manners, customs and religions.[5]

Lively interest in Japan as a prospective mission field was openly discussed by Church leaders for the first time in 1872, triggered by the visit to Utah of a prestigious Japanese delegation then touring the United States. This group, which came to be known as the Iwakura Mission was favorably impressed with the people of Deseret, as were the Mormons with them. When Church President Lorenzo Snow announced the opening of Mormon missionary work among the Japanese on April 6, 1901, he indicated that this decision had been influenced by his first highly positive encounter with members of that race during the visit of the Iwakura Mission to Salt Lake City twenty-nine years before.

Elder Heber J. Grant of the Quorum of the Twelve was appointed as the first mission president to Japan. He and three companions arrived at Tokyo Bay on the morning of August 12, 1901, to commence their labors. A succession of mission presidents and missionaries continued the mission to 1924, but conversions were remarkably few. When Heber J. Grant became president of the Church, he closed it.[6] A total of eighty-eight Mormon missionaries labored in Japan between 1901 and 1924. Of these, one died and sixteen were sent home early because of illness or transgression. Among the Japanese for the same period, 174 were baptized, twenty-seven of whom either died, moved out of the country, or were excommunicated from the Church.

Gaps and differences in language and traditional culture between the Mormon elders and the Japanese people were only part of the problem. There was an inadequate number of missionaries assigned to work (no more than twenty served in the country at any given time); and, more important, because of a newly rising spirit of national self-confidence among the Japanese people—marked also by a new sense of manifest destiny and xenophobia—all forms of Christianity became suspect. Mormonism was Western, and in view of the prevailing ethnic pride, there seemed no need to look to its young American emissaries for guidance.

After more than two decades of Mormon proselytizing in Japan, Elder Lewis H. Moore wrote home from Sapporo to his family in Vernal, Utah, on August 31, 1923 (just two days before Japan suffered its greatest earthquake disaster of all time), in an obviously dyspeptic mood:

> *This people are certainly a stiff necked bunch. Something will have to happen to humble them before they will receive the Gospel as they should.... There are only one or two who are real saints and are willing to work, and do their part. But after considering the time since this mission was established in nineteen one, about twenty years ago, it almost discourages one....*
>
> *Something is going to cause their downfall, of that I am certain. It's in the air so to speak. They are getting all together too proud and ambitious. And when the fall comes it will be a hard one. It will have to almost wipe them off the earth in order to break their pride.*

Mormonism had failed to take root in Japan. And it was the same story for The Church of Jesus Christ of Latter-day Saints in all other areas of Asia during the nineteenth century. Asia was too far away. For the missionaries, simple survival was an almost overpowering problem. They were lonely and isolated. They often had little or no guidance from the Church leadership at home. They found barriers of language and culture insurmountable, and except for the Japan Mission elders had neither opportunity nor ability to teach the gospel in the native language to native people. Indeed, nineteenth-century Mormon missionaries spent most of their energies in introverted work—concerning themselves with other Americans and Europeans on the scene—rather than in meaningful communication with the indigenous population. The local people were not ready; the foreign missionaries were not prepared. Conditions were not ripe for Mormon success in Asia. But all of this was to change drastically in the aftermath of the great new upheaval known as World War II.

The American entry into Asia during World War II has been of critical importance for the Church. It brought the mainstream Church into close contact with the oriental world. Wars in Japan, Korea, the Philippines, Vietnam, and elsewhere in Asia introduced American LDS servicemen, and with them the restored gospel, to the people of those lands. After rendering long and continuous leadership to Church developments in Asia, Elder Gordon B. Hinckley of the Council of the Twelve observed in 1968 that the dark tapestry of war has had its silver lining. Mormon GIs established bridgeheads for the Church, and "a marvelous membership" has developed out of "the sweet fruit of seed once planted in dark years of war and in the troubled days immediately following." World War II opened the way for an unprecedented era of Church growth in Asia.

When Edward L. Clissold was dispatched by the First Presidency to reopen missionary work in Japan in March, 1948, there were 153 native residents of Asia on the records of the Church. By 1951 this number had reached 979; by 1965 it had climbed to 17,979; and by the end of 1975 had risen to the impressive total of 71,710. In 1951 the ratio of Mormons to non-Mormons in Asia was 1 to 1,739,010. By the end of 1975 the disparity had been reduced to one Mormon for every 56,263 non-Mormons in that most populous part of the world.

Changing conditions in Asia and changes within the Church in recent years have both accounted for the marked contrast between Mormon missionary results in Asia before and after World War II. In Japan, in the aftermath of war, the people faced American occupation forces with mixed feelings of wonder and fear. Japan had been defeated, and all Asia had suffered devastation. Ancient traditions had been disrupted, disparaged, and damaged. The gods of Japan, including the emperor, had failed. The people had fallen into soul-searching humility and distress. Throughout Asia the people were in great need of hope and love and were ready for alternatives to the past. It was a day of opportunity for the Church. In the timetable of the Lord (to paraphrase a statement from President Ezra Taft Benson given in 1970),[7] this was the day for Asia.

In Korea and the Philippines, where growth has been exceptional, the Church has benefited from the peculiar largess of historic Catholic and Protestant missionary work. When in 1965 Latter-day Saints in the Philippines celebrated the fourth anniversary of the opening of those islands to LDS missionaries, that year also marked the four hundredth year since the beginnings of Catholic work in that country. More than 90 percent of the Filipino people were already at least nominally Christian by the time the first Mormon missionaries arrived. Likewise, in Korea the native population had already been substantially exposed to Christian ideas, phraseology, and scriptures and had already allowed legal sanctions and social toleration for Christianity. Before the first Mormon missionaries arrived in Seoul in April of 1956, nearly 10 percent of the Korean population had already joined one of the Protestant faiths. Unlike conditions elsewhere in Asia, in these two countries Christians occupied positions of prominence and power. To be American, to be Christian, and to speak English were all positive factors in the acceptance of Mormonism in postwar Korea and the Philippines.

Growth had accompanied expansion into new fields of labor. In 1965 there were three missions and no stakes of the Church in Asia; by the end of 1975 there were sixteen missions and five stakes (the latter in Japan, Korea, and the Philippines). The principle of physical gathering to America—the land of Zion—had been enlarged to include gathering to Zion communities—stakes of Zion—throughout the world. Zion was now being earnestly established in Asia. For the first time, Church members in Asia were encouraged to build up the Church on a permanent basis within their own countries, to learn to lead, to establish and administer the stakes of Zion within their own ranks, and to enjoy the full fruits of the gospel at home.

So much for changing conditions in Asia that have facilitated the growth of the Church there since World War II. Let us turn now to changes within the Church that have also helped.

A primary key in the phenomenal unfolding of the work of the Lord in recent years has been a new effort to take the Church to the people in "outlying" areas of the world—including Asia. Within the framework of this policy of decentralization, resident General Authorities are now living on the scene in Asia; and area conferences have brought the leading brethren of the Church into repeated personal association with local members. In 1975 alone, President Spencer W. Kimball and other General Authorities presided over conferences in the Philippines, Hong Kong, Taiwan, Korea, and Japan. For the first time thousands of native Saints were able to see, hear, and feel the personal presence of the living President of the Church. This has been of incalculable benefit in providing opportunities for identification and participation in the affairs of the Church.

This opening Asian society and more expansive involvement on the part of the Church have combined to produce a rapid growth in membership. In part this has also been facilitated by some traditional Asian beliefs. Consider, for example, that since concern for the dead moves so deeply and traditionally among the people of Asia—including commitment to family and ancestors—the promotion of work for the dead among Latter-day Saints has met with enthusiasm there. History-making excursions, some at great sacrifice, to the Hawaiian Temple have been readily planned and carried out. All this has facilitated the development of leadership and the establishment of stakes. And it is an example of ways in which native values have strengthened the message of the gospel among the people.

From the vantage point of the Asian panelists on this symposium, traditional Asian culture is a double-edged sword. Entrenched traditions are frequently an obstacle to the spread of the gospel. But we also know they can sometimes help.

At the deepest levels, one cannot fully know the Church in Asia by reference only to outside or foreign influences. The growth of the Kingdom in that vast and diversified area is reflected in and through the lives of the local members. At best, an outsider's view is always blurred by differences in language, nationality, ethnicity, and tradition. The history of the Church in Asian countries is essentially the story of the struggles, frustrations, beliefs, and achievements of individual Chinese, Japanese, Korean, Indonesian, Thai, Indian, and Filipino members. Questions of what has been accomplished and how best to move ahead are illuminated most clearly in the experiences of the native Saints. The story of Dr. Kim Ho Jik in Korea is an illustration in point.[8] He has left his mark; he is a type that many others have exemplified in their own ways. The power of his life, of his faith, and of his knowledge has withstood all tests and is a mark of the fundamental key to Mormon success in Asia.

Kim Ho Jik was the first Korean to be baptized into the Church. He was probably the most distinguished and influential native of Asia thus far. More than any other single man, he was the father and prime moving force in the establishment of the LDS missionary work in Korea.

Born into a Confucian home in north P'yongan Province on April 16, 1905, he sought the truth from early boyhood. His search first led him to Ch'ondogyo, a native eclectic faith much in vogue at the time, and later to Buddhism. These failed to satisfy him. In 1925 he joined the Presbyterian Church and served as an elder for a period of time. Here again his spiritual needs were unfulfilled. Thus, he resolved to journey to America with a dual purpose in mind: to seek out the "real religion"—the one that would satisfy his conscience—and to gain further knowledge in nutritional science.

Before going to America, Kim Ho Jik had received his undergraduate education at the Suwon Agricultural and Forestry College and at the Tohoku Imperial University in Korea. Between 1950 and 1951 he attended Cornell University at Ithaca, New York, where he received his M.A. and Ph.D. degrees. It was during this time that a member of the Church, Oliver Wayman, reached out in friendship to this Korean student and invited him to attend Latter-day Saint meetings. One day Brother Kim asked Brother Wayman if he had any literature that would tell him about the tenets of his faith.

I quote from Brother Wayman's recollection of that incident:

Knowing that he was a devout and studious Presbyterian, I gave him a copy of Dr. James E. Talmage's Articles of Faith. *Within a week he had read the book and asked for more. He told me it was the best book on the gospel he had ever read and that he believed it thoroughly. I gave him a copy of the Book of Mormon, which he read in a very short time. He accepted it as the word of God along with the Bible, but said the Book of Mormon was much easier to understand and more complete. Clyde Richards and I encouraged him to attend our services and he agreed. However, we found that our services were just a short time earlier than the Presbyterian services. So, he would come to our sacrament meeting and leave during the latter part of the opening exercises to attend his own church. This continued until I left.*

On the day I was leaving Cornell, I met him in the corridor as Clyde and I were talking. I felt impelled to ask Dr. Kim if he knew why he had left his home, family, and a good position in Korea to come to the U.S. . . .

I then bore my testimony of the gospel and told him that it was my opinion that the Lord had moved upon him to come to America at the opportunity presented to him in order that he might receive the gospel and take it back to his people in preparation for a great missionary work to be done there. He had received the gospel but had been unwilling to accept it through repentance and baptism, but, he wanted to carry the truths he had learned to the Presbyterian church for its reform. This I informed him would not work and that if he refused to do the work the Lord had for him to do, another would be raised up in his place. I have seldom felt the Spirit as strongly as I did at that time and knew that what I was telling him was true. That was the last time we saw each other.

Dr. Kim read the Book of Mormon again; the Spirit bore witness to him of its truth. In the summer of 1951, he was baptized in the Susquehanna River near the place where Joseph Smith and Oliver Cowdery had been baptized. As Brother Kim came up out of the water, he reported that the inspired testimony of Brother Wayman was substantiated by a voice saying to him: "Feed my sheep, feed my sheep."

On the flyleaf of his triple combination, under the record of his baptism, he later wrote the notation: "Words Given—Feed my Sheep." Shortly thereafter, he was ordained a deacon, and three weeks later a priest. In September of 1951, he returned home to take up an influential career and to become a key in the development of the Church in Korea.

When Dr. Kim returned to Korea, he was immediately given positions of high responsibility in education and government. These included:

president of the National Fisheries College in Pusan; vice-minister of education in Syngman Rhee's cabinet; chief Korean delegate to UNESCO, where he represented Korea in India and other foreign assignments; professor at various universities; and dean and president of several colleges. He also served as dean of the College of Animal Husbandry at Konguk University and president of the Seoul City Board of Education. He authored six highly regarded publications. The latest at Cornell University, in March 1951, was entitled "Device of High Protein: A Low-Cost Diet for Orientals."

One Sunday while Dr. Kim was vice-minister of education, Korean President Syngman Rhee sent his secretary in the president's personal car to find Brother Kim and bring him to the presidential palace to discuss an important matter that had arisen. The secretary found Brother Kim teaching a Mormon Sunday School class. Brother Kim told him he would have to wait until Church was over before he could accompany him. When Brother Kim finally met President Rhee, he was chastised for causing such a delay. Brother Kim explained that because of the importance of his assignment as a Sunday School teacher, he had to finish his lesson before he could answer the summons. Whereupon President Rhee patted him on the shoulder and said, "Chalhaeso!" (You did well.)

Brother Kim was a widely acclaimed authority on nutrition, and particularly the nutritional value of the soybean. As a result of this expertise, he was asked to represent Korea in the United Nations' Food and Agricultural Organization meetings in India in August, 1959. He took advantage of the plane trip and some of his leisure time there to carry out part of his New Year's resolution to reread the Book of Mormon. Mosiah, chapter 20, was marked with the date *August 8, 1959.*

Less than a month later Brother Kim suddenly died.

Having heard the voice speak the words that had been uttered to other disciples long ago, "Feed my sheep," Brother Kim had lived long enough to serve as a vital instrument in bringing the gospel to Korea and to assist the Church to gain a foothold there. He was an inspiration to a predominantly young membership. There are many who still cherish his counsel to them as well as experiences of association with him in humble places where many of lesser fame would not have gone.

Kim Ho Jik of Korea was the first of a whole generation of first-generation Mormons of Asian ancestry whose experience and training qualify them to interpret the problems facing the Church in Asia from a native vantage point. Augusto Lim, Rhee Ho Nam, and Seiji Katanuma, whose reports follow, are additional examples.

THE CHURCH IN THE PHILIPPINES

Augusto Lim

I am honored to have been invited to participate in this symposium, and I hope I will be equal to the responsibilities given me to present some ideas about the challenges and problems facing the Church in the Philippines.

In 1961 four missionaries started the work in the Philippines. Later, in 1967, the first Philippine Mission was organized. At present, we have a membership of approximately 22,000 Saints, with close to 400 missionaries serving in two missions. We also have a stake in the greater Manila area.

The Church in the Philippines, just as in so many other areas newly opened for missionary work, is composed of Saints from a lower economic class of people. I would say that probably less than 5 percent of the members come from either the upper or middle classes. The majority are from the working class, from the ordinary people of the country, and, in general, they are rather poor. We estimate the average monthly income of a Latter-day Saint family in the Philippines to be about $60.00 (U.S.).

Although we find the various Church programs to be as timely and as relevant to our needs in the Philippines as they are to the Saints in Utah, we cannot afford them. Thus we face serious problems in implementation. With the rapid growth of a membership that is poor economically, people in our wards and branches simply cannot buy the many manuals, publications, and other teaching aids so important to the operation of the Church. The Filipino members are not able to acquire Church materials, such as family home evening manuals, Church magazines, and other publications that you people in Utah take for granted.

In addition to our serious economic problems, we also face serious language problems. The Philippines is the third largest English-speaking country in the world. However, this fact is misleading because only 20 to 25 percent of our Church members, whose ancestral language, generally, is Tagalog, have a working knowledge of the English language. The rest, 75 to 80 percent, are barely able to communicate in English. Most of our members are only sufficiently fluent to gain enough testimony to want to be baptized into the Church. But they are not able to fully use or understand the instructions and programs of the Church because these are written in English. While a fourth of our people can handle English, the rest must depend on the interpretations of these people for a knowledge of the gospel and the procedures of the Church.

All of this affects our capacity to train leaders and helps to explain why we are currently experiencing a shortage of trained leaders who can properly administer and explain Church programs. As I look at it, since English is the official language of the Church in the Philippines, and since no more than 25 percent of the members can effectively use that language, our choices for leadership are limited to a small percentage of the people who join the Church.

The phenomenal growth of the Church in the Philippines simply adds to this problem. We now have 400 missionaries in the field, two full-time missions, and an average of 300 baptisms every month. With less than 400 missionaries we baptized more than 3,000 new converts in the Philippines in 1975. We simply do not have enough trained leaders to keep pace with this fast growth of the Church.

Another continuing problem for us is the lack of sufficient physical facilities in the Church. We add a ward or a branch each month. The condition of the Manila Stake is an example of the dilemma this poses. With a present membership of 4,676, we have only three buildings in the entire stake. Fortunately, we have received letters from Salt Lake City stating that two other buildings should be under construction by the end of the year or early next year. We definitely lack physical facilities conducive to worship and to the study of the gospel. Obviously, this is not the fault of the Church at large but simply a problem related to the depressed economic condition of the Filipino Saints. They are not earning enough to pay for the implementation of the programs of the Church.

Studies made in the Philippines point out that 65 percent of the income of an average Filipino family goes for food, 25 percent goes for housing, and the remaining 10 percent for all else—transportation, clothing, education, tithing, Church budget, building fund, temple fund, fast offerings, and all such things. You can imagine the problems we are facing.

The Manila Stake presidency has pondered and prayed about these problems at great length, and we have come to the following conclusions:

1. Church materials should be made available to as many members in the wards as possible by having the Church allow us to purchase them for a price that would be within the means of the members. We have suggested that if a lesson or administrative manual costs $4.00 (U.S.), it be given to us for one peso, or less than 14 cents.[9] We feel that if the Church will allow us to secure these manuals at this reduced price, the wards and branches will be able to acquire all the manuals they need to implement fully the programs of the Church. Many of our

members who do not now have access to Church publications in their homes to help them build their testimonies would thereby be able to have them.

2. Now, if this reduced-cost plan is not possible, we would like to suggest that the local Church be allowed to publish its own publications in the Philippines. Possibly we could be selective and, with the approval of the Brethren, pick up from the different publications of the Church those items we think will be relevant to our needs. These would be sold or distributed to the members at a price within their reach. We could economize by reducing some of the costs for unnecessary illustrations and embellishments. In some ways we are doing this in the stake right now, and we are gradually overcoming this one leadership problem.

3. In addition to finding ways to make the literature of the Church available to our members, we feel, at this stage, that the Church should start considering teaching the gospel and conducting meetings in the native languages.[10] In this way the missionaries would be able to teach the gospel to all the Filipino people, not just a small portion of them. When we decide to do this, I can assure you that the growth of the Church in the Philippines will exceed anyone's imagination. But right now we are reaching only a small percentage of the people. If meetings and Church publications and materials were in the local languages of the people, we would have better and more meaningful activities in the various Church units; we would have more members actively participating; we would have fewer people sitting around on the sidelines because of their limited facility in the English language.

4. As for physical facilities, our Church program must be better tailored to meet the needs of the Saints: buildings must be constructed at a cost within our means. Right now in the Philippines we have buildings as beautiful and as expensive as any you see in Bountiful or Provo. But, as I have already explained, you people here have a much higher income than we have. We do need buildings, but we need buildings we can afford to build and maintain. For example, we have a stake center in Manila. We love it; we appreciate the concern of the Brethren in providing this magnificent edifice for us. We have been told that the Saints in the Philippines should have the same facilities as the Saints in Utah. This is good, and we appreciate this thoughtfulness. But this has created a big problem for us—the problem of paying for a building we cannot afford. As a stake president, I must solve this problem; it is part of my responsibility. I am getting white hairs for that reason.

5. These suggestions are merely temporary; I know they do not provide permanent solutions. Since it seems that the poor economic condition of the people is the main cause of many of our problems, we feel

we should have the Church welfare program at work in the Philippines. We should introduce it (*to* the Filipinos *in* the Philippines), and see to it that it works to affect the lives of the members. Special emphasis should be placed on career development. Members should be encouraged and helped to gain academic degrees and acquire vocational and technical skills and training. Moreover, we should institute an employment placement program so that our members can become employed. Those who are underemployed or unemployed must find means to have sufficient income for their needs. On this final note I thank you very much for inviting me here, and I bring you the heartfelt greetings of the Filipino Saints.

THE CHURCH IN KOREA

Rhee Ho Nam

It is indeed a great honor for me to speak as an invited guest on this special occasion during the Brigham Young University centennial year. It happens that we are also now commemorating the Korean centennial of opening its doors to the modern world to end its long isolation as a hermit kingdom. Since opening up to the influence of the Western world, Korea has changed almost beyond recognition. Yet, beneath this modern changing Korea runs a stream of traditional culture, like a deep river originating in the ancient mountains. Korean culture links the old and the new, the past and the future. Korea, the real Korea, is the totality of that ancient stream whose end is not in sight. The old ways of thinking remain strong in the minds of most people, regardless of their education or rank.

Koreans have been very conservative in their thinking and have traditionally adhered to the old customs of Buddhism and Confucianism; yet they received the restored gospel during the Korean War, which lasted three years, from 1950 to 1953. That war did much to alter old value systems. Without these values, a cultural vacuum was created which necessitated substitutions. The Mormon religion, brought by a handful of servicemen during the war, has been easily accepted by the Korean people. The answer to Korea's mental and spiritual vacuum was Mormonism. Since the introduction of the Church into Korea, only a quarter of a century has passed, yet the Church has grown amazingly both in quantity and quality. There are nearly 11,000 members in thirty different cities, sixteen Church-owned chapels, nine wards, and two branches of the Seoul, Korea, Stake; and there are over thirty branches in the five districts encompassed within the Seoul and Pusan missions.

I would now like to point out several concerns and problems facing the Church in Korea today. As I have indicated, the Korean way of life is deeply rooted in traditional culture, but tradition is changing rapidly, and the people are becoming aware of new alternatives in modern ways of life. Despite this positive attitude toward change, members of the Church are often caught between the conflicting patterns of the old and new, between tradition and modern values, and sometimes between gospel values and traditional Korean culture. By way of illustration, let me mention three special concerns: (1) marriage, (2) *chesa* (ancestral worship), and (3) entrance examinations into higher education. I select these three problems because they concern particularly the young people of the Church. If the Church is to grow, we must keep our young people in the faith. If we can properly understand and educate the young, we shall have a promising future.

Marriage

The choice of a marriage partner in Korea was traditionally managed by the parents of the prospective bride and groom. In our society today, it is still not made without first consulting what we call *kunghap*. The *kunghap* tradition is rooted in ancient Chinese theories based upon the Five Elements (Korean, *ohaeng;* Chinese *wu hsing*) theory and sometimes on the combination of the so-called ten common time factors and the twelve *ti* (in Chinese *chee*) or animal trait factors. By properly pairing these, Koreans say, one can determine one's destiny, which is therefore often thought to be linked with the year, month, day, and hour of one's birth.

Certain astrological and zoological signs for the year, month, day, and hour are thought to bring a fortunate and happy life, and some others do not. For example, parents of a daughter born in the year of the horse will have a problem choosing a husband for her. This is rooted in the belief that any woman born in the year of the horse is totally undesirable. The chance of her marrying into a higher class family is almost nonexistent. You girls here born under the year of the horse are lucky to live in American society. I also tell some of the girls in our country who are born in the year of the tiger to go to some Western society so their chances will improve.

Because of these marriage practices, we have had a sad experience in my stake. One of the sisters who belongs to the First Ward, Sister Kim, happened to meet a young man from the Seventh Ward, Brother Pak. They sat in Church, they grew to like each other, and later they decided to get married. So the young man informed his parents that he would like to marry Sister Kim who, like himself, was a member of the

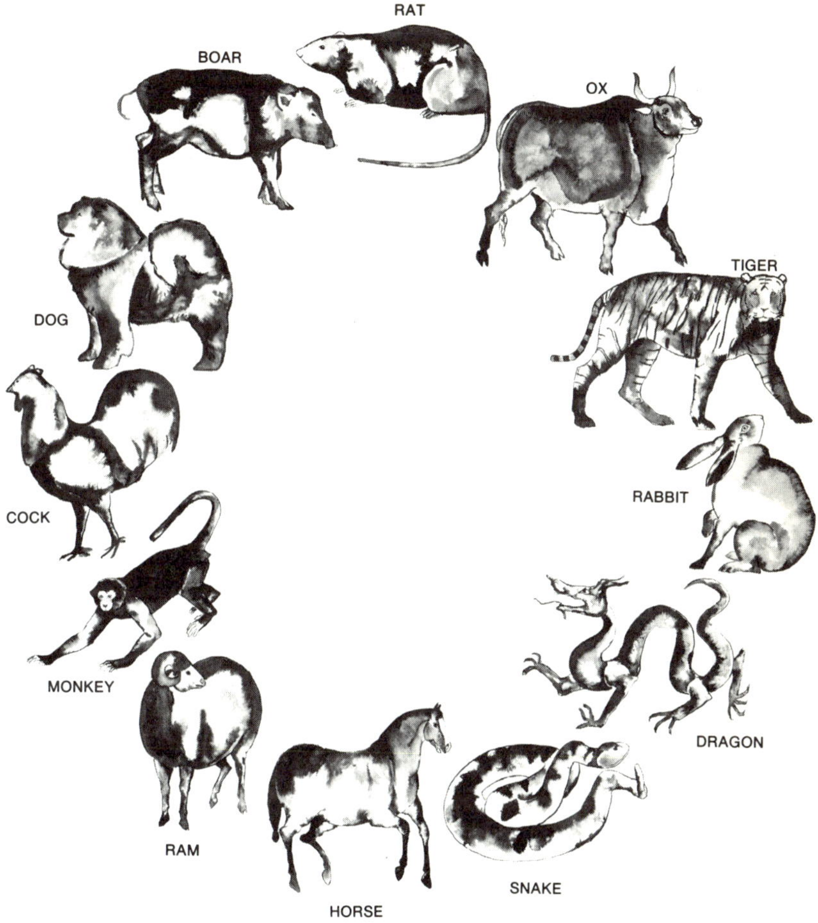

FIGURE 8. ANIMALS OF THE ASIAN ZODIAC. INTRODUCED ABOUT 220 A.D., THE TWELVE ZODIAC ANIMALS ARE ASSOCIATED WITH THE TWELVE "TERRESTRIAL BRANCHES," WHICH, WHEN LINKED TO THE TEN "CELESTIAL STEMS" IN VARIOUS COMBINATIONS, FORM PART OF A SIXTY-YEAR LUNAR CYCLE, *ILLUSTRATIONS BY M. CORINNE GEERTSEN.*

Church. The parents were very happy, and they invited the girl to their home. During the course of the conversation, his mother asked her about the year, month, day, and approximate hour of her birth. Then the following day she went to see the people who check *kunghap*. She found that the young lady was born in the year of the tiger, which would not fit well with her son's birth pattern. So they decided not to bring the young lady into their family. If they were to do so, they believed she would certainly become a widow. For this reason Sister Kim lost a potential husband. Bishop Kim Cha Bong of the First Ward had to have a long interview with the two young people, and I happened to be involved in this matter, too. So some traditional customs are a problem for us. The Church emphasizes that members should marry members. In American society you find a young woman or a young man and you get married. But in our society this traditional way of thinking, the *kunghap* idea, prevents us from freely doing as we may want.

Ancestral Worship

Now, secondly, I wish to talk about ancestral worship—what we call *chesa*. In ancient Korea the practice of worshipping one's ancestors had its development with the worship of a heavenly god. The legendary founder of Korea, Tan'gun, was said to have been the son of God. Sacrifices were offered to this heavenly being after the reaping of the year's harvest. Extending down to the present day, ancestral worship is plainly evident in the manners and actions of most older Koreans and has left an indelible mark in the social patterns of Korea. Despite the economic urgency of implementing modern science and technology, Koreans still show more concern with manner than with matter. That is, they are more concerned with outward form than with inside content. Even though Confucianism and Buddhism have become weak in recent years and remote from the everyday life of the Korean people, and even though Christianity is newer and more active, the philosophy of Confucius still influences the lives of more Koreans than the teachings of any other religion. And it has reinforced Korea's deep reverence for its ancestors.

The custom of ancestral worship does not now cause a serious problem for the Korean Saints. Due to the genealogy program, the members can trace their family tree and pay respect to their ancestors by helping them obtain eternal life in the celestial kingdom. Recently, the Korean people have begun to take an interest in the genealogy program of the Church.

It was not always that way for Church members. I remember that Brother Cha, who was baptized in Seoul in 1957, was the eldest son of his family. In Korea's traditional society eldest sons have special functions to perform. He left the Church because he was responsible for carrying out family ceremonies, including ancestor worship, and the Church does not believe in the bowing before people, or food, or any engraved things. Unfortunately, when he left the Church, we had not introduced the genealogy program into Korean society. We have found that it is compatible with Korean concern for ancestors.

Entrance Examinations

I want to say something about entrance examinations into higher education as a special Church problem in Korea. At present, parents place their children into a ruthlessly competitive school system, where they are expected to survive a series of examination hells. By enduring these hells the youngsters attempt to bring honor to their family and assure their own future employability.

Higher education generally does not prepare students for a special type of job. It is only a general qualifying factor that opens doors to a broader spectrum of job opportunities in business, industry, or government. Many such jobs have little or no relationship to the field of education or specialization the student has mastered. Yet having a high degree in any specific field is an important thing. Better, if the degree is obtained from a prestigious school, the graduates can generally be assured of preferential job placement and subsequent advancement. Seldom, therefore, do students overlook the difficult examinations, nor do they forget that only those graduating from the best schools stand a good chance in the job market.

There are fifteen universities, fifty-four colleges, and 198 secondary schools in the Seoul area alone. Church members attend all of these. Tuition paid monthly at the secondary schools and grammar schools is extremely high. With this background, let us examine a typical school day for one of our Korean LDS high school students. His day begins at 4 a.m. with breakfast and a brief review of the day's studies. By 6 a.m. he is on his way to school aboard an overcrowded city bus. He spends the day at school with ten-minute intervals between eight classes before returning home at 5 p.m. After a quick dinner, his parents begin tutoring him to try to give him extra preparation for examinations. When this extensive homework is completed, he is fortunate to receive four hours of sleep before starting the schedule again the next morning.

This schedule, similar to that required to pass the national level examination in order to graduate from college, is difficult, but it makes Korean students extremely well read. Therefore, because of their vigorous and demanding schedule, we Church leaders are caught on the horns of a dilemma. On the one hand, we want our Latter-day Saints to succeed in the highly competitive educational system that takes much time and energy; on the other hand, of course, we want our youngsters to attend their Church meetings and to develop strong testimonies. We have not yet fully succeeded in resolving this problem in Korea.

I visited Japan a few years ago and while there met with several Japanese students who were preparing to go into higher education. They had a saying then in Japanese: *yonto goraku. Yon* means four, with the idea that if you sleep four hours, you'll be able to enter the university you desire. *Goraku* carried the idea that if you sleep five hours you will fail. Before coming to Salt Lake City on this trip I returned to Japan, to Ōsaka and again talked to some of the students. I said *yonto goraku de ne*. They said, "No, no, we don't say *yonto goraku,* anymore; we say *santo yon desu*"—which means if you sleep three hours you will be able to succeed, but if you sleep four hours, you won't pass the examination. Well, Japan is worse than Korea on this. Our students now might have four hours' sleep, but we are in the stage of going from *yonto goraku* to *santo yon de*. It's a transition stage.

I am a member of the Fifth Ward of the Seoul, Korea, Stake, and we have a woman member named Yoon Chang-sook. She is a well-educated woman from a well-to-do family. She has two sons and a married daughter. One of her sons graduated from Kyonggi High School, one of the best in Korea. Now this young boy wanted to enter Seoul National University, which in our country is considered to be the Korean version of Harvard. He spent many hours and days preparing. Upon graduation from high school he took the exam to enter the engineering college of the university. But he failed.

Oh, this young man was so ashamed! He thought he had brought shame on all his family. His mother became inactive, knowing that everybody would know that her son had failed. She did everything she could to try to help her son go to a big-name school. We had other universities. But this young man was so stubborn, he was determined to go to Seoul National University. He took the exam another year, and he failed again. But the third year he passed. My wife and I were sleeping one night—it was almost midnight—when the telephone rang. I said "Hello," and a voice came, "President Rhee?"

"Yes, speaking."

"This is Sister Yoon from the Fifth Ward."

"Oh, yes; what can I do for you?"

"No, there is nothing you can do for me. Our son passed!"

The following day we had a stake presidency meeting. With me were my two counselors, executive secretaries, and others, and after the meeting I said:

"By the way, Sister Yoon's son passed the examination to enter Seoul National University."

"Oh, we know; we heard."

"Why," I said, "she just called me last night."

"Well, she called us about midnight, too."

She called everyone, starting from the stake president, to the first counselor, the second counselor, and right on down. By the next morning, everybody knew. This is a simple indication of what it means to Koreans to gain entrance into higher education. Competition is terribly severe. So I urge you students at BYU, those who are attending without going through the difficult exam hell, to study very hard, for you are lucky to be living in your own situation.

I will just spend one more minute. Since the seminary and institute programs were introduced in Korea in September of 1972, enrollment has grown extensively. Today we have 973 seminary students and 1,589 who attend institute. We have five full-time and three part-time faculty members. The problem facing the leadership of the seminary program in Korea is convincing parents that having their children attend seminary is not a waste of time. This is particularly difficult when the parents are not members of the Church. Many potential students, especially nonmembers, have declined the opportunity to attend institute classes because there are many demands on their time. Of course, the Church has been in Korea only a few years. This situation will improve. The future of the seminary and institute programs in Korea is bright. It is our responsibility to see to the education of the youth. While the Church is still in its infancy in Korea, the youth of today constitute the generation that will bring forth the first generation of Mormons to be born and raised in the Church. It is to this current group that our energies must be directed. They must be motivated to go on missions, to marry in the Church, and to put the Lord first.

THE CHURCH IN JAPAN

Seiji Katanuma

Since Commodore Perry visited Japan in 1853 with three iron vessels to open Japan's window to the West, the United States has introduced many things to my country. If someone asked me which of all these things has made the Japanese people happy, I would say baseball and

Mormonism. And with the area conference in Tokyo last week, the Church in Japan seemed to reach a new high plateau in its history. There we enjoyed the announcement that a Tokyo Temple would be built. Since then we have felt that the Church in Japan is enjoying a period of hope and happy expectations.

The Church is prospering in Japan. Today we have many wards and branches, and we are proselyting in many areas. That is why the name of The Church of Jesus Christ of Latter-day Saints does not sound so strange to the Japanese people anymore. Aside from growth, the number of family convert baptisms has made surprising increases in recent years, and the number of investigators over thirty years old is increasing greatly.

As Japanese members, we should understand that we have great new opportunities. To meet these, we must enthusiastically promote the gospel and Church programs much harder than ever before. Yet we have to be careful and realistic. If we look back on the history of Japan, we find that religious sects have been persecuted wherever they have grown large. I believe our Church cannot expect to be an exception. The Church in Japan stands in a delicate position. In other words, the eyes of the Japanese public are gazing sharply at the growth of the Church. We have many wonderful programs with definite goals. However, in order to realize the full blessings of these programs, we must understand how best to implement them in our unique Japanese culture. I would like to illustrate this by three cases.

First case. A certain brother, whom we will call Brother Yamada, recently moved from one town to another. He was asked by the community people to work with them to clean up the community streets. But it was Sunday. He refused because he had to preside over meetings in Church. Then a PTA meeting was held on the following Sunday. He could not attend that, either. His wife also had a Church responsibility on that occasion. Later, Brother Yamada and his wife were asked again to work at the PTA offices. But Brother Yamada refused the request because he had to conduct twenty-two meetings a month as a branch president. In the meantime, he was eager to teach the gospel to his neighbors. If you were his neighbor and were not a Mormon, what would you think?

Second case. Shūkanyomiuri, a weekly magazine, had a special issue last October, in which the following comment was noted:

Christians say the Mormon Church of the United States is on the march. You can see that the Church in Japan has been gaining public attention; but on the other hand, Japanese society regards this Church as a Church of the United States.

What do you think of this?

Third case. A young elder wanted to become a missionary. Of course his bishop encouraged him. He returned to his home in Hokkaido during the New Year's vacation, where he told his father, who was not a member of the Church, about his desire to become a missionary. His father became angry and opposed his desire. But the son's timing was poor. As it turned out, he appeared thoughtless and inconsiderate because he had talked to his father on Ōmisoka day, that is, December 31. The last day of the year has special meaning to the Japanese people. They take a bath to purify themselves and make preparations to welcome the new god of the coming year with a special dinner. The son seemed to be indifferent toward this tradition. In view of this, can we expect that his father and relatives would be interested in the Church?

Now I would like to show you some magic—great, mysterious magic. When you have to carry several items, such as books, how do you do it? What do you use? In Japan we often use a *furoshiki,* a large scarf. We sometimes use it as a necktie, and even as an umbrella; and if there are no books or other materials to wrap in it, we can carry it in our pocket. It is very easy and convenient. The use of the furoshiki is one example of many distinctive Japanese characteristics. Americans may want to carry things on their backs or in their arms. But in our society, it is natural and almost instinctive to use a furoshiki. Our approach to this and to many other everyday situations is different.

That is why I would like to suggest that although the gospel will never change, the way in which it is presented can be different. As Japanese Saints, we must first serve the communities in which we live. This is good not only for effective missionary work but also for making our neighbors understand what kind of people the Mormons are. Second, we have to erase the image of an American Church in our society. Third, we must be more effective in learning how to live the gospel in our different cultural setting.

Comments, R. Lanier Britsch

I am sure all of you, along with me, have been greatly stimulated by these three discussions. Several weeks ago Elder Neal Maxwell used a phrase that I think is helpful for us in dealing with the problem of intercultural adaptation that our speakers have emphasized. He talked of "programs versus principles." By "program" he meant the outward manifestations of the faith such as the style of buildings and personal appearance, but he also implied that he was concerned with changeable programs of the Church. By "principle" he meant those beliefs, doctrines, ordinances, and absolutes that cannot be changed or tampered with. Both elements—programs and principles—are important to the Church, and both have an effect upon the growth of the Church.

I think first of all we should recognize that Brother Lim's approach has been primarily concerned with programs or outward forms—the physical elements, you might say. Brother Lim spoke primarily about the problems of making the Church operable in his native society.

On the other hand, Brother Rhee spoke in a different light. His discussion dealt with the problem of the conflict of principle versus principle. By this I mean that he has placed before us problems that relate to traditional Korean or Confucian principles as they conflict with principles of the gospel. When you start talking about the difficulty a person has because of ancestor worship, that is an important example of principle versus principle. He spoke about the traditionalist point of view, something that has been part and parcel of their society, something that has been the very basis of their value system, something upon which they make their basic decisions.

Brother Katanuma spoke about the difficulty we run into when we begin pitting programs against principles. He suggests that we might change the outward trappings of the faith, but at the same time he insists that we should not change the principles.

Let me make one further observation, and then I will ask questions, and Brother Palmer can follow later with others. I did a little figuring as Brother Lim was discussing the problem of finances in the Philippines. Probably many of you did a little bit of quick calculating in your minds also. What is the current price of the *Ensign?* I think it is about five dollars a year. We are talking about paying almost forty pesos to subscribe to the *Ensign.* This amounts to about 8 percent of a man's monthly income to subscribe to a basic Church magazine. By comparison, this would be the same as an American family with a $9,000 annual income spending sixty dollars for the same publication; that is, 8 percent of a monthly wage of $750. Do you see a problem there? If someone wants to buy a copy of Elder Bruce R. McConkie's *Mormon Doctrine,* the cost of getting that one Church volume exceeds 15 percent of the average monthly income of a Filipino Saint.

Now I have a question, Brother Lim. What kind of building would you suggest could be constructed in the Philippines that would make it possible for the Saints there to afford being members of the Church and have the kind of physical facilities they need?

Augusto Lim

I am not an architect or a builder, and so it is really difficult for me to answer. I am generalizing when I say that what we have right now in the Philippines are buildings that are too expensive. I am not suggesting the construction of a hut or a building that would be made out of materials that would not last. Our buildings are intended to last. I am trying to say that we want to have buildings that are not like what we have (which are similar to what you see all around you) but nevertheless buildings that will last. I do not know what kind of building this would be. But that is what we want. I hope someone can help us design such a building.

Comments, Spencer J. Palmer

I do not know how you have felt about the comments of these three brethren from Asia, but for me this has been more than an intellectual exercise or an academic experience. I have been thrilled by their affirmations of faith and by their candid, realistic, and penetrating approaches to problems facing the Church in Asia. At last it seems we have arrived at the age in our development here when we have begun to listen to Asia and to Asian members of the Church. We have begun to counsel together, and I am grateful for what I have learned from these leaders today.

I have two principal comments. One: Asia is obviously diversified, not only in physical and technological ways, but in traditional values, customs, and beliefs. The Philippines is different from Korea and Japan. And the priority needs of Church members are not the same everywhere, in part because the Church has longer and larger developments in some areas than in others.

Brother Katanuma was concerned with publicity, a sense of public awareness in Japan. As a Church we have been in Japan much longer, and (thanks in part to a strong LDS Nisei community in Hawaii and elsewhere, and to a more highly developed economic and industrial order in Japan than in other countries of Asia) our communication with the Japanese people has been more immediate and substantial over a longer period of time.

President Lim is concerned with basic bread-and-butter issues—the challenges of implementing Church programs among a people who are both relatively poor and new to the Church. On the other hand, speaking for another people in another area of Asia, President Rhee is primarily concerned with the juxtaposition of the restored gospel and established elements of Korean tradition. President Rhee suggests that his native culture is two-edged. Some of its elements are inimical to the gospel, and they are stumbling blocks for those who wish to extend the influence of the Church in Korea. But others—like *chesa* (ancestral worship)—are compatible.

Two: It struck me as ironic that a stake president in the Philippines was appealing to a Mormon audience here in America for greater tolerance of simplicity and frugality—and for the right to build only that which the people could afford or practically use. He is asking us to not pressure his Saints there to live beyond their means. I say this sounds ironic because the Mormon pioneer heritage is precisely marked by its insistence on values of hard work and thrift. His is a plea for recognition of Filipino conditions and needs, with the implication that one of the challenges of the contemporary Church from the vantage point of Asian members is how best to respond to demands for uniformity in the programs and procedures of the worldwide Church. In a sense, this Asian leader is asking us to return to our historic roots.

There is a suggestion here that bigness tends to demand uniformity, that today there is a danger in the expanding Church of less responsiveness to contextual needs in different places in the world. I was surprised by President Lim's suggestion that he feels he is being pressed into consenting to the construction of buildings that Filipino Saints cannot afford to build and maintain. I know that Elder Hinckley, the Asian area supervisor, strongly advocates economy in the construction of new buildings. I was also intrigued by Brother Katanuma's questions regarding national consciousness and nationalism, of the need in Japan for a de-Americanization at certain levels in selected ways in communicating the message of the gospel to the Japanese people.

I share his interest and concern for greater doctrinal and scriptural understanding of the special contributions the Lord has in mind for his children in Japan.

For years I have been fascinated by questions regarding the relationship of the gospel to the diverse cultures of mankind. Therefore I was pleasantly challenged by President Rhee's discussion of Korean *chesa*. It would be interesting to find out from him what counsel he gives his Korean members on this subject. Does he feel it appropriate for Asian Latter-day Saints to cooperate with their relatives and friends in honoring the dead, in praying before the spirit tables of deceased ancestors, and in offering them food and drink in accordance with ancient family rites? Your response to this might well shed light on general principles members should follow in determining the relationship of the gospel to traditional societies elsewhere in the world.

Augusto Lim

Responding to Spencer Palmer's question, I would like to explain that I brought up this matter of our inability to buy manuals, our lack of facilities, and underemployment because I believe the gospel in its fullness is difficult to practice under Filipino conditions. The members do not have the tools or necessary equipment, so to speak, to effectively build their testimonies.

These problems are not the only problems, by any means, but we are a new Church in the Philippines. We are new in Asia. The Church has been in the Philippines barely fifteen years. Because of the limited time, we have many problems in building leadership and in meeting daily needs. Once in my monthly personal priesthood interview with one of the bishops, he told me that the young people have already accepted the fact that in this life it is almost impossible to acquire an education. It would be almost impossible for him to be employed in an establishment that would give him wages sufficient for his needs. Therefore, he has given up trying to improve his economic condition. We anticipate that the next generation of Filipino Saints will be better off economically—that we will have more lawyers, more doctors, more engineers, more mechanics, more agricultural specialists.

Rhee Ho Nam

I was asked how I helped our members in Korea to observe their ancestor worship. First, to make a long explanation short, I think we must emphasize the genealogical program in our society. This will solve the problem. When we say *chesa,* we place the food on the table. Rice, soup, vegetables, meat, and salt are spread out. Wine is an essential thing. Then you prepare a paper that indicates people believe their father's or grandfather's spirit will indeed enjoy the food. It is a memorial service during which family members bow respectfully to their deceased relatives. This is in conflict with the teachings of our Church and the Lord, before whom we should be bowing.

Now, I believe something that President Kim Ho Jik said. If your parents or other members of your family want to have food, let them have it. Let them place it on the table. A member of the Church may bow, but he is not bowing to the spirit of his father or grandfather. We should pay respect to our fathers or grandfathers because we were able to receive life and temple endowments through gifts and labors. As an expression of appreciation and respect, we may bow. But Korean Latter-day Saints cannot supplicate the spirit of the dead, or the food, or the paper that is placed on the offering table. This explanation helps some people, but it will not satisfy everyone. Since all of us in Korea are converts to the Church—none was born in the Church—we must wait until our children, the second generation, grow up. They are the first ones to be born into the Church; and when they grow up, we want them to be married in the Church. I hope my boy will marry my second counselor's daughter. When I interview bishops and high councilors I often ask, "How is your daughter?" "How is your son?" I ask them to educate them in such a way that, when my daughters (and I have three) grow up and I want a son-in-law, we do not have to look all over town. We can trust others of our Korean leaders to have like goals and to grow alike in the gospel. When their children marry in the Church, they will have fewer problems because they will have a common philosophy. This second generation is our hope for the future. I keep telling everyone, "Let's have no evil-speaking of any brother or sister, because we are all going to be in-laws in the future!"

Seiji Katanuma

I was impressed and also sorry as I listened to President Lim, because his situation is about the same as it was twenty years ago in Japan. I remember that sad situation. I have been in the Church for twenty years. But to tell the truth, I have at times been frustrated because I have sometimes felt there is a lack of understanding among those who implement the Church programs concerning various situations the local members are actually facing. The Church leaders in Japan want to adopt many Church programs directly from America where they were first implemented. However, the situation in Japan is quite different from that in America and, accordingly, the Church programs must be adopted to the realities of the Japanese culture. With this kind of feeling, I have, with my requests and recommendations, occasionally felt like a "thorn in the side" of my mission president.

Questions and Answers

Question

President Lim, what about the language problem? Are you going to be able soon to get into Ilacano and Tagalog?

Augusto Lim

There is now a national language based on Tagalog. It is the language spoken in Central Luzon in the Manila area. I am not very sure about the exact number of people who communicate well in Tagalog. But I think it would be safe to say there are ten to twelve million people. The Philippines is not a small country; it has over forty million people. And the country is divided into regions. The Tagalog-speaking region alone could easily be a mission in itself, it's such a big region. The biggest, however, is the Visaspan-speaking region; we have close to fifteen million people speaking the language. Again, this could be an ideal mission in itself. Then we have the Ilacano, probably with about eight million people, and the Chalarda people—probably four to five million. Because the government is really pushing the idea of a national language, it seems to me that the Church should now start planning ahead. We should keep pace with what is happening in the country, because in the next ten or fifteen years, a big majority of our people will be Tagalog speakers. That language is now being taught as a medium of national instruction in the elementary grades and also in public high schools. A strong move is now underway to use the national language as a language of instruction even in colleges. And this has gained ground in the last few years. If we began mission work in Tagalog, we could certainly reach millions of the people whom the missionaries cannot reach at the present time.

Footnotes

1. Interesting details relating to the missions of William Willis, Hugh Findlay, Joseph Richards, and Robert Skelton may be found in B. H. Roberts, *A Comprehensive History of the Church of Jesus Christ of Latter-day Saints,* 6 vols. (Salt Lake City: Deseret News Press, 1930) 3:389; and R. Lanier Britsch, "The Latter-day Saint Mission to India: 1851–1856," *BYU Studies* 12 (Spring 1972):262–78. Additional materials are in Spencer J. Palmer, *The Church Encounters Asia* (Salt Lake City: Deseret Book Co., 1970).

2. Roberts, *A Comprehensive History,* 4:72–73.

3. Britsch, "The Latter-day Saint Mission to India," p. 275.

4. Protestant Christianity helped shape the pseudo-Christian T'aiping movement (1851–64), perhaps China's greatest politico-agrarian upheaval. Tens of millions of people lost their lives. See Eugene Powers Boardman, *Christian Influence upon the Ideology of the T'aiping Rebellion* (Madison, Wis.: University of Wisconsin Press, 1952).

The T'aiping bore a chiliastic stamp, suggesting certain iconoclastic religious and even supernatural resolutions of the crises facing China at the time. Christian missionaries in China were largely ambivalent in their response to the T'aiping rebels—some looked upon them as harbingers of a promising future, while others were suspicious and apprehensive. In the end, this movement did not bode well for Christianity in China.

5. Portions of Stout's letter are cited on the *Deseret News* (Salt Lake City), December 22, 1853, p. 3; and in Spencer J. Palmer, *The Church Encounters Asia* (Salt Lake City: Deseret Book Co., 1970), p. 28.

6. Additional details on closure of the Japanese mission may be found in J. Christopher Conkling, "Members without a Church: Japanese Mormons in Japan from 1924 to 1948," *BYU Studies* 15 (Winter 1975):191–214; and R. Lanier Britsch, "The Closing of the Early Japan Mission," *BYU Studies* 15 (Winter 1975):171–90.

7. Ezra Taft Benson, address in *Report of the One Hundred Fortieth Annual General Conference of the Church of Jesus Christ of Latter-day Saints,* (April 4–6, 1970) (Salt Lake City: The Church of Jesus Christ of Latter-day Saints, 1970), pp. 127–32.

8. I am grateful to F. Ray Hawkins, President of the Seoul, Korea, Mission of the Church, for assistance on biographical information relating to Dr. Kim Ho Jik.

9. Seven pesos and fifty centavos are equivalent to the U.S. dollar.

10. A discussion of the languages of the Philippines is taken up in the question-answer section that follows.

CULTURE AND THE GOSPEL

INTRODUCTION

Gordon C. Whiting

The four presentations making up this section share a concern for subjective culture. Subjective culture leaves aside the physical artifacts of human behavior and concentrates upon those nonmaterial elements that, for a particular group, give meaning to its shared norms and values.

Shared norms and values within a culture have the side effect of creating a wall against other cultures, which are often seen in negative terms. Notice the reaction of a learned Chinese gentleman of a bygone age, confronted with the phenomenon of the European:

These "Ocean Men," as they are called, are tall beasts with deep sunken eyes and beaklike noses. The lower part of their faces, the backs of their hands, and, I understand, their entire bodies are covered with a mat of curly hair, much as are the monkeys of the southern forests. But the strangest part about them is that, although undoubtedly men, they seem to possess none of the mental faculties of men. The most bestial of peasants is far more human, although these Ocean Men go from place to place with the self-reliance of a man of scholarship and are in some respects exceedingly clever. It is quite possible that they are susceptible to training and could with patience be taught the modes of conduct proper to a human being.[1]

The implicit part of subjective culture comes into our awareness best when we are confronted by beings whom we recognize as like us in genetic heritage but who behave in ways that to us are curious. Even should we come to fathom with our intellect these peoples' culture, our negative *feelings* will not easily desert us. Such ways are not, in our view, the sensible nor the most appropriate way for a proper human being to behave.

If we merely comprehend parts of an alien culture, and that only upon conscious effort, our experience will not be comparable to that of the natives. They move in the sea of culture as their first, rather than second, nature. It is not merely the culture's parts but the nature of their integration—the culture's structure—that determines its place in the life of those who bear it. As Robert Lynd points out, "the significance of structure for a culture may be suggested by the analogy of a Gothic cathedral in which each part contributes thrusts and weights relevant not only to itself alone but to the whole."[2]

The presentations of this section are concerned, however, with a more precise focus than subjective culture. They deal with communication across cultures. When messages transcend cultural boundaries, much that within a single culture can be taken for granted rises to impede understanding. Communication suddenly becomes quite problematic. The immediate hurdles are obvious: languages and other subtle and profound symbol systems are not shared. Literal translations are laughable or appear as gibberish. When other translations are tried, how shall one judge if or when equivalency of thought has been achieved? Even norms and strategies for signaling understanding differ. What shall a Westerner make of a Chinese's smile and nod? What shall a Chinese businessman make of a Westerner's obvious disdain for ceremony and proper form? Even with common purposes and the best will, each party to a complex intercultural transaction is liable to feel uncertainty, puzzlement, irritation, and estrangement. "Why does he always fail to do what he should? What real relationship do we have? Why can't he behave properly and see the obvious demands of the situation and task? How refreshing it will be to return home and have sensible, predictable people to work with again!"

Of course, these feelings are not universal, and it is the fervent hope and expectation of all the authors of this section that, by adherence to correct principles and through the mediation of the Holy Ghost—that most powerful facilitator of communication—messages will bridge cultural chasms and will result in both proper understanding and enriching human relationships. Further, it might be hoped that the experience will prepare all parties for a deeper appreciation of the "culture" latent in the gospel itself.

In one way or another, all the presentations here concern themselves with precisely what those principles may be. As in most such tasks, it is easier to point out the negative than the positive. We and others have already stumbled across much that fails to aid the realization of intercultural communication. We are hence warned away from the negative more often than we are directed to what has been demonstrated as positive and sure.

In the first essay, Spencer J. Palmer lucidly outlines five ways of accounting for religious parallels in highly diverse cultural settings. Two of these, which he terms the diffusionist and the common-human-predicament approaches, have been the principal secular explanations of cultural similarities. They also have served efforts by agnostics to debunk religious claims to divine communication. Without denying some validity to the diffusionist and common-human-predicament explanations of these similarities, Palmer enlarges the range of possibilities by discussing three uniquely religious perspectives that do allow for the divine in history. Although he does not insist on assigning precise weights to the relative importance or validity of each of the five categories of explanations of cultural resemblances, Palmer does so clarify the issues that the way is prepared for a detailed analysis of the significance of any rationale selected for a communication strategy devised to reach particular populations.

Palmer also seems to hope that cultures themselves may be vehicles of expression which, however different in form, have a capacity to convey similar content when attuned to the gospel culture itself. Perhaps an analogy to language is permissible. The Adamic language's potentials and efficiencies may only be approximated by subsequent languages. Nevertheless, we believe salvation is possible and the gospel expressible in the full range of languages now extant. Similarly, no present human culture approaches the perfection of the culture of heaven, but to the extent the fullness of the gospel supplants their missing parts and substitutes their erroneous or satanic elements, we may all be saved out of them.

Truman G. Madsen provides a fascinating treatment of religious symbolism and also points out the difficulty of fitting Mormon symbols into the usual categories. In his view Mormonism both reforms and reformulates symbols, doing so through revelation. Thus the usual tangles and difficulties that human reflection frequently leads one to are often resolved as by a "[sharp] . . . two-edged sword, . . . dividing asunder . . . both joints and marrow" (D&C 6:2; see also D&C 11:2; 12:2; 14:2; 33:1). The similarity between religious symbols and their referents is not quite analogic or iconic but rather reinactive. Yet none of these categories properly states the case, for Madsen notices that the flexibility of the religious symbol system in any given culture entails the possibility of context radically altering meaning, as when the biblical serpent serves as symbol for both evil and good.

As important as it is for religious symbols to convey sentiments and feelings, Madsen very properly points out the necessity of their being intelligible and having understandable content. Messages received from heaven are not devoid of content; they are not just sentiment and feeling. And while mortals may only partially grasp their content, what they do grasp should be intelligible as well as profoundly moving.

Seiji Katanuma provides an opportunity to experience a mode of organization, argument, and thought process from another culture. His thesis stresses the importance of a system of writing. Together with other influences, and to a degree we find hard to imagine, he believes this accounts for the emergence of a culture dependent upon sight and mental images derived from visual experience. The cultural tendency is toward an aesthetic-emotional grasp of reality. If we nod agreement to the dictum "I think; therefore I am," the Japanese in Katanuma's homeland might find more convincing the statement "I see and realize beauty; therefore I and others are." Without disputing the common human heritage that all people share, Katanuma does present evidence for differences in connotations and expectations. But this is misstated, for it sounds argumentative and analytical, something that does not characterize his essay. Katanuma *presents* the thesis and some examples he finds illustrative of it, then turns to some specific recommendations for a more visual approach to teaching the gospel among the Japanese people. His discovery of scriptural parallels to the mode of thought he recommends as appropriate for presenting the gospel of Jesus Christ in Japan is striking. It is an instance of the ways in which diverse cultures can contribute depth of insight to our appreciation of God's word.

In Gordon C. Thomasson's essay, he strongly embraces one of Palmer's five explanations of similarity among religions, arguing against the proposition that Mormonism is explicable as a product or even a reflection, in its essentials, of Western culture and consciousness. At the same time, he is at pains to show that Mormonism is no more oriental than occidental. He claims that it bursts all the usual cultural categories and classifications. It seems to him uniquely acultural, even though it has the characteristics of integration, pattern, symbolic transmission, and a specific value system—all the necessary and sufficient conditions of a culture. Indeed, it is the culture of heaven, adapted in some nonessential way, perhaps, to our stage of development and presented so that we may come to an understanding and to greater conformity with it; nevertheless, it is unique. What critics have regarded as evidence of incredible eclecticism and syncretism, Thomasson sees as convincing evidence of divine origin.

In Thomasson's view, the gospel's fullness fills out the gaps left in every culture, while also crowding out elements that are satanic or that fall short of the divine. Cultures have something to repent of as well as something to complete before they come up to the gospel standard. Thomasson's thesis argues for the assimilation of Saints from every culture into a common gospel culture where national origin provides only interesting variations on a common theme of allegiance to divinely ordained or revealed values, patterns, assumptions, and moral-spiritual realities.

Footnotes

1. Cited by Robert T. Oliver, *Communication and Culture in Ancient India and China* (Syracuse, N.Y.: Syracuse University Press, 1971), pp. 4–5.

2. Cited by A. L. Kroeber and Clyde Luckhohn, *Culture: A Critical Review of Concepts and Definitions* (New York: Random House, Vintage Books, 1952), pp. 333–34.

MORMON VIEWS OF RELIGIOUS RESEMBLANCES*

Spencer J. Palmer

In studying the religions of the world, scholars customarily make elaborate comparisons of the differences and similarities they find. Particularly has this been the case in comparisons of Christianity and the various faiths of Asia and the Middle East, such as Hinduism, Buddhism, and Islam.

As for the differences the scholars find, the most fundamental one, from one perspective at least, is between the great biblical religions (Judaism, Christianity, and Islam) and the religions of India (e.g., Hinduism). In comparing these religions, one sees a clash between biblical theism (belief in one God who is personal, worthy of adoration, and separate from the world but continuously active in it) and monism (be-

*In modified form this lecture was printed in *Brigham Young University Studies* 16, no. 4 (Summer 1976): 660–81, in a special issue of selected centennial lectures.)

lief that god, mind, and matter are undifferentiated). Christians thus appeal to a God who is Creator and Lord of all. Hindus, on the other hand, look for unity with an impersonal divine principle. This carries with it grave differences in the evaluation of the world and history. The biblical religions accept the world as real, as having a definite origin, and moving towards a definite termination at some future date; however, for the Hindus and other Monists the world is *maya*, illusory, the present phase being a beginningless and endless series of cycles. The biblical faiths take pride in the fact that they have a historical basis: the exodus from Egypt, the Crucifixion under Pontius Pilate, the Hegira.[1] For the monists, general philosophical ideas replace historical events. Hence, the Hindu doctrine of man is metapsychological, a piece of subtle and—so it would seem to Latter-day Saints—unsubstantiated analysis.

For Latter-day Saints, perhaps the most acute conflict has still to be mentioned. Gotama Buddha, the founder of Buddhism (c. 530 B.C.), may say that the difference between his way and that of the Jew, Moslem, or Latter-day Saint is so great that he must deny that the word religion is really common to all. Gotama acknowledged no God at all, but only gods who, like men, are caught in the net of *karma;*[2] no future life, but only the bliss—or extinction—of Nirvana;[3] no soul, but only the legacy of one life bequeathed to another that falls heir to it; no prayer, but only meditation as a form of spiritual discipline; no grace, but only man's resolve to tread the Noble Eightfold Path to the end. The ultimate doctrines of Buddhism, like those of Hinduism from which it sprang, are negative and pessimistic in terms of their response to the worth of this mortal life and the individual as the locus of value. Since Buddhists believe that underlying reality is one inclusive mind or stream of consciousness, Christ and judgment are imaginary, irrelevant, or "untrue." Could there be more serious conflicts and discrepancies than these?

But the restored gospel does not contradict Buddhism on every hand. In fact there are between the two a number of remarkable resemblances. Both Christ and the Buddha believed that covetousness and lust were at the root of human suffering; that men must shake the dust (the cares of this world) from the mirror of their minds and seek to nourish the spirit of the inner man; both declared that freedom lies in following a way of life free from cruelty, falsehood, killing, stealing, and unlawful sexual relations.

Aside from those ethical teachings similar in Buddhism and Mormonism, parallels between the life stories and the reported sayings of Jesus and Gotama have intrigued the followers of these two religious leaders, as well as secular scholars at large, at least since the time of St. Jerome. Leaving aside for now the credibility of the narratives and comparing only commonly accepted beliefs, how should Latter-day Saints explain the following resemblances?[4]

1. Both Jesus and Gotama were foreordained in a preexistent spirit world to come forth at a particular time, after preliminary examination and selection of the most favorable family, country, race, and mother into which to be physically born.

2. Both entered the womb of their mother in a miraculous manner, having no mortal father.

3. Both were born into a world whose inhabitants' bodies had become coarse and gross and who had lost much of their original brilliance because a being of an inquisitive nature had commenced eating a debilitating food.

4. Both had births accompanied by special heavenly illuminations.

5. Both were recognized in infancy by respective religious leaders as persons of great promise, with special missions to perform among mankind.

6. Both visited holy temples in their youth and displayed unusual precocity and wisdom before their elders.

7. Both launched their ministries early in their thirtieth year following periods of fasting and solitude.

8. Both gained disciples under a fig tree.

9. Both were severely tempted by an Evil One (Mara and Satan).

10. Both selected a council of special disciples and joined with them in carrying out their religious ideals by way of example.

In addition to these historical agreements, further similarities in thought and phraseology between the gospels of the New Testament and the Dhammapada of Buddhism include the following:

1. From Christ: "Now do ye Pharisees make clean the outside of the cup and the platter; but your inward part is full of ravening and wickedness. Ye fools, did not he that made that which is without make that which is within also?" (Luke 11:39, 40).

From the Buddha: "What is the use of platted hair, O fool? What of the raiment of goat-skins? Within thee there is ravening, but the outside thou makest clean."[5]

2. Christ: "Strait is the gate, and narrow is the way, which leadeth unto life, and few there be that find it" (Matthew 7:14). [Elsewhere there are similar biblical analogies: "Our soul is escaped as a bird out of the snare of the fowlers; the snare is broken, and we are escaped" (Psalm 124:7).]

Buddha: "This world is dark, few only can see here; a few only go to heaven, like birds escaped from a net."[6]

3. Christ: "Let them alone: they be blind leaders of the blind. And if the blind lead the blind, both shall fall into the ditch" (Matthew 15:14).

Buddha: "As when a string of blind men are clinging one to the other, neither can the foremost see, nor can the middle one see, nor can the hindmost see. Just so, methinks, Vasettha, is the talk of the Brahman's verse in the three Vedas."[7]

4. Jesus told the woman of Samaria that his salvation is as "living water" (John 4:10–14); in Saddharma-pundarika (the Lotus Sutra), Gotama compares salvation to "water for all."[8]

In the face of such religious similarities and parallels, what explanations do Latter-day Saints have? Are these and other agreements imaginary? Are they only coincidences? Are they simply remarkable illustrations of poetic license, or of distortions of language and culture at the hands of faulty translators? Should they be explained by reference to the similarity of circumstances under which both Christ and Buddha taught? Have the Buddhist legends and teachings derived certain of their elements from Christian sources? Or must Christians accept the allegation that certain things in the Gospel records have either derived from the earlier Buddhist legends or from another common ancient source? For Latter-day Saints, who are eager to see their faith disseminated worldwide and to see it effectively implanted among all peoples, and yet who wish to accept and encourage anything that is "virtuous, lovely, or of good report or praiseworthy"(Article of Faith 13), questions of religious comparison between the cultures of man, East and West, are of great significance. Do religious elements that seem harmonious or even universal spring from a common source when once the pure gospel of Jesus Christ was known to our fathers? Are similarities to the gospel simply satanic substitutes, counterfeit attractions suggesting that all roads lead to heaven? Or are there other explanations possible? How do Mormons handle non-Mormon religious beliefs, values, rituals and symbols that seem to be not only compatible with true gospel principles but in some cases even appropriate manifestations of them? Are such resemblances an advantage or a disadvantage to those declaring a unique Latter-day Saint message?

Acting on the premise that religious similarities are indeed ubiquitous in the world, how have Mormons generally approached them? In this paper I shall examine five basic Mormon views of religious resemblances, the first two of which have been less argued and much less developed among members of the Church.

1. Primordial Images—Echoes of a Preexistent State.

In Mormon theology human predispositions of thought and feeling may be viewed as "echoes of eternity," since all men lived together under common conditions with God in a premortal spirit world. After quoting Wordsworth's famous "Ode: Intimations of Immortality . . .", which suggests that the minds and spirits of mankind come to earth "Not in entire forgetfulness, . . . /But trailing clouds of glory do we come/ From God, who is our home," Joseph Fielding Smith comments that "there may be times when flashes of remembrance of these former days come to us."[9] Then he quotes Orson F. Whitney, a former member of the Council of the Twelve, who explained that more than once, upon hearing a noble sentiment expressed, though unable to recall that he had ever heard it until then, he found himself in sympathy with it, was thrilled by it, and felt as if he had always known it. Elder Whitney referred to the Savior's statement that "My sheep know my voice," concluding that those things that are true and instinctively beautiful appeal to men everywhere because we were all acquainted with the gospel in a previous life before we came here, and it is this that gives it a familiar sound.[10] President Joseph F. Smith "heartily endorsed" Elder Whitney's observation that common experiences in the antemortal spiritual life predispose, influence, and guide human thoughts and preferences in this life, for "we often catch a spark from the awakened memories of the immortal soul, which lights up our whole being as with the glory of our former home."[11]

Of course this is not the same as Carl Jung's view of the "collective unconscious," but there is much in that scholar's discussion of "basic archetypes" that nonetheless seems congruent with the Mormon view of preexistence and that might well help explain resemblances of thought and belief among mankind. Jung taught that a symbol can express itself among large masses of people simultaneously.[12] He saw parallels with mythological motifs among his patients. For example, a very young child would recite a dream to Jung which exactly paralleled some ancient Persian myth. The child could not have been taught the myth, for very few people who were not classical scholars even knew of it. After considerable study and deliberation, he found that general story outlines of myths were identical across cultural heritages that had no possible chance of contact. He concluded there is a common, almost instinctual disposition among all men—including civilized men—to symbolize identical themes in their religious myths. Why are the story lines of religious fantasy and experience so common among all men? In 1919 Jung developed the term *archetype* to account for these expressions of "collective psyche." He did not suggest universal symbolism, but he did suggest universal archetypes. He did not see these archetypes as conscious images of the mind, but they did stand in the deepest reaches of the unconscious. He called them "primordial images"—congenital preexistent images—believing that the mind has inherited an *a priori* disposition to work in a certain way. The psyche is not passive; it is an active agent in the framing of meaning.

From a Mormon point of view, similar ways of thinking and acting can easily be interpreted as deriving from our existence with God; and perhaps the so-called "psychic unity" of man that has been argued by so many may indeed go back to our preexistence, to our primordial, native intelligence. President Smith, Elder Whitney, and so many others of us in the Church from time to time have talked about "glimmers" and the "thin veil." We say that thoughts rise in our minds to make us feel we have experienced this, felt that, or believed something else. And such "echoes of eternity" seem to be the common experience of mankind. Having common beginnings in the spirit world, naturally we should expect, if only at times in faint and wistful ways, common manifestations of those beginnings with God. In his 1973 Commissioner's Lecture, Truman Madsen concluded that only something of such magnitude can account for conscience and the full phenomenon of other powers inherent in man:

> *Though presently a veil is drawn over specific images of that realm—we do not now recall our name, rank, and serial number—there is built in us and not quite hidden a "collective unconscious" that is superracial in character, a pool of such vivid effect, such residual power in us, that our finite learnings and recoveries are at best a tiny aftermath.*[13]

And it is in this that one should be able to find explanations of resemblances in the beliefs and religious experiences of man.

2. The Devil Invention Theory

Milton R. Hunter draws attention to the devil theory in his book, *The Gospel through the Ages.* Many of the pagan practices were so similar to those of early Christianity, says Hunter, that many Christian apologists have concluded all this had to be the work of the devil. Elder Hunter points out that in about A.D. 150 Justin Martyr, after describing the Lord's Supper as given in the Gospels, reportedly remarked: "The wicked devils have imitated [it] in the mysteries of Mithra, commanding the same thing to be done." Tertullian, another Christian teacher (A.D. 160–220), claimed that "the devil, by the mysteries of his idols, imitates even the main part of the divine Mysteries. . . . He baptizes his worshipers in water and makes them believe that this purifies them from their crimes." And 1300 years later, "Las Casas (A.D. 1474–1566), A Spanish Catholic missionary, observing that the ceremonies of the [American] Indians closely resembled those of the Christians, concluded that the devil had arrived in America ahead of the Christians and implanted in the minds of the natives many teachings closely akin to Christianity." [14]

In this view, the devil has exerted a powerful influence upon men in counterfeiting the true principles and ordinances of the gospel. Lucifer has fostered many clever imitations in an effort to lull mankind into satisfaction with partial truths and to weaken the appeal of divinely authorized teachers. In the words of Jacob, the Book of Mormon prophet, men can become angels to a devil, for Satan, who beguiled our first parents, is capable of stirring up the children of men with dreadful works of darkness by transforming himself "nigh unto an angel of light" (2 Ne. 9:9).

Thus, similarities to the gospel are considered Satanic substitutes—counterfeit attractions suggesting, among other possibilities, that all roads lead to heaven.

3. Diffusion

Among Latter-day Saints, by far the most popular and compelling explanation of religious resemblances is the belief that religious elements appearing to be harmonious or even universal sprang from a common source after the pure gospel of Jesus Christ was known to all our fathers. Adam, the first man, was taught the fullness of the gospel. In turn he taught it to others. But men, yielding to the temptations of the evil one, sinned and departed from the truth. The original, true doctrines were changed and warped to suit the appetites of evil, ambitious men. Thus the principles of the gospel have appeared in more or less perverted form in the religious beliefs of mankind. The gospel was again taught to the world in its purity in the days of Jesus Christ. Again, willful men changed the doctrine, and a host of Christian parties came into being. The many religions among the human race are an evidence of the magnitude of apostasies from the simple, easily understood revelations of God.[15]

The pioneer Mormon study of Mormonism in a world religious setting was Thomas C. Romney's. Consistent with his diffusionist approach, he suggested that doctrines of trinity as applied to Deity reach back into the remotest past and are universally espoused. The numerous examples of trinitarian belief among ancient Egyptians, Mesopotamians, Babylonians, and Sumerians are all reflections of an original authentic model—the Father, Son, and Holy Ghost.[16] Romney argued that both blood and bloodless sacrificial offerings of the Vedic gods of India (Indra, Gonesha, Varuna, Visnu), the libations to Confucius in the traditional ceremonies of the state cult of China, the sacrificial offerings to the gods of the ancient Greeks and Romans, as well as those many Jewish and Christian sacrifices for the purpose of placating the wrath of the deities or of placing the worshippers in happy accord with unseen and ineffable powers are all evidences of "common bonds of union"—universal religious patterns—that in the main at least "sprang originally from a common source."[17] Anciently men offered sacrifices without really knowing the historical roots of their own practices. These roots are found in the original sacrifices of Adam and his posterity, which were in similitude of the sacrifice of the Lamb of God, even Jesus Christ. The scripture explains:

And after many days an angel of the Lord appeared unto Adam, saying: Why dost thou offer sacrifices unto the Lord? And Adam said unto him: I know not, save the Lord commanded me.

And then the angel spake, saying: This thing is a similitude of the sacrifice of the Only Begotten of the Father, which is full of grace and truth (Moses 5:6–7).

In like manner, the diffusionist view holds that the doctrine of reincarnation, transmigration, and rebirth in Hinduism, Buddhism, Jainism, and Sikhism is actually a modified and "strange type of immortality." Romney points out that the early Rig Veda, the earliest book of the Indo-Aryans, makes no mention of reincarnation. This belief developed much later. Only after the people were forced to face the enervating climate of the region of the Ganges, the myriads of insects and other forms of animal life, and the difficulty of extracting a decent living from the soil did a new drab outlook upon man's present existence develop.[18] And this new negativism vitally affected the Indian view of immortality. Life was no longer an experience to be thankful for, another step in the process of eternal development which, if rightly lived, would lead toward God. In a widening disparity, the ultimate goal of Nirvana in Hinduism and Buddhism is a form of annihilation to be reached only after countless incarnations during which the soul gradually attains the power to negate the desire to live. This is not eternal individualized progress.

Elder Alvin R. Dyer, another exponent of the diffusion view, concludes that religious confusion in the world has resulted from deviations from established principles, from mutations of original truth. Items: The Hindu worship of Dyaus Pitar, a nature god of the sky or heaven, can be thought of as "a legendary perversion of the teachings of Abraham and Moses concerning preexistence and of God our Eternal Heavenly Father."[19] Despite the original illustriousness of the teachings of Confucius and Lao-Tzu[20] and the mystical and ornate rituals of earlier Buddhism, all of which seized the instincts of the Chinese race, there have been long periods of transition that have resulted in a "universal apathy" among that people. All life and vitality in the religious thought and sentiments of the Chinese have now disappeared;[21] so also have they from Hinduism, Zoroastrianism, Taoism, and Islam, they having fallen under "the lash of departure" from their own original doctrines. Modern Taoism is quite different from the high theories of its founder. It presents a pathetic history. It started with some admirable features of truth, but it has degraded fearfully into polytheism, demonolatry, witchcraft, and occultism. Shinto has become so vague as to be undefinable in the minds of either priests or philosophers.[22] Originally a pure and righteous "law of the birthright" existed among the families of the ancients. This patriarchal order was established by God. It was a call to responsibility. Through a long process of mutated developments, this great principle was later expressed in southern Asia as the Hindu caste system. And in like manner, the Moslem belief in *jihad,* or holy war against the unbelieving infidels, and the sense of superiority associated with state Shinto in Japan—by which the Yamato race claimed an inherent right to rule over others by force and bloodshed if necessary—are all decadent expressions of the ancient law of the birthright.[23]

By far the most influential and effective Mormon spokesman of a diffusionist view is Hugh Nibley of Brigham Young University. In all his prodigious scholarship, there is an underlying view of an unchanging God who in his dealing with man follows a constant pattern. God repeatedly reveals his will, his unchanging truth, to selected peoples of the earth. Resemblances and ties that seem to exist among all the religions of antiquity reappear in history primarily because of a pattern of divine restorations and human apostasies. And since the teachings and powers of God to chosen peoples have often been deliberately imitated in every age of the world, and in other ways disseminated among men, a diffusion of truth from a single center has continued to recur. What has been done in one dispensation has often been foreshadowed in another. In Nibley we have an eschatological pattern of history which is also prominent in Jewish and Christian scriptures and in apocryphal writings as well: "the periodic repetition of certain characteristic events—a 'visitation,' as it was called, from heaven; the making of a covenant; the corruption and wickedness of men, leading to the breaking of the covenant; the bondage of sin, then the coming of a prophet with a call to repentance; the making of a new covenant; and so around the cycle."[24] God is at the helm of history. Thus, at the base, religious parallels are rooted in the mind and will of God, in repeated revelations. Parallels between the history of the restored Church and the doings of the ancients are not consciously contrived imitations; the analogies that can be drawn between the sufferings, wanderings, and spiritual aspirations of the Mormon pioneers and those of the people of ancient Israel cannot be drawn because the former wanted it so. The Mormons were pushed around entirely against their own will. All along, the whole history of the Church has been the will of God. Resemblances to earlier beliefs and experiences have an extraordinary force among Latter-day Saints because they have not been intentional and they actually are the fulfillment of prophecy.[25]

In a recent book, faced with resemblances between the LDS temple endowment ceremony and ancient Egyptian endowment rites, Nibley sees these as an example of countless parallels, many of them instructive, among the customs and religions of mankind. But they are imitations of earlier gospel models, and little more. The Egyptian rites "are a parody, an imitation, but as such not to be despised. For all the great age and consistency of their rites and teachings, which certainly command respect, the Egyptians did not have the real thing, and they knew it."[26]

4. The Common Human Predicament

There are Mormons who believe that the diffusion theory explains religious parallels only in a limited way. They readily agree that God revealed original principles and ordinances of the gospel and bestowed the authority and power of the priesthood to Adam, and that in the course of time, as populations expanded and as peoples moved away from one another and became independent, they took with them some of their original features and applied them in new settings. But to these Latter-day Saints this is a handy explanation that fails to cover much of the ground. At best such a view explains common religious forms only within limited geographical areas.

William A. Wilson, the Mormon folklorist, observed that if all stories develop out of the original story in the Garden of Eden, then we should be able to find in the Bible account all the materials that have generated other stories as they fragmented and broke into parts.[27] But this cannot be done. Moreover, folklore studies indicate that certain kinds of stories and beliefs are limited to particular peoples. They do not circulate worldwide. In a study of folk beliefs among peoples of the Indo-European languages, that is, from Ireland to India, one can find common themes. Wherever Indo-Europeans have traveled, parallel beliefs have been widely diffused. Similar ideas can be found in North America, South America, and other parts of the world by travelers who have taken them there. But such diffusion is limited; elements of Indo-European folk tales, for example, are not found in Southeast Asia. Diffusion from a single source answers only part of the problem of religious parallels worldwide.

The view here is that certain things are fundamental to all human beings—arising out of the common human predicament—and explain many of the similarities of thought and practice so widely experienced here on earth. All men face problems of birth, life, sex, disease, death, joy, disappointment, and grief. All men ask, Why must we die? Why must we be sick? Why must we grow old? Why must we suffer? What happens after death? Common beliefs and practices arise from the common predicament of man in responding to his circumstances. Parallels to the experience of Job in the Old Testament are everywhere.

This polygenetic view that religious beliefs and rituals have arisen spontaneously and independently in various countries but have generally followed uniform patterns of development offers special insights into the use of religious symbols, rituals, and ordinances among mankind. Mircea Eliade, the great professor of comparative religion at the University of Chicago, says that human actions have no intrinsic value. Human actions become valuable only insofar as they unfold according to divine patterns. If human life is to have any ultimate meaning it must somehow transcend this human predicament. It must somehow become identified with the transcendental, the divine. If things remain earthly, they have only limited earthly value. Eliade concludes that human beings all over the world carry out festivals, rituals, and ordinances as an aid and an effort to transcend the ordinary human predicament.[28] Victor Turner and others speak of these as "periods of timeless time," wherein men, through the language of ritual, transcend the arbitrary human world and connect themselves, their relationships, their institutions, and their social order with something beyond this life.[29] Thus, religious symbols are the means by which they establish contact with the divine. And without such ordinances and rituals the provisional and arbitrary arrangements of this world have no ultimate value. If life is to have intrinsic value, it must be derived from some external transcendental source. People all over the world realize this. And this common realization brings about similarities in religious belief and practice.

Since our mundane world has no ultimate meaning until it is connected with something beyond this, frustration and pain are relieved primarily through extraordinary rituals and symbolic expressions. And in this, God is not a God of one point in time or of one people or even of one genetic line.

Latter-day Saints may be exclusive in ways they are not aware of all the time. Other peoples have basic operating principles in their religious systems that find expression in terms of their own cultural idiom. We differ from these people culturally; the vehicles of our expression are different. But when we deal with others at similar levels of meaning or seek to communicate according to similar principles rather than expect to use similar cultural idioms, we reach common ground. We find similarity. Thus Merlin Myers has observed that it may well be that for the celestial kingdom the symbolic vehicles and the underlying principles must be adapted to each other in ways that preclude variation there.

No doubt there are cultural vehicles that are peculiarly adapted to the celestial order of things. Truth can be given expression in a variety of cultural and symbolic vehicles, and can provide valid functions and services for those who receive them, but the cultural symbols of man can also be regarded as vehicles to aid people in reaching higher means of expression in the celestial kingdom. Within the Church there are instrumentalities by which such levels of insight are encouraged and achieved.[30]

In the 84th Section of the Doctrine and Covenants the Lord explains that the greater priesthood holds the keys of the mysteries of the kingdom and that "without the ordinances thereof, and the authority of the priesthood, the power of godliness is not manifest unto men in the flesh" (D&C 84:21).

John A. Widtsoe repeatedly emphasized that man lives in a world of symbols, some not so beautiful and pleasing, but that their forms are of relatively little consequence. In the end, it is what they suggest and teach that counts: "No man or woman can come out of the temple endowed as he should be, unless he has seen, beyond the symbol, the mighty realities for which the symbols stand."[31]

Those Mormons who give credence to "the common human predicament" view find superiority in the rites and ordinances of the priesthood, but at the same time peoples all over the world are trying to accomplish similar goals within the framework of their own world view. They have their symbols and ordinances, too, and through these symbols they seek to transcend their earthly predicament. These people seek to break through this mundane realm and realize the supernatural by means of them. In other words, all men bear the stamp of the entire human condition; the similarities of their concern and their response to the needs and conditions of this life are not essentially questions of either divine or nefarious forces emanating from another world but of the harsh realities of this one.

5. The Light and Spirit of Christ

In Mormon theology the spiritual influence emanating from God is not confined to selected nations, races, or groups. All men share an inheritance of divine light. Christ himself is the light of the world; even those who have never heard of Christ are granted the spirit and light of Christ. In the Book of Mormon Christ told the brother of Jared, "In me shall all mankind have light" (Eth. 3:14). In a revelation to Joseph Smith, the Lord explained:

Whatsoever is light is Spirit, even the Spirit of Jesus Christ.

And the Spirit giveth light to every man that cometh into the world; and the Spirit enlighteneth every man through the world, that hearkeneth to the voice of the Spirit (D&C 84:45–46).

And in the "Olive Leaf" revelation of 1832 we are told that this Light of Christ

proceedeth forth from the presence of God to fill the immensity of space—

. . . [It is the light] by which all things are governed, even the power of God who sitteth upon his throne, who is in the bosom of eternity, who is in the midst of all things (D&C 88:12–13).

If any man acts according to this inspiration, he progresses from grace to grace, learning precept upon precept, until he receives full enlightenment.[32] That every man ever born enjoys the light of Christ was reiterated by Brigham Young, who taught that there has never been "a man or woman upon the face of the earth, from the days of Adam to this day, who has not been enlightened, instructed, and taught by the revelations of Jesus Christ."[33] This allows each individual to recognize truth, and the associated results often lift men to new and higher insights than were traditionally known among a given people.

Since God has thus inspired men of all cultures and creeds, the possibilities are staggering. Such religious reformers as Martin Luther and John Wesley—despite their personal frailties and errors—may be looked upon as instruments of God's will. Likewise, a whole continuum of Christian mystics in medieval European history, some of whose ideas seem at times closely to resemble Mormon teachings today, show the extent to which they separated themselves from the "orthodox" thought of the Catholic Church. These include St. Francis of Assisi and St. Bernard de Clairvaux, to name only two. Also, Christian devotionalism represented by Thomas à Kempis's *The Imitation of Christ* (1426), on the way in which a true Christian should behave, and the development of Christian art and architecture in Russia beautifully express a diffusion of inspiration and light among the peoples of Europe.

Among Hispanic people living in Europe as well as in the Western Hemisphere, contributions to civilization are monumental and countless.

In the fields of literature and painting the works of Diego Rivera and Rufino Tamayo, as well as of Francisco Goya and Diego Velásquez are celebrated worldwide for their illuminations and beauty. From Spain, Miguel de Cervantes' classic, *Don Quixote,* has provided inspiring insights that have encouraged and sustained men of all lands to seek for betterment in life. Mexican achievements in establishing the first university in North America and in publishing the first book in the Western Hemisphere (in 1539 by Juán Pablos) have been a great blessing to all those who have been able to come under their influence.

Columbus and the Pilgrims were moved upon by the "Spirit of God" to sail to the New World. The founding fathers of the United States were also moved upon by the Spirit. Great western scientists and poets were likewise inspired.[34]

It follows, then, that God inspires not only non-Mormons but also non-Christians as well, including "heathen" philosophers, religious leaders, and peoples. God has raised up inspired teachers and great reformers in various cultures throughout history—not only Jewish and Christian spokesmen. In this Mormon view, all peoples and even all religions possess elements of truth. To illustrate, all of the following religions or philosophies profess a statement of moral principle in essentially the same wording as the Christian golden rule: Judaism, Hinduism, Buddhism, Sikhism, Zoroastrianism, Islam, Shinto, Socratic Philosophy, Confucianism, Taoism, and Jainism. John Taylor affirmed: "The Catholics have many pieces of truth; so have the Protestants, the Mahometans, and Heathens."[35] George Albert Smith reiterated this theme,[36] and Brigham Young observed:

> *"Do you suppose the Hindoos have the light of the Spirit of Christ?" I know they have; and so have the Hottentots, and so has every nation and kingdom upon the face of the earth, even though some of them may be cannibals.*[37]

Latter-day Saints believe that America was divinely prepared as a haven for the establishment of The Church of Jesus Christ of Latter-day Saints, that Columbus was inspired to discover this promised land, and that the Constitution of the United States was instituted of God. But they also teach that the Omnipresent Spirit moved upon the thinkers of Greece and Rome and upon the Protestant reformers of European history. Likewise artists and thinkers in Asia have been moved upon by inspiration from God: Ferdosi of Persia; Kalidasa, Asoka, and Gandhi of India; Mencius, Tu Fu, and Po Chiu-I of China; Sejong of Chong Mongju of Korea; Bashō and Chikamatsu of Japan; and José Rizal of the Philippines, to name only a few at random. God's Spirit has rested upon other inquiring and imaginative men who have produced incomparable Shang bronzes, T'ang pottery, Sung landscapes, Koryo celadons, magnificent buildings, mosaics, paintings, and sculptures in India and in the Middle East; it has also led to the invention of Arabic numerals and the Indian zero, and in China, Korea, and Japan to the spinning wheel, paper, the first ironclad ships, the foundations of modern chemistry, and the first printing presses with moveable type.

Although some Latter-day Saints may believe that God's operations are confined to their Church, according to the teachings of the Church leaders this belief is a mistake, for God operates among his children in all nations.[38] The living prophet and president of the Church communicates God's will to those within the Church and to all men who are prepared and able to listen; for those outside the Church God often employs other spokesmen. Brigham H. Roberts explains, "It is nowhere held that this man [the living prophet] is the only instrumentality through which God may communicate his mind and will to the world."[39] All who seek God are entitled to further light and knowledge, regardless of historical or cultural setting. Thus, John A. Widtsoe's view helps explain the impetus for various religious developments:

Spiritual outreachings are not peculiar to one country. Instead, in every land men have sought the gifts of the spirit.... Men have arisen in every land, who have tried to formulate the way to happiness, for the benefit of themselves and their fellow men.... The religions of Egypt, China, India, and Persia, are examples.[40]

Brigham Young believed that even idolatry arises from the actions of men of faith.[41]

Orson F. Whitney taught that Zoroaster, Mahavira, Gotama Buddha, and Confucius "were servants of the Lord in a lesser sense, and were sent to those pagan or heathen nations to give them the measure of truth that a wise Providence had allotted to them" and that they, along with others, "have been used from the beginning to help along the Lord's work—mighty auxiliaries in the hands of an Almighty God, carrying out his purposes, consciously or unconsciously."[42] Brigham H. Roberts summarizes:

While the Church of Jesus Christ of Latter-day Saints is established for the instruction of men; and is one of God's instrumentalities for making known the truth, yet he is not limited to that institution for such purposes, neither in time nor place. God raises up wise men ... of their own tongue and nationality, speaking to them through means that they can comprehend; not always giving a fulness of truth such as may be found in the fulness of the gospel of Jesus Christ; but always giving that measure of truth that the people are prepared to receive. Mormonism holds, then, that all the great teachers are servants of God; among all nations and in all ages. They are inspired men, appointed to instruct God's children according to the conditions in the midst of which he finds them. Hence it is not obnoxious to Mormonism to regard Confucius, the great Chinese philosopher and moralist, as a servant of God, inspired to a certain degree by him to teach those great moral maxims which have governed those millions of God's children for lo! these many centuries. It is willing to regard Gautama Buddha as an inspired servant of God, teaching a measure of the truth, at least giving to these people that twilight of truth by which they may somewhat see their way. So with the Arabian prophet, that wild spirit that turned the Arabians from worshiping idols to a conception of the Creator of heaven and earth that was more excellent than their previous conception of Deity. And so the sages of Greece and of Rome. So the reformers of early Protestant times. Wherever God finds a soul sufficiently enlightened and pure; one with whom his Spirit can communicate, lo! he makes of him a teacher of men. While the path of sensuality and darkness may be that which most men tread, a few, to paraphrase the words of a moral philosopher of high standing, have been led along the upward path; a few in all countries and generations have been wisdom seekers, or seekers of God. They have been so because the Divine Word or Wisdom has looked upon them, choosing them for the knowledge and service of himself.[43]

George A. Smith believed that Mohammed "was no doubt raised up by God on purpose to scourge the world for their idolatry."[44] Parley P. Pratt, in a general conference address, declared:

With all my prejudices of early youth, and habits of thought and reading, my rational faculties would compel me to admit that the Mahometan history and Mahometan doctrine was a standard raised against the most corrupt and abominable idolatry that ever perverted our earth, found in the creeds and worship of Christians, falsely so named.[45]

Moses Thatcher, another member of the Council of the Twelve of the Church, was "struck by the profound philosophy, pure morality, and comprehensiveness exhibited in the writings of Confucius and Mencius [and] the Chinese sages" as divinely inspired, far-reaching, and heavenly doctrines.[46] Likewise, in a KSL radio address in 1927, Elder Matthew Cowley expressed his belief that "Confucius understood the doctrine of repentance" and that on the basis of his teachings on purity and virtue "one would almost believe that the gospel was borrowed from Confucius."[47]

Thus, in this Mormon view, God has inspired men to think and write according to the conditions in the midst of which he finds them; Islam,

Hinduism, Taoism, Confucianism, Shinto, and Buddhism have within them inspired and inspirational principles, and the peoples of these lands will be judged by God in accordance with their individual willingness to abide by them, as they are not totally subversive of gospel values, but are striking evidence that God has spoken "to all nations of the earth" and that mankind will ultimately be judged by that which they have been inspired to receive, at least until a fullness of the gospel has been provided.[48] For in the words of Alma, the Book of Mormon prophet, the Lord grants "unto all nations, of their own nation and tongue, to teach his word," and counsels in wisdom to provide them with all that he feels is appropriate "according to that which is just and true" (Alma 29:8).

James E. Talmage saw authentic comparisons between Mormonism and Buddhism, believing that the latter provided a constructive path that could consistently lead upward to the fullness of the restored gospel:

> *We believe that man may advance in righteousness and become more nearly perfect; even as the followers of Buddha teach, that by the* "Holy Path" *[Hināyāna] or by the* "Pure Path" *[Mahāyāna] men may walk in the light and become Buddha.*
>
> *We believe as you do, my beloved readers in Japan, that some will follow the path of* Hinayana, *and others the higher road of* Mahayana—*each choosing for himself, according to inclination and capacity; and, sad to say, yet others use that God-given freedom of choice and follow the path of sin that leadeth downward to perdition.*[49]

The distinction thus made is significant and impressive, and it is in effect the difference between the Mosaic law and the gospel of Jesus Christ. Better to live by Hināyāna—in obedience to the stern commands, "Thou shalt" and "Thou shalt not"—better to do good through hope of reward and eschew evil through fear of punishment than to do evil and reject good. But better still, far better is it to absorb the spirit of righteous law—to walk by Mahāyāna—to make right living the natural mode of life, and through inspiration and divine love, rather than because of the law's demands, rise to exalted rank.

Conclusion

Each of the five Mormon views elaborated here provide useful and meaningful insights into questions of religious resemblances. But none of them covers the whole ground alone, and all of them together fall short of explaining all such parallels. My own feeling is that only inspiration from the Lord can provide the answers as to which of these five possibilities should be dominant in a particular case. Regardless of the relative importance of each of the five in a particular setting, we must decide from a tactical point of view whether the work of the Church will be more effective if we emphasize the diabolic nature of the similarities between the gospel and the native faiths or if we emphasize the heritage of the pre-earth life or of the light of Christ or of a partially accurate deposit of a faith and truth from ancient times or of whatever else. But this much is certain: the view one takes has important implications for the future of the Church.

Our reactions to religious similarities not only influence our perceptions of the religions of Asia but also our feelings for missionary work in that part of the world. With even a little familiarity with other religions, we can be much impressed by what seem to be duplications of elements usually assumed to be totally unique to the restored gospel of Jesus Christ. To come upon these parallels in the remains of cultures long dead (Assyrian, Egyptian, Babylonian, Ugaritic, and others) is one thing. To come upon them in the scriptures of living world faiths that compete with us for the hearts and minds of men—Buddhism, Hinduism, and Islam—or in Confucian and Taoism teachings honored among the Chinese, Koreans, and Japanese—may be more difficult to handle. A little such familiarity with non-Christian religions can breed confusion and concern. And some may be tempted to turn to sheer relativism, to believe that one faith is as good as another, or that all faiths express the same truth in variant cultural trappings.

This is one of the pitfalls often associated with polygenetic "human predicament" and "Light of Christ" approaches to the whole problem of religious resemblances. Some men have seized upon the resemblances of Christ to other men of his age and to other so-called hero figures of all time and upon resemblances between Joseph Smith and Mohammed or some other religious leaders to prove that these two are simply two of many. That makes the Savior and the Prophet much easier to explain. Hugh Nibley has warned us that by diligent research one can match all the Christian teachings with the teachings of others; and these have been pointed to repeatedly by students of comparative religion in order to bring Christ and his prophets down to the level of everyday experience and supplant the miraculous and unsettling by the commonplace and reassuring. As to the process of gaining a sure knowledge of the Lord and his Prophet, I heartily agree with Nibley's colorful and cryptic statement:

One does not compose music with a sliderule, and the divinity and truthfulness of Christ were never meant to be proved by history, since we are told from the beginning that that knowledge comes to one only by direct revelation from the Father in heaven.[50]

I find one aspect of the diffusionist approach particularly challenging to Mormon students of comparative religion: Diffusionists tend to think in terms of dispensation patterns as a framework for understanding the religious experience of mankind. At least by implication we are told that the human story is a conflict between two states of mind, between those who have been rebellious, indifferent, or hostile to God and those who have been custodians of truth—the lovers of God. This is the yardstick by which the various religions may be measured. Therefore, in each case we must ask ourselves how much a religion has preserved of the primitive, original revelation—and what its known historical links are. After Israel (Judaism), how should the great religions be ranked? Should first place be assigned to Zoroastrianism, because it hands on and recasts a tradition of remote antiquity, of severe truth and high morality? Should Zoroaster be followed by the *rishis* of the *Vedas*, Brahmans by birth, who spring from Seth's descendants by one line, a class of men chosen by God who, though somewhat crippled or degenerated, are still devoted to God's service, as E. L. Allen has contended?[51] Or, on the other hand, shall we agree that among the nations of antiquity who stood nearest to or at least very near to the source of primitive revelations from God, the Chinese must hold a distinguished place? Among the Chinese are there not many remarkable vestiges of eternal truth to be found in their classical works and in their time-honored religious traditions?[52] As Latter-day Saints begin seriously to investigate the source of Japanese religion and lay claims of finding extraordinary links between them and the peoples of the Old Testament and Book of Mormon, does this require a significant revision of our perceptions of that people's place in the unfolding of God's work in the latter days, as so many of our students have suggested in recent years?[53]

Among those Latter-day Saints who underscore the manifestations of God's influence among all men on an independent and personal basis—either through his Spirit or in response to common needs and problems in the human condition—the universality of God is stressed. The whole race of man—in every land, of every color, and in every stage of culture—is not only the offspring of God, but in the vast compass of his providence all are being supported by his love to reach within the limits of their powers a knowledge of the Supreme. Not only in this is God thought of as having a more universal and direct involvement in the lives of all his children on an individual basis, but also the sense of community among human beings is enhanced. On the other hand, diffusionists tend to stress the eternal struggle between truth and error, between eternal truth and local culture, between God's chosen people and those who are not so chosen, between the revelations of God and the ways of the world. Implicitly, this calls for a primary focus on the ways in which Latter-day Saints are different from others, rather than upon their common humanity or their dependence on a common Father. Among diffusionists there is always the temptation to construe a narrow, exclusive, and arrogant view of themselves and of the Church that militates against true brotherhood—the pure Love of Christ—the expansion of Zion in the "nethermost" places of the earth, the full acceptance of gospel values in alien heathen cultures, and full recognition that the God of Israel is also the God of the whole earth.

For those of us who seem ready to see God's handiwork throughout the world and even in the lives of wise teachers, poets, philosophers, and scientists and who are happy to believe that they all have a work and mission under an overruling Providence, there are two final cautions I should like to make. First, although the Spirit and power of Christ is manifest worldwide, this is not to suggest that the founders and teachers of the great religions of man have a full endowment of either light or power. They have not. They did not receive the gift of the Holy Ghost or the keys and authority of the Holy Priesthood, and without these they could not receive revelation and authority to perform more than preparatory principles and ordinances for their people. Gotama Buddha has been a light for Asia, but he could not be the light of the world. He was not appointed or empowered to that position. I believe that Mohammed was an inspired man, a prophet without priesthood, who performed a particular mission at a special time among a people with special needs. But God has a living prophet who heads up his universal kingdom in the earth—The Church of Jesus Christ of Latter-day Saints. The President of the Church is God's mouthpiece—a universal mouthpiece, endowed with the keys of presidency over all affairs dealing with a fullness of God's power and authority throughout the earth.

As Latter-day Saints we cannot dismiss Buddhism out of hand simply as a false religion. The light of Christ shines in it, too. But there is danger here. A friendly and appreciative approach to non-Mormon religions in Asia carries with it an intrinsic temptation to think that in places like Thailand we must at least symbolically, if not literally, dress the Mormon missionaries as Buddhist monks. But recognition of religious parallels does not imply the need for advisability of such a course. In seeking for that which is "virtuous, lovely, and praiseworthy" within the native faiths, we are not seeking accommodation or compromise. Others have tried this with no effective benefit. There is no value to the Church or to the people of Asia in allowing Jehovah to be accepted into the Buddhist pantheon; and there is no gospel benefit in having Jesus Christ identified as an avatar of a Hindu god, as an incarnation of the Buddha, or in any way less than the Son of God, "the only name given among men" whereby we must be saved. But despite the prospect of this negative result, the positive implications of using good things in Asia as building blocks for bringing people into a fuller realization of their own spiritual possibilities must not be ignored.

Footnotes

1. In Islam the flight of Mohammed from Mecca in A.D. 622 is known as the Hegira.

2. *Karma,* in Hinduism and Buddhism, is the force generated by a person's actions that determine his future spiritual condition, both in this life and in succeeding ones. Good deeds lead toward liberation—Nirvana—and bad ones to a continuation of an individual's transmigration but in progressively inferior states of existence and worse conditions of pain and suffering.

3. Nirvana is the term used primarily to refer to the state of release or salvation in Hinduism, Jainism, and Buddhism. Literally the word means "extinguishing" a flame. Although Gotama Buddha rejected the idea of the existence of gods and individual souls, he did believe in *karma.* Therefore, related to the Buddhist doctrine of rebirth and *karma,* an individual's series of lives is compared to the lighting of successive lamps, one lamp after another. The "relighting" goes on as long as the individual has desire and individual consciousness and is subject to care, pain, and external reality. The state of Nirvana is reached when desire and individual consciousness are extinguished and a state of oblivion—and therefore bliss—has been achieved. From this state the individual, or the stream of consciousness, will be reborn no more. An individual's movement towards Nirvana is typically attained by treading the Noble Eightfold Path, which includes not merely ethical self-training but also techniques of contemplative mysticism such as yoga.

4. These are drawn from W. Woodville Rockhill, trans., *The Life of the Buddha and the Early History of his Order* (London: Kegan Paul, Trench, Trubner & Co., 1884), which is derived from Tibetan works in the Bkah-Hgyur and Bstan-Hgyur, the Tibetan Tripitaka.

5. Dhammapada, 394, in *The Sacred Books of the East,* ed. and trans. F. Max Muller, 14 vols. (New York: Scribner's, 1901), 12:90. Hereafter cited as *SBE.*

6. Dhammapada, 174, *SBE* 12:48 (pt. 2).

7. Tevijja Sutta 1:15, quoted in S. H. Kellogg, *The Light of Asia and the Light of the World* (London: Macmillan and Co., 1885), p. 136.

8. Saddharma-pundarika, trans. H. Kern, *SBE* 10:118–141.

9. Joseph Fielding Smith, *The Way to Perfection: Short Discourses on Gospel Themes* (Independence, Mo.: Zion's Printing and Publishing Company, 1943), p. 30.

10. Ibid., p. 45.

11. Orson F. Whitney, "The Undiscovered Country: A Dissertation on Spiritual Themes," *Improvement Era* 23 (December 1919):101.

12. J. F. Rychlak, *Introduction to Personality and Psychotherapy* (Boston: Houghton-Mifflin, 1973), pp. 143–47; see also C. G. Jung, *The Collected Works of C. G. Jung,* 17 vols., ed. Herbert Read, Michael Fordham, and Gerhard Adler (London: Routledge and Kegan Paul, 1953–73); see particularly volume 9, *The Archetypes and the Collective Unconscious* (1959), and volume 11, *Psychology and Religion: West and East* (1958).

13. Truman G. Madsen, *Conscience and Consciousness,* Commissioner's Lecture (Provo: Brigham Young University Press, 1973), p. 5.

14. Justin Martyr, *Apologia,* as cited in Milton R. Hunter, *The Gospel Through the Ages* (Salt Lake City: Stevens and Wallis, 1945), p. 40.

15. Which is the theme of John A. Widtsoe's introduction to Thomas Cottam Romney, *World Religions in the Light of Mormonism* (Independence, Mo.: Zion's Printing and Publishing Company, 1946).

16. Ibid., pp. 64–65.

17. Ibid., pp. 217–26.

18. Ibid., pp. 78.

19. Alvin R. Dyer, *This Age of Confusion* (Salt Lake City: Deseret Book Co., 1964), p. 15, footnote.

20. Lao-Tzu was the founder of Taoism, i.e., followers of the way of nature.

21. Dyer, *Age of Confusion*, p. 98.

22. Ibid., pp. 105–10.

23. Ibid., p. xiii.

24. Hugh Nibley, *The World and the Prophets* (Salt Lake City: Deseret Book Co., 1954), pp. 213–14.

25. Ibid., pp. 214–15.

26. Hugh Nibley, *The Message of the Joseph Smith Papyri: An Egyptian Endowment* (Salt Lake City: Deseret Book Co., 1975), p. xii.

27. Tape-recorded interview with William A. Wilson, March 1976.

28. See Mircea Eliade, *Cosmos and History* (New York: Harper Brothers, 1959).

29. Victor Witter Turner, *The Drums of Affliction: A Study of Religious Processes among Ndembu of Zambia* (London: Oxford University Press, 1968). See especially p. 5ff.

30. I am indebted to Professor Myers, not simply for his insights, but for the insights he has stimulated within me in our taped discussions.

31. John A. Widtsoe, "Temple Worship," *Utah Genealogical and Historical Magazine* 12 (April 1921):62.

32. See Charles W. Penrose in Brigham Young et al., *Journal of Discourses,* 26 vols. (London: Latter-day Saints' Book Depot, 1854–86), 22:85. Hereafter cited as *JD.*

33. Brigham Young in *JD,* 2:139.

34. This is elaborately emphasized by Charles W. Penrose in *JD,* 23:346.

35. *JD,* 1:155.

36. George Albert Smith, an address in *One Hundred and Second Semi-annual Conference of The Church of Jesus Christ of Latter-day Saints,* 2–4 October 1931 (Salt Lake City: The Church of Jesus Christ of Latter-day Saints, n.d.), p. 120.

37. *JD,* 2:140.

38. *JD,* 24:61.

39. In B. H. Roberts, *Defense of the Faith and the Saints,* 2 vols. (Salt Lake City: Deseret News, 1907), 1:514.

40. John A. Widtsoe, "Is There a Master Race?" *Evidences and Reconciliations* (Salt Lake City: Bookcraft, 1947), vol. 2, *Gospel Interpretations* (1947), p. 216.

41. *JD,* 6:194.

42. Orson F. Whitney, an address in *Ninety-First Annual Conference of The Church of Jesus Christ of Latter-day Saints,* 3–6 April 1921 (Salt Lake City: The Church of Jesus Christ of Latter-day Saints, n.d.), p. 33. See also Forace Green, comp., *Cowley and Whitney on Doctrine* (Salt Lake City: Bookcraft, 1963), pp. 292ff.

43. Roberts, *Defense of Faith and Saints,* 1:512–13.

44. *JD,* 3:32.

45. *JD,* 3:40.

46. Moses Thatcher, "Chinese Classics," *The Contributor* 8 (1887):301.

47. Matthew Cowley, "The Gospel of Repentance," KSL Radio address, Sunday evening, 31 July 1927.

48. Cf. 2 Ne. 29:7–12.

49. James E. Talmage, "In the Lineage of the Gods," *Improvement Era,* 8 August 1905:726–27.

50. Nibley, *The World and the Prophets,* pp. 16–17.

51. E. L. Allen, *Christianity among the Religions* (Boston: Beacon Press, 1961), pp. 61–62.

52. One delightful example of this proposition is Gerrit Gong's, "We Are Waiting the Impact of Chinese Ancestor Worship," a typescript with slide illustrations, which argues that the Chinese have enjoyed the spirit of Elijah (i.e., a great tradition of salvation for the dead) from times of remote antiquity.

53. This is a popular theme among some Japanese Latter-day Saints, and particularly among *nisei* Japanese and missionaries returned from Japanese fields of labor. Some of the ramifications are suggested in my article, "Did Christ Visit Japan?" *Brigham Young University Studies* 10 (Winter 1970):135–58; see also "The Japanese Search for Identity," in my forthcoming book, *Every Nation, Kindred, Tongue, and People.*

THE ROLE OF RELIGIOUS SYMBOLISM: EAST AND WEST

Truman G. Madsen

Q. What are we to understand by the four beasts, spoken of in the same verse? [Revelation 4:6.]

A. They are figurative expressions, used by the Revelator, John, in describing heaven, the paradise of God, the happiness of man, and of beasts, and of creeping things, and of the fowls of the air; that which is spiritual being in the likeness of that which is temporal; and that which is temporal in the likeness of that which is spiritual; the spirit of man in the likeness of his person, as also the spirit of the beast, and every other creature which God has created (D&C 77:2).

And behold, all things have their likeness, and all things are created and made to bear record of me, both things which are temporal, and things which are spiritual; things which are in the heavens above, and things which are on the earth, and things which are in the earth, and things which are under the earth, both above and beneath: all things bear record of me (Moses 6:63).

It is widely held today that religious symbols have a unique power. Their influence transcends symbols that are mainly social, political, or literary, as, for example, the black belt, the flag, or the father-motif in

Dostoevsky. Religious symbols depend for their life on immersion in the sacred. Their most authentic impact occurs because of what Rudolf Otto calls the "numinous"—an aura of holy associations that evoke fascination, wonder, awe.[1] But we live in a thoroughly secularized world. Contemporary man has moved far from the assurance of a universe that "lives and breathes" in a divine aura. The result is that religious symbols fail to enlighten or grip many people as, in the mornings[2] of their glory, they once did. In his book *The Sacred and the Profane,* Mircea Eliade has traced this almost universal desacralization—this loss of meaning and power in sacred symbols. His discussion centers on four main ancient symbols—sacred space, sacred time, human emancipation, and transformation.[3] Latter-day Saints know that these symbols come together with immense vitality in our modern temples.[4]

Whether due to the decline of the numinous or not, sacred symbolic life, so characteristic of both Eastern and Western religions, has itself declined and has brought many efforts at diagnosis—attempts to explain the trouble and perhaps to do something about it. Among the different approaches, two main efforts have been attempted at therapy. One is reformation—an attempt to peel away and discard accretions and distortions of traditional symbols in favor of a return to the original or primordial symbol. (This effort may, in the end, be scholarly guesswork.[5] But in just this spirit, Protestant reformation movements, in order to reenthrone biblical faith, discarded five of the seven Roman sacraments.) Yet one may cut away the withered leaves and branches of a tree only to find that the trunk or, worse, the whole root system is dying. So a second effort at therapy is reformulation—the taking of more or less living symbols and translating or refurbishing them in more contemporary modes (to translate, for example, the language and symbolism of the New Testament into contemporary symbolism), as Rudolf Bultmann attempts to do in his project of demythologizing texts. He claims he is "purifying" the text of its merely historical and time-bound cosmologies and saving only its truly religious power in the vocabulary of present-day philosophy.[6] The gain may also be a loss, as, for example, when Bultmann denies the resurrection but offers the "resurrection-faith."[7] Moreover, "the contemporary" philosophical vocabulary may be weaker. Compare the title of Luther's hymn, "A Mighty Fortress Is Our God," with a modern equivalent—"A Nuclear-Fallout Bomb Shelter is Our God." In the end, the substance of symbolism may disappear under its new clothing; grafting may replace the original.[8]

Mormonism presents another way of approaching the problem of therapy—the way of restoration—which at its heart is the fresh, flowing, living stream of present revelation. One outcome of this surge of religious birth and rebirth over a century and a half has been to dissolve and transcend many of the twists and mutilations of past symbolic usage. But notice that the process does not utterly exclude the two therapy efforts described above. It embraces them. It revivifies the old texts and, in the result, includes elements both of reformation and reformulation. Of course, new scriptures have been uncovered and revealed—new symbols, new covenants, new ordinances. Yet at root, what is new is also somehow everlasting: "things which have been kept hid from before the foundation of the world" (D&C 124:41).[9]

In this paper I shall treat four main aspects of religious symbolism from the Mormon perspective:

1. some unique roles of religious symbols;
2. the close similarity between key religious symbols and things symbolized;
3. the flexibility of religious symbolism in tension with divinely assigned meanings as we have received them through the restored gospel; and
4. three dangers that face us as we encounter the symbol-systems of other religions.

Unique Roles of Religious Symbols

Religious symbols have multiple effects. Much contemporary discussion stresses their grip on our feelings and our will, rather than on their enlightening or information-giving roles. But from our Mormon heritage, whether symbols are verbal-scriptural or ceremonial-artistic, we see that they have been capable of reaching both mind and heart—for several reasons. First, religious symbols, as our temple worship all by itself should demonstrate, are more expressive of the depths of man than merely prosaic or conceptual statements.[10] Second, they have what may be called a "cosmic condensation" role—a power to pull into one emblem or concerted enactment whole clusters of meanings.[11] Third, religious symbols, unlike other modes of expression, can speedily become surrogates or substitutes for what they symbolize. For oaths sworn on symbolic bibles people have shed blood. One may bow down with idolatric consecration to an inanimate object as if it were itself divine.

The expressive, condensing, and surrogate power of religious symbols reflects a primary etymological meaning of the word "symbol"; it means "bringing together." Symbols unite the perceiver and the perceived. They make accessible to the senses an intelligible set of religious meanings. They likewise unite the fragmented self. When we gather in a sacramental service, we are usually more "at one" with ourselves and others and with the Master than at other times. Our symbolic involvement is more than conceptual or imaginative, and more than memory. Symbols have an almost uncanny power to bring together levels of meaning otherwise neither fully plumbed nor mastered—hence the moot question of whether Christ's use of symbols, as, for example, in the parables, is intended to reveal or conceal. Most often parables do both. Something is instantly apparent, but no matter how deeply one probes, something is always beyond immediate grasp. Take, for example, the wheat and the tares (D&C 86).[12]

That leads to another unique role of religious symbols—they give access to the highest as well as the subtlest qualities, powers, and relations of life. As John A. Widtsoe writes of the temple.

The endowment is so richly symbolic that only a fool would attempt to describe it; it is so packed full of revelations to those who exercise their strength to seek and see, that no human words can explain or make clear the possibilities that reside in the temple service. The endowment which was given by revelation can best be understood by revelation. . . .[13]

Thus, from our highest symbolic experiences come great insights, new levels of understanding, and also a heightened self-awareness and a sense of being in touch with the truly Divine.

The Similarity Question

But are our religions symbols, even those of scripture, "coined"? Are they not somewhat capricious and conventional? Could not any given symbol be substituted for another that would serve just as well for any intended meaning? And is the origin of symbols to be thought a spontaneous one (because a little study of the world's religions suggests that any segment of reality can stand, by our own intentions, for anything else)?

The many levels of symbolic usage make this question difficult. Probed to its roots, however, the Mormon heritage seems to point to our acceptance of a dispensational or diffusionist understanding of symbolic origins. Hence we accept that in the beginning unity and coherence existed in the symbols and symbol relations God gave to man. Accordingly, we expect, and in some measure find, that fragments of that unity and coherence, though broken down into disorganized blocks, are found over the entire world of religion.[14]

If we are startled at the apparent uniform types and all-but-universal spread of these symbols, we must postulate not only a uniform source but also a certain subtle uniform reception. Symbol receivers as well as the symbol transmitters have a certain common undergirding of intelligence and spirit: for all our differences—radical differences—we have the same basic apperceptive capabilities, understanding things as we perceive them in light of our previous experience. "For man is spirit," says a modern revelation, and "that which was from the beginning is plainly manifest unto them" (D&C 93:33, 31). Locked in us is more than what Jung called the "collective unconscious," which Paul Tillich often regarded as the "Symbol-making factory" of both religion and the arts.[15] For us, symbol comprehending has much to do with original perception—premortal and powerful—presently submerged in cosmic amnesia, yet giving us a deep tendency toward things with a "familiar" quality or ring. Many interpreters of the religious consciousness agree on this: there is something almost invincible about religious symbols. Through the centuries they have tremendous staying power and seem only replaceable by other religious symbols. Even though they be consciously, rationally, and devastatingly criticized or deliberately abandoned, yet in the depth-self they recur. Thus, whatever the contemporary decline of religious interest, there is still a primordial and perennial impact of gospel symbolism. There are still reverberations below the surface awareness. Some archetypes may, as Jung believed, be universal, regardless of the variations of time, cultural divergence, and idiosyncratic temperament.[16]

Both the Roman Catholic and Greek Orthodox traditions in the West and the Taoist, Hindu, and Buddhist religions in the East asserted a radical discontinuity between the nature of this world and the nature of the divine or the "transcendent" realm beyond—Heaven, the Atman, the Tao. This is called "an infinite qualitative distinction." On this view nothing on earth is really similar to anything beyond. The consequence for theories of religious symbolism is the view that we must either understand these symbols negatively (saying only what the real beyond is *not,* never what it is) or analogically (saying what the relationship is *like,* never what it is). Thus all religious expression must be "broken," qualified, or denied. It must never be "taken literally."[17] The luxuriant paintings on the ceiling of the Sistine Chapel, for example, tell Roman Catholic theologians nothing about the nature of God. And these theologians in turn teach that people must, in the end, look beyond the paintings. Yet Catholicism and other dualistic religions in both the East and West have been most prolific in their creative embellishments of symbolic expression and in their inclusion of symbols in worship and teaching.

In marked contrast, Mormonism asserts that the earthly and the heavenly are, in fact, similar. And it testifies that in the life to come not only the "soul" of man (often defined in other religions as an undifferentiated and immaterial thing) but man's body and senses, in direct touch with his depth-awareness, will be transformed and enhanced, not negated.[18] Yet Mormonism has often been suspicious of, if not hostile to, the use of religious symbolism, and hesitant to ascribe more than one level of meaning to scriptural interpretation. This suspicion is more remarkable when one considers the full-flowering symbolic richness of LDS doctrines and ordinances, especially those presented in the temple.[19]

Some of this hesitancy to use religious symbolism is no doubt culturally conditioned. John Dillenberger, for example, observes that a large proportion of nineteenth-century Mormon converts were British or Scandinavian. These countries maintained a pervasive hostility to continental painting, sculpture, and architecture, especially as they flowered in France and Italy. He speculates that had the majority of our Mormon converts come from these aesthetic centers in Western Europe, our attitudes toward religious art would have been markedly different.[20] But whether or not one accepts this reading, there is something both Hebrew and Christian in the Mormon anxiety about symbolism. It arises from a long and melancholy history of abuse, even tragic abuse, of religious symbols.

The Flexibility of Symbols and Divine Intent

Mormons are often characterized as biblical and scriptural "literalists." But this is a half-truth. In our sacred literature as well as in much that we say and do, we are indeed speaking not metaphorically but historically; not attempting to penetrate helpful myths but to report actual events; not trying to ritualize or tokenize real suffering, real service, and real processes of salvation, but to live them and make them part of our lives. But for these very reasons we should be the last to underestimate the meaning and power of symbolic expression. For from beginning to end our heritage is replete with expressive symbols.[21] Like all authentic religionists, we are anxious to avoid idolatry. But for us, symbols may be close to that which they symbolize. This is the outcome of our eternalism, that heavenly and earthly are in crucial ways similar, "that which is spiritual being in the likeness of that which is temporal" (D&C 77:2). Because of this, a symbol may both *stand for* and *be* what it symbolizes. Thus earthly symbols may do more than represent heavenly realities. They may actually present them. They may, as Victor Warnach puts it, *disclose* as well as *signify*.[22]

To illustrate: the name *god* is a functional symbol for the divine. The word itself may fulfill some of the roles earlier ascribed to religious symbols. Whether spoken reverently or profanely, it has an impact of shape and sound that is remarkable and moving.[23] But there is a symbol for God that is closer in nature than these letters or sounds. It is man himself. Man, despite his present finitude, is closer in nature to the Divine than any letters or sounds. He has both a distinct affinity and a distinct relationship with the Divine. Man is an embryonic god. All other attempts to symbolize the nature, attributes, and relations of God, useful though they may be, are misleading unless man, the living symbol, is kept in his preeminent symbolic position. We recognize that man is to be "added upon" (a different thing from the Eastern notion of being "subtracted from") until he is that consummate personality of which Jesus Christ was prototype and prophecy. Christ is, to use a lovely phrase of Eliza R. Snow, the "great fac-simile."[24]

In this matter, the Mormon faith appropriates the biblical roots of Judaism. In the Torah, the same Hebrew words that forbid making any likeness or icon or graven image of the Lord God also convey their justified existence. Thus Abraham Joshua Heschel warns for his Old Testament tradition that unless religious symbols are God-given, they may quickly become idolatric substitutes for divine reality and lose their effectiveness.[25] Yet he insists it is thoroughly Hebraic to say that man is created in the likeness and image (in the *tselem* and the *demuth*) of God. This identification makes sense of both the law and the prophets of the Old Testament. For viewed both in spirit and body man is considered *the* symbol, and by that process, *the* extension of God himself. Thus even the body of a criminal condemned to death must be reverenced (see Deut. 21:23). Many rabbis view man's body as the "icon" of God (see Tselem Elohim in Genesis 1:27 as rendered in the Hebrew language). Cleanliness of body is a reverential and ceremonial act. The commandment, "Ye shall be holy: for I the Lord your God am holy" (Lev. 19:2) covers more than "Ye are mine." It says "Ye are me"—the extension of me—"therefore, be what I am: holy."

Jesus Christ manifests and extends this primal insight. He teaches that man must treat others as himself and himself as he treats others—both as divine. Hence, "inasmuch as ye have done it unto one of the least of these my brethren, ye have done it unto me" (Matt. 25:40). His modern revelations only intensify the recognition: "Man was . . . in the beginning with God" (D&C 93:29). In all this there is no denial of man's corruptibility. Man as fallen and mortal is a mere seedling and, at times, a decaying seedling at that. But it is because he falls from a divine nature that this fall is so radical and the need for regeneration and transformation so all-inclusive.[26]

Much symbolist theology of our time arises from an anxiety, even an obsession, to preserve the holiness of God by insisting on his radical transcendence from man, his detachment, his state as "utterly beyond."[27] The mission and commission of Latter-day Saints is exactly the reverse:

to honor and glorify his name and his very nature in the earth; not to escape but to transform this world and its inhabitants into God's glorious condition and likeness. That is our deepest motivating force. It is what gives man both freedom and dignity. It places him in a position of dominion over all that is in and upon and above the earth. For Mormons to lose sight of this truth and our own symbolic relationship to the Divine is to forfeit our image and betray our potential.[28]

If Mormons should not fear but rather more effectively employ religious symbols, we nevertheless must be careful in our attitudes toward them. One way to approach the discussion on this point is to ask what we should avoid in symbols and symbolism. We are to avoid the hasty conclusion that symbols are merely conventional and arbitrary and utterly removed from anything literal. We are to avoid detachment and loss of similitude, or the development of a sentiment that there is power but no truth in symbols. We are to avoid seeing the symbol without seeing through it to the living God. And what are we to affirm? That symbolic fruits require literal roots. Symbols only edify when God's spirit is present. A proper spiritual reunion, especially in his ordinances, therefore occurs only when he by his Spirit *is* present. In this sense symbols do "participate" (a favorite term of the depth-psychologists) in that which they symbolize.[29] Both symbol and the symbolizer are transformed by the Spirit—that is the indispensable source of their light and life and power. That is their true efficacy. Thus for us the soundest response to the secularizing or desacralizing trends of our time is not an argument. It is seeking the infusion of the Spirit in all the religiously symbolic words and acts of our lives, even those considered most menial or base.[30]

But once we know what a symbol stands for, may we not dispense with it? On that impulse many Western and Oriental minds idealize a perfect language—silence. Silence, it is claimed, is the only mode of expression where ambiguity and confusion are utterly removed. But deep in our heritage is the record and the promise of a perfect language (which, no doubt, may include silence). When we ask ourselves what a perfect language might be, it is illuminating to ask what frustrates and defeats us in our present languages: confusion about what one names or points to, inability to initiate or elicit duplicating feelings in the hearer, and fragmentation—losing one's grip on the fullness of reality by the paralysis of analysis, i.e., "breaking things down" into bits and pieces. But reflection will lead us to see that, in the end, only if the persons who communicate are themselves endowed with a spiritual form of communion will language do, however remarkable it may be. Once again we are driven to the need for unity, a direct connection or even identification of the originator and the instrument. And only then can we say that "he that preacheth and he that receiveth, understand one another, and both are edified and rejoice together" (D&C 50:22). Such language can be "mighty even as thou art, unto the overpowering of man to read" (Ether 12:24). This is the "pure language" prophesied of by the ancient prophet Zephaniah (Zeph. 3:9).[31]

If this is true, then the incessant search in our time, both in Western and Eastern cultures, for symbolic innovation—the attempt to overcome the alienation of outworn symbolic traditions—is, regardless of its imaginative and creative strength, doomed to fail. The communication process must be enveloped in the power of God. And it is therefore universally true, as the Master put it: "I am the true vine, . . . ye are the branches: He that abideth in me, and I in him, the same bringeth forth much fruit: for without me ye can do nothing" (John 15:1, 5). Those who have any living and direct touch with Christ sense his hand and are impressed with endless symbolic reminders of his influence everywhere. Those who lack direct touch see him nowhere.

Literal and Divine Symbols

In light of the above discussions, let me now illustrate concretely the range and power of symbols that both stand for and are what they symbolize on the one hand and, on the other, give us a direct connection with the Divine.

Take the symbol of the serpent. The Book of Genesis applies that symbol with all its coordinate meanings to the deceiver, the adversary, "that old serpent, the devil." In the Garden drama, it is he who deceives, beguiles, poisons, and kills. His condemnation is radical: to crawl in the dust (and no modern English expression is more contemptuous than "a snake in the grass"). Yet strangely, it is a serpent, a lifeless brazen serpent at that, which Moses lifts up in the wilderness as a saving mechanism. Simply to behold that serpent is to receive life, protection, healing.[32] Thus a symbol for evil and death becomes a symbol for the highest good, even for life itself.

In the New Testament, far from abandoning this symbol, Jesus makes it the symbol of wisdom ("be . . . wise as serpents"—Matt. 10:16). Then, having identified himself as embodied light and truth, the creative logos of the world, Jesus identifies himself with the serpent: "As Moses lifted up the serpent in the wilderness, even so must the Son of man be lifted up" (John 3:14). "And I, if I be lifted up from the earth, will draw all men unto me" (John 12:32). Through this image Jesus promises deliverance and sanctification to those who receive him and his way. Hence the powerfully suggestive statement about the bruising of heels and the crushing of heads. And one of the gifts or fruits of his transforming Spirit is that his disciples shall take up dangerous, even poisonous, serpents and not be harmed (Mark 16:18).

In the Eastern religions there are whole cults of the serpent, but with the same ambivalence or antinomy between death and life. In much Eastern iconography, the serpent and the dragon symbolize temptation and evil; but for some Chinese religions the dragon is likewise the spirit of change and growth and, indeed, of life itself. One finds the same contrast in the religions of Egypt, where the serpent is the enemy and yet is overcome by another serpent-symbol, the flaming sword. As we study the walls of the tombs of Thebes, we see the vision of the Egyptian ceremonialists that man's very salvation comes by his passing through the furls of a serpent's body. In Mesoamerican culture, likewise, the snake is portrayed as the archenemy. But there is also a redeemer figure, and he, the savior-god, is himself a feathered serpent—Quetzalcoatl.

The feathering reminds one of the cryptic observation of Joseph Smith that even to dream of flying signifies deliverance and triumph, a prophetic sign that "the word will be received with power."[33] Elsewhere the Prophet writes that wings are symbols of power "to move, to act" (D&C 77:4). In viewing Christ this way one sees him as the living word, the messenger "with healing in his wings" (Mal. 4:2), or, more Hebraic, in his hands and feet. Christ descends below all things and then ascends above all things, reversing the effects of the fall and the curse of man. The same images recur in modern revelation. At least twelve times the Lord begins and ends revelations with the statement, "I am Alpha and Omega, the beginning and the end, the first and the last" (see D&C 19:1, 35:1, 38:1, 45:7, 54:1, 61:1, 63:60, 68:35, 75:1, 81:7, 84:120, 112:34).

In ancient religions, the serpent biting its own tail becomes a sacred circle on which are often inscribed the first and last letters as in the Greek alphabet. The ring thus formed is a symbol of eternal lives, a cosmogony and cosmology of the "never-ending." The glorified serpent, then, is both origin and consummation. And his priesthood, named after Melchizedek, himself a redeemer type (see the Inspired Version of Heb. 5:6–8) is without beginning of days or end of life (see Heb. 7:3, iv).

One may disagree with these hasty tracings of the serpent symbolism. But one thing is clear: in *our* sacred sources, the serpent is the symbol of both the lowest and the highest. And that surprising resolution of grand opposites can be extended to a thousand and one other examples throughout the religious world.[34] In this harmonizing of opposites it can be seen how a symbol for evil and death can become a symbol for the highest good and life, and how it can become not only a representation of a religious idea but a presentation of the Divine itself.

But now the question becomes more urgent: how do we know what a symbol is intended to mean and to do? How do we avoid abuse and even inversion? A partial answer is that the Doctrine and Covenants, as well as the last great discourses of the Prophet Joseph Smith, frequently use a key word—namely, "key." It is significant that the "keys of the kingdom" are keys both of understanding and of authority and power. Contrary to all the noncognitive theorists, intelligibility *is* essential to symbolic power, as also is symbolic power essential to intelligibility. "I know not," says Adam when he is asked why he is offering up animal sacrifices, "save the Lord commanded me." But in the presence of the charismatic angel he is then taught, "This . . . is a similitude of the sacrifice of the Only Begotten of the Father, which is full of grace and truth" (Moses 5:6–7). From that moment on, understanding increases with symbolic power. And Adam has divine authority for offering sacrifice in the appointed way.

The implication is clear. Mere interest in or use of symbols is not enough. One must also be in touch with the Divine that generates and empowers those symbols with their *intended* meaning and function. All the major world religions make a distinction between the initiate or neophyte and the adept or master. Symbols are seen as stages on life's way. But to the genuine master, mystery is less and less mysterious. For us, the ceremonies of transformation that enable a man fully to know God are the ceremonies that enable him to reunite with—indeed, to become—God.[35] And in that there is intention, not merely accident.

An example of how original purity of intent can be garbled is in rampant Oriental ancestor worship. One can see this as an obsessive mixture of creature and Creator, an idolatric enslavement to the dead and gone. Regalia and ritual attend the family-oriented Chinese New Year—a symbolic reinforcement of this tradition. How seriously are such symbols taken? One answer: The father of a girl who had accepted the gospel of Jesus Christ brought her before her family. Ceremonially, with three incense sticks, he burned and probed her arm until it sizzled. Then in a special incantation designed to sever her from the family, he withdrew her name from the family list; and in prayer he implored the ancestor-spirits not to punish the family for her defection.

But behind his act, as also the artifacts, the photos, the relics, and the altars that are part of so many crowded Chinese homes (most with smatterings of beliefs from Buddhism, Confucianism, Taoism, and some Western Christian amalgamations) is this: the undercurrent conviction that the dead are influenced by ceremonial acts of the living. To neglect the dead and the wishes of the dead is to cause them to become devils, thrust down to suffer, consigned (and confined?) in a netherworld. Does not this apparent distortion hide a kernel of inspiration? That we break family bonds and neglect our progenitors at the peril of our own salvation?[36]

But now I turn to a whole constellation of symbols in which the reverse is the case—where overbeliefs and underbeliefs, or what Duncker calls the "pattern of situational meanings,"[37] not only qualify symbol usage but dominate and even reverse their original meanings. Here ceremonial similarities conceal differences in fundamental belief.

In Tibet, China, and Japan, there is a variation of Buddhism known as Tantric. It aspires to a condition "beyond Samsara" (illusion) and Nirvana (bliss). Harvard's Professor Kenneth Chen insists that this condition is not, as viewed in some forms of Buddhism, a cessation of consciousness. It is a state of awareness that is achievable through *mantras* or ceremonies to be both chanted and acted out. Four main gradations or transitions in the ceremonies involve symbolisms of right and left, light and darkness, the reception of vital wind, and male and female. The recital of proper syllables is viewed, as in Hindu tantras, as the mechanism of transformation into god or goddess. The entire production of the world is represented in miniature, and the mantras are placed on different parts of the body with a view to bodily purification. It is believed that a microuniverse is somehow situated in the human body and that each body has its counterpart, a *mudra,* or color. Male and female, the *upaya* and *pragna,* must simultaneously come to enlightenment or thought-illumination and this unity must precede the creative process. Great affection (*raga*) promises intense and transcendental bliss that both binds and liberates (seals and fulfills?). It is taught that without this oneness of thought and emotion all acts become evil. Man's and woman's *merudana,* or spinal cord or skeleton-bones, are compared to "the mount of ascent." Lotus blossoms are placed in the laryngeal, cardiac, and lumbar regions. Ritual words are spoken as the attention is focused on the neck, the heart, and the navel. This plexus theory culminates in the belief that the cerebral plexus (forehead) finally possesses all virtue.

It is tempting to say of all this that we are seeing ceremonial or initiatory symbolisms close in meaning to the glorification of sacred marriage and eternal family life that are part of authentic Christianity and contemporary temple marriage in the restored Church. Indeed, some Western minds are quick to take these symbols—and the literary and artistic expressions on the walls of temples—as a degenerate aberration of original symbols. Perhaps they are right. However, I believe we must look deeper—look into the underlying belief pattern itself. When we do, we find that much of original Buddhist metaphysics is superimposed on all this symbolism. The metaphysics and the belief patterns that spring from them—though split into various schools—involve much stress on the early yogacarin doctrine that the world is utterly unreal, that both the perceived and the perceptor are illusory.

Tantric Buddhism, so interpreted, seeks a transcendent negativism, an arriving (where man is a verb and not a thing) at absolute essence-lessness. The wise man thus initiated is to view himself as "without change, appearance or duality as pure vacuity" and nature as viewed as "infinite, nondual consciousness."[38] That comes close to the total negation of the Mormon axioms of an uncreate, self-existent universe where individuality is eternal, the intensification of life real, extinction impossible, and space and time and their relationships real even for God. Apparent similarity in Tantric symbols turns out to be contrast and antinomy.

Dangers of an Encounter with Other Symbol Systems

In the encounter of symbol systems, many world religious movements can teach us lessons of what to avoid. Consider Islam, a missionary-minded religion that has penetrated almost every land and clime. One may ask whether its expansion has used its own congenial and expressive symbols. The answer of most scholars is that it has not. There is instead much watering-down and accommodation. Technically, Islam claims no priesthood or sacraments and little that is distinct. Moslems share with other religionists a deep fear of images and idols, this in spite of a physicalistic approach to religion. As a result it has often been observed that Islam is without many great artists, especially in painting and sculpture, though its architecture and geometric symbolisms are sublime. Of course, there are organized symbolic prayers, and the doctrine of the five "pillars" can be thought of as symbolic. But even here the stress is functional. The Moslems have settled for the teaching of certain beliefs without the symbols and rituals.

On the other hand, the Church of England, now going through an agonizing reassessment of its traditional prayer book, has from earliest times been elaborately sacramental. "High Episcopal" has meant high ceremonial. Today, in part as a result of the "Liturgical Revival" among Protestants generally, the communion or the Last Supper has been brought into every phase of life, even into work parties and church-sponsored Cub Scout meetings, many times a week. And discussion of the symbolism flourishes. Yet a recent inquiry into the "actual beliefs" of Episcopalians showed that less than 5 percent of the movement's communicants held to the traditional teachings of Anglican theology and philosophy. Here is ritual without belief.

These two tendencies—beliefs without symbols and rituals, or symbols and rituals without beliefs—each may become a religious extreme that we should avoid. Yet these tendencies in Islam and the Church of England are seen in many other movements today; and they pose a threat to us. I therefore now turn to three generalized warnings. I call them (1) radical dualism, (2) pragmatism, and (3) pan-symbolism.

Radical Dualism

We have seen that dualisms, and untenable dualisms, permeate most religions. In the West, for example, are Platonist distinctions of static forms versus the changing flux of perception. In the East the Mahayana Buddhist transforms the ethical beginnings of Buddha into a metaphysical hierarchy that makes the earth nothing and Nirvana everything. In our own theological parlance is the constant distinction between mind and body, between sacred and secular, between earthly and heavenly, between man and god. Within limits these distinctions are useful. But in our encounter with world religions we must strive day and night to avoid the massive classical and historical blunder that asserts that "this world" and "other world" realms are utterly unlike. Religion is degraded to the degree that it builds itself on such dichotomies, because the result is an unpiloted flotilla of symbols. Under these conditions religionists whistle in the dark without even the conviction that what they are whistling is a tune.

In contrast we should continually remind ourselves that the restoration teaches an axiom of continuity. Earth is a high symbol for heaven because each is in process of becoming heaven. (Orson F. Whitney is said to have remarked that one could learn all there is to know of celestial love by studying the ocean.) Time is an adequate symbol of eternity because time is indeed a moment of eternity, and duration will extend to eternity. The body is an appropriate symbol for the spirit because it is in the express image of the spirit and vice versa. The family is a glorious symbol for eternal life because godly life is embodied in eternal family. There is then no absolute distinction between literal and symbolic. Thus to the pseudo question "Is your meaning literal or symbolic?" the appropriate answer is "Usually both." Every word and every symbol has at least one denotation and a mass of connotations. There are, in symbolic usage, primary, secondary, and tertiary meanings. All these combined give a symbol its power. Translation of a symbol into literal propositions will always mean some loss, but not total destruction; and translation of propositions into symbols will mean intensifying the roles we have here outlined.[39]

Pragmatism

In the Orient, especially among the Buddhists, many questions are skirted, avoided, or blanked out by simply maintaining at a profound level (what many Western minds say is a superficial one) that "these questions do not matter." For the Buddhist, for example, the hard question of whether there was in any sense a creator of "Samsara" (illusion) is often viewed as futile. The Buddhist's overall concern is to cope with suffering compassionately, and his overall method is to deny the final metaphysical or ontic status of suffering, and to abandon all attachments, seeking the extinction of desire (Nirvana).

In American culture there is evidence that fewer people care about the truth of religion than about the good or usefulness of religion. One gathers this is in part because of a widespread critical skepticism, reinforced by existentialism, stating that no process in any field can arrive at significant truth. If, therefore, religion matters at all, it must matter on other grounds. These turn out to be practicalistic or utilitarian. Questions of meaning and truth are transformed into questions of usefulness and worth. How often we hear, "We're all seeking the same thing; as long as we're sincere we'll come out all right. What matters is how we live here." Such a trend is manifest in the behavior of a woman I saw enter a temple in Taiwan. She went through a token ceremony of prayer with something of the same expression one sees on the faces of people who are dropping nickels into slot machines. She later confirmed my hasty judgment by explaining that if she did not get her wish she would soon go to another temple. Here we see no vision of self-transformation and few convictions of the import of ultimate questions.

Truth, of course, will always have practical impact; we shall know truth by its fruits. But it does not follow that whatever "works" is therefore worthwhile or, even in a relativistic sense, true. Within limits we have individual permission to invest our own symbols with "given meaning." ("It mattereth not what ye shall eat or what ye shall drink when you partake of the sacrament, if it so be that ye do it with an eye single to my glory" [D&C 27:2].) And in like manner we may invest our own meaning in given symbols (in temple worship we are encouraged to offer up our own most holy desires [see D&C 95:16]). But in the approach to God, not just anything—however sincere—will do. The warning to avoid insoluble mysteries is combined in the Prophet Joseph Smith with the admonition, "I advise all to . . . search deeper and deeper into the mysteries of godliness."[40]

Pan-symbolism

The notion is widespread that symbolism frees man from the need to think logically and consistently, thereby removing him from a mental "straight jacket." Such a notion often derives from the tendencies of radical dualism and pragmatism noted above, i.e., that in religion we are dealing with an utterly transcendent something, or that religion is a practical matter with no strictly true or false doctrines. Following on this, pan-symbolism, as seen by writers as varied as Julian Huxley, Curt J. Ducasse, Phillip Frank, and John Herman Randall, among others, asserts that as all religions have a kind of common, often sociological or psychological root of attraction they should all be given equal status. This is so even though their doctrines and beliefs are incompatible with each other. Interestingly, until recently many scientific and analytic writers held that religion was noncognitive and therefore meaningless. Now, with the pan-symbolism thrust, we are hearing that religious symbols have meaning but that all such meaning is bound to be paradoxical, and the paradoxes are to be glossed over.

Clinical psychologist Jerome Frank, himself an agnostic, has suggested that people's religious sentiments may be processed through their right cerebral hemisphere (which is nonverbal), but that their perceptions of religious meaning come through the left hemisphere (verbal) and from there are translated into dogma, signs, and symbols. The translation is always sufficiently distorted so that disagreement between experience and interpretation is inevitable.[41] The result is a symbolic tower of Babel. The tendency now is to say "never mind."

Here again the Mormon position must remain unequivocal—namely that paradox or self-contradiction does not signify truth, but error. Attempts to warp or bend superficial resemblances into some conglomeration are in the end futile. It is the insight of Joseph Smith that in every falsehood there is something of the sparkle of truth. That is a profoundly important recognition. But from it we should not slip to the notion that there need not be coherence in our symbols or our belief—just a pastiche of pieces that are forced to a contrived overlap, some pieces upside down and others right side up. Not so. The perfect relationship with Christ emerges from the restoration of divine truth; and divine truth, properly understood, is consistent with itself.

We come then to the final plea for reconciliation. It is often said that there are two kinds of mind: one sees unity in diversity, and the other sees diversity in unity. Our missionaries of the future will be under necessity (for we cannot communicate unless we know others' language, including symbol-language) to bring to bear their deepest inspiration and most disciplined study in both the verbal and symbolic languages of the world's religions. As they seek to transform lives, they may turn the multifaceted prisons of various symbol systems into prisms of Christ's truth and Christ's power; turning dead into fruitful trees, turning husks into living corn. Goethe once said that one "who wishes to understand a painter must go to the place where the painter works. We must do so, if only in empathetic imagination.

Meantime, if we avoid both the superficial rejection and the superficial embrace of East-West difference, we shall become far more communicative, far more tolerant, and far richer in our own religious depths.

Footnotes

1. Rudolf Otto, *The Idea of the Holy,* trans. J. W. Harvey, rev. ed., (London: Oxford University Press, 1929), ch. 3–6.

2. There has been more than *one* dispensation and more than one outpouring and downpouring.

3. Mircea Eliade, *The Sacred and the Profane,* trans. Willard R. Trask (New York: Harcourt, Brace and Co., 1959). Eliade summarizes: "the *completely* profane world, the wholly desacralized cosmos, is a recent discovery in the history of the human spirit." One consequence is that modern men are cut off from the sacred or, at least, find it increasingly difficult to rediscover the religious dimension (p. 13).

4. See, for example, Hugh W. Nibley, "Christian Envy of the Temple," *Jewish Quarterly Review* 50 (October 1959 and January 1960):97–123 and 229–40.

5. The scholarly effort to recover the "original intent" of symbols and symbolic usage arrives, at best, at probability statements.

6. Rudolf Bultmann, *Kerygma and Myth* (New York: Harper & Row, 1961). See especially the chapter entitled, "New Testament Mythology."

7. For a critical account of Bultmann's project see Ronald Hepburn, "Demythologizing and the Problem of Validity," in Antony Flew and Alasdair MacIntyre, eds., *New Essays in Philosophical Theology* (New York: Macmillian, 1956), pp. 227–42.

8. This is one of the profound lessons of the allegory of the tame and wild olive trees (Jac. 5–6). Neither the branches nor the roots are to be too much tampered with. Grafting is a dangerous but sometimes a life-saving and life-giving affair (Jac. 5:73).

9. Joseph saw this dispensation as the gathering of all dispensations that would "revolutionize the whole world." (*TPJS,* p. 366.) "New and everlasting" is a contradiction in terms; unless the all-new is also the all-old; unless, in short, it is eternal.

10. Refer to my "Three Theories of Religious Language," *Brigham Young University* Studies 2(Spring-Summer 1960):227–40.

11. Consider as examples the cosmic implications of the signing of a treaty, the salute to an officer, the placing of a crown, or touching the shoulder with a sword. Consider also the temple as a miniature universe; consider how much is contained in the symbolism of the bread and wine in the sacrament, or the symbolism of olive oil.

12. T. W. Manson has observed that Jesus adjusted his teaching mode to the condition of his hearers. To the critical, the bitter, he often answered questions with questions. To those who received him and his initiatory ordinances, he taught and presented himself in direct intimacy. To those between these two extremes he taught in parables. See *The Teaching of Jesus* Cambridge: Cambridge University Press, 1963).

13. John A. Widtsoe, "Temple Worship," *Utah Genealogical and Historical Magazine* 12 (April 1921):63.

14. See, for example, such phenomenological studies as Francis Huxley, *The Way of the Sacred* (New York; Doubleday, 1974).

15. See Carl Jung, *The Undiscovered Self* (New York: New American Library, 1958). See Paul Tillich, *Systematic Theology* (Chicago: University of Chicago Press, 1951–63), 1:131, 170. Also Paul Tillich, *Dynamics of Faith* (New York: Harper & Bros., 1957), pp. 41–54. An astute criticism of Tillich's notion that all religious language must be symbolic, and that religious symbols point beyond the "subject-object distinction" is Paul Edwards, "Professor Tillich's Confusions," *Mind* 74(April 1965):197–206.

16. Jung reports that a girl of eight had a series of uncanny dreams whose images were baffling even to her psychiatrist-father. Jung claims to find in these dreams twelve religious archetypal motifs dealing with the stages of creation, the origins of the world, initiation and rebirth, transformation, apocatastasis (or restitution), destruction, and restoration. So far as Jung could determine, the girl had received little or no apparent conscious teaching on these things. Carl G. Jung, *Man and His Symbols* (New York: Doubleday, 1964), p. 69ff.

Compare Jung's "Transformation Symbolism in the Mass," in *The Mysteries*, Eranos Yearbooks, Bollingen Series, vol. 30, no. 2 (New York: Pantheon Books, 1955), p. 329. "Self-recollection is gathering together of the self.... This approximation to the self is a kind of repristination or apocatastasis, in so far as the self has an 'incorruptible' or 'eternal' character on account of its being pre-existent to full consciousness."

17. For the problems this dualism poses see Ronald E. Santoni, ed., *Religious Language and the Problem of Religious Knowledge* (Bloomington: Indiana University Press, 1968), pp. 129–97. Both Hināyāna and Mahāyāna Buddhists offer literal characterizations of Nirvana. But these are most negative: "inexpressible," "unconstituted," "not avhava" (absence), "inconceivable." But it seems clear that individuality ceases. Such metaphorical language is used as "like a flame returns to pure fire." But this, it is claimed, is "beyond anything whatsoever perceived or cognized." Many forms of Western Christian mysticism are likewise negative. See E. J. Thomas, *The History of Buddhist Thought*, 2d ed. (New York: Barnes & Noble, 1951), pp. 230–48, and *The LIfe of Buddha as Legend and History* rev. 3d ed. (London: Routledge & Kegan, Paul, 1949).

18. In its positive estimate of the flesh and its unequivocal insistence on the physical resurrection as a step up, a transforming and redeeming process, Mormonism cuts between the standard options of materialism vs. spiritualism and idealism vs. naturalism. Equally radical is the notion that the spirit-body is itself physical in character and that this is not a contradiction of terms.

19. Ordinances, especially temple ordinances, recapitulate man's entire existence. See Widtsoe, "Temple Worship," pp. 49–64.

20. John and Jane Dillenberger have been joint-fellows of a study of nineteenth-century American religious art. John Dillenberger observed to me personally: "There is something of everything in Mormonism." More accurately, there is something of Mormonism in everything. For a study of how style and form manifest particular religious concerns see Jane Dillenberger, *Style and Content in Christian Art* (New York: Abingdon Press, 1965).

21. In the first chapters of the Book of Mormon, for example, there is interweaving of a vision-revelation of the ministry of Christ and the many-leveled symbolism of the Tree of Life. And note the following comments on "types and shadows:" Mosiah 13:10; Al. 13:16; 25:10, 15; 33:19; 37:45; Eth. 13:6; and 2 Ne. 11:4—"All things which have been given of God from the beginning of the world, unto man, are the typifying of him."

22. Victor Warnach, "Symbols as Vehicles of the Sacred," *Ways of Being Religious*, ed. Frederick J. Streng, Charles L. Lloyd, Jr., and Jay T. Allen (Englewood Cliffs, N.J.: Prentice-Hall, 1973), pp. 149–55.

23. The name of God properly pronounced was sacred, even unspeakable, in Israelite history. Exact sounds of the vowels are believed able to penetrate the veil as no other sound. Thus the very structure of names, given and spoken, has religious significance beyond the ordinary.

24. Eliza R. Snow, "Again We Meet around the Board," in *Hymns,* (Salt Lake City: The Church of Jesus Christ of Latter-day Saints, 1948), no. 242.

25. Abraham Joshua Heschel, "Symbolism and Jewish Faith," in *Religious Symbolism,* ed. F. Ernest Johnson (New York: Harper and Brothers for The Institute for Religious and Social Studies, 1955), pp. 56–62.

26. Commenting on the figurative use of "beasts" in the Apocalypse of John, Joseph Smith taught: "A beast is never used to represent the Church but man in his degenerate state having become like brute Beasts." But the figures are also literal. In the Revelation, "John saw things in heaven, beasts, women, etc. ... he saw (as the Hebrew says) the images of Beasts. Rev. 5:13 proves that John saw Beasts in Heaven and heard them speak praise to God (though we) do not know what language they speak." "Joseph Smith Papers," April 1843, Church Historical Department, Salt Lake City. Cf. Joseph Fielding Smith, comp. *Teachings of the Prophet Joseph Smith,* (Salt Lake City: Deseret Book, 1938), pp. 290–92; hereafter cited as *TPJS.*

27. This is the view of extreme mysticism, Western as well as Eastern. Revelation, on such a view, is by strict definition impossible, except "revelation" that the mystery is mysterious. And all theology, including symbolist theology, is viewed as an attempt "to say the unsayable."

28. On this score it is interesting that the Inspired Version of the Bible modifies the so-called Pauline dualisms, especially in the Book of Romans. The war is not between flesh and spirit, but between the unregenerate flesh and inspired spirit. For the Christ-reborn man, the objective is not to keep oneself unspotted from the world but "unspotted from the vices of the world" (James 1:27, IV).

29. There is a widely-held distinction between "spectator awareness" and "participative awareness." See for example, Kurt F. Reinhardt, *The Existentialist Revolt* (Milwaukee: Bruce Publishing Co., 1952), pp. 228–43.

30. This, I take it, is the intent of the modern admonition: "Nevertheless thy vows shall be offered up in righteousness on all days and at all times" (D&C 59:11). Man is himself described in modern revelation as a living temple (see D&C 93:35). The building of one is symbolic of Elijah: "The power of Elijah is to that of Elias what, in the architecture of the Temple of God, those who seal or cement the stone to their places are to those who cut or hew the stones, the one preparing the way for the other to accomplish the work." "Joseph Smith Papers," Church Historical Department, Salt Lake City, Utah, Discourse of Sunday, March 10, 1844. Cf. *TPJS,* pp. 335–41.

31. Music reaches levels of awareness that words cannot. It is therefore interesting that Joseph Smith said that Adamic language was spoken *and sung* by our first parents, suggesting that speaking was singing, or that in the speaking there was something musical. On one occasion when Elizabeth Ann Whitney sang in the Adamic language, the interpretation was "rejoicing and praise to the great Author and Giver of good." See "General Meeting of the Relief Society," 17 July 1880. Church Historical Department, Salt Lake City, Utah. A related question is whether writing can ever be as moving as speaking or singing.

32. Alma says of this, "a type was raised up in the wilderness," meaning a type or symbol of the Son of God. Few understood, he writes, and many would not even look, too hardened to believe (or to recognize?) that "whosoever would look upon it might live" (Al. 33:18–21).

33. *Latter-Day Saints' Millennial Star* 20:423.

34. For a study of serpent-symbolism in ancient mystery cults and parallels in Greek, Roman, Phoenician, and Gnostic writings, and their echoes in the Christian world, see Hans Leisegang. "The Mystery of the Serpent," *The Mysteries,* pp. 194–260.

For the Egyptian treatment of this ambivalent symbol see Hugh W. Nibley, *The Message of the Joseph Smith Papyri* (Salt Lake City: Deseret Book, 1975), pp. 177–81.

35. "I assure the Saints," said Joseph Smith, "that truth, in reference to these matters, can and may be known through the revelations of God in the way of His ordinances, and in answer to prayer" (*TPJS* p. 325). Recent research (for example, by Johannine scholar Raymond E. Brown) suggests that the use of the term "mystery" in the New Testament can often be properly read "ordinances." That identification is clear in D&C 84:19–21. See Raymond E. Brown's *The Semitic Background of the Term "Mystery" in the New Testament* (Philadelphia: Fortress Press, 1968).

36. Deep in Judaic tradition is the concept of collective responsibility—the idea that the whole nation, the whole of Israel, exists as one identity, and that all individuals must be regarded in its sacrifices, its guilts, its blessings. (The idea that "they without us cannot be made perfect"?) Hence the seriousness of being cut off, or severed.

37. Karl Duncker argues that ethical clashes that seem irresolvable because of emotion or custom may at root be ideational. The question is "What does a person think he is doing when he performs a certain act?" See his "Ethical Relativity," *Mind* 48(January 1939):39–57. The question applies to ceremonial as well as ethical behavior.

38. S. N. Dasgupta, *Introduction to Tantric Buddhism* (Cambridge: University Press, 1955).

39. On the translatability question, see Paul Henle's "Metaphor" in *Language, Thought, and Culture,* ed. Paul Henle (Ann Arbor: University of Michigan Press, 1958), pp. 173–95.

40. *TPJS,* p. 364.

41. Jerome Frank, "Sources and Function of Belief Systems" (paper delivered at the American Psychological Association Annual Convention, Washington, D.C., September 14, 1976.

MORMON DOCTRINE AND TRADITIONAL JAPANESE PATTERNS: SUGGESTIONS FROM A CULTURE OF SIGHT

Seiji Katanuma

Language is the vehicle of culture, and words are an index for culture. It is confirmed knowledge that language is the key element for the understanding of culture. It provides the system of "phonetic symbols for the expression of communicable thought and feeling."[1] Hence we may reasonably assume that a proper approach to taking the gospel to another culture should be made through a historical and psychological understanding of the target culture's language. Such an approach for the Japanese people is now possible, largely, if not completely, by research on the consciousness of the Japanese people's usage of *Kanji* (Chinese characters). We shall see how a proper knowledge of this is important to the successful expansion of the Church in Japan.

Starting from relevant information about language and culture, let me discuss several features of the Japanese language and show how these relate to Japanese culture and tradition and, ultimately, to the thought patterns of the Japanese people.

We will need to go back to the ancient and uncertain times of Japan in order to know how the Japanese began to employ Kanji. The written Chinese characters the ancient Japanese first began to use represented, in Chinese, monosyllables. For example, the Chinese will merely say "*Wo gei ni*" (我給你), three syllables which mean "I give you" in English. But the same sentence in Japanese takes eleven syllables: "*wa-ta-shi-wa-a-na-ta-ni-a-ge-ru*." Thus the ancient Japanese people's use of Kanji was quite different from that of the Chinese. Accordingly, Kanji as a symbolic system was, in fact, a very indirect and clumsy system of writing for the ancient Japanese people. The history of the use of Kanji has been in essence the long attempt to develop a unique system of symbolism based on the sounds and meanings of Japanese words while utilizing Chinese characters for their written expression.

As sounds multiplied and time went on, the Japanese gradually acquired many Kanji. *Manyoshu* (Collection of Ten Thousand Leaves), which is the oldest and largest anthology of Japanese poetry (dating from approximately A.D. 313–759), is the real evidence showing progress in the art of writing with Kanji. Here is a poem from that anthology attributed to the Emperor Yuryaku, who lived from A.D. 418 to 479. You will note that in this example the ancient Japanese put one Kanji to each Japanese syllable.

ko mo yo mi ko mo chi fu ku shi mo yo
籠毛與 美籠母乳 布久思 毛與

mi bu ku shi mochi kono oka ni na tsuma su ko
美夫君志持 此岳尓 菜採 須兒

ie ki kana na nora sa ne sora mi tsu
家吉閑 名 告 紗根 虚見津

Yama to no kuni wa o shi na be te ware ko soore
山 跡 乃國 者 押 奈戸手 吾 許曾居

shi ki na be te ware ko so ore ware ko so wa
師 吉 名 倍手 吾 己曾座 我 許背歯

nora me ie o mo na o mo
告目 家 呼 毛 名 雄母

(籠: basket 毛: hair 與: give 美: beauty 母乳: mother's milk)

The following is a translation[2] of the poem that has *not* been done by taking the meaning of each word like "basket," "hair," "give," "beauty," "mother's milk."

> Your basket, with your pretty basket,
> Your trowel, with your little trowel,
> Maiden, picking herbs on this hillside,
> I would ask you:
> Where is your home?
> Over the spacious Land of Yamato
> It is I who reign so wide and far,
> I myself, as your lord, will tell you
> Of my home and my name.

Here is another poem by Yamabe no Akahito, who died about A.D. 736. In this one we see that each syllable does not require a separate Kanji.

kudara *no* *no*
百濟 野 乃

hagi no
芽

furu *e* *ni*
古 枝 尓

haru *matsu* *to*
待 春 跡

ori *shi* *uguisu*
居 之 鸎

naki *ni* *ke* *mu* *kamo*
鳴 尓 鷄 鵡 鴨

The translation is as follows:[3]

> In Kudara field
> upon the withered branches
> of lespedeza,
> waiting long for spring to come,
> has the uguisu sung?

As the centuries passed, the ancient Japanese people came to intertwine Kanji with their thoughts and feelings. Kanji thus grew from a descriptive language to a symbolic system which facilitated their expressing freely what they thought and felt. Accordingly, the more the Japanese became familiar with Kanji, the more they came to recognize its features not as mere sound units but also as meaning-carrying units. Hence each Kanji could take on polysyllabic representation, examples of which we saw in the second poem above. In such a development of recognizing Kanji we may presume that the ancient Japanese could feel the Kanji as an ideograph. For this reason, a poet wrote "我妹子我" which is pronounced *wa ga mo ko ga*, meaning "my lover" in English. The poet wanted to embrace his lover by writing two *ga* (我)—which means "I" in English—one on each side of his lover, *moko*. In this manner, as the ideographic features of Kanji became associated with the Japanese way of thinking, Kanji led the Japanese language to the development of complex symbols expressing sentiment and feeling.

My next explanation is an extremely serious one. If I am asked what the Japanese word *kikan* means to me, I find that many *kikans*, as sounds, begin to run parallel in my brain to many Kanjis. The word *kikan* is dissociated from any particular meaning and is only intelligible to me when I see the Kanji for the word. The reason I get into a cold sweat with the word is that there are twenty *kikans* in Japanese, each with three syllables: ki-ka-n. It is for this reason that we feel such an attachment to the Kanji usage. Our language does not work well without it.

As a further illustration, Junichiro Tanizaki, one of the best modern novelists in Japan, could not help using a nuance evoked by both *Kanji* and *Kanamoji*.[4] In his book *Bunshō Tokuhon*, he described this as follows:

It is a tangible fact that words in Kanji and words in Kana have a nuance which seems deeply to affect the content. We do well to admit that writers should be very careful how and when they use Kanji, and just the same with Kana.[5]

Tanizaki's sure grasp of this subject matter in our language clearly helps explain why protests arose against the Japanese National Railroads for its proposal to change the Kanji names on the signboards of each railroad station going into Hiragana. One man expressed his worry whether he could see the station name when he passed by in an express train. For him, Kanji was not the letters to read but the letters to see. I should like to stress that his predicament is not unlike that of most Japanese.

The important point is that no matter who he may be, a Japanese is led in interpretation *from sound to shape*. Broadly speaking, through seeing Kanji, Japanese people have developed an expression much more strongly connected with seeing than hearing; and that trend has generated vigorous energy within the specific features of Japanese culture. It is my opinion that the Japanese have become accustomed to a unique pattern and way of understanding through seeing Kanji and that, because of this, they are now in a different position from Westerners, most of whom seem to develop their language patterns and way of understanding through hearing. It may be a crude way of putting the matter, but I should like to call our culture one of sight.

Is there any relationship between this so-called culture of sight and the traditional Japanese patterns? Although my exposition has aspects that are unclear, I should like to say yes. The ancient Japanese eyes (accustomed to seeing Kanji as Chinese characters coming originally from graphic symbolism) seemed to have genius for grasping things in a picturesque way. Some examples follow, starting first with a quote from the ancient *Nihongi* ("The Chronicles of Japan").

But in that Land there were numerous Deities which shone with a lustre like that of fireflies, and evil Deities which buzzed like flies.[6]

This description seems to be a painting to express what the deities were. The traditional Kanji characters used in that literary "painting" should be enough to explain why the Japanese people saw nature not scientifically or analytically, but rather picturesquely.

Here, from "Makura no Soshi" ("Pillow Sketches"), is another good example:

In spring, I love to watch the dawn grow gradually whiter and whiter, till a faint rosy tinge crowns the mountain's crest, while slender streaks of purple cloud extend themselves above.

In summer, I love the night, not only when the moon is shining, but the dark too, when the fireflies cross each other's paths in their flight, or when the rain is falling.

In autumn, it is the beauty of the evening which most deeply moves me, as I watch the crows seeking their roosting-place in twos and threes and fours, while the setting sun sends forth his beams gorgeously as he draws near the mountain's rim. Still more is it delightful to see the lines of wild geese pass, looking exceeding small in the distance. And when the sun has quite gone down, how moving it is to hear the chirruping of insects or the sighing of the wind!

In winter, how unspeakably beautiful is the snow! But I also love the dazzling whiteness of the hoar-frost, and the intense cold even at other times. Then it is meet quickly to fetch charcoal and kindle fires. And let not the gentle warmth of noon persuade us to allow the embers of the hearth or of the brazier to become a white heap of ashes![7]

And the following poem by Ikkyu, one of the Zen priests[8] who had constantly speculated upon the philosophical subject of "What is the heart?" also has a good deal to say about this point, especially about the religious implications. Yet Ikkyu did not look at the subject as would Socrates, Aristotle, or any of the other Western philosophers. He merely composed a poem and said:

And what is it, the heart?
It is the sound of the pine breeze
there in *the painting.*[9]

I have offered value judgments on some characteristics of Japanese culture and language, and I have given some examples that allow us certain observations and interpretations. Before abstracting the schemata of the traditional Japanese patterns from these examples, however, I should like to tell you about Buddhistic paintings in the early days of the history of Japan, an artistic school that developed extraordinarily in our country. One of these famous paintings is of a mountain called *Shumisen* (*Sumeru* in Pali) and another of a mountain called *Ryojusen* (*Grdhrakuta* in Pali). The former was imagined as the highest mountain in the center of the world, the latter as the mountain on which Gotama preached the Nirvana. The last painting I must mention is one called *Azabu Sansui Ga* (the painting of a mountain and a river on a patch of hemp) which also shows the Nirvana.

In pursuing the traditional Japanese patterns of language and thought, I should like to ask why in Japan so many paintings symbolic of the religious world could be so extraordinarily well elaborated. The way the ancient Japanese acquired their way of thinking is the key. Buddhist priests in the early days of Japan reasoned that there were no other symbols than those paintings by which to preach the Nirvana to the Japanese people because those people were traditionally in a culture of sight saturated by Kanji to which they had become accustomed.

Before discussing further, let me provide a summary of the traditional Japanese patterns through the examples I gave you.

1. Generally speaking, the Japanese people characteristically think and understand by proceeding from "sound" to "shape" as the center of their consciousness.
2. For this reason, they are apt to feel secure only when they have a concrete "image" monitoring between "sound" and "shape".
3. They also have a patterned behavior to see things around them more emotionally than scientifically or analytically.
4. It is a distinguishing fact that the Japanese people's way of understanding is not logical, as in the example of the Zen priest Ikkyu.

Starting from these points, as you can readily understand, our methods of teaching the gospel in Japan have become much more advanced than ever before. Because of the "culture of sight" it is possible for us to use to great benefit some very spiritual films like *Man's Search for Happiness, Meet the Mormons, Christ in America,* and *Ancient America Speaks.* And then each of the missionaries has his flipchart with him to reinforce the concepts of the Uniform System for Teaching Families. Such a method should be given much attention in the future, because of its appropriateness to the way of thinking and understanding I have already explained. There is no doubt that we must develop and refine this method. The point is how to satisfy the demands of Japanese epistemology.

For this purpose, let me speak briefly about the Uniform System for Teaching Families, which contains nine topics (including fifty-five main concepts) as follows: (1) Family Home Evening; (2) The Restoration; (3) Eternal Progression; (4) Continuing Revelation and Individual Responsibility; (5) Truth versus Error; (6) Baptismal Challenge; (7) Obedience to the Lord's Commandments Brings His Blessings; (8) Our Relationship to Christ; (9) Members in the Kingdom. This is spiritually a well-organized form for helping those who have never been touched by the gospel. If, however, proper attention were given to the Japanese culture of sight, this Uniform System would be organized as a visible rather than verbal system. The main form of communication would therefore be visual. The reason why I boldly say so is that verbal communication, particularly through conversation, seems to be inflexible for preaching the gospel, particularly to the Japanese, but perhaps also to other nations.

For Japanese, at least, it is much better to make visual aids the main communicative system and use verbal communication only as a supplement. There are several reasons I would like to review and further explicate. First, the Japanese people are fundamentally not good at verbal communication. An example can be found in the Japanese version of the Uniform System. The English says: "And that's why our *conversation* today can help you and your family—each of you—to know and feel a personal relationship with the Master." (Before explaining this point, please just imagine that this would be the first time that most Japanese would be listening to the gospel.) The Japanese translation of this passage is as follows: "*Watashitachi wa sono koto ni tsuite* ohanashi *shi, kazoku no minasan ga Shu to kojinteki na kankei ni aru koto o shiri, mata kanjite itadakitai to omotte imasu.*" The key words to consider here are those emphasized in each passage—*conversation* and *ohanashi,* the latter allegedly being a translation of the former. When we consult an English-Japanese dictionary to find the Japanese word for "conversation," the dictionary gives us "kaiwa," "danwa," "zadan," and "kaidan." That is all. The word "ohanashi" does not appear. What, then, is the meaning of the word "ohanashi"? The sound "o" is a prefix to indicate respect and politeness. And "hanashi" means "to tell a story." Did the translator make a mistake with such a simple word? Of course not. He probably felt that the word *conversation* strictly translated by such words as *kaiwa, danwa*, and so forth did not fit into the Japanese mentality.

What do you Americans do when you want to initiate a conversation? You ask, and the person you ask can frankly say no, and does so more frequently than saying yes. I also know that you can ignore hierarchical differences among you. You just call one another "John" or "Seiji." You sometimes touch a man on the shoulder, knee, or hand to stress your thought. In this manner you can have a real conversation. On the other hand, we Japanese people, after bowing with much care so as not to be impolite or inappropriate, begin to speak quietly and never express ourselves too much.

The second reason why the gospel should be communicated with a visible rather than verbal system is because verbal communication seems to be too logical for the Japanese. This is, of course, closely related to the fact that Japanese never express themselves verbally too much. Most Japanese like to understand in the way that Ikkyu did rather than the way Socrates would do in a "dialogue."

In the third place, it is true that some concepts in Mormon doctrine are so unfamiliar to the Japanese people that they are difficult to fit into the Japanese way of thinking and understanding.

Finally, it is also necessary that the so-called new visible Uniform System should be aimed at helping the communication of the gospel not only across cultural barriers but also among people in a given single culture. Hence, for Japan there should be at least two visual-aid additions: one, to show the whole life of Jesus Christ, the other to show the heart and substance of the genealogical program.

As for Christ's life we have little in the Uniform System about him, except the following paragraph:

From his premortal life, Jesus was born into the world. His mother was Mary and his father was God, our Heavenly Father, under whose direction Jesus had created this world. When he was just thirty-three years old, evil men, who hated him because he taught that he was the Son of God, had him nailed to a cross. After several agonizing hours he died, and his body was taken by his friends and laid in a tomb. When they returned early in the morning of the third day, they found that his body was gone from the tomb. Angels who were there told his friends that he had been resurrected—that he was no longer dead!

With respect to genealogy, we must help the Japanese to grasp the reality of the gospel for the dead, for whom they have a special feeling of respect and attachment anyway.

If such a visual methodology as I have proposed were to be created and effectively used, we would still have to deal with the verbal communication accompanying those well-ordered and organized films. In this the missionaries could make the new system more helpful for teaching each of the concepts by having a tape recorder wherein a native speaker would make a verbal communication to supplement the visual aids (which should remain the main system of communication). This would not be a translated language from American documents but rather the living native tongue expressing the concepts presented in the system of visual communication established for the standard Uniform System. We should then not need to worry about the deviation from the truth of the gospel.

By our employing this system, the following advantages may be obtained:

1. It would be possible to get to the implicitly real in a given culture.
2. Through proper understanding of the people in a given culture, it would be possible to help to a greater degree those who are going to be led to the understanding of the gospel.
3. In the meantime, the people would be able to establish their lives uprightly according to the rules and the commandments and the doctrines of the Church by being taught immediately what is correct or wrong in their traditional cultural patterns.

Let me introduce two examples that will enlighten us on how to grasp real communication.

1. Missionary: Believest thou that there is a God, Mr. Tanaka?
   Mr. Tanaka: I do not know what that meaneth. Is he of such kind that I may see him?
   Missionary: Probably, not always. However, he will surely appear to you if he wants to do so.
   Mr. Tanaka: Does he resemble *Ame no Minakanushi no Kami?*[10]
   Missionary: I do not know what that meaneth. But I think he doth not resemble a god of the gentiles such as thou toldest me.

2.:Missionary: Wilt thou hearken unto my words, if I tell thee by what power I do these things? And this is the thing that I desire of thee.

Mr. Tanaka: Yea, I will believe all thy words.
Missionary: Believest thou that there is a God?
Mr. Tanaka: I do not know what that meaneth.
Missionary: Believest thou that there is a Great Spirit?
Mr. Tanaka: Yea.
Missionary: This is God. Believest thou that this Great Spirit, who is God, created all things which are in heaven and in the earth?
Mr. Tanaka: Yea, I believe that he created all things which are in the earth.

A comparison of these two examples of missionary work is profitable. The first case is not uncommon in my country. Mr. Tanaka, on this occasion, tried to tie the God the missionary was trying to explain to him with the vested concept of a god he has already had. His understanding was cut off halfway, and it may be imagined that he will become uneasy about understanding what the missionary told him. The latter example, on the other hand, seems to be a good one of how to help a person who has a different cultural background. This is a real-life case: the missionary is Ammon, one of the greatest missionaries in the Book of Mormon; Mr. Tanaka is Lamoni, the king ruling over the land of Ishmael (see Al. 18:22-29).

The Western denotation is not always the Japanese denotation, and the Western connotation is not always the Japanese connotation. Your best expression is not always best for us. An understanding on the part of the missionary of a different culture and tradition when he is transmitting the gospel enables us to feel a faint breath of God, too, for the message has a better chance of getting to the heartstrings and emotions of a people.

Footnotes

1. Edward Sapir, *Culture, Language, and Personality* (Berkeley and Los Angeles: University of California Press, 1966), p. 1.

2. Ralph Hodgson, trans., *Anthology of Japanese Literature,* comp. Donald Keene (Rutland, Vt.: Charles E. Tuttle Company, 1955), p. 33.

3. Kenneth Yasuda, trans., *Land of the Reed Plains* (Rutland, Vt.: Charles E. Tuttle Co., 1972), p. 25.

4. The characters for the Japanese phonetic syllabary.

5. Junichiro Tanizaki (1866-1965), born in Tokyo, known as a novelist in the succession of traditional Japanese literature.

6. *Nihongi,* trans. W. G. Aston (Rutland, Vt.: Charles E. Tuttle Co., 1972), p. 64. *Nihongi* or *Nihonshoki* were compiled by Toneri Shinno, Ono Yasumaro and others in A.D. 720.

7. Sei Shōnagon, *Makura Zōshi,* trans. W. G. Aston, as quoted in W. G. Aston, *A History of Japanese Literature* (New York: D. Appleton and Co., 1899), pp. 106–107. The original was written by a Court Lady, Sei Shōnagon, in approximately A.D. 1000.

8. Ikkyu (1394–1481), a Zen priest in the middle of the Muromachi Period (1392–1573).

9. As quoted in Yasunari Kawabata, *Japan the Beautiful and Myself,* trans. Edward G. Seidensticker (Tokyo: Kodansha International, 1968), p. 54 (italics added).

10. Ame no Minakanushi no Kami, the Chief Deity in the center of Heaven in the *Kojiki* (Chronicle of Ancient Matters) compiled in A.D. 712.

TEACHING ACROSS DISPENSATIONS: A COMPARATIVE RELIGIONS PERSPECTIVE ON THE CHALLENGES OF BEING A WORLDWIDE CHURCH

Gordon C. Thomasson

As a preface to my topic, I should like to refer to the recent addition to the standard works of the Church: the Lord's 1836 revelation to Joseph Smith, "Heirs of the Kingdom." Few texts are as potentially useful in helping us understand our place in today's expanding Church and in setting the tone for this symposium. In that revelation the Lord tells us, by implication, that the majority of the inhabitants of the celestial kingdom will be individuals who died before they arrived at the age of accountability. Most of those individuals, given what we know about world population and comparative infant mortality rates, will have been born into a non-American culture. Hence it is clear that even though in this dispensation the gospel has not existed in its fullness among all other races and cultures, the Lord's plan has included an important place for these groups. How many of the Lord's choicest spirit children obtained physical tabernacles and experienced mortality among those peoples? What a beautiful, and perhaps sobering, basis upon which we can begin to appreciate all other races, religions, and cultures, as we prepare to take them the fullness of the gospel.

As we move to fulfill our responsibility of teaching the gospel to more of our Father's children who live on the other side of the religious and cultural gaps that exist between them and the dispensation of the fullness of times, we face numerous challenges. I want to outline some of them. My method is not to talk about a specific and well-defined topic, for the work that will make such a discussion possible has yet to be done. Rather, I seek to begin to define the topic, to draw a number of tangents, as it were, and let those tangents suggest the outline of a circle. One might say I am pounding stakes in the corners of a field we must plow if later we wish to sow and to reap. Much of the land I intend to plow is virgin soil; but some of it may also be sterile. Not certain which condition may prevail, I make no pretension of suggesting what decisions the Brethren should make on specific issues of this discussion. At most ours is the task of providing, given our limitations, the best data we can. My efforts derive from taking the gospel of Jesus Christ as I understand it, and my testimony, through ten years of graduate study on subjects relating to religion.

The phrase "across dispensations" means that the peoples to whom we are to deliver the fullness of the gospel have been influenced by religions that have their origins, at least in part, in apostasies from the many previous dispensations of the gospel. Reaching them is somewhat analagous to the hypothetical task of a present-day North American teaching the gospel to, say, the Galatians of the fourth century A.D. Because of the difficulties implied, we can learn certain lessons that might aid us in our task: We must (1) correct our own and others' misconceptions about the origin, form, and content of the gospel message, (2) carefully define Christ's real message, (3) understand the problems intrinsic to teaching his message across dispensations, and (4) understand the people we are to teach. I also suggest (5) some new methods rooted specifically in important LDS gospel perspectives that may aid us in understanding the gospel message and teaching it to people of widely differing cultures, religions, and value systems. Of course, in all this we must seek the Lord's guidance through the Holy Ghost if our efforts are to be useful. Our efforts, nevertheless, are necessary.

Correcting Misconceptions about the Origin, Form, and Content of the Gospel Message

Joseph Smith was a revolutionary. I do not use the word in the narrow political sense but rather in the same way we apply it to Copernicus.[1] Both men revolutionized certain patterns of thought prevalent in their time. For his part, the Prophet—more than restoring a religion, instituting a new social system, coining a new language, and fathering what Thomas F. O'Dea described as "a native and indigenously developed ethnic minority"[2]—went so far as to reject the core or center of Western consciousness. He elaborated in its place something we might call a gospel-centered consciousness, which creates a whole new view of, and way of speaking about, the universe(s),[3] to say nothing of generating a new and different *Weltanschauung* or world view. And for traditional Christianity, Joseph Smith's "heresy" is much more significant in implication than was Galileo's crime of merely failing to "save the appearances."

The revolutionary mode of Joseph Smith notwithstanding, almost no one in the scholarly world considers the results of his work unique. Instead, we usually find them discussed in terms of environmental determinants or some other sort of intellectual pigeonholing. When we accept or fail to analytically challenge such scholarship, we mislead others and deprive ourselves of the insights to be gained from an accurate understanding of the uniqueness of the Restoration. Such insights should also facilitate a more effective teaching of the gospel message to other cultures. Let us examine critically several common ways by which the uniqueness of the gospel is explained away.

Environmental Determinism

Many discussions of Mormonism offer explanations of Joseph Smith's work based on some form of environmental determinism. Usually some aspect of the Restoration is classified and described as a result of environmental forces supposed to have influenced the history of religions in America as well as the course of the Prophet's life. There are serious flaws in many of the assumptions underpinning such arguments. Consider, for example, that *all* the "elements" existed in the environment in which Alfred Nobel (1833–96) grew up; all the chemicals he combined were well known by his contemporaries. But when Nobel combined seemingly commonplace elements with other everyday items in a new and unprecedented configuration, he launched a revolution in ideas about chemistry. Yet it would be foolish to say that one of Nobel's creations—dynamite—was little more than a product of history. On the contrary, it was a product of Nobel who created a revolutionary synthesis from commonplace elements. So it was with Joseph Smith, although as to whether his creative power derived from inspiration and revelation from God we can only bear testimony.

The elements of a religiocultural system do not exist in isolation any more than do elements of a chemical compound. On the contrary, they interact as part of a whole, and to define one element independent of the part it plays and ignore the way it is unavoidably and significantly different as it develops and is articulated within a system in relation to the other elements is to engage in trivia. When one constituent part is removed from its *Gestalt,* when a symbiotic relationship is ignored, when one member is removed from its ecosystem, any description of it must miss the vital essence of that thing. And when Mormonism as a whole is viewed in contrast and in interaction with other religiocultural systems, its uniqueness is as undeniable as it is informative.

In 1832 Alexander Campbell, angered at the loss of Sidney Rigdon (one of his important followers) and Rigdon's Kirtland congregation, polemized against Mormonism by offering one of the first environmental explanations of the Book of Mormon. Referring to many religious and social questions of the time, Campbell argued that the Book of Mormon contained "every error and almost every truth discussed in N. York for the last ten years."[4] Though subsequent writers do not always exhibit Campbell's antagonism to Mormonism, 140 years later Sydney Ahlstrom, quite devoid of Campbell's particular sort of bias, could still parrot that the Book of Mormon was a reflection of "the total social and spiritual situation of the 'burned-over district' of western New York."[5] As I have stated elsewhere, however,

such an approach ignores the fact that where parallels occur they almost invariably relate to what are perennial questions—themes which recur in countless religious histories—and are by no means unique to the Burned-over District.[6]

If the Book of Mormon treats some themes that recur in countless religious histories (yet not all the themes are by any means predictable), if Mormonism provides answers for the types of questions one could expect almost any religion to face, what of it? That similar religious themes and questions may be found in a variety of religions is hardly significant. The kinds of answers that are given, however, are significant. And it is there that environmental explanations of Mormonism and the Book of Mormon begin to break down. Let us review several environmental explanations that deserve scholarly debunking.

Camp-Meeting Religions

There was a time when writers could get away with explaining Joseph Smith in terms of camp-meeting religion.[7] However, over the years that argument became less satisfactory to Mormonism's antagonists (as environmental determinants of Mormonism always seem to become as one learns more about the hypothetical determinant and its supposed result). Recently, for example, we saw an anti-Mormon, Wesley Walters, do an about-face, rejecting camp-meeting type explanations. He had worked for years to show that camp-meeting revivals did not occur in Palmyra in 1820 and that Joseph Smith's history and his religion are therefore false.[8] Reluctant to say that the Reverend Mr. Walters did not look at the evidence very well, though his anti-Mormon bias is as obvious as Campbell's, I will simply say that he, rather than Joseph Smith, was conditioned by environmental determinants to look for big camp-meeting revivals with large numbers of conversions (and the type of excesses Joseph Smith condemned at Kirtland—a strange turn-around in itself) as the trigger to Joseph's first vision. And Walters could not find any.

On the other hand, within two months of my arrival in the "Burned-over District" (to do research on Southeast Asian religion, not Joseph Smith), I accidentally heard of Allen Wesley Coates; and in February of 1974 two friends and I interviewed him and his brother-in-law, Tobias Edwards. Mr. Coates, a non-Mormon native of Palmyra, ninety-five at the time, told us an interesting story: His grandfather Coates had been a deacon in the Manchester Methodist Church; young Joseph had worked for Deacon Coates; he was a good worker; the deacon had taken Joseph to a "revival" *at the church* just before Joseph "had his vision."[9] So there was a revival. But what influence did it have?—that is a more meaningful question. Yet the point is that Joseph's religion cannot be predicted (or understood) from a knowledge of "Burned-over District" culture, revivalism, or camp-meeting religion.

Fundamentalism

One often hears that Mormonism is fundamentalist. There is a great deal of literature on religious fundamentalism in the United States. But no one can seriously read it and still consider Mormonism to be fundamentalist. On the superficial level someone will say, "But you take certain Bible narratives to be literally true, and that's fundamentalism." And if you stop there, it is; but no fundamentalist will or can accept the qualification of existing scripture "as far as it is translated correctly" (see Articles of Faith 8), or the idea of additional scripture, or even the Mormon understanding of the first verse of Genesis, based on Joseph Smith's translation of the Hebrew, which reads, "At the beginning ... the *Gods* [Elohim], *organized* ... the heavens and the earth" (Abr. 4:1; italics added). And these are only three of countless differences in structure and content between Mormonism and fundamentalist Christian religions. No one can do more than label (or libel) Mormonism when he speaks of it as being fundamentalist. Whether we talk about historical or contemporary fundamentalism, as soon as specifics are cited, the comparison breaks down.

Puritanism

In a similar way we are told that Mormonism is puritanical, especially about sex, and that here the religion was also heavily influenced by traditions in its environment. If *puritanical* is simply used pejoratively, it deserves to be ignored; but when a supposed scholar uses the word to explain Mormonism, one can only wonder. Let me illustrate. Before Parley P. Pratt's conversion, Puritan norms drove him to quasi-monasticism in his cabin on the Ohio frontier; he was trying to get away from the guilt of his love for Miss Thankful Halsey, which in "Puritan" thought reflected a displacement of one's love from God to a degraded human, and was thus seen as a type of idolatry.[10] Joseph Smith, on the other hand, taught Pratt "how to prize the endearing relationships of ... husband and wife" and how to appreciate the "eternal union of the sexes in those inexpressibly endearing relationships ... which are at the very foundation of everything worthy to be called happiness."[11] Neither Joseph Smith nor Brigham Young can be shown to have taught puritanical doctrine. Insofar as puritanical ideas exist as a current within Mormonism, they are post-Restoration imports. Yet the importation is not surprising. As I suggested years ago, we ought to write a history of the Church sensitive to the central fact that up through the 1950s "the Church's history is one of the conversion, assimilation, and reeducation of in large part Calvinist Protestants."[12] That reeducation process is always problematical; it takes a long time, even for the likes of Parley P. Pratt.

Old ideas, such as the still-current false doctrine that sex exists only for procreative purposes, die hard. In 1849 in a meeting of the Council of the Twelve, Parley P. Pratt asked several questions about "connections between spouses." Brigham Young responded first with an observation that

many inhibitions regarding marriage ... resulted from the individuals' early gentile environment—then he stated: "As to sexual connection during pregnancy, just as they please about that, they could suit themselves."[13]

Converts may have brought Puritan ideas with them into Mormonism and may retain them to the present day ("even unto the third and fourth generations"), but unless and until such ideas can no longer in any way be distinguished from the gospel, until the church as a whole accepts and "canonizes" (as it were) the "doctrine"—to call such persisting hangups the *Restoration* is an exercise in literary creativity, not history. If such syncretism ever does occur, then, of course, we have a real problem.

The Book of Mormon on Monarchy

Outsiders often misperceive elements such as puritanism as part of the restored gospel because of a less-than-accurate treatment our own LDS spokesmen have given the matter. Richard L. Bushman tells us of a specific case in point, showing how scholars have viewed the antimonarchical sentiments voiced in the Book of Mormon as environmentally determined by American post-Revolutionary War Rhetoric. Yet Bushman demonstrates how a careful study of the Book of Mormon text exhibits no such correlation.[14] But the chapter headnotes, added much later, do imply such a correlation; and many non-Mormons made their judgments of outside influence based on the headnotes to the chapters rather than on the text itself.

Masonry

In a similar vein, scholars dealing with topics such as Masonry and Mormonism would have few problems if they were really to compare such topics with adequate data. The fact that correlations can be made between Mormonism and Masonry is insignificant compared with the correlations that can be made with much more ancient traditions[15] that were not a part of Joseph Smith's "information environment."[16] To suggest that *A* (that is, Masonry) was significantly related to *B* (Mormonism), or to imply that *A* may have influenced *B*, especially when minimal research would also show that if *A* somehow did influence *B* it resulted in *B's* looking more like *C* than *A* will almost certainly lead to misunderstandings among Mormons and non-Mormons and to the perpetuation of such views in scholarship generally.[17] I have yet to find an environmental explanation of Mormonism that, when pursued, does not beg or raise more questions than it answers, nor one that escapes the problems inherent in such types of "if I were a horse I would do . . ." and "just-so story" explanations of religion that E. E. Evans-Pritchard so effectively critiques in his *Theories of Primitive Religion.*[18]

Environmental determinists will continue to theorize. Yet to the degree that Mormonism is accurately described and studied, their theories will become more and more obviously absurd. For example, rather than challenge the validity of the mounting body of evidence in favor of the authenticity of the Book of Mormon, environmental determinists may follow the amazing lead of Åke V. Ström in his "Red Indian Elements in Early Mormonism." In this work Ström held that "it is not impossible that an Indian nurse or neighbour could have furnished the receptive boy [Joseph Smith] with old Lenape material" that found its way into the Book of Mormon and Mormonism.[19]

Whether one studies Mormon economics, Mormon city planning, or Mormonism's peculiar complex of *rites de passage,*[20] environmental explanations are inadequate because, as Evans-Pritchard said:

> *We have to account for religious facts in terms of the totality of the culture and society in which they are found, to try to understand them in terms of what the* Gestalt *psychologists called the* Kulturganze, *or of what Mauss called* fait total. *They must be seen as a relation of parts to one another within a coherent system, each part making sense only in relation to the others, and the system itself making sense* only in relation to *other institutional systems, as part of a wider set of relations.*[21]

While every individual is in some degree influenced by his environment, the only times environmental determinants have been found to provide significant and viable perspectives into the origin of Mormonism are when they serve a negative function. The indisputable message of the First Vision was that there was an alternative to the environmental influences troubling the young Joseph. Often we find Joseph Smith responding to other religious ideas and practices, using them as foils against which to make gospel concepts clear by contrast. While such environmental factors can "elicit" principles of the gospel, such an influence can hardly be said to have created them.

The Difficulty of Comparative Approaches

I have argued that Mormonism is unique and cannot be explained by its environment. But can we help people to understand something unique simply by explaining it in terms of itself? Obviously this is harder than drawing parallels between it and something known. Yet, while generally less mischievous than environmental explanations, comparative discussions of Mormonism that would shed authentic light on the religion, if we use Evans-Pritchard's criteria, are difficult to produce. One main problem is that there can never be a one-to-one correspondence between the elements of different religious systems, let alone the languages that are used to describe them or to make them function.[22] Let us look at the problem of languages as a simple illustration of the dilemma.

Full translation from German into our Germanic-based English language is often effectively impossible. As Professor Ernst Benz expressed it:

> *And how can one possibly express in English the meaning of the German* Geist? *All the terms available—spirit, ghost, mind, reason, reasonableness—prove to be inadequate. They imply at the most one single element of the complex German term* Geist. *More difficult still proved to be the attempt to translate ontological terms. In trying to give the different meanings of* sein, Wesen, Wesenheit, Wesenhaftkeit, Substanz, Essenz, *not to speak of translating terms like* Nichts, Nichtsein, Nichtigkeit *and* Ungrund, *I met repeatedly with the adamant resistance of the English language. . . . But this difficulty of translation of one European language into another is a simple matter compared to the attempt to translate a European language into an Asiatic one.*[23]

And when we move from discussing the same system in different languages to describing one system to persons of other systems, or in terms of other systems, the language and conceptual problem becomes compounded. Moreover, explaining two systems in terms of a third, even a hypothetical one, is no more certain. Ideal types, theoretical reconstructions of the history of religions—whatever the methodology, we face problems in communicating an accurate picture by the comparative method.

Eduard Meyer studied and wrote about Mormonism, compared it to Islam, and put both within the framework of his own theoretical understanding of religion. Few scholars have been more broadly prepared to attempt such a comparative task. Yet no one takes Meyer's work seriously today, and the manifold ways in which it unintentionally misrepresents Mormonism have been amply discussed.[24]

The most formal attempt to explain Mormon theology by the comparative method was described by its author as:

a comparative commentary that is intended simply to differentiate Mormon doctrine from the classical Christian theology. . . . Comparisons are solely in the interest of facilitating an understanding of Mormonism.[25]

Even this careful attempt fails because its author has been trained in (as have most of us) and relies on a language and logic—and I mean standard English and Western logic—that are in many ways unsuitable for a discussion of Mormonism.

Let me illustrate. Some years ago I participated in a seminar on comparative religions under Matthias Vereno, an Austrian phenomenologist and historian of religion. While the main focus of the seminar was methodology, specific presentations dealt with various religious traditions. I chose to discuss Mormonism. Having received a great deal of training in methodological approaches to the study of religion (with as diverse scholars as Thomas F. O'Dea and Mircea Eliade) I had—on my own—stepped back and applied methods and models ranging from Van Gennep's to Husserl's to the restored gospel as I understand it. The results were astounding to me, and I therefore determined to explore others' reactions to my conclusions. Since all those participating in the seminar were familiar with the work of and had studied with O'Dea, I knew that I would have to find an approach that would cause them to question his thoughtful but nevertheless thoroughly Western approach to Mormonism.[26] I would also need to make them question their generally environmental determinist view of the Restoration as a product of the "Burned-over District" of upstate New York.

I began my discussion by asking those present what they could conceptualize as the end-product of Marx's classless society, given the possibility of such a society's being realized. After a short discussion, it was agreed that people would be moral and just, and that they would approach some sort of behavioral perfection. At that point I suggested that while the "necessary" social revolution progressed to a classless society, we might also expect scientific revolutions to continue, such as we have seen in the progress of medicine in previous decades. The ultimate question confronting medicine would eventually be why cell tissues lose their ability to reproduce themselves with vigor and why what we call aging therefore occurs. If human tissue could be made to continue to reproduce itself, barring accidents or new diseases, mankind would become effectively immortal. I then asked the group what word in the English language would most accurately describe a person who was both morally perfect and physically immortal. Their uncomfortable answer was that such a being might be called a god.

At that point I introduced the members of the seminar to Brigham Young's explanation to Lorenzo Snow concerning the nature of God: "as God was, so are we now; as he now is, so shall we be."[27] It took all that to partially break through a communication barrier. It was just as Professor Benz had written in relation to an understanding of Buddhism:

From Christian lecterns and pulpits we hear proclaimed in noisy and confident terms detailed information concerning the essence of god, ... [but] our traditional theological ideas and concepts of God are a serious obstacle in understanding. . . .[28]

Even after commenting on the intended literalness of Brigham Young's theomorphic anthropology and the implication that, for Mormons, God's existence preceded his essence, there was still a great deal of puzzlement among members of my seminar group with their Judeo-Christian background. So I continued my presentation by elaborating on B. H. Roberts's "Limitation in the Attributes of God" (those being his eternity, immutability, omnipotence, omniscience, and omnipresence).[29] Someone then commented that this radically finite (to say nothing of evolutionary) theism really could not even be compared to Alfred North Whitehead's speculations.

I then tried to make the point that to study Mormonism one had to determine what it was *not!* Thus I presented them an opportunity to attempt to bracket the many presuppositions they held. I intentionally left them to ponder (along with brief descriptions of Mormon views of evil, cosmology, and authority) how the gospel could be described except through a methodological approach that recognized and tried to appreciate this unique phenomenon in terms of itself.

Rejecting the Already Shaken Foundations

In considering further ways to correct our own and others' misconceptions about the origin, form, and content of the gospel message, we should keep additional observations in mind. The main point to be made in beginning a study of Mormonism, either for missionary teaching or scholarly purposes, is that it rejects, and must be understood as rejecting, the very foundations of Western consciousness. Consider the amazing verbal tendency of Greek-influenced cultures and languages that in turn have influenced us. Consider also the incredible influence on our thinking of Platonic (and neo-Platonic) idealism and Aristotelian either/or logic. Disregarding for now any possible linguistic "deep structures," these factors have a greater influence on our language and thinking (and this includes speakers of standard English, all of Europe's culture groups, and those non-Westerners who have received Western-style educations, especially on the higher levels) than any others. Yet it is precisely these foundations—Platonic idealism and Aristotelian either/or logic—that Joseph Smith rejected as he became involved in the process of the Restoration. This involved more than the mere rejection of specific traditional religious concepts; e.g. "there is no such thing as immaterial matter" (see D&C 131:7–8). The Prophet's denial of a meaningful distinction or qualitative difference between spirit and matter underlies and is woven throughout the entire belief-structure that is Mormonism, from our concept of the nature of God(s) to our material conception of the celestial kingdom, and thereby illustrates his radical departure from the established ways of thinking about many things. Mormonism, insofar as it could have a "systematic theology" (which is a good example of an obviously inappropriate Western concept, due to the necessary open-ended nature or incompleteness of a process-like expanding gospel based on continuing revelation), is logically quite consistent and coherent within itself. Section 131 of the Doctrine and Covenants, while written in 1843, does not reflect any change in approach—only a making-explicit of that which is found throughout the Latter-day scriptures.

On the other hand, Augustine (A.D. 354–430), one of the key figures in the transition from classical antiquity to the Middle Ages, like most of his thoroughly Hellenistic Judeo-Christian counterparts (to say nothing of his predecessors or those who followed him), "read the books of the Platonists and had been set by them towards the search for a truth that is incorporeal, [he] came to see Your [that is, God's] invisible things which are understood by the things that are made,"[30] thereby effectively splitting God from man and the universe. Not so with Joseph Smith, who rejected such alienating bifurcations.

Along with rejecting the radical otherness and incomparability of God (a function of either/or logic as well as idealism), Joseph consistently gave answers to gospel questions that were of a *both/and* rather than an *either/or* nature. He had ample experience with such an approach in the Book of Mormon. Take the question of the morality of war. Rather than an either/or or a man-based situational ethic, we find in the Book of Mormon an affirmation of "absolutes" that depend on and are relevant only to the particular situation, and determinable only through continuing revelation.[31] Late in Joseph's life we are not surprised to find him articulating the eternally subordinant though somehow not inferior relationship we have with him whom we call God the Father by discussing the idea of there being a plurality of Gods. Indeed, throughout the teachings of the Restoration we find a consistent and coherent though non-Aristotelian approach.

These kinds of differences constitute the essence of the Restoration's "heresy." It is not a simple differing on specific doctrinal points or social practices, but a thoroughgoing and constant rejection of the Greek philosophical foundations of Western religious and secular thought. And it is here that we find the most basic flaw in virtually all discussions of and attempts to translate and teach Mormonism. The failure to recognize that Mormon thought cannot be validly approached or adequately analyzed with the same categories usually applied to Western thought plagues individual Mormons as well as scholars. Western categories simply will not work. To use them results only in distortion.

East Is East and West Is . . .?

What, then, is Mormonism? What, as my title suggests, is to be taught across dispensations? And why is the task of teaching such a challenge? We have begun by saying that Mormonism is a fundamentally non-Western religion (in that it rejects the foundations of Western thought). But we must immediately qualify that by saying that its being non-Western does not necessarily place it in the same category with an Oriental, Asian, African, or native American religion either; for while all of these are non-Western religions, their relationship to the gospel is no more straightfoward than is that of the so-called Western religions. Besides, because of increased East-West contacts, these categories are today less useful than ever.

The categories are less useful because diffusion is again increasingly being recognized as one factor among many which must be accounted for in history. But even the diffusion model cannot be a simplistic one—with culture-patterns repeated in xerox-type copies radiating out in ever-spreading waves from a single center to one society after another. Moreover, it is also recognized that mere contact of one culture with another is not so important as influence, and that in most contacts where influence also occurs the influence is often two-way. Thus models must be rather complex in order to be informative.[32] Whether we speak of Judaism before Alexander the Great (when it was considered an Oriental religion), or the influence of Greco-Roman art in developing a pictorial vocabulary in Buddhism (which in large part molded the Mahāyāna tradition), or the presence of (almost certainly Indian) gymnosophists in second- and third-century A.D. Alexandria, diffusion must be taken into account. And while we can debate with Sir Mortimer Wheeler as to the degree of "imprinting" that resulted from diffusionary "impacts" in the particular case, to ignore the interrelatedness of Old World cultures, East and West, has been a fool's venture ever since Sir Aurel Stein documented the old land silk routes from Rome to China. So, too, more than spice flowed along the land and sea routes from Europe to Southeast Asia—as images of Roman deities dug up at Oc-Eo on the Southwest coast of Vietnam testify. Finally, the link of the New World to the Old—of the Western to the Eastern hemisphere—is also becoming more evident every day.

In the past, discussions of diffusion, like discussions of Mormonism that employ other types of environmental determinist arguments, were unproductive precisely because the "explanations" were given as final answers to put an end to discussion. In earthly probation, though we are unique individuals, the main test is *how* we exist in interdependent relationships with God, his children, and the earth. There will always be contacts with the world, and what is important is the *quality* of the interactions that occur—not whether they occur—how we influence others, and if we allow ourselves to be influenced by them. Mere contact does not prove influence, as Christ tried to point out to those who criticized his dining with sinners and publicans (Matt. 9:10–13). And even though contact has occurred and a resemblance exists between the actions of two groups or persons who came in contact, that does not prove one significantly influenced the other. Environmental factors *can* have influence, but it rests with anyone who suggests such relationships to prove: (1) that contact in fact occurred, and (2) that significant influence resulted from the contact. But, given that we exist in interrelation with other groups, how can we most effectively reach and influence them without compromising the integrity of the gospel? First, we must understand the gospel.

There Is More to Language Than Meets the Ear: Defining the Nature and Essentials of Christ's Real Message

A Mormon Language

Superficially, Mormonism looks familiar to the Western eye. Rather than invent a whole new language and vocabulary, which no one could have begun to understand and to which no one would have listened, Joseph Smith, for teaching purposes, used conventional Western (standard English) words or signs, though one finds that he often gave completely new symbolic connotation or meaning to those words.[33] Consequently, we might note that the study of Mormon English has barely begun to reflect the radical implications of the gospel message to outsiders, who are almost uniformly unaware of their ignorance. And Mormons, too, until recently in the main raised and educated in standard English-speaking, -reading and -writing cultures, often do not distinguish the degree of mismatch between gospel language, their Mormon English, and their neighbors' standard English.

On the most obvious level, the word "God" occurs throughout Latter-day scriptures, but the meanings a Latter-day Saint attaches to that word bear no relation to what one might find in a traditional Christian lexicon. And so it is throughout Mormonism. Whatever topic is broached, new definitions are offered and consistently used in Latter-day scriptures. To understand Mormonism one cannot turn to Webster (not even to an 1828 edition of Dr. Webster's *American Dictionary of the English Language,* which, given the evolution of standard English since that time, would seem to have more relevance to Joseph Smith's writings than modern editions), but rather must search out the particular and often multiple new meanings which Joseph gave for traditional words in the texts themselves.

In formulating his new definitions, Joseph also took a non-fundamentalist approach to scriptural language as well. Here is an example both of revealed new definitions and inspired interpretations: "It is written *eternal damnation;* wherefore it is more express than other scriptures, that it might work upon the hearts. . . ."[34] The "expressiveness" or symbolic content of the word is a "mystery" which has impact upon its hearers and can motivate them to repent, but the semantic "mystery" is subsequently explained, explicitly in this particular case.[35]

So, upon a different cognitive foundation, rejecting Plato and Aristotle, a new basis for perceiving the universe is constructed. New definitions for what are therefore effectively new words are taught in the scriptures and other writings within the context of this new logic, grammar, or syntax, and a new world view results. On these foundations, to the degree that a true convert to Mormonism is effectively taught, fellowshipped, and linguistically socialized—insofar as Mormon concepts of God, man, space, time, justice, agency, and responsibility are internalized and lived—a new person with a new mental frame for perception of the interrelationship of self with the universe results—a new culture and a new religion that cannot be explained simply in terms of the old.[36] The gospel is distinctly outlined in 3 Nephi 27:13–21, but like the "baptismal interview" in Mosiah 18:8–10, *all* is said, but in a skeletal way that we must flesh out. A quick glance at the gospel would suggest seemingly familiar shapes and contours, but close scrutiny reveals that not a single dimension or angle is really comparable with other religions because of the radically different foundation upon which the structure is edified.

A Viable Curriculum

If we are to present Mormonism correctly to the world, we must emphasize the concept "fullness" as we understand it in the phrase "fullness of the gospel." We understand this as a filling out of, or adding to, the religious truths others already have. It was for fullness that the Lord instructed Joseph Smith to join none of the sects of his day, thereby making it possible for him to be instrumental in restoring the gospel.

This idea of "adding to" and "completing" is best expressed by B. H. Roberts, who said of the interpretation given by many Mormons to Joseph Smith 2:18–19 (and 1 Nephi 14:10ff.),

It is quite possible that we ourselves have not understood the true relationship in which we stand to the religious world.[37]

As Roberts labored to point out, the first vision was in no way intended to "proclaim the universal corruption of individual Christians," nor was 1 Nephi 14 meant "to stigmatize the Church of Rome as the church of the devil."[38] Indeed, while on the one hand we proclaim several major dispensations of the fullness of the gospel throughout human history and numerous individual and group apostasies from the fullness of the gospel in every dispensation, we also assert that in all "lands and in all ages God has not left himself without witnesses among them [all nations and races of men], but has raised up prophets among them who taught them at least some measure of the truth—perhaps all they could accept and incorporate in their lives."[39] Thus:

"Do you suppose the Hindoos have the light of the Spirit of Christ?" I know they have; and so have the Hottentots, and so has every nation and kingdom upon the face of the earth. . . .[40]

We must not lose track of the fact that all peoples on the earth have the same Heavenly Father and that while cultures and peoples have grown apart, all of us nevertheless trace our genealogy to common earthly parents. Accordingly, all of us have a birthright to the light of the Spirit of Christ, and all of us are exposed to its influence in one degree or another.

You may go among the Pagans, or among all the nations there are, and they have their religion, their sacraments, and ceremonies, which are as sacred to them as ours are to us: they are just as precious and dear to them, though we call them heathen. They are idolatrous worshippers; yet their religion is as sacred to them as ours is to us. If they live according to the best light they have in their religion, God is God over all and the Father of us all; we are all the workmanship of his hands; and if they are ignorant, filled with superstition, and have the traditions of the fathers interwoven like a mantle around and over them, that they cannot see any light, so will they be judged; and if they have lived according to what they did possess, so they will receive hereafter.[41]

Our message is certainly not Western culture nor is it a political message.[42] Speaking of what is today called "nationalism," an editorial in the *Millennial Star* stressed:

This national feeling is another feature of "Gentilism." "Gentilism" breaks up the family of man, and divides them off into parties and nations, having contrary interests.

"Mormonism," on the other hand, unites the family of man, by drawing them from all nations and parties . . . What has one nation to boast over another? . . . There are good and bad . . . qualities in all nations. . . . All real Saints, when they receive the Gospel, will readily relinquish party spirit and national feeling, and count such things as the distinctive ornaments of Satan's kingdom.[43]

Toward a Viable Method for Teaching Christ's Message across Dispensations: Some Problems We Face

We must, then, know what we are going to teach, and what not; then we must learn how to teach, and, if we wish to be successful, this will vary with every group we approach. Far more is necessary than translation and transculturalization as they have been discussed up to now.[44] As one long-time staff member of the Church's Translation Services Department said:

Right now we can safely say that the translations of the various Standard Works are different in each language in which they are translated.

We fear and tremble. We wonder if the Gospel is preached the same way in my country and Japan and any other country. That's where our fears are.[45]

At the beginning of this article I stressed that one aspect of a religion cannot be studied in isolation from or taken out of the context of the system in which it exists as a whole without serious distortion in understanding resulting. That same limitation often exists when we attempt to remove one symbol, one word, or one concept from a culture and use it as an equivalent to one of our own concepts for translation and teaching. Whatever the meaning we might attempt to assign to a borrowed word or symbol, the new meaning will not automatically cause the old word to lose its other meanings and implications that derive from its place within its original cultural and linguistic context. It will still generate associations in the minds of its perceivers that refer back to its nongospel origins or implications.[46] The greatest problem this poses for the Church is that such an uncritical conceptual amalgam could erode the basic truths of the gospel.

The Danger of Syncretism

Improper choice of symbols for transmitting a message is one of several causes of religious *syncretism* (the con-fusing, or fusing together of religions—what one Sinologist recently described as "chop suey" religion). Religious syncretism is one of the most constant and yet least systematically studied phenomena in the history of religions. Most scholars prefer to study one tradition as if it ran the course of its existence as a logical unfolding of itself, like the opening of a single lotus, rather than as if it were one of many flowers in a field that can cross-pollinate, reseed themselves, and constantly change. The former approach avoids the necessity for scholars to work constantly to broaden their education. For the believer it permits an assertion of the purity of his tradition. But syncretism is always a possibility of which the scholar must be aware and a danger of which the believer must beware.

I am conscious of the seeming paradox implicit in asserting the importance of syncretism while having previously said that environmental determinism is useless for explaining the Restoration. This is, however, more than a declaration of faith. I do not deny that outside forces can potentially influence the subsequent development of Mormonism, and where they *in fact* can be shown to be operant we cannot ignore them. But that requires real historical work, documenting that both contact (impact) and influence (imprinting) did occur, as well as the significance of that influence. To explain, let me contrast two examples. No one denies that Richard Ballantyne, a Presbyterian convert, organized the first Mormon Sunday Schools. No one denies that he did so based on his knowledge of how Sunday Schools operated outside the Church. Subsequently the Sunday Schools have become a major gospel-teaching institution of the contemporary Church. Did the adoption of this institutional type produce, however, any significant changes in the overall belief system of the Church? They did not. The Thirteenth Article of Faith affirms Mormonism's openness to good ideas. But can certain ideas be adopted without qualitatively changing the essential nature of the Church?

Let me, by contrast, be more specific. Shinto "Sunday Schools" have arisen in modern, post World War II Japan. These have been patterned after and were developed as a (defensive) response to Christian proselytization and Sunday Schools. Is the adoption, by "Shrine" Shinto, of such an institution qualitatively comparable to the Mormon adoption of a Sunday School system? From all I can see, in a word, no. The overall LDS Church structure, with its priesthood governance, already contained a place for auxiliaries. No radical changes were needed to add this new program. On the other hand, no comparable formal administrative organization existed within Shrine Shinto under which Sunday Schools, let alone a formal curriculum, could be developed. The perceived need for systematic institutionalized instruction in Shinto necessitated the creation of entirely new rational-bureaucratic structures in what was previously an institutionally amorphous religion. The probability of qualitative changes in Shinto resulting from beginning a Sunday School program is very different from the Mormon case.

Contacts occur constantly between religions, especially where one is of a missionary bent. The question is the significance of such contacts. As Whitney Cross said of Shakers in the "Burned-over District":

Mops, seeds, and presumably other Shaker products found a market in western New York towns, but cultural exports are more difficult to trace. Any direct influence from Shakerism upon later religions in the region must apparently be assumed rather than proved.[47]

With all these qualifications, syncretism does occur, and from an institutional point of view, that fusing which would qualitatively change the gospel message must be avoided if the purity of the gospel is to be preserved.

Syncretism can take many forms and can result from different and varied circumstances. It is usually the unintended result of well-meaning attempts to disseminate a particular religion. The most common problem occurs when symbols are adopted from the prospective converts' culture; all too often the old meanings cling to the symbols and are gradually absorbed into the new religion.[48] One should not imagine, however, that religious leaders cynically sit down and say something like "Let's see how we can corrupt our teachings to make them 'sell' to these people." It is more likely that available words and symbols are used because they seem, at first glance, most adequate to the task, and only over the passage of many years do the syncretizing effects become obvious, if they are even noticed at all.

Kyanzittha, the late eleventh-century ruler of Burma, sought to unify his kingdom politically through both military and religious means. In his attempt to convert Burma to Theravāda Buddhism, however, he "found by experience (like the Indo-Greeks of Gandhāra) that the most effective way to teach them Buddhism was to give them a large number of images to worship."[49] This attempt succeeded in part, but rather than making Theravāda widespread, the result was:

*Buddhism of a wide syncretistic kind, embracing not only Mahāyānism and the earlier Tāntric schools of east Bengal, but also the old Vedic and Brahmanic cults (excluding sacrifice), especially Vaisnavism, whose influence was deep in Lower Burma, both among Mon and Pyu; heedful also of the old Nāga-worship of the north, of native Burmese animism . . . of the clan-spirits (*kindok*) and spirit-mediums (*doṅ*) of the ancient Mons, perhaps even of aboriginal totemism . . .*[50]

Among the nominally Theravādan Burmese of today, aspects of all of these systems survive. Where syncretism has occurred, certain elements survive in form only, bereft of their original meanings like the Christmas tree, of whose pagan origins most of us are aware but few can explain. Other elements preserve a vitality of their own, having "bent" the system to conform to their original meanings.

The following illustrations raise another set of problems. The Council of Trent (1545–63) prohibited what they had found to be confusing iconographic practices, such as the depiction of the "Holy Trinity," seen here, or as three distinct but identical figures. This picture is from Cuzco, Peru, and originates in the late seventeenth or early eighteenth century. It is derived from similar illustrations that date as far back as at least the fifteenth century. In spite of the best efforts of the Roman Church, this sort of artistic statement persisted for centuries. Now, whether or not one is trinitarian in belief is irrelevant to the point I want to make. The Catholic Church had a concept they wanted to teach, and like *all* concepts it was subject to misinterpretation. From their point of view it did get misinterpreted, and it got into print and into the minds of their people.

FIGURE 9. THE HOLY TRINITY.

FIGURE 10. THE *TRIMURTI*.

In the second illustration we see a classical *Trimurti* sculpture of Brahmā the creator, Visnu the preserver, and Siva the destroyer, from Elephanta, India. Let us suppose it were our task to communicate a trinitarian message in Latin America or India. Knowing in advance the various religious concepts of those cultures, how would you go about teaching a message about the Father, the Son, and the Holy Ghost without your hearers understanding you in terms of such mental constructs as the *Trimurti* or the Cuzco Trinity?

It is a mistake to suppose that Mormons need not be concerned with this problem. For a long time our own missionary program in Hong Kong used the same Chinese character (*shan*) for "God the Father, God the Son, or God the Holy Ghost."[51] I have no idea how much re-fellowshipping had to take place to erase the misunderstandings that must have generated. As the study of early Christianity has progressed, aided by the discovery of the Dead Sea Scrolls and the Nag Hammadi Coptic-Gnostic library, it has become obvious that Christian history, in Robert M. Grant's words, "will require a fairly complete rewriting."[52] If anyone had the Spirit and was an inspired teacher of the gospel, it had to have been the early apostles. But time and again the New Testament and the recently discovered documents reflect that their hearers often misinterpreted the message on the basis of their own background and experience. To say that was of no consequence to the early Church is to blind oneself to history; and to suppose that the Spirit, without our best efforts today, will automatically prevent such distortions coming into our teaching is wishful thinking.

Syncretism and the Former-day Saints

Let us review some of the history of syncretism in Christianity after Christ's death. We do this from the perspective of non-Mormon scholars. First, Werner Jaeger:

Among the factors that determined the final form of the Christian tradition Greek civilization exercised a profound influence on the Christian mind.[53] *... In the apostolic age we observe the first stage of Christian Hellenism in the use of the Greek language [in the New Testament]. ... The language question was by no means an irrelevant matter. With the Greek language a whole world of concepts, categories of thought, inherited metaphors, and subtle connotations of meaning enters Christian thought.*[54] *Thus, as Philo used to say, ... "the old coin is put to use again by giving it a new stamp."*[55]

Adolf Harnack explored much the same problem:

The influx of Hellenism, of the Greek spirit, and the union of the Gospel with it, form the greatest fact in the history of the Church in the second century. ... About the year 130 ... the religious philosophy of Greece began to effect an entrance, and it went straight to the centre of the new religion.[56]

Again, Mircea Eliade, speaking of initiation rituals, wrote:

As a universalistic religion, Christianity was obliged to homologize and find a common denominator for all the religions and cultural "provincial-

isms" of the known world. This grandiose unification could be accomplished only by translating into Christian terms all the forms, figures, and values that were to be homologized. . . . For our purpose it is important to note that, together with Neo-platonic philosophy, the first values to be accepted by Christianity were the initiatory themes and the imagery of the mysteries. . . . [Christianity] came in the end to borrow from the liturgies and the vocabulary of the Hellenistic mysteries.[57]

These patterns persist into the present, and they resulted from honest efforts to teach Christianity to people of other cultures. After discussing certain passages of scripture that are effectively impossible to "translate" into some languages, E. E. Evans-Pritchard made this point:

Missionaries have battled hard and with great sincerity to overcome these difficulties, but in my experience much of what they teach natives is quite unintelligible to those among whom they labour, and many of them would, I think, recognize this. The solution often adopted is to transform the minds of native children into European minds, but then this is only in appearance a solution.[58]

The fact is that incorrect transmission and religious syncretism can be found occurring where and whenever we find two or more religions in contact with each other. The question becomes, how can it be minimized and corrected? Before grappling with that question head-on, however, let us turn first to a discussion of a concept that will aid our understanding people in such a way that a conscious attempt to avoid syncretism might be made more meaningful. I call it the "Dispensation Gap."

The Dispensation Gap: Understanding the People We Are to Teach

The phrase "teaching across dispensations" has reference to the fact that the gospel message of the "dispensation of the fullness of times" must be taught, whenever a non-Latter-day Saint is taught, across what we might call a dispensation gap. Virtually all the other religions of the world, all the cultures we know, owe their origin, if we trace back far enough, at least in part to one of countless individual and collective apostasies that have occurred in the past. In most cases that origin has to some degree influenced their present-day religious beliefs and behavior. This is especially the case with those aspects of religion—ritual and symbols—that are more a part of the collective consciousness and community experience and are therefore less subject to change than are the necessarily more individual meanings or connotations assigned to religious matters. When we teach, especially as a worldwide Church, we must remember that we are trying to bridge a chasm between where we are and where they have come to be.

It would be naïve to suggest that the religions of which I speak have developed in an uninterrupted direct line. Certainly individual creativity, honest misunderstanding, poor teaching, syncretism resulting from contact between the many religions that have broken off from the gospel, and divisions within those religions as well all account in part for the diversity of religions today. We must also add to that the fact that God reveals to every people within the context of their religion and culture and possibly by some of the aforementioned means as much truth as they are willing and able to live. To all of these peoples, whatever their circumstance, we are charged to deliver the fullness of the gospel—not to destroy the truths they have preserved or have had revealed to them, but rather to supplement and amplify the truth they have. That is our task.

Symbols and Teaching

In order to teach people the fullness of the gospel we must communicate with them, and to do that we must use symbols just as Joseph Smith was obliged to use them during the Restoration. John A. Widtsoe perhaps says it best:

We live in a world of symbols. We know nothing, except by symbols. We make a few marks on a sheet of paper, and we say that they form a word, which stands for love, or hate, or charity, or God or eternity. The marks may not be very beautiful to the eye. No one finds fault with the symbols on the pages of a book because they are not as mighty in their own beauty as the things which they represent. We do not quarrel with the symbol G-o-d because it is not very beautiful, yet represents the majesty of God. . . . We live in a world of symbols. No man or woman can come out of the temple endowed as he should be, unless he has seen, beyond the symbol, the mighty realities for which the symbols stand.[59]

So symbols must be used. And our theoretical understanding of the history of religions suggests what may well be the ultimate problem in choosing the right symbols. Other religions, languages, and cultures are composed of many and varied symbols, all of which are pregnant with meanings. Some of these symbols have their origin or derive their meanings from past dispensations and revelations from God; and at first glance they seem the best choice for a translator. But being part of a system, they have clinging to them conceptual accretions from ages past. They are like old wineskins that are perhaps not too stretched but which contain many potential contaminants of the new wine of the gospel message. So, often the "best" possible choice for translation and teaching from a dictionary point of view, will, in the context of the religio-cultural system as a whole, be an unacceptable choice. At times the problem is obvious, as was the choice in Spanish-speaking countries to use the word *sacerdocio* for priesthood, but substitute *presbîtero* (presbyter) for the more obvious *sacerdote* to avoid our priests in the Aaronic Priesthood being thought of in the same terms as Catholic priests, who were referred to by that name. How does one begin to sort out this general kind of problem and make the right choices, know when to coin a new word, or gloss a text? I believe there is a way to cut the Gordian knot.

Professor Ernst Benz has written how the sociologist Joachim Wach attempted to "contribute to a better and more positive interpretation of religions on the basis of a new conception of 'general revelation,' and to press toward a profoundly theological understanding of the inner structure of the history of religions."[60] Professor Benz has also stated that he covets a clear intuition himself, "a clear insight into the earlier stages of the religious consciousness of mankind. I should like to know the way in which man has passed through these stages up to the present and how they lie submerged in the depths of our humanity in some form that is now barred and veiled from us."[61] These are laudable goals, and I should like to suggest that there are perspectives from which such vision is possible for all of us.

Translating and Teaching

Perhaps the best starting place for approaching the problem of teaching peoples of other cultures is in Hugh Nibley's discussion "Translated Correctly?"[62] Written for the general reader, it puts many problems in perspective—especially the common misconception that translation is a word-for-word or sentence-for-sentence procedure. I would go so far as to suggest a general *rule of thumb* for judging translations of latter-day scriptures: the closer the number of pages in a translation approximates the number in the original, the worse the translation! It is one thing to translate scientific documents into another language, for the scientists who read the translated documents—aside from having an essentially common educational background—usually share an agreed and commonly understood technical vocabulary designed to equate to the original languages. But scriptures are intended as often as not for investigators and new converts who do not know the meanings of our words. And all this combines with other problems—faults that are "the mistakes of men" about which Nephi speaks, as well as biases in the languages of those whom we seek to teach—to cause great difficulties in transmitting an accurate picture of the gospel message. So, restating my *rule*, the more thoroughly we do what is usually called glossing our texts—explaining our intended meanings—the better they will be. There will be problems, though. On that we can count.

Some sixty-six years ago, B. H. Roberts gave a discourse titled "Men the Avatars of God."[63] As the discourse is developed, an English reader can probably avoid the confusion that might result from Roberts' loose use of the word "avatar"—which one dictionary gives as meaning "incarnation of a Hindu deity." But I doubt we would ever want to use that word in a tract in India. By the same token, the first translation into Indonesian of "Joseph Smith Relates His Own Story" had the Prophet receiving the first vision on the occasion of performing a *salat* (the five daily prayers Moslems should perform). That problem was quickly corrected. However, the Bible in Indonesian (I would say almost unavoidably) uses the word *Allah* for God, and in a country which is at least in large part Moslem, one can guess the amount of reteaching and unteaching this word is going to necessitate with our converts.[64] Explaining genealogical and temple "work for the dead" in Southeast Asian countries and helping people to distinguish it from "ancestor worship" will be a completely different task than even the one faced in Confucian-influenced countries.[65] In Bali, for example, the rituals performed long after the death of a relative are understood to be necessary for that soul's eternal progress. And while we find that these and other practices have an almost familiar ring to them, to suggest an equivalence between such concepts and ours is sure to mislead those we teach. Taking another example, there is an almost unbridgeable difference, linked only by the coincidental use of the English word *meditation*, between principle-centered meditation such as has been recommended to us by General Authorities, where the focus is on better understanding of gospel precepts and of our relationship to God, and the incredible popularizations and perversions of Yogic disciplines so common today. These disciplines, even in their nonperverted and noncommercialized forms, are part of a mystical tradition whose real purpose is not to better understand the gospel, but to achieve a union with a "being" or nonbeing who can fill the entire universe and yet dwell in one's heart.[66]

While at the beginning of this conference John L. Sorenson suggested some metaphorical rafts, teaching people in other cultures is, at best, like navigating a narrow and shoal channel that has swift tides and is lined with rocks. If we make the passage we will pass many wrecks that have tried and failed. We may run up on a sandbar and need help to get off. It will not be easy; of that much we can be sure. With that said, I would like to suggest that we have some maps that could help us chart our way.

New Methods

Much has been made of 1976, the year of our symposia, as both a BYU centennial and a U.S. bicentennial year. I should like, in that dual context, to suggest that LDS scholars consider adopting, or at least testing, the value of hypotheses that are in effect a declaration of independence from the world's scholarship. I am in no way suggesting that we have all the answers or that we are or will be excused from gaining every tool, learning every language, and studying all the very useful work that is and has been done by others. Rather, I should like to suggest that it is well past the time that such essential tools and background should have been acquired and high time we began to investigate questions with the additional information available to us. We need to test out the usability of gospel-based perspectives for the study of religion, such as those outlined by Spencer J. Palmer. These can help us better our understanding *per se*, and possibly facilitate the inspired transmission of the gospel message to all the world.

Let me give an example. Through the first three decades of the twentieth century we find that a number of LDS scholars left Utah to study religion, principally at the Divinity School of the University of Chicago. I think the great tragedy of their honest attempts to learn at that time (and problems resulting from that generation's efforts persist up to the present day) is that biblical scholarship was then, as much as now, divided up into camps. And so some of the LDS students chose either the side of Protestant biblical fundamentalism or (in terms of approach to the text) the liberal camp. And they brought what Brigham Young would have called their "sectarian wranglings" back to Zion.[67] From what I have read of these men and from conversations and correspondence I have had with some of them and their students, I can safely say that it never seemed to dawn on them, to the ends of their lives, that the gospel might have provided other perspectives which would have handled the data equally well or better but avoided the problems and contradictions of Mormonism implicit in the positions they adopted. By way of contrast, Hugh W. Nibley, who perhaps coincidentally did not go to a divinity school to get his Ph.D., took another approach. If we examine his method for the study of scriptures, we find that he developed an approach to the study of ancient texts which deals as effectively with preserving and illuminating the essential message in the scriptures as it does with obvious textual problems and issues, such as multiple authorship and redaction, that exist in the Bible. His method, if I can capsulize it, is to approach the scriptures using the history we have of the development of scriptures *in* the Book of Mormon (as well as parallels with what we know of the development of modern LDS scriptures) as a set of possible hypotheses or models which might help us to understand the development and meaning of other texts.[68] When I studied under Dr. Nibley, I learned to look at religions and test out whether other LDS perspectives added to my understanding. Later, at another university, I applied one such method when I was studying under a non-Mormon scholar in a seminar on Nag Hammadi documents. I argued for a ritual-based interpretation of those texts—which went completely contrary to the scholarship of that time.[69] S. Kent Brown and Wilfred Griggs have subsequently worked with that same professor. He has now become one of the leading proponents of a ritual interpretation of those texts.

In many different cases I have found that hypotheses derived from gospel perspectives on the history of religions have aided immeasurably in understanding other religious phenomena, and non-LDS scholars have often agreed, at least with the conclusions so reached.[70]

So, I am urging that specifically LDS perspectives for the comparative study of religions be explored as means to meet the challenge of teaching across dispensations. For example, it is time that we take our understanding of the pattern of dispensations and apostasies that have occurred throughout history and use that as one theoretical framework in which to examine, as distinct entities, each of the various religions, its history and beliefs, seeking to comprehend the cultures and peoples we wish to teach. We must test out, however, whether or not in fact we can come to a better understanding of the truths they know, of their symbol systems and worlds of meaning. If we succeed, with the help of the Holy Ghost, such knowledge can be an aid in bridging the gap that exists and make possible an effective teaching of the fullness of the gospel that will be a blessing to them and to us, avoiding many nets that have ensnared such attempts in the past.

I am aware that similar, though far from identical, approaches to the study of religion have been tried in the past. Consider the case of the American Indian. As early as 1724, J. F. Lafitau, S. J., a French priest, wrote "The Customs of the American Savages Compared with Those of the Ancient Times,"[71] which explored similarities in religious beliefs and came to the conclusion that these resulted from the original revelation given to Adam and Eve. Many explanations have been attempted, for "from 1492 curiosity was rampant in Europe about America. Authors such as Swift and Voltaire satirized the mania which produced and sold countless fictional and real literary descriptions of voyages of discovery, exploration, conquest and colonization."[72] After 1492 people began asking whether or not the indigenous peoples of the Americas could have been left without a knowledge of the gospel. On these debates the very lives of many Indian peoples hinged.[73] As non-Western religions were studied and became better known, and especially after Hindu religious texts became available in the late eighteenth century, two camps arose. One camp, as Evans-Pritchard put it, "sought, and found, in primitive religions a weapon which could, they thought, be used with deadly effect against Christianity."[74] On the other side, while I grossly oversimplify the picture, there arose scholars who attempted to understand the history of religions in terms of their belief in Christianity. Perhaps the best-known and best of these is the ethnological search for and study of an *urmonotheismus* (original monotheism) which is most commonly associated with the Vienna school of Wilhelm Schmidt. This is not the place to detail this or any of the other many attempts to understand religious phenomena.[75] Suffice it to say that up to now no one has systematically attempted to explore the overall history of religions using as possible explanatory models LDS concepts such as that of the dispensations and apostasies of which we have record throughout history. A brief survey of one aspect is to be found in Hugh Nibley's "The Expanding Gospel,"[76] but this piece, though highly praised by even some non-Mormons, only points the way.

A Tentative Conclusion

I have attempted to sketch out a few of the ways in which we (as LDS scholars) need to correct our own misunderstandings about the Restoration, define the essentials of the gospel message, understand the problems inherent in the task of teaching, get to know the peoples we are to help teach, and take advantage of the resources we have available to teach them. All this is easily said. A great deal of effort will be required to meet the challenges, and perhaps the most significant asset we can have will be flexibility, along with a willingness to learn from others' mistakes.

On this last count there are, of course, abundant examples. Consider the following one: after India won her independence, a significant effort was made to create village councils and train leaders as a foundation for local government. Similar institutions had existed prior to the colonial period, but had been suppressed or neglected to the point of extinction. Democracy in India required the rebuilding of local leadership resources, styles, and skills. From this the Community Development program was born. Taking the Indian program as a model, international development agencies began essentially identical programs around the world. Many programs failed, for a number of reasons. Consistently, though, one factor emerged: local needs and differences were being ignored in the effort to impose a single pattern everywhere because it worked in one place. In Indonesia, Community Development programs were rejected by the government, and with good reason, because indigenous institutions and styles of leadership, particularly adapted and appropriate to their culture, already existed. Not only was Community Development redundant, but it was inappropriate; and many of its proponents were so inflexible they failed to see that local *means* might be more effective than imported styles to achieve a given *end.*

Beyond the eternal essentials of the gospel, we also must be flexible and open to the potential appropriateness of local ways to achieve gospel ends. That this will be difficult for us is nowhere more obvious than in popular attitudes toward music in the Church. In countless meetings one can hear people comment on the comfort and security they have felt, traveling around the world, when they heard the hymns of Zion being sung, regardless of the language. I know from personal experience that it does make a Westerner feel secure, but at what cost? For many non-Western converts the diatonic four-part hymnal tradition that early Church members brought with them from Protestantism leads or prepares them to worship in the same way as did the Latin Mass for the majority of Roman Catholicism's communicants in recent centuries. Latin "mystified" worship and helped to create an atmosphere of awe, fear, and wonder precisely because it was so alien to the congregations' cultures. It is true that the *language* of our hymns is the vernacular, as far as they are translated correctly, but language is at best a part, possibly even the lesser part, of worship through music. People attempt to unite together to praise the Lord. To do so effectively, however, each individual must feel *one* with the Saints. If the "song of the righteous" is to rise as a collective prayer unto God (D&C 25:12), the sincere expression of all participating, then those congregated must to some degree be capable of understanding the communication they initiate, which necessarily includes the musical setting of such prayers. Just as some virtuosic classical music, however artistic, is not conducive to worship for many American Saints, so too Western hymns leave many non-Western members out of what is to be a community experience, with little alternative but to parrot musical forms as foreign and unintelligible to them as the Latin Mass was to pre-Vatican-II Catholicism. Virtually every culture has particular forms of musical expression appropriate for addressing God. Perhaps these might be adapted as legitimately to the worship services of non-Western Saints as the hymnal tradition of apostate Europe was adopted for ours.

It is my prayer that, as the Church expands, we as individuals will be able to maintain flexibility and be open to the range of possible alternatives in areas such as leadership styles, musical forms, missionary plans, and teaching methods that other cultures offer. I feel there is a significant lesson to be learned in the change from ward teaching (with its fixed lessons, narrow purpose, and relatively inflexible structure) to home teaching (with its focus on the needs of the particular family and whatever methods are appropriate to meet them). One can speculate on the possibility that ward teaching is to home teaching as standardized missionary lessons are to . . . *X?* The potential benefits seem enormous. To take advantage of them, however, we must go to work in earnest.

A world of data has been compiled, and we have some unique and possibly productive tools with which to explore and make sense out of that data. But we must begin to do so, or it will avail us nothing. If the historical models and data the scriptures provide are indeed useful to us, as they have in some cases proved to be for even non-Mormon scholars, then how much more might we gain by a serious effort to use what we have been given, not only for the sake of learning itself, but for the purpose of doing that which must be done—meeting the challenge of being a worldwide Church and in a truly effective way teaching across dispensations.

Footnotes

1. Copernicus's *Revolutions of the Heavenly Bodies* provided new conceptual and astronomical centers for man's self-understanding. Application of the word "revolutionary" is equally justified in the case of Joseph Smith and religion. Moreover, given the evolving direction of industrial capitalism and "rugged individualism" in Joseph Smith's lifetime, he must also be recognized as a social revolutionary. I stress this, notwithstanding the superficial scholarship of anti-Mormons, too many "neutral" (in the sense that they agnostically treat all religions equally) non-Mormons, and naïve, overspecialized, and often uncommitted Mormons, all of whom dismiss the Restoration in whole or in part as a product of the "Burned-over District." Shortly after delivering this paper I received Volume 44 (March 1976) of the *Journal of the American Academy of Religion* and was both surprised and pleased to read Samuel S. Hill, Jr.'s "A Typology of American Restitutionism: From Frontier Revivalism and Mormonism to the Jesus Movement". Hill recognizes The Church of Jesus Christ of Latter-day Saints as the exemplary, if not unique, *type* of "Institutional Restitution." His analysis merits citation. The LDS Church, the Mormon people, "stands as the most radical or revolutionary of all the American enterprises aiming toward building the Church on earth. . . . One has to say finally that it is not classifiable with any other branch of Christianity, since it is its unique self, quite distinct—and of course separate—from all traditional ecclesiasticism" (p. 69). Noting that to merit the name "revolutionary" a movement must have a comprehensive program, he states: "Comparable developments are necessary to foment a religious revolution, namely, a multidimensional, many-faceted alteration in patterns of polity, belief, behavior, and community. Mormonism's claim to being truly revolutionary is ratified by the comprehensiveness of its departure from existing traditions and the novelty of its new configuration of dimensions. . . . Clearly the Latter-day Saints live by a unique and significantly different theology separating them from all other Christians, as

well as within a distinctive institutional framework" (p. 70). Hill's article is a refreshing change from what has been the norm among scholars.

2. Cited from Thomas F. O'Dea's foreword to Nels Anderson, *Desert Saints: The Mormon Frontier in Utah* (Chicago and London: University of Chicago Press, Phoenix Books, 1966), p. xiv. See also Thomas F. O'Dea, *The Sociology of Religion* (Englewood Cliffs, N.Y.: Prentice-Hall, 1969), p. 70. A more recent commentator recognized that even today "culturally this [the Mormon Region] is the best defined region in the nation" (Raymond D. Gastil, *Culture Regions of the United States* [Seattle and London: University of Washington Press, 1975], p. 237). The entire chapter "The Mormon Region," pp. 237–43, is worthy of attention. In the foreword to this same book Nathan Glazer wrote: "One should be as undesirous of having the distinctive Mormon region, for example, disappear into a homogeneous American mass, and lose its remarkable combination of high fertility, low infant mortality, high education, and highly developed nongovernmental self-help institutions as of seeing a variant of some food disappear . . ." (p. x).

3. We recall here Walter Sullivan's discussion of the shock that would result for most religions of the world if life is discovered in outer space. Mormonism was specifically mentioned as being relatively prepared for such an event in comparison to other groups. See the chapter "What If We Succeed?" in *We Are Not Alone*, rev. ed. (New York: McGraw-Hill Book Co., 1966), p. 287.

4. Alexander Campbell, *Delusions: An Analysis of the Book of Mormon* (Boston: n.p., 1832), p. 13, cited in Whitney R. Cross, *The Burned-over District: The Social and Intellectual History of Enthusiastic Religion in Western New York, 1800–1850* (New York: Harper Torchbooks, 1965), p. 145.

5. Sydney E. Ahlstrom, *A Religious History of the American People* (New Haven, Conn.: Yale University Press, 1972), p. 503.

6. Gordon C. Thomasson, "Daddy, What's a 'Frontier'?: Second Thoughts on the Environment That Supposedly Produced the Book of Mormon," a paper delivered at the Brigham Young University Book of Mormon Symposium, Provo, Utah, April 25, 1970; circulated through Mormon Heritage (Santa Barbara, Calif.: 1970), p. 2, and available in the BYU Library, Special Collections. Compare also Milton V. Backman, Jr.'s review of Ahlstrom: "Mormonism as an Eddy in American Religious History," *Dialogue: A Journal of Mormon Thought* 8 (Spring 1973): 106–9.

7. For the most recent discussion of this general topic, see Dickson D. Bruce, Jr., *And They All Sang Hallelujah: Plain-Folk Camp-Meeting Religion, 1800–1845* (Knoxville, Tenn.: University of Tennessee Press, 1974).

8. Wesley Walters, "New Light on Mormon Origins from the Palmyra Revival," *Dialogue: A Journal of Mormon Thought* 4 (Spring 1969):60–81. See also Richard L. Bushman's cogent reply in the same volume, pp. 82–93.

9. Oral history interviews on 13 February 1974 with Allen W. Coates and Tobias Edwards, being transcribed by the Manuscripts Division, Harold B. Lee Library, Brigham Young University. An interesting check on Mr. Coates' story comes from his brother-in-law, Tobias Edwards. The two are personally estranged, but in a separate interview Mr. Edwards confirmed the essential details of Mr. Coates's narration as accurate and a valid reflection of Coates family tradition as he had also heard it from his wife (Allen W. Coates' sister). Local officials held meetings in their churches, even though no full-time preacher was available. When a particularly well-known circuit-riding preacher arrived in the area, several days of meetings might ensue—a real revival, but not a camp-meeting. Today, the only hook upon which Mr. Walters can hang his argument is *his* definition of what constitutes "an unusual excitement on the subject of religion" and how many conversions are necessary to be considered "great multitudes" (Joseph Smith 2:5) by a teenage boy. For four of Joseph's family to become Presbyterians was more than sufficient to create a "time of great excitement" (Joseph Smith 2:8) in the home itself, especially considering Jo-

seph, Sr.'s attitudes. Add to this the tendency of many who proselyte to count "birds in the bush" and use "everybody's doing it" arguments to convince the hesitant to "get on the bandwagon," and the question becomes moot. Ultimately, Mr. Walters is saying that because 1820 statistics do not meet *his* twentieth-century criteria for large-scale religious excitements, Joseph Smith's history is false. For a mature man to make such a point of disagreeing with an adolescent's perception of scale is ludicrous scholarship.

10. See for instance Edmund S. Morgan, *The Puritan Family: Religion and Domestic Relations in Seventeenth-Century New England* (New York: Harper and Row, 1966), pp. 48–49; see also pp. 49–64.

11. Parley P. Pratt, Jr., ed., *Autobiography of Parley Parker Pratt,* (Salt Lake City: Deseret Book, 1972), p. 297. The two texts are presented in reverse order for stylistic clarity only.

12. Gordon C. Thomasson, "Thoughts on Mormon 'Neoorthodoxy'," *Dialogue: A Journal of Mormon Thought* 5 (Winter 1970):123. One obvious value to such a history will be the perspective it provides as more of the Church's converts come, in the near future, from Spanish-speaking Catholic populations, and in the more distant future from Asian non-Christian peoples. The effective assimilation and reeducation of these convert populations will face the Church with entirely different problems than did the mostly northern European Christian converts of the past. This task of "religious education" (far beyond mere "fellowshipping") will be reflected necessarily in the whole Church. Talks by General Authorities, lesson manuals, and Church publications at any given time in history can be seen as reflecting on and responding to those problems facing the majority of the Church's membership. In the future the Anglo-Europeans in the Church will have to adjust to a very necessary change in teaching priorities and to being "out of the limelight." Another history well worth doing could focus on the outside issues to which General Authorities addressed themselves in previous generations, putting their remarks into context for the first time for modern readers. B. H. Roberts's discourses are an obvious case in point, but every General Authority to some degree has had to respond to the problems of his day, and just as the headnotes in the Doctrine and Covenants and the *History of the Church* illuminate Joseph Smith's writings, so too such a history, well done, could open up many aspects of the gospel to us. One good example is to be found in Brigham Young's positive reactions to Darwinism and Christianity's embarrassment over the same issue, Brigham Young et al., *Journal of Discourses* 26 vols. (London: Latter-day Saints Book Depot, 1E55–86), 14:115–16 hereafter cited as *JD*.

13. Brigham Young Manuscript History, May 1849, p. 70. Of course, by the time that pregnancy could be diagnosed with certainty in those days (the possibility of super-fetation being rare enough, and after the third month, virtually nil), a second conception was known to be impossible. Thus, Brigham Young was clearly rejecting the idea that sex existed only for purposes of reproduction, and coincidentally reminded Pratt of the nongospel origin of such attitudes. But if Mormonism is not puritanical, neither is it accurately described in the sadly ahistorical *Sex and Marriage in Utopian Communities: Nineteenth Century America* by Raymond Lee Muncy (Bloomington and London: Indiana University Press, 1973), ch. 9 and 10.

14. Richard Bushman, "The Book of Mormon and the American Revolution," *BYU Studies* 17, no. 1 (Autumn 1976):3–20.

15. For a beginning on this topic, see appendixes 1–4 in Hugh Nibley, *The Message of the Joseph Smith Papyri: An Egyptian Endowment* (Salt Lake City: Deseret Book, 1975).

16. See especially my discussion of Joseph Smith's potential "information environment" in "Daddy, What's a 'Frontier'?"

17. A typical example of this is Bryan Wilson's article "Mormonism" in the current edition of the *Encyclopedia Britannica.* Along with stating that Joseph Smith got the temple ordinances from Masonry, a few of the other historical canards perpetuated in this supposedly reputable source include that Brigham Young's defiance of federal authority started the

Utah War and that Brigham Young was responsible for the Willie and Martin handcart company disasters. Until LDS scholars specifically respond to such "scholarship," the myths will continue to circulate.

18. E. E. Evans-Pritchard, *Theories of Primitive Religion* (Oxford: Oxford University Press, 1965). This text is more useful than any other I have encountered for understanding the major types of errors made by students of religion. Every student of Mormonism, whether from an anthropological, sociological, psychological, or historical perspective, would benefit by reading it.

19. Åke V. Ström, "Red Indian Element in Early Mormonism," *Temenos: Studies in Comparative Religion* (Helsinki) 5 (1969): 163. See my comments on this article in "Daddy, What's a 'Frontier'?", p. 4, and note 6A.

20. See my manuscript in process, "'What Are Your Names?' The Teaching Function of Gospel Ordinances," which shows that the coherent complex of *rites de passage* found in the Church does not qualitatively differ, as far as structure goes, from the naming of babies through temple ordinances. For a study that does justice to Mormon economics as a unique system, see Gordon E. Wagner's "Consecration and Stewardship: A Socially Efficient System of Justice" (Ph.D. diss., Cornell University, 1977).

21. Evans-Pritchard, *Theories of Primitive Religion*, p. 112, italics added. The use of foreign language terms in quotes such as this one highlights the need for sensitivity to original meanings. While one could give quick English "translations" for such words, equivalents are much more difficult to find, and the foreign word, left untranslated, at least serves to warn the reader that there is much more there than meets the eye. Perhaps the best explanation of cultural particularity and the essential impossibility of a simple-minded "machine" translation is found in 2 Nephi 25:1–6, where Nephi elaborates on the necessity of our studying "cultural anthropology" if we hope to understand the scriptures: "there is none other people that understand the things which were spoken unto the Jews like unto them, save it be that they are taught after the manner of the things of the Jews" (verse 5). The Book of Mormon is far ahead of most present-day scholarship, let alone that of 1830, in its definition of this problem.

22. As Werner Winter wrote in his essay "Impossibilities of Translation," "While languages may be similar to each other, they are never identical.... The system of form and meaning in language A may be similar to that in language B, but is never identical with it. [Winter acknowledges the triviality of this tautology, but many lose sight of the fact that if the systems of form and meaning were identical we would be talking about one language and not two.] This statement has a very simple, yet very important corollary: *There is no completely exact translation.* "[eds.] W. Arrowsmith and R. Shattuck, in *The Craft and Context of Translation* (Garden City, N.Y.: Anchor Books, 1964), p. 95. See also essays by John C. Alleman and myself, and others, in the proceedings of the *1973 Conference on the Language of the Mormons* (Provo, Utah: Language and Intercultural Research Center, Brigham Young University, 1973).

23. Ernst Benz, "On Understanding Non-Christian Religions," in M. Eliade and J. Kitagawa, eds., *The History of Religions: Essays in Methodology* (Chicago and London: University of Chicago Press, 1959), p. 117. The more completely religious language is understood, the more obvious it should become that the only way a person or machine can provide a quick or simultaneous translation of religious subject matters, barring direct revelation from God, is if they provide a superficial or an incorrect translation. And it is the complexity of the problem that has resulted in no fewer than some eight editions of the Book of Mormon in German, to cite but one example.

24. For a discussion of Eduard Meyer's *Ursprung und Geschichte der Mormonen* (Halle: Verlag von Max Niemeyer, 1912), see Hugh W. Nibley's "Islam and Mormonism—A Comparison," *The Ensign*, March 1972, pp. 55–64. For a general examination of false parallels of Mormonism and Islam, see Arnold H. Green and Lawrence P. Goldrup, "Joseph Smith,

an American Muhammad? An Essay on the Perils of Historical Analogy" *Dialogue: A Journal of Mormon Thought* 6 (Spring 1971):46–58. It would be well to add that Islam, while "Oriental" in that it originated east of the Mediterranean, maintains a continuity with its Hellenistic counterparts, later Judaism and Christianity. This becomes increasingly evident as one sees how Islam is transformed in its manifestations east of the Indus, especially in Indonesia.

25. Sterling M. McMurrin, *The Theological Foundations of the Mormon Religion* (Salt Lake City: University of Utah Press, 1965), p. x.

26. Thomas F. O'Dea, *The Mormons* (Chicago and London: University of Chicago Press, Phoenix Books, 1964).

27. Thomasson, "Thoughts on Mormon 'Neoorthodoxy,'" p. 126. Original citation in Brigham Young Manuscript History, 16 February 1849, pp. 19–20.

28. Benz, "On Understanding Non-Christian Religions," p. 121. President Spencer W. Kimball has said, "The sharing of the gospel often requires us to cross language and cultural barriers .... I am under no delusion, brethren, to think that this will be an easy matter without strain or that it can be done overnight, but I do have this faith that we can move forward and expand much faster than we now are," "when the world will be converted," *The Ensign,* October 1974, pp. 12–13. President Kimball here challenged us to "lengthen our stride" and meet our responsibility to spread the gospel. He also said, "It seems to me that the Lord chose his words when he said 'every nation,' 'every land,' 'uttermost bounds of the earth,' 'every tongue,' 'every people,' 'every soul,' 'all the world,' 'many lands,'" p. 5. One of the keys to accomplishing this goal is to "prepare the message in the native languages," p. 11. This will require far more work than we have expended in the past.

29. B. H. Roberts, *Seventy's Course in Theology,* 4 vols (Salt Lake City: Deseret News, 1911), 4:69–71. The standard English and Christian definitions of these terms are the result of two millennia of councils, philosophical analyses, theological debates, schisms, and compromises. All of these terms, as used outside of Mormonism, can be seen as partaking of a general Greek spirit. If one searches Latter-day scriptures, as well as Joseph Smith's commentaries on various Biblical passages, however, it becomes clear that he gave and employed definitions in all his writings that contradicted the normal Christian definitions. Beyond the qualifications or redefinitions Roberts indicates in his text, other crucial limitations or Mormon definitions of these terms include the following: that God's "eternity" must be qualified by the fact that man is "coeternal" or "coequal" with God and uncreated, that God's "immutability" can be understood with regard to His perfection in adherence to principle, but this does not change the fact that he has not always been as he now is, that God's "omnipotence" does not include the power to force men to accept exaltation, that God's "omniscience" must be qualified by the fact that there would have been a time when God was as we are now, by implication not knowing "all," and moreover, in Roberts' words "not that God is omniscient up to the point that further progress in knowledge is impossible to him; but that all knowledge that is, all that exists, God knows" (p. 70), and the obvious point that "omnipresence" must be totally redefined in accord with the fact that we say God has a physical body. These specifically Mormon definitions are consistent in their rejection of Greek definitions of perfection which see matter as hopelessly corrupt, all change as evil, and God necessarily (by either/or logic) the exact and total opposite of the mortal condition. Finally, as Roberts states, "It ought to be constantly remembered that terms absolute to man may be relative terms to God, so far above our thinking is his thinking; and his ways above our ways" (p. 70). The Mormon "heresy" is thus complete, and not accidentally, as we shall see below, because it rejects the logical premises from which traditional definitions were derived.

30. *Confessions of St. Augustine* (New York: Sheed and Ward, 1942), book 7:20, p. 152.

31. See my essay "In Good Conscience," in G. Thomasson, ed., *War, Conscription, Conscience and Mormonism* (Santa Barbara, Calif.: Mormon Heritage, 1972), pp. 87–89 and

notes 46 and 47, available in the BYU Library, Special Collections. A rejection of Greek presuppositions and logic does not mean, of course, that the gospel is either irrational or nonrational. It simply means that a different logical structure is built upon a distinct foundation (continuing revelation). For discussions of non-Greek systematic, rational conceptual systems compare F. Th. Stcherbatsky, *Buddhist Logic,* 2 vols. (New York: Dover Publications, 1962); Hajime Nakamura, *Ways of Thinking of Eastern Peoples: India, China, Tibet, Japan,* ed. Philip P. Wiener (Honolulu: East-West Center Press, 1969); and Michael Cole and Sylvia Scribner, *Culture and Thought: A Psychological Introduction,* (New York: John Wiley & Sons, 1974).

32. For an elaboration of a possible diffusionary hypothesis see my discussion in "Togetherness in Sharing an Umbrella: Divine Kingship, the Gnosis, and Religious Syncretism" in the proceedings of the 1975 Welch Lecture Series, 26 March 1975, footnote 12, available in the BYU Library, Special Collections. One clear example of diffusion to which insufficient attention has been paid is the inevitable synthesis of Hagoth's Lehite culture with the Malayo-Polynesian cultures of the Pacific.

33. See also my essay "A Study of Mormon Language, Religious Language, and Rhetoric" (Santa Barbara, Calif.: Mormon Heritage, 1970), available in the BYU Library, Special Collections; various readings in the proceedings of the *1973 Conference on the Language of the Mormons,* the *Conference on the Language of the Mormons 1974* (Provo, Ut.: Language Research Center, Brigham Young University, 1974), and the proceedings of the past several symposia on *LDS Intercultural Communications and Language Concerns.*

34. D&C 19:7. A great deal of time has been wasted on what are trivial aspects of Mormon English—institutional or bureaucratic terms—which change quite frequently. "Mormon English" that truly changes one's world view includes, on the other hand, definitions of words like *God* (the First Vision, D&C 130:22), *eternal* and *endless* (D&C 19), *priestcrafts* (2 Ne. 26:29), etc. One of the most revealing definitions given by Joseph Smith is the one he offers for "power." It dissolves the logical problems that God's being "all good" and "all powerful" have created for those in the Judeo-Christian tradition who acknowledge the existence of evil, without denying the reality of evil. When God's *power,* or the *power* of the priesthood, is defined in D&C 121:41ff (cf. Moses 6:61), it becomes obvious that God has all the "power" that can be exercised righteously and maintained through eternity, and it is evident that he is "all good" precisely because this is the only power he does exercise. The traditional problem of evil is troublesome only if one accepts the Greek premise that God has the kind of coercive power to force men and the elements, which in fact characterized Satan's plan. Even in "commanding" the elements, Jesus said "peace, be still" (Mark 4:39). In this regard, see my manuscript in process, "All their *creeds* were an abomination in his sight."

35. D&C 19:8ff. While the doctrinal implications of this specific section are quite widely understood, with even non-Mormon commentators being aware that we reject traditional ideas of hell, few have gone beyond the immediate doctrinal import of the verse to reflect on the implications of the Lord using language for its psychological impact rather than specific semantic content. How many other words are similarly used? While this passage does not necessarily allow for the allegorical interpretations so common in Christianity, it highlights the necessity of searching the scriptures and other sources for Joseph Smith's definitions rather than casually assuming one's personal command of the English language is adequate for understanding the scriptures. We acknowledge the imperfection of scriptural texts, the unavoidable ambiguities of Standard English, the necessity of learning precise Mormon English definitions for many words, the possibility that words are used with intentionally multivalent meanings with specific messages for those "that have ears to hear" (see my discussion on this point in note 12 of my essay, "Mormon Symbols: Structure of Mormon Consciousness and the Basis of Mormon Communication Activities, Mormon Language, and Mormon Arts," in the *1973 Conference on the Language of the Mormons,* p. 79), and the implication of D&C 19 that some words are intentionally used as "mysteries." Given such problems, the necessity of the Spirit for understanding all "scripture"

(including as defined in D&C 68:4) becomes more obvious. The often-repeated warning that the time will come when no man or woman can live on borrowed light is obviously necessary if for no other reason than that every communication is susceptible to private interpretation, and even one who seeks to be blindly obedient must have the Spirit to know, in fact, exactly what it is they are told to be obedient to—otherwise they can in no way be certain that they are doing anything more than being blindly obedient to their own private interpretations!

36. See especially John L. Sorenson, "Mormon World View and American Culture," *Dialogue: A Journal of Mormon Thought* 8 (1973): 17ff. Of specific interest is Sorenson's reference to the work of Clyde Kluckhohn which suggested a greater congruency between the value systems of Mormons and Zuñi Indians than with the Anglo- and Spanish-speaking populations studied (pp. 18ff.). A *Weltanschauung,* or world view, is not a set of facts or ideas about reality, but rather is a classic example of a whole which is greater than the sum of its parts. A world view is an integration or synthesizing of past experience that serves as a frame for perception and interpretation of reality. World view is personally dynamic and changing in response to experience but, due to shared learned concepts, can be said to have some degree of uniformity within a culture. As a person comes to accept the gospel and integrate its principles into his or her life, all previous ideas will accordingly be modified and come to correspond more closely to what Sorenson terms a Mormon world view. The core of the gospel, of course, is not culture-bound, but because many of us have not completely assimilated a gospel world view and lack a full understanding of the gospel, we attach nonessentials to it, or fail to transmit it fully. We, like the writers of the Book of Mormon, are often producers of "faults" which "are the mistakes of men" (Book of Mormon, title page).

37. From B. H. Roberts, "The Relationship of the Church to the Christian Sects: The Doctrine of Two Churches Only," *Defense of the Faith and the Saints,* 2 vols. (Salt Lake City: Deseret News, 1907–12), 1:27.

38. Ibid., p. 25.

39. Ibid., p. 12. It should by now be clear that I am using the term "dispensation" to refer not just to "major" dispensations of Adam, Enoch, and others, but to "minor" dispensations of Alma and others, and "partial" dispensations of truth from God to every people, giving them all they could accept and incorporate in their lives, as well. These partial dispensations are important for understanding the religions of those to whom we must convey the fullness of the Gospel.

40. *JD* 2:140.

41. *JD* 6:293.

42. See, for example, LaMond Tullis, "Mormonism and Revolution in Latin America," *Brigham Young University Studies* 16, no. 2 (Winter 1976):235–49.

43. "Party Spirit," *The Latter-Day Saints' Millennial Star* 8 April 1854, p. 210. Such emotions have, of course, . interfered with propagation of the gospel message, possibly more than any other form of intolerance. We have yet to reach Heber C. Kimball's standard: "I am not national nor sectional, and God forbid that I should be, for I have that Spirit that delighteth in the welfare and salvation of the human family. And when I have that Spirit about me, can I be national? You never knew that feeling to be in me for I abhor it. I will not bow my head to that national spirit, nor to any spirit that is not of God"(*JD* 4:278).

44. See the various discussions in the aforementioned *Conference on the Language of the Mormons* proceedings. As an example, the passage "Feed my sheep" (John 21:16) might be translated into a Lapp language using some word equivalent for "sheep," but since their culture contains no data for understanding the interrelationship of shepherd and sheep, all the rich implications of the text are lost. *Transculturizing* the text might involve substituting the word "reindeer," but while this is a closer fit to the culture than sheep, and some understanding might result, to fail to look into the place of reindeer in

the religious system—to ignore the religion-based semantic content of the word—is to leave the door open for countless non- or antigospel connotations to enter our communications. Ultimately the whole religious culture of the group we wish to communicate with must be understood before we can translate with confidence.

45. Roger Dock in *1973 Conference on the Language of the Mormons,* p. 88.

46. Those who still think translation, transculturization, and transmission of the gospel into other languages for other people is a simple task would do well to reflect on the fact that old wineskins (and we can liken wineskins to symbols), both because they are weakened and already stretched to their limit through the fermentation of the wine they originally contained, and because they contain residues of the old wine which can taint or cause the new wine to ferment in an unacceptable way, are unusable for new wine. If a second-hand wineskin, or a borrowed symbol, is to be used again, it cannot already have been semantically filled and stretched to its limits, and one must make certain that a purification process takes place so that none of the old content remains to infect the new.

47. Cross, *The Burned-over District,* p. 33. While Cross here recognizes it is far more difficult to prove diffusion than to assume it, on other occasions he is not so careful to qualify his statements, especially those about Joseph Smith. Others have been equally careless, claiming, for instance, that Joseph got the idea for the law of consecration from communistic experiments at Kirtland, ignoring the fact that the law of consecration is hardly even comparable to what was going on in Kirtland, to say nothing of the fact that alternative economic systems are recorded in 4 Nephi which was published in 1830, long before Joseph had heard of the Kirtland experiment. Similarly, scrambled logic and carelessness with data to make environmental determinist "cases" are found in many discussions; some, for example, refer to the Book of Mormon as anti-Masonic, ignoring the fact that the overall pattern of temple worship is outlined in the Book of Mormon text, and then conclude that Joseph acquired the ordinances from Masonry in the 1840s. Two other common confusions of data are the strange sequence of influences supposed to have worked on Joseph Smith's attitudes toward blacks in the mid-1830s, and discussions of polygamy that ignore the clear though limited authorization it is given in Jacob 2:30. Such discussions as these reflect at least extreme carelessness, and at times, a bias perhaps better described as malice.

48. Religious syncretism can also serve the needs of a political state. See "Sharing an Umbrella."

49. Gordon H. Luce, *Old Burma—Early Pagán,* 3 vols. (Locust Valley, N.Y.: J. J. Augustin, 1969), 1:361.

50. Ibid., pp. 72–73.

51. Marcellus S. Snow, "Translating Mormon Thought," *Dialogue: A Journal of Mormon Thought* 2, (Summer 1967): 57; see also pp. 55–57. Compare also Robert J. Morris, "Some Problems in [of] Translating Mormon Thought into Chinese," *Brigham Young University Studies* 10, no. 2 (Winter 1970):173ff.

52. Robert M. Grant, *Gnosticism and Early Christianity* (New York: Harper Torchbooks, 1966), p. 1.

53. Werner Jaeger, *Early Christianity & Greek Paideia* (London, Oxford, and New York: Oxford University Press, 1969), p. 4.

54. Ibid., pp. 5–6.

55. Ibid., p. 9.

56. Adolf Harnack, *What is Christianity?* trans. Thomas B. Saunders (New York: Harper Torchbooks, 1957), pp. 200–201. See also pp. 206, 220–21 and 263ff.

57. Mircea Eliade, *Rites and Symbols of Initiation: The Mysteries of Birth and Rebirth* (New York: Harper Torchbooks, 1965), p. 121. A recent trend towards attempting to in-

tegrate various Hellenistic, pseudo-Pythagorean, alchemical, astrological, and nineteenth-century European evolutionary anthropological theories with the gospel is to be found in Albert Roustit, *Prophecy in Music: Prophetic Parallels in Musical History,* trans. John A. Green (France: n.p., 1975). The book's reception seems to be a function of its readers' ignorance of their own tradition's relationship to the book's intellectual foundations.

58. Evans-Pritchard, *Theories of Primitive Religion,* p. 14. Rudolf Otto, in *The Idea of the Holy* (London, Oxford, and New York: Oxford University Press, 1967), makes reference to a parallel problem: "Once enunciated and understood, the ideas of the unity and goodness of the divine nature often take a surprisingly short time to become firmly fixed in the hearer's mind.... Frequently, thereupon, the hearer adapts the religious tradition that has hitherto been his to the new meaning he has learned," (p. 139).

59. John A. Widtsoe, "Temple Worship," in *Utah Genealogical and Historical Magazine* 12 (April 1920):62. We have no choice but to use symbols, of course, since all communication uses symbolic forms. It is well past time, however, that we become more self-conscious about and careful with the symbols we use. "The 'mighty realities' of which Widtsoe speaks are available only through the ministrations of the Holy Ghost. It is *our* responsibility to communicate the symbols." "Mormon Symbols," p. 76.

60. Benz, "On Understanding Non-Christian Religions," p. 115.

61. Ibid., p. 131.

62. Nibley, *Message of the Joseph Smith Papyri,* pp. 47–55.

63. B. H. Roberts, *Defense of the Faith and the Saints,* 2:395 The word *avatar,* while meaning an incarnation, refers to any one of multiple incarnations of gods in many forms, human and nonhuman. Another term which might be useful were it not for its other implications is *Yuga,* which could be used for *dispensation.*

64. The problem of Bible translations promises to become more complex in the future. Translators necessarily quote scriptural citations in speeches by General Authorities as well as articles in Church publications from the version of the Bible used in their language. Often, however, the logic of the original statement is based on what President Joseph F. Smith called a "distinction without a difference" in the King James text. In English several different words might be used, whereas only one is employed in another language—*Geist* being a prime case in point—and the remarks are therefore confusing at best. While a great deal of confidence has been expressed in the King James translation as, in the past, the best English translation available, it should not be forgotten that Joseph Smith said that the Martin Luther German translation of the New Testament was superior to the King James, and scholarship is continuing to improve other foreign-language translations. The Church consistently uses the more modern translations in non-English contexts, and the deficiencies of the King James text will increasingly cause problems in the future. Added to this is the fact that the most commonly used version of the Bible in the Church today is Joseph Smith's Inspired Revision (or at least parts of it—the Book of Moses, Joseph Smith 1, various commentaries on the Inspired Version in the D&C [76, 77, etc.] (and texts from the brass plates in the Book of Mormon. And it is possible that the 1960 revision of de Reina and de Valera's Spanish Bible will someday displace the King James text from second to third most commonly used Bible in the Church. Soon some hard decisions must be made concerning ways to assure uniformity in Bible-based instruction in the Church.

65. As this conference brought out, Korean ancestor-worship can be converted into acts of respect without compromising the gospel or the culture. Those who object to the adaptation of such patterns might do well to reflect on the origins of the Western custom of putting flags and flowers on graves. There is no essential difference between the two. Along these lines, LDS scholars might benefit from following the reappraisals now being done of Matteo Ricci's sixteenth-century attempts to Sinicize the Roman Catholic Mass, which seem to have been far more valid and viable than scholarship prior to Vatican II could guess, with the documents then available.

66. While R. Lanier Britsch tried to clarify many such possible parallel values in his recent article, "Latter-day Saints and Eastern Religions: A Few Thoughts on Bridge Building," *The New Era,* October 1975, pp. 7–8, the unavoidable brevity of that article leaves many misunderstandings that exist in the Church unresolved. At least one missionary of my acquaintance currently in Southeast Asia still has not come to understand that transcendental meditation, which he began to practice before joining the Church, does not correlate positively with gospel principles. While I have extensive notes on this problem, it will be some time before an article can be produced which specifies the fallacy in such disciplines from a gospel point of view.

67. For one side of this story, see Russel B. Swenson, "Mormons at the University of Chicago Divinity School: A Personal Reminiscence," *Dialogue: A Journal of Mormon Thought* 7 (Summer 1972):37–47. See also Ralph V. Chamberlin, *Life and Philosophy of W. H. Chamberlin* (Salt Lake City: Deseret News, 1925), ch. 7, for another case in which Church members fought over two worldly positions rather than seek out a gospel perspective.

68. Hugh Nibley, *Since Cumorah: The Book of Mormon in the Modern World* (Salt Lake City: Deseret Book, 1967). See especially his discussion of Isaiah, p. 147. For another such fertile LDS alternative to the world's interpretations, see John L. Sorenson's unpublished manuscript "The 'Brass Plates' and LDS Biblical Scholarship."

69. See my "The Gospel of Philip," circulated privately (Santa Barbara, Calif.: Mormon Heritage, 1971), available in the BYU Library, Special Collections.

70. On several occasions I have given noted scholars articles written by Dr. Nibley which related to their work, and asked them to respond. While the articles were written from a specifically Mormon perspective, all agreed that the logic and evidence were clear and compelling, and generally agreed with the conclusion as well. In one case, the scholar questioned stated that Nibley's grasp of his own field was superior to his, and went on to ask if it would be possible for him to recruit Nibley to teach at his own institution—one of the world's most prestigious universities.

71. Cited in Jan de Vries, *The Study of Religion: A Historical Approach,* trans. Kees W. Bolle (New York: Harcourt, Brace & World, 1967), p. 76. After one has read the already recommended Evans-Pritchard volume, this is a useful complement for the serious student.

72. Thomasson, "Daddy, What's a 'Frontier'?", p. 7.

73. Lewis Hanke, *The Spanish Struggle for Justice in the Conquest of America* (Philadelphia: University of Philadelphia Press, 1949).

74. Evans-Pritchard, *Theories of Primitive Religions,* p. 15.

75. Ibid., pp. 102–4ff; also *The Study of Religion,* pp. 120ff.

76. Hugh Nibley, "The Expanding Gospel," *Brigham Young University Studies* 7 no. 1 (Autumn 1965):3ff. See also his collection of articles that appear in the pamphlet *When the Lights Went Out: Three Studies on the Ancient Apostasy* (Salt Lake City: Deseret Book, 1970).

SECULARIZATION AND THE GOSPEL

INTRODUCTION

Douglas F. Tobler

The loaf to be leavened by the gospel message in the 1970s and beyond has acquired a different shape and texture from that worked by the Saints and missionaries during the first century and a half of our history. Whereas once, not long ago, most people in Western civilization ordered their lives and judged their deeds by the maxims of the Judeo-Christian traditions, now they choose from a smorgasbord of man-made philosophies, or they believe simply in the materialism of this world. For them, what is real is the here and now. Whereas, within the memory of those living, Mormonism was castigated for not being a "Christian" faith, now whether it is perceived as Christian or not makes little difference to those who believe that religion in general and Christianity in particular are irrelevant to the contemporary human condition. Scarcely two decades have passed since one sincere Mormon missionary, armed with memorized Bible scriptures designed to persuade doubtful and uninformed Austrians and Swiss that he was bringing them the original Christianity, found himself, like many missionaries before and since, brusquely rebuked by the responses: "What is the Bible? Who cares what the Bible says? Religion is a big swindle. If God exists, how can he allow so much suffering in this world?" Only gradually did it dawn on the missionary that this new world did not share his values and assumptions. God no longer played a substantial role in people's lives. Nietzsche, it seems, had, for these people, been proven right: God was dead, and man had killed him through unbelief. Alma had seen this kind of people: they "live without God in the world" (Mosiah 27:31).

This process of secularization, one of the dominant features of the modern world, has been eloquently defined by Ernst Benz in the following essay. It is, he says, "the disappearing of the concept of the Holy, the negation of the transcendent origin of our world and our human life, the desacralization of social and private life, the limitation of our self-understanding on a merely rational and worldly concept of the rules of our social and private life and of our situation in the natural universe, with the general tendency to eliminate the rest of religion also from the marginal areas where it still survives, especially from the ethical field."

Thus, slowly, over the years, a changed and changing society with different values has appeared. What was formerly agricultural and rural is now urban and industrial; whereas before, education was reserved for an intellectual aristocracy, now surging masses press against the doors of schools and universities throughout the world. Prosperity and technology, reason and science have joined with apostate forms of Christianity to create a man-centered rather than a God-centered world. Not surprisingly, our society has become obsessed with preserving this mortal life at all costs; for many people it is all there is. When all of man—individually and collectively—is perishable; where faith in a hereafter is weak or seems impossible; where *Angust*—the dread of the unknown—hovers over a world aware of its ability to destroy all that lives and breathes; this, indeed, is a world different from the past. Ironically, the age of space exploration has become an age of spiritual confinement to this planet. We have the ability to fantasize about other worlds but lack the faith to prepare for them.

Equally ironic is the first-time attraction of the secularized Western world to the unique religions, traditions, and practices of the East. Yoga, transcendental meditation, and a variety of Eastern cults seem to those bound to this earth a means of transcending in the here and now their unhappy and uncertain condition. It is a kind of mystical asceticism which confirms the relentlessness of the quest for meaning in life.

The challenge is to bring a knowledge of Christ to this secularized generation. We may do so by gaining an understanding of the ways in which modern men think, then help to create the conditions wherein the gospel message can be articulated for them and the Kingdom made to flourish.

The symposia essays that follow are an attempt to consider some areas where the Church is in, but not of, the world. Professor Ernst Benz, a noted European scholar, sees Mormonism as offering a positive kind of secularization, a unique example of how Christ can be made real in this world. This is one of the first accounts by non-American scholars to see Mormonism as theologically legitimate and worthy of both scholarly and ecclesiastical attention.

In the second essay, Robert S. Jordan calls attention to the political challenge: how does the Church pursue its universal mission in the midst of a plethora of politics—some democratic, some authoritarian, some communist, some stable, some fragile—but all exercising some form of jurisdiction over souls to be won for the faith. Here, as in the other essays, we see that God and man work together to fulfill the destiny of the Kingdom.

Our third offering in this section explores the relationship of economic organization, society, and freedom. If it is true that both the Church and its members thrive best in free societies and that economic freedom is basic to those societies, should the Church be interested in promoting that freedom? In a provocative and positive manner, James R. Kearl and Clayne Pope suggest some ways that in our present world this might be done.

Finally, Douglas F. Tobler, in discussing philosophical Marxism, shows why it has become so attractive in a world where generations of a new breed of truth seekers, unaware of the gospel, are existentially casting about for something to believe in. What has given Marxism in its various formulations such unusual magnetic appeal? What does the gospel offer to those to whom Marxism has emotional, philosophical, and spiritual appeal? How may we show those inclined to philosophical Marxism how the gospel can answer their needs and show them the way to the dignity, human justice, and personal happiness they seek? How may we show them, in a way in which they will listen, the superiority of the gospel of Jesus Christ over all man-made philosophies, not only for questions about life after life, but of life now, too?

The large audience at the secularization session of the expanding Church symposia at which these papers were presented also heard comments by Elder Neal A. Maxwell and Louis C. Midgley. The session then concluded with a vigorous question-and-answer period, which reached a climax in the poignant, spontaneous testimonies of several members of the audience who, having thought they had found their answers to life in the philosophies of men, had found their way out of a shadowy past into the gospel light. The comments by Elder Maxwell and Professor Midgley and the question-answer exchange follow Dr. Tobler's essay.

MORMONISM AND THE SECULARIZATION OF RELIGIONS IN THE MODERN WORLD*

Ernst Benz

The secularization of religions in the modern world is one of the themes most discussed among the scholars of sociology, of theology, and of history of religions of today. I had the privilege of attending two of the main international discussions of that theme, the "Salzburger Humanismusgespräche" (January 1976) in Rome. The general impression of both colloquies was that of a happy confusion, which is very typical of conferences of learned specialists. Some sociologists taught the imminent definite collapse of religion; others admitted that this decay seemed to be unavoidable in the present situation but that there may be a small chance of the survival of religion in case of unpredictable catastrophes. Marxists like Ernest Bloch attacked Christianity because the Roman inquisition burned thousand of witches, and even neo-Marxists like Max Horkheimer came back to the theme of burnt witches, as if Christians through centuries had done nothing else than to burn witches.

But just this impression of happy confusion encourages me to condense the broad variety of contradictory statements into some very few and I hope understandable concepts:

There is one basic understanding of the secularization of religions in the modern world that is very widely spread among the leading groups of modern sociologists: that religion in all its historical forms is more and more disappearing from modern society and from the consciousness of modern man, which means that modern life and secularization are identical. Secularization concerns not only the shrinking influence of religious institutions—especially of the institutional churches—on public life but also the diminishing influence of religion on the self-understanding of modern man and especially on his ethical behavior. Secularization in this broadest sense is desacralization—the loss of the consciousness of the holiness of life not only in the social structures but

*A forum address delivered March 30 1976 at Brigham Young University and printed in the Centennial Lecture issue of *Brigham Young University Studies* 16, no. 4 (Summer 1976): 627-39. Several editorial modifications were made for the benefit of monolingual English readers.

also in the private sphere of man. Of special importance is the assertion that this process is irreversible, that it cannot be stopped any more, and that means religion has no future at all; it still survives as a vanishing phenomenon in some marginal fields of society, in some areas of cultural hinterland, but its destiny is sealed.

This concept of secularization seen from the standpoint of the history of modern ideas sounds, in spite of its claim to be based on facts and critical observations, a little suspicious because of its surprising resemblance to the concept of religion developed by Karl Marx in the footsteps of Ludwig Feuerbach. According to Marx, religion is necessarily dying out as the result of the progress of the socialist society, and this dying out of religion is irreversible because religion is based on an idealogical self-deception of man that keeps him in the state of an opiatic dream of a pretended better beyond, hindering him from settling his life in this world by his own force and from building up here the perfect socialist society.

Yet it would be dishonest not to admit there are some real historical reasons for the rise of a strong process of secularization in modern times. This process began in its conspicuous form in the time of the Enlightenment of the seventeenth and the eighteenth centuries as a direct consequence of and reaction to the terrific religious wars, during which the Christian gospel of love was thoroughly compromised by the fighting Christian churches themselves. There arose sharp criticism of the traditional religions and of their established institutions among the leading spirits of the epoch. The criticism of religious doctrines and institutions in this "First Enlightenment" was at first represented by only a small minority of intellectuals and scholars; but with the spreading of the modern natural sciences and the extension of public education into the modern school and university system in the following centuries, we reach today the epoch of the so-called "Second Enlightenment," which implies that the merely rationalistic and scientific interpretation of nature, history, and man has now reached the broad masses and modeled the whole consciousness of modern society. We have to admit the religious institutions were themselves the main reason for and the stumbling block to the general criticism of religion because of the discrepancy between their own theological pretensions and highly sublime self-interpretation on the one side and the deficiency in their practical behavior on the other side.

As a matter of fact, secularization is a phenomenon typical of all living world religions, for Judaism and Islam as well as for Hinduism and for Buddhism. There are some peculiarities among the different types of secularization in the religions in question, and very interesting studies exist about the typical form of secularization, for example, in Hinduism and Buddhism, but we cannot enter today into the details of this side of the problem. I suggest we limit our inquiry to the secularization of modern Christianity, with a special consideration of Mormonism.

Let us begin with a critical distinction, which is the more necessary as most sociologists have not taken it into consideration. Basically two types of secularization exist.

The first one is the type already mentioned at the beginning, the disappearing of the concept of the holy, the negation of the transcendent origin of our world and our human life, the desacralization of social and private life, the limitation of our self-understanding to a merely rational worldly concept of the rules of our social and private life and of our situation in the natural universe, with the general tendency to eliminate the rest of religion also from the marginal areas where it still survives, especially from the ethical field.

But a second type of secularization is typical and essential for Christianism. The main idea of the Christian faith is God's self-manifestation in this our world through Jesus Christ, and God's self-realization in this our world through the power and the gifts of the Holy Spirit. And this involves a quite different, positive type of secularization, which means God's way of secularization. In a pointed formulation we could say: secularization is the way of divine incarnation. God's will, God's power, God's spirit penetrate the matter of the world to model and shape it according to his own will—for modeling mankind, for building up his kingdom. Martin Luther says in his commentary to the first chapter of Genesis: "The Holy Spirit does not like to move always upon the face of the waters like a goose; he wants to penetrate and work."

Considering this type of secularization, we must as historians admit that Mormonism is the best example of this positive secularization of the Christian gospel, because it was driven from its very beginning by the aim to prepare and even to anticipate the promise of the coming kingdom of God. Mormons were so strongly and directly and so verbally convinced of the reality of the message of Christ—"The kingdom of heaven is at hand" (Matthew 3:2)—that they began to anticipate it on American soil by cultivating vast areas, by building city after city in which they gathered their people as citizens of the coming kingdom of God. The persecution and the destruction of their holy places drove them finally into the western desert, and there they fulfilled the most admirable and astonishing work of making the desert blossom under the most atrocious exterior conditions of nature, of climate, of absence of material resources.

Let me put for a moment the Mormon concept of the kingdom of God into the framework of Christian eschatology in general. In the time of Jesus three different types of eschatological expectation existed in Israel side by side:

The first one was a merely political hope to overcome the Roman conquerors and to reestablish an independent Jewish state under the guidance of the Messiah in this world with the center in Jerusalem. The Messiah was expected to be a political leader, sent by God, who, by the help of God's miraculous power, would fulfill his work of liberating the people. In the New Testament we find several examples of such cases of Messianic political rebellions trying to expel the Romans from Israel and to build up an independent Jewish state. Jesus himself was condemned by the Roman political authorities and sentenced to death as such a Messianic rebel.

Another more pietist group of believers did not expect the foundation of an earthly kingdom of a political Messiah but the coming of the heavenly Kingdom, the manifestation of the heavenly Jerusalem, brought down by the heavenly "Son of Man"—the appearance of the new heaven and the new earth, in which the chosen people of all times and generations participated in the state of resurrection. But these two different forms of expectations and of hope were not so clearly separated from each other in the hearts of the believers.

We find very soon, already in Saint Paul's letter, a third kind of expectation: A resurrected Christ will return to this earth in glory and will establish with his chosen people a kingdom for a thousand years on this earth, a millenium, and will rule the world with them during the time in which Satan is bound. Only after a thousand years of the rule of Christ will the rest of the promises of the Apocalypse be fulfilled: the last visitation of the Church of Christ, the last judgment, the resurrection of the dead, the coming of the new heaven and the new earth, and the appearance of the heavenly Jerusalem with its golden gates and its wall of diamonds, jasper, and emeralds and with its river of the water of life.

We can observe during the long history of Christianity that this expectation of the Millennium fascinated the Christian believers much more than any other merely abstract theological concept of the kingdom of God because it excited much more the human hope of salvation and of fulfillment of the divine promise; it fascinated much more the human imagination; it impelled much more the human energies to work directly for the coming of the kingdom of God, it inspired much more the purpose to accelerate its coming by human collaboration and to prepare for and even to anticiapte it here in this world.

This expectation of the millennium produced quite unexpected political and social consequences. Already in Jesus' time there were people who tried to take the kingdom of heaven by force (see Matthew 11:12). Sometimes this millenarian movement also took the form of a political revolution, as in, for example, the millenarian movement of Thomas Müntzer, the revolutionary contemporary of Martin Luther. Müntzer was convinced that it was necessary to eliminate first the enemies of the Kingdom of God, the princes and the bishops of this time, by the power of the sword, accelerating so by an open rebellion the coming of the kingdom of God. His revolt was shot down by the artillery of the Protestant and Catholic princes and bishops.

The Mormons differed from all other millenarian movements of Christian history for two reasons:

First, their program to assemble the chosen people of God in their own empire or kingdom or state or church was realized under the colonial conditions of the United States, first in the Middle West, and later on in the Far West. There was at that time still empty land enough to build up a holy state of their own by the work of their own hands and to extend this planning of their own church-state or state-church even to the enormous size of "Deseret," covering most of the western territories of the United States to the coast of the Pacific Ocean.

But there is a second still more striking peculiarity of Mormon millenarianism: in the Book of Mormon the traditional eschatology finds its new geographical center in America. The traditional idea of the Christian "Heilsgeschichte"—history of salvation—with its center in Jerusalem, in Palestine, in Asia Minor, in Europe, gets a new pole in America—first in Jackson County, Missouri, and then in Salt Lake City in Utah. The sacred history of the redemption of mankind, described in the Old and the New Testament, finds its parallel in the sacred history of America, described in the Book of Mormon. Europeans generally do not understand very clearly what that means, and I always had some difficulty in explaining it to my students. Prior to Joseph Smith, America as a continent seemed to be in a certain sense excluded from the traditional biblical history of salvation. America is never mentioned in the Bible. For the Puritan immigrants, America was the wilderness, including the American Indians, a wilderness provided by God for European religious refugees to plant a better church in the desert, better than the older European churches corrupted by popes, bishops, and kings. The American continent appeared to the European immigrants as a wild place of refuge, a wilderness without history, a *tabula rasa* offered by God for a new beginning. The historical consciousness of the Puritans was always that of immigrants.

The Book of Mormon provides a supplementary description of God's deeds on the American soil. America in the Book of Mormon is no more considered as a wilderness devoid of history but has its own long history of people and tribes and generations, including the whole pre-Columbian period; and this history of America is sacred history, history of salvation from its beginning. Even the history of the Jews finds its parallel on the American continent by the presence of the lost ten tribes of Israel or at least of some part of them. This was one of my first experiences in this country. In 1960 I had an invitation to be a guest professor at Harvard Divinity School. At that time the visa regulations were still so complicated that they gave me an immigration visa. So I had to go to the immigration office at Boston. I was waiting there for a long time in the midst of a crowd of Italians, Syrians, Greeks, and other newcomers. On the wall of the office I discovered a poster, representing the famous Indian chief standing on the rock at the coast of Plymouth, looking at the approaching Mayflower and crying: "Hey, foreigners!" It was a very pleasant comfort for all these timid newcomers to discover that this continent is populated by foreigners like them, with the only exception of the Mormons, who belong together with the Indians to the old-timers of this continent.

That means the Mormons are the only true Americans with a fully developed American historical consciousness, without any immigrant minority complex. They belong to their American continent from ancient times, not only from the late Mayflower times. This historical consciousness directly inspired, for example, the studies of pre-Columbian archaeology and enthnology that are so highly developed at this university. And I would say Mormons alone of all the rest of Americans have the privilege to celebrate not only centenaries like the latecomers of this continent but millenaries of American history and prehistory if they want to do so. Mormonism is the producer and the most realistic and practical result of the positive way of secularization of the gospel of the kingdom of heaven at hand in America, including, at the most advanced point of secularization, the printing of their own dollar bills of the Kirtland Safety Society Antibanking Company, signed by Joseph Smith, Israelite.

Now, I have talked about the two types of secularization, and I have to underline that there is a danger also in the positive line of secularization. The process of secularization in the sense of developing the original impulses of the gospel, of the power of the Holy Spirit, can proceed so far into worldliness that it comes in its advanced state to an interruption or a loss of contact with the original or heavenly source and with the heavenly aim. The vision of the heavenly kingdom of God may disappear and may be more and more absorbed by a merely social, technical, economical interpretation of the aim of mankind. "Vertical eschatology," the expectation of the kingdom of heaven which is "at hand," turns over into a merely "horizontal eschatology," the expectation of the perfect society of this world only.

Both dangers are threatening Christianity today. In the second half of the nineteenth century an American of German origin, Walter Rauschenbusch, discovered and propagated the so-called "social gospel," which influenced very quickly modern Protestant theology. The heavenly kingdom no more seemed to be relevant; the main aim of Christian theology was said to settle first the material social needs of this world. And evidently it was necessary in that time of industrialization to emphasize the social responsibility of the Christian churches in a socially and economically changing world, but some theologians went so far in this program of the social gospel that they forgot the everlasting gospel of the heavenly kingdom. Today we hear day by day from the newspapers about the worldwide activity of the Ecumenical Council of Churches to help underdeveloped countries to overcome their social troubles, an activity based on merely social and even political understanding of a so-called "theology of liberation" including revolution and terrorism; the whole activity seems to move more and more in the line of a merely "horizontal eschatology" with all its political consequences. This danger of forgetting the heavenly origin and the heavenly aim of the gospel is evidently also threatening Mormonism today. I am not entitled to talk in the name of Mormonism, and I want to avoid the slightest suspicion of arrogance to do so, but after all my studies of the religious sources of Mormonism and of the fascinating history of The Church of Jesus Christ of Latter-day Saints, and of the modern research works on Mormon eschatology, I have the impression that Mormonism keeps in its own traditional understanding of Christian life and thought three basic concepts that are sources of permanent spiritual reinforcement and could be antidotes to overcome this danger of a wrong secularization:

The first is the concept of the everlasting gospel, which we find in the Apocalypse of St. John and which is so strongly emphasized in the Book of Mormon and in the prophecies given to Joseph Smith, recorded in the Doctrine and Covenants. It means that the basic promise, the primitive power, the original spirit and force of the gospel of Jesus Christ is not exposed to decay, to corruption, or to depravation in any sense of the word. This everlasting gospel includes the permanent duty of universal mission, as it is said in the Apocalypse itself; and the same appeal to the permanent duty of universal mission is also expressed by Joseph Smith in Doctrine and Covenants 133:36–38:

And now, verily saith the Lord, that these things might be known among you, O inhabitants of the earth, I have sent forth mine angel flying through the midst of heaven, having the everlasting gospel, who hath appeared unto some and hath committed it unto man, who shall appear unto many that dwell on the earth.

And this gospel shall be preached unto every nation, and kindred, and tongue, and people.

And the servants of God shall go forth, saying with a loud voice: Fear God and give glory to him, for the hour of his judgment is come.

This order demands the continuity, the permanence, and the universality of the spreading of the everlasting gospel, which represents an effective antidote against the theory of the irreversible secularization of religion.

The other point of resistance, of attack, and of reconfirmation against the dangers of wrong secularization seems to me to be the insisting upon the promises of the permanent presence of the gifts of the Holy Spirit. Today we can observe in the midst of the crisis of Christianity and of the different Christian churches the completely unexpected rise of the so-called "charismatic movement" or "pentecostal movement," emerging in the different traditional Christian denominations, even in the Roman Catholic Church. Many Christians, disappointed by the general progress of secularization of their own church, begin to rediscover the reality and the power of the gifts of the Holy Spirit, which were forgotten or neglected or ignored in the different churches sometimes through centuries. If I look into the history of Mormonism, I discover that The Church of Jesus Christ of Latter-day Saints insisted from the very beginning of its dramatic history on the powerful presence of these gifts of the Holy Spirit; they never forgot them or ignored them. Other Christian churches are beginning to rediscover the imposition of hands, forgotten and ignored through centuries. Mormons practiced it permanently from the beginning. They understood their whole history as guided by the presence of the Holy Spirit in the form of prophecy, of advice, of confirmation, of warning, and—let us use an otherwise unfashionable word—of miracles. What the charismatic movement propagated as their new discovery can already be found in the seventh Article of Faith of The Church of Jesus Christ of Latter-day Saints, formulated by Joseph Smith: "We believe in the gift of tongues, prophecy, revelation, visions, healing, interpretation of tongues, etc." Mormons always preserved a very living feeling amd consciousness of the presence of the Holy Spirit and of the activity of his gifts, above all of prophecy as a living element of the guidance of the Church. Prophecy is more than mere adaptation, more than compromise; it is the way of divine guidance through the dangerous deserts and rocky mountains of human history, it inspires and enables the believers in the future as it did in the past to prepare and to anticipate so far as possible the coming kingdom of God.

There is still a third concept, which may preserve Mormons better than others from the wrong way of secularization. This is a concept in which they distinguish themselves from all other Christian denominations. It concerns the understanding of the religious origin and destiny of man. It is the idea of the incarnation of preexisting spirits in human bodies. But this incarnation is understood in a completely different sense than we find expressed, for example, in the Hindu concept of incarnation. Man does not come into this our world as a victim of his thirst for life, and the incarnated soul is not understood to be a victim of a theft by which his heavenly garment, the heavenly pearl, is stolen from him; incarnation is not considered a catastrophe, caused by sin committed in an earlier life, but the human soul descends from heaven into this bodily world to get the unique chance to advance in the grand scale of being, in which he is to move in the eternal worlds. The spirit descends into a body of flesh and bone because of the great council in heaven, in which God shows the human soul the possibility to develop his force and his knowledge in full consciousness of all the difficulties awaiting him there. To this knowledge belongs also the knowledge about death. The spiritual beings pressing for incarnation know very well from the beginning that the passing of death belongs to the tasks in whose performance man has to stand the test in this world. This great council is put before the free spirits for their decision. In a free decision man enters the way of endless progression, and with the full knowledge of all the risk of it, the great law of increasing complexity, the law of endless development of all his powers in the midst of a universe becoming increasingly complex. In this concept of man there is practically no place for the sense of the loss of the consciousness of the transcendent origin and aim of man. Denying his heavenly origin, would deny himself, would deny the sense of his life, the meaning of the community of man in which he lives, the sense of the universe in which he dwells.

This is actually, as I think, the main argument against the assertion of the end of religion and the irreversibility of its secularization. This assertion ignores and even offends practically human nature itself. Man is not only the *homo faber,* the technical man, not only the industrial and economical man, *homo economicus,* but also from the beginning the *homo religiosus,* the religious man, the man who has a *sensus numinus,* an inner sense, described in the Book of Creation by the words: "And God said, Let us make man in our image, after our likeness. . . . So God created man in his own image" (Genesis 1:26–27). The will to develop this image of God, the will to perfection, the will to reach the end of the development of all his power given him from above is deep-rooted in man's life; hope and the aim of perfection are a basic element of life itself.

This allows me to add still a few words about the centenary of this university. With respect to the University of Marburg, which is my university, the oldest Protestant University in the world, founded as a Protestant university in 1526, it could be said that the Brigham Young University is a relatively young institution. But this would be an inadequate consideration. If we consider the circumstances of its rise, it is a really admirable and unique foundation. Let us look at others. The Spaniards arrived in America in 1492, and they founded their first university forty-six years later in Santo Domingo in 1538; other universities were established in 1551 in Mexico and in Lima, 1562 in Guatemala, 1573 in Bogotá, and 1598 in Cuzco. They founded them fifty to 100 years after their arrival, and that in spite of the fact that they had at their disposition all they needed for such academic foundations: learned scholars, who were monks and could easily be sent out by obedience, maintained by their monastic organizations; and excellent libraries and printing presses at home, providing them with all the necessary materials for study and education and with the full traditional system of academic training.

The Protestants in America were a little faster in building up an educational system at academic level: the Pilgrim fathers arrived in 1620; Harvard College was founded in 1636, sixteen years later. The Puritans also had the opportunity to import directly their scholars and their books from England and to adopt the continental academic traditions directly from the other side of the ocean.

For the Mormons the task of building up a system of higher education was much more difficult. They were poor people, persecuted from the beginning, but even under these circumstances they started in Nauvoo a university that was destroyed during the brutal expulsion. But with an indefatigable resoluteness they came back to this plan here in Utah in spite of the fact that they were fully occupied with the enormous difficulties of colonization of the country and the daily need of survival in the desert. One generation after the arrival at the Salt Lake Valley they had their own university, which reached very soon the standard of the highest academic institutions of the country. This university had to be founded under the most difficult outer circumstances, far away from the academic foundations of the East Coast. Even after the construction of the railway they had to build up their system of higher education under the greatest sacrifices.

They could do it, because for the founder of this university, Brigham Young, education was of central value in his religious thinking, a main part of religious life itself, intimately connected with his idea of eternal progress, of permanent perfection. For him education was included in the order of Jesus Christ: "Be ye therefore perfect, even as your Father which is in heaven is perfect" (Matthew 5:48). His concept of education has its roots in its understanding of the highest aim of man, the aim to become perfect. "Intelligent beings are organized to become Gods, and become associated with the highest intelligencies [sic] that dwell in eternity. We are now in the school, and must practise upon what we receive."[1]

In that sense he proclaimed for his people the program to reach the highest possible standard of knowledge as an essential element of the gospel. And he says:

Not only does the religion of Jesus Christ make the people acquainted with the things of God, and develop within them moral excellence and purity, but it holds out every encouragement and inducement possible, for them to increase in knowledge and intelligence, in every branch of mechanism, or in the arts and sciences, for all wisdom, and all the arts and sciences in the world are from God, and are designed for the good of His people.[2]

I was very much surprised to discover in Brigham Young's writings the interpretation of a biblical idea very much discussed among the pietists of my own country in Wurtemberg, the concept of sin against the Holy Ghost mentioned in St. Matthew 12:31: "Wherefore I say unto you, All manner of sin and blasphemy shall be forgiven unto men: but the blasphemy against the Holy Ghost shall not be forgiven unto men." There were some pietists who were very much terrified by the atheistic and merely materialistic development of modern sciences, and sometimes they understood the warning of Christ against the blasphemy of the Holy Ghost as a warning against modern science. Brigham Young ignored such an anxious attitude. He says in his genial interpretation:

If we continue to learn all that we can, pertaining to the salvation which is purchased and presented to us through the Son of God, is there a time when a person will cease to learn? Yes, when he has sinned against God the Father, Jesus Christ the Son, and the Holy Ghost—God's minister: when he has denied the Lord, defied Him and committed the sin that in the Bible is termed the unpardonable sin—the sin against the Holy Ghost. That is the time when a person will cease to learn, and from that time forth, will descend in ignorance, forgetting that which they formerly knew. . . . They will cease to increase, but must decrease. . . . These are the only characters who will ever cease to learn, both in time and eternity.[3]

So his concept of education, and with it his concept of the aim of a university, is included in his concept of perfection, which opens the human mind and fills it with a real love of knowledge and joy of wisdom. In our time, when all kinds of reform programs of education are elaborated all over the world, based on a more or less totally secularized understanding of human nature, I find it inspiring to discover in the discourses of the founder of this university words that encourage students, teachers, and scholars to study and view learning as an essential element of the perfection of man and of human society with its outlook on the kingdom of God, the kingdom of heaven. Let me close with this ecumenical statement of Brigham Young, underlining the right way of secularization and preserving it from its going wrong:

How gladly would we understand every principle pertaining to science and art, and become thoroughly acquainted with every intricate operation nature, and with all the chemical changes that are constantly going on around us! How delightful this would be, and what a boundless field of truth and power is open for us to explore! We are only just approaching the shores of the vast ocean of information that pertains to this physical world, to say nothing of that which pertains to the heavens, to angels and celestial beings, to the place of their habitation, to the manner of their life, and their progress to still higher degrees of perfection.[4]

This concept of education is unique for this Brigham Young University and is worthy to be celebrated forever.

Footnotes

1. Brigham Young et al., *Journal of Discourses,* 26 vols. (London: Latter-day Saints Book Depot, 1855–1886), 8:160. Hereafter cited as *JD.*

2. *JD* 13:147.

3. *JD* 3:203.

4. *JD* 9:167.

THE POLITICAL CHALLENGES: MORMONS, GOVERNMENTS, AND POLITICS

Robert S. Jordan
with
Parley W. Newman, Jr.

Let me say at the outset that it is a pleasure for me to participate in this symposium. I personally have enjoyed the various sessions. Being a member of the Church whose career has been away from Utah and, to some extent, away from the United States, I find it refreshing to come back and to see the trends of thought that are going on and to feel the liveliness in the discourse as reflected in these colloquia. That is why I feel honored to have the opportunity to be here.

Earlier discussions in the symposia have already touched on the general subject of the Church within the context of the international political scene. Obviously it is a subject we cannot avoid. I want to continue this discussion and focus it in several selected ways. These include the problems of political confrontation and adaptation, political ideology, human rights, population control, and the communications revolution.

The Dilemma of Confrontation and Adaptation

The Revolutionary War of 1776 not only freed the American colonies from British political control, but it also severed their connections with many European social institutions. The nineteenth century therefore became a time of great experimentation as the new nation struggled to create a set of political and social institutions fitted to its unique conditions. The same was true as it sought to redefine and develop a new relation with God outside the norms of standard European religious orthodoxy. As a consequence of all this upheaval, people became serious listeners and thinkers about important religious questions. Many people were therefore receptive to the gospel when the Lord restored it in 1830. But while the restored Church survived, and indeed thrived, virtually all other religions and communal movements that sprang up at this time have withered, and most have vanished.[1]

It has been suggested by a number of observers that the Church survived the nineteenth century in America because of its remarkable ability to adapt to new surroundings and circumstances.[2] To the outsider, this represents an interesting example of social adaptation and internal cohesion; to the member, it is a reflection of continuous revelation combined with fundamental rationalism.[3] This is an appealing point, for it shows the Church as a dynamic institution, growing and adapting to meet new circumstances, with its strength deriving not from the rigidity of its doctrine but from the flexibility of its response to new and challenging circumstances.[4]

Confrontation between the Church and the surrounding society, given the central role of persecution in LDS history, is not a new theme for Mormons. But if not new, today it is certainly unfamiliar to most Latter-day Saints of North America, who have adapted well to mid-twentieth-century life. Their dress, conduct, modes of life—or life-type—while somewhat different, blend not unfavorably with those of their non-Mormon neighbors. Persecution has disappeared, and life is generally comfortable. But herein lies a danger: adaptation that is too complete leads to assimilation; and assimilation, perhaps more surely than persecution, can lead to disintegration. Some people wonder if we have already become an "aristocratic" American church, confident and comfortable in our twentieth-century American setting but propelled by our doctrine to confront the diversity of mankind.

But the problem of political confrontation versus social adaptation poses some very real and serious questions for members of the Church. It is easy to hold that the Church must preserve its essential qualities and doctrines while modifying less essential features to meet changing needs, but reconciling the two is more complex. Many Mormons, through inspiration and reason, have sought to know what is essential and cannot be altered and what can in fact be modified to fit new circumstances. An early pioneer posture of no "entangling alliances" may yet give us clues as we expand throughout the world and as our members become more and more aware of various national, social, and ethnic aspirations alien to the American experience.

Even though in its early days the Church experienced sharp tensions between itself and the established political order, today, in the United States, this tension is not readily apparent. The official policy of the Church seems to support established national governments, and especially those where the right to proselyte is not forbidden. In this respect the declaration of belief in Section 134 of the Doctrine and Covenants is often cited, part of which holds that:

We believe that all men are bound to sustain and uphold the respective governments in which they reside, while protected in their inherent and inalienable rights by the laws of such governments; and that sedition and rebellion are unbecoming every citizen thus protected, and should be punished accordingly . . . (D&C 134:5).

What is not always understood today is that such statements were originally issued not only as an expression of belief for the instruction of the membership, but also to allay the fears of non-Mormons who saw the political organization of the Church as potentially counter to American political institutions.[5] In the early days of the Church and until the time of the Manifesto, Church members were committed to fulfilling the prophecy of Daniel not only in a spiritual but in a political sense. At the center of the Kingdom's *political* organization was the Council of Fifty, eventually to become the central political organ of the world to prepare for the Second Coming. The Saints believed this political transformation was to be accomplished by peaceful and voluntary means. But this concept of peace and voluntarism was not understood or accepted by the gentiles, who saw the Mormons as a threat to their established political system. This gave a genuinely revolutionary quality to Church doctrines that is not generally known or appreciated by many Church members today.

The Saints have not wholly abandoned the idea of a theocratic government but tend to believe that it will not be instituted on a global basis until after the Second Coming. A century ago, however, members felt that the political expansion of the Church was an inherent part of the restoration of the gospel. As an example of this belief and its implications, consider the following statement by Parley P. Pratt concerning the dispensation of the fullness of times as opened by Joseph Smith to prepare the way for the Savior's return:

> *That dispensation will fulfill the times of the Gentiles, restore the kingdom to Israel, gather home their twelve tribes, organize them into a theocratic government, that is, a government founded and guided by prophets, priesthood, visions and revelations. . . . To this dispensation, all nations must submit.*
>
> *All merely human religions or political institutions, all republics, states, kingdoms, empires, must be dissolved, the dross of ignorance and falsehood be separated, and the golden principles of unalloyed truth be preserved, and blended for ever in the one consolidated, universal, eternal government of the Saints of the Most High, and all nations shall serve and obey him.*[6]

In contrast, the Church, at least for the present, has largely put aside its political aspirations. But even so, and in the context of the declaration of belief regarding government and laws contained in Section 134 of the Doctrine and Covenants, some intriguing fundamental questions remain. For example, is it proper to rebel against a government that violates the laws of God and the inalienable rights of its citizens? Our own Revolutionary War would seem to give a positive answer to that question. Or, more broadly, when should members confront a national government and when should they remain silent and perhaps, in Mark Twain's phrase, run the risk of being guilty of the lie of silent assertion? How should we Mormons respond to United States national policies that conflict with Church doctrines and also with the policies of other nations where increasing numbers of our Mormon brothers and sisters live? And what are the political implications for the Church as it seeks to expand on a global basis? These are serious questions for which there are no ready answers, as an examination of some of the most urgent political problems of the day clearly reveals.

Because we live in a secularized and secularizing world, the dangers inherent in political confrontation and social adaptation will be constantly with us. Now, as never before, Mormon leaders in all lands are seeking inspired answers to these most difficult questions.

The Church and Political Ideology

The declaration of belief noted above has generally been given broad application to mean that while members of the Church are encouraged to support the enactment of laws that protect essential freedoms, the Church does not deny the legitimacy of national governments and does not advocate their overthrow. Certainly, in our lifetime, it has been relatively tolerant and uncommitted in passing judgment upon other governmental forms. There is, however, one important exception, and that is communism.

In the early 1960s, for example, Elder Ezra Taft Benson described communism as "slavery, immorality, atheism, terrorism, cruelty, barbarism, deceit, and the destruction of human life through a kind of tyranny unsurpassed by anything in human history." He also said that the members of the Church should "accept the command of the Lord and treat socialistic-communism as the tool of Satan." And at the same time, the First Presidency of the Church went on record with a strong statement:

We call upon all Church members completely to eschew communism. The safety of our divinely inspired constitutional government and the welfare of our Church imperatively demand that communism shall have no place in America.[7]

The above statements on communism appear quite clear: the forces of evil, ignorance, and slavery are arrayed against those of freedom and justice, and no quarter can or should be given. The position of prominent leaders of the Church is unequivocal. Most American political leaders are equally as strong in their opposition to communism at home. However, it is current U.S. foreign policy, albeit debated, to seek forms of detente and rapprochement with the two bastions of communism, the Soviet Union and the People's Republic of China. The primary reason is the fear of America's national leaders that in the nuclear age there would be no victor in an all-out nuclear war, and therefore some accommodation would seem not only reasonable but prudent. Similarly, through the promotion of trade agreements and cultural exchanges, American national leaders hope that the differences between communist and capitalist societies can be reduced and that perhaps some of the liberalizing aspects of the American political and economic system will find their way into the Soviet-socialist bloc and Chinese political systems. But will they? And is there not a danger of a reverse influence?

In the circumstances, what approach can we Mormons adopt? If we categorically oppose economic and diplomatic relationships with political systems we view not only as alien but evil, we appear to challenge a fundamental foreign policy assumption of the United States government. While that might bother some American Mormons, Saints in other lands are less likely to be concerned. On the other hand, should we accept the premise of present American policy in the hope that some positive gains may be realized as by-products, such as an increase in the measure of freedom of peoples living under communist regimes, including in particular freedom of religion and, eventually, greater opportunity for missionary work? Can we not find a justification for preaching the gospel to such "closed" political systems without appearing to compromise our political stand?

As regards noncommunist authoritarian political systems, it may well be that the secularization that has been going on everywhere during the past half-century is breaking the monopoly of traditional Christianity and thereby creating proselyting opportunities for the Church that otherwise would have taken much longer to bring about. In other words, do we find ourselves in an ambiguous position where new forms of government present opportunities for the Church rather than foreclosing opportunities?

Compounding the problem further is the fact that throughout the world the idea of democracy as practiced in the United States and defended by the Church is on the decline. In Latin America, for example, two elected governments recently fell—Chile and Argentina—bringing to eight the number of nations there now under military rule. Latin America has been described as "the growing graveyard for democracies," reflecting the fact that only Venezuela and Colombia have elected governments and that the government of the latter is tottering on the brink of collapse.[8]

Elsewhere in the world the prospects for democracy are equally bleak. In Africa and Asia some form of authoritarian rule rather than democracy represents the general mode of governmental organization. India, long the bastion of Western-style democracy in Asia, appears to have preserved its democratic institutions, but it is the exception rather than the rule, and even there the temporary cessation of democratic practices under Indira Gandhi may prove to be an ominous sign for the country. Only in Western Europe, North America, and the Pacific (Japan, Australia and New Zealand) does Western-style parliamentary or representative democracy remain.

Many of the Western European governments, while retaining their elected parliamentary institutions, have in fact been moving toward the adoption of various forms of state-centered economic and social systems. Sweden and Great Britain are good examples of this movement. In these nations as well as to some extent in our own, government of elected representatives is giving way to bureaucratic government, albeit not without misgivings. A recent example can be seen in the appeal in the bicentennial U.S. presidential election campaign of those candidates—Carter and Reagan—who represented themselves as anti-government, i.e., against what was portrayed as a federal encroaching bureaucracy on the lives of the citizenry.

Concurrent with the worrisome trend away from representative democracy is the diminishing ability of the United States to influence the course of international politics. The United States is exerting a lessened impact in the world economic sphere. This is constantly reflected in the work of the United Nations, where time and time again the representatives of the United States in major political organs have adopted, though with great difficulty, postures, attitudes, and policies that ten or fifteen years ago they would not even have considered.

With the emergence of the European Economic Community (EEC) and Japan and the development of third-world (Asia, Africa, Latin America) economic blocs and pressure groups—the Organization of Petroleum Exporting Countries (OPEC) and the United Nations Conference on Trade and Development (UNCTAD) being the more visible examples—the global economic power of the United States has diminished considerably. The United States is no longer the only major exporter of technology and capital. Moreover, the country now must compete with a growing number of nations, both as a seller and as a buyer. In fact, the relative industrial capacity of the United States in relation to that of Western Europe and Japan is slipping year by year. This lessened economic and political impact leads other nations to seek political as well as economic models elsewhere.

The Church has continued to defend the concepts of political freedom as they are expressed in the American Constitution. For example, in the November 1975 General Conference Elder Benson told a worldwide audience that the members of the Church were "the nation's watchmen." "No other people," he said:

collectively love the Constitution and honor it and hold it as a divinely inspired document as do the Latter-day Saints. The duty of the watchman is to watch over his people.... Have your youth enough of the fires of freedom kindled in them to withstand the darkness? ***We must teach them in our homes, churches and schools. The sound must go across this land from one end to the other.***[9]

But in a world that is becoming increasingly pluralist—politically, economically, and hence ideologically—can the Church meet the challenge to defend these concepts while still pressing the missionary work forward in countries where full political freedom does not exist? That task must be pursued with superb skill and under the inspiration of the Lord. For the Church is becoming, in fact, a worldwide church and, in many countries, certain political concepts embedded in the doctrine may be seen as an American export or be viewed as a potential threat to the established political system or at the least be seen as doctrinally irrelevant. In any event, we must work to preserve the United States in freedom and liberty so that the Lord's purposes for the Church as a whole can be fulfilled.

The Church and Human Rights

Closely related to the Church's political orientation and its relations with national governments is one of the major political issues of the day—the question of human rights. Consider some of the provisions of Section 134 of the Doctrine and Covenants: "We do not believe that human law has a right to interfere in prescribing rules of worship to bind the conscience of men, nor dictate forms for ... devotion" (v.4). Men possess "inherent and inalienable rights" (v.5). And "we believe that no government can exist in peace, except [its] laws are framed and held inviolate as will secure to each individual the free exercise of conscience, the right and control of property, and the protection of life"(v.2).

And in our own time the leaders of the Church have reaffirmed the LDS commitment to the principles of individual rights and freedoms. For example, Elder Hugh B. Brown, then a member of the First Presidency, spoke strongly in favor of these rights:

We say again, as we have said many times before, that we believe that all men are the children of the same God, and that it is a moral evil for any human being to be denied the right to gainful employment, to full educational opportunity, and to every privilege of citizenship, just as it is a moral evil to deny him the right to worship according to the dictates of his own conscience. . . .

We call upon all men, everywhere, both within and outside the Church, to commit themselves to the establishment of full civil equality for all God's children. Anything less than this defeats our high ideal of the brotherhood of man.[10]

Yet the ideals proclaimed by the Church and other institutions concerning the brotherhood of man and the right of every individual to his liberty and freedom of conscience all too often encounter national practices that run counter to them. Perhaps the first national practices to spring to the mind of Latter-day Saints are the repressions by the Soviet government of its people as described by expatriate author, Alexander Solzhenitsyn. Here the Church may deal with the problem directly and openly; it would be surprising if a Church that believes in continuous divine revelation and an atheistic authoritarian political system were not critical of each other.

But on another level the issue may be less forthright, as, for example, the repressions that occur in many of the quasi-totalitarian governments of the right that abound in Latin America and Asia but that nevertheless allow the Church considerable religious freedom of operation. Because of our doctrinal adherence to the dignity of man and therefore to human rights and freedoms, should we, through our local representatives abroad, press for civil rights and political liberties and defend the inalienable rights of all God's children? If so, would we run the risk of antagonizing a national government that could all too easily turn its repressive measures against Church members?[11] Many countries have political systems that allow them to engage legitimately in political repression. That is true, in fact, for the overwhelming majority of nations. When is it better to confront and when is it better to remain silent? Which moral principles are worth defending before the world, and what risks are worth the potential cost that incurring them entails? To use a biblical analogy, when do you accuse the king of adultery and when do you refrain from speaking? (Cf. Matthew 14:1–11 and Luke 23:6–9.)

Population Control and Birth Control

Population control and birth control, though obviously related, are not necessarily the same thing. The former generally refers to a set of governmental policies designed to reduce the rate of population growth within a country. Birth control, on the other hand, refers more specifically to the decisions of couples to limit the size of their families. Both types of control are becoming more and more accepted, particularly in countries that have become notably secularized and economically advanced. In other countries, for example India, national governments have sometimes made strenuous efforts to reduce the rate of population growth through birth control measures, even to the point of conducting mass sterilization programs. The Church's position on population, as far as its own members are concerned, is quite clear: we are urged to have large families, circumstances permitting. The Church's position with respect to nonmember populations is less clear, though the general Mormon attitude seems to be that population is not the serious problem many make it out to be. Support for this attitude is drawn from scripture—"For the earth is full, and there is enough and to spare" (D&C 104:17)—and from a belief that God has a plan for the tabernacling of his spirits with which man should not tamper. The advent of the Millennium when the wicked will be destroyed is sometimes seen as a solution to population problems.[12] And then there is the commandment, which has never been rescinded, to replensih the earth. With regard to resource pressures, a prevailing attitude is that population increase can be cared for through increased production, resource reallocation, and a willingness to establish the right priorities.[13]

The Church's position with regard to population has occasionally come under fire for failing, in the minds of its critics, to come to grips with actual physical circumstances. But whatever may be the merit of such criticisms, it is not the position itself that is the heart of the political difficulties being examined here but rather that the Church may find itself directly in the middle of delicate international political ebbs and shoals, to say nothing of reefs. In many countries where population control has become a tool of national policy to achieve social ends, teachings of the Church encouraging large families could run directly counter to these national policies. Thus, once again some members may face an unpleasant dilemma: if they accept the teachings of the Church and advocate large families, they may risk sanctions against themselves and the Church. What should or can be done in these circumstances? The choices, unfortunately, may not be easy.

With regard to birth control, the Church has taken an unambiguous stand. Early in 1969 the First Presidency issued a statement regarding the official Church position. Two key paragraphs of this statement are as follows:

We seriously regret that there should exist a sentiment or feeling among any members of the Church to curtail the birth of their children. We have been commanded to multiply and replenish the earth that we may have joy and rejoicing in our posterity.

Where husband and wife enjoy health and vigor and are free from impurities that would be entailed upon their posterity, it is contrary to the teachings of the Church artifically to curtail or prevent the birth of children. We believe that those who practice birth control will reap disappointment by and by.[14]

Within the body of Church doctrine are many reasons why members should rear large families, in addition to the commandment given to Adam and Eve. This is not the place to review those teachings; the point, rather, is that the teachings of the Church on birth control could carry with them important implications for the Church's relations with national governments.

In addition to such economic pressures as inflation, the cost of education, and increasing job insecurity and persistent unemployment, some national policies are already construed to favor those with small families. These are specific governmental policies and programs and not merely the unofficial social pressures often brought to bear on individuals. For example, United States income tax laws, although perhaps not intended to be punitive, are seen by some to discriminate against large families, in that the exemptions permitted do not approach the cost of child support. And in fact they also discriminate against marriage. Couples who choose to live together rather than marry can, depending on their level of income, save from several hundred to several thousand dollars a year on their taxes. To cite one example, the well-known CBS news program "Sixty Minutes" once reported the case of a couple who, every year, fly to a Caribbean island shortly before the end of the year, obtain a divorce, then return to the United States to file tax returns and remarry.

It is also possible that, in spite of substantial opposition from civil rights groups, including the American Civil Liberties Union, the federal government will take steps to limit the number of children that can be born to welfare recipients, especially single women. Should this in fact become a reality, it would constitute a vitally important and potentially dangerous precedent for the intervention of the federal government in the private lives of its citizens.

For the moment, however, United States policies with regard to population limitation do not constitute a direct challenge to the Church teachings on the importance of the family. More important are social and economic pressures likely to be reflected in future policies. National policies in several other countries can, however, present a potentially critical area of strain between the Church and national political authority. This potential conflict exists because, in contrast to the position of the Church, the prevailing conventional wisdom in most countries is that the "population explosion" represents a critical issue that must be faced openly and immediately. The president of the World Bank, Robert McNamara, for instance, compared the population "bomb" to the nuclear bomb and described it as "a central determinant of mankind's future, and one requiring far more attention . . . than it is presently receiving."[15] Given the assumptions non-Mormon observers bring to this question, the logic of their position is not difficult to understand. At present rates of growth, and assuming demographic changes associated with economic development and modernization, the population of the world, which reached 4 billion in 1975, will be roughly 6.5 billion in the year 2000. By the year 2020, the world will have reached a net reproduction rate of 1.0 (the minimum replacement level), and by the end of the 21st century will have attained a stable population of about 11 billion, or a little less than 3 times the present population.

What such a population would mean for global conditions, is of course, not known. But in a world whose resources, at the present rate of consumption, appear already to be under considerable pressure, it does not appear that conditions, especially in the developing world would be better than they are now, and are likely to be far worse. Even if quick action is taken on a massive scale so that the replacement level of 1.0 is reached in the year 2000 instead of 2020, the world population would eventually stabilize at about 8 billion. This is still a very large figure, one that reflects the long lead times governing population trends. But the difference between this figure and that of 11 billion is significant, and, precisely because of the long lead times involved, for many people the problem becomes a particularly insistent one.

Not all people or governments share this view, however, and for this reason population control is one of the most hotly debated and divisive issues confronting the international community. On one side are those developed nations, such as the United States, Canada, and West Germany, who are currently at or are about to achieve zero population growth. These countries argue that the rapid population growth of many developing countries puts tremendous pressure on food supplies and undermines development efforts. They assert that this will be true despite the "green revolution" that has permitted food production to keep pace with increases in population, albeit somewhat behind in terms of distribution. Further increases in the use of chemical fertilizers (especially in view of the energy crisis), pesticides, and mechanized farming techniques could create a situation wherein food might be available; but its increased cost, derived from the application of these modern techniques, could make it prohibitively expensive for these nations. In this sense, a rise in food cost might be a bigger danger than a reduction in supply.[16]

As many developing countries view the issue, it is probable, however, that population growth will outstrip food production. Thus third-world governments see themselves faced with two unhappy choices: either control population growth or deplete national foreign currency reserves to purchase ever more expensive food, thus risking, ultimately, insolvency and famine. In this connection, today the United States and Canada, both zero population growth countries, produce more of the world's export grain and by the end of this century could continue to be the primary international suppliers. This would give these two countries tremendous international impact and influence as they decide who shall receive food and who shall not.[17]

Another strand of the argument for population control is that in developing countries attempting to develop a modern industrial capacity, surplus production must be reinvested in the economy if growth is to be achieved. It is self-defeating, however, if marginal increases in production are offset by concomitant increases in population that consume the excess production rather than permit its reinvestment. Thus, many governments see limiting population growth as a way to help achieve industrial development and, as a not incidental by-product, to increase the standard of living of their citizens. Many developing countries, however, do not share this view of the relationship of population control and economic development. Instead, they view Western calls for such efforts with deep suspicion, fearing they reflect a form of neocolonialism the developed nations are using to preserve the current international economic order. These countries perceive population growth as an essential element of their industrial growth, providing new consumers and an expanding labor force. These developing countries, thus, are seeking to expand their populations.

These countries also point to the fact that an individual in an advanced industrial state can consume about five times as many resources as a person in a developing country, and thus they argue, perhaps with considerable justification, that population growth in their countries does not carry the same ultimate economic implications; instead, population control by some countries may make possible, in humane terms, better lives for growing populations in other countries. Further, they stress that what is needed is not population control but a more equitable redistribution of the world's wealth. In this same vein, though in less drastic form, the United Nations has been carefully studying the problems of population at the international level.[18] Aspects of secularization other than birth control—social and economic changes associated with modernization and industrialization, for example—may actually play a more important role in determining demographic trends within a society. For example, in a recent speech on population control, Mr. McNamara suggested five steps governments of developing countries might take to reduce population growth:[19]

1. Reduce current infancy and child mortality rates sharply.
2. Expand basic education and increase the proportion of girls in school.
3. Increase the productivity of smallholders in the rural areas, and expand earning opportunities in the cities for low income groups.
4. Put greater stress on more equitable distribution of income and services in the drive for economic growth.
5. Above all else, raise the status of women socially, economically, and politically.

It is clear, therefore, that the Church's position on birth control is not the only element that may bring it into conflict with the secular world. The conflict could be much deeper and could reach to the very nature of modern society. The challenge is clear: How can Church members deal with the secularizing trends on all fronts of modern society that may already be shifting the values of some Church members, both old and new, away from the Church's teachings on birth control? It is of no small moment that family planning has become a subject of intense debate among many younger Church couples, and in fact several studies have revealed that a high percentage of these couples are practicing birth control.[20]

The Church and the Communications Revolution

The Church's more recent global orientation, set against the backdrop of its traditional American national setting, can create tensions within the Church between an American-dominated center and a periphery extending in many directions worldwide. Since early times, the Church has possessed a centralized, somewhat authoritarian organizational structure, although of late there have been substantial changes made in the direction of organizational decentralization. This centralization has been possible largely because, until only recently, the population of the Church was small and was concentrated for the most part in the Western United States. And even during the more recent period of the Church's rapid international growth, centralization remained possible because of the concomitant growth in communication and transportation systems permitting instantaneous contact with, and travel access to, any part of the globe. But now that the Church has become significantly larger and more pluralist in composition and practice, this new pluralism argues in favor of a more decentralized administrative system. The Church, through its regional programs and stress on local program initiative, has vigorously responded to these needs, although the results of the experiment in several areas are inconclusive. And indeed the reconstitution of the First Quorum of Seventy may reflect an increasing centralization of Church operations. But decentralization internationally might afford a degree of administrative flexibility that can help lower the possibility that American national political values will become intertwined with the application of Church programs abroad. Whether or not this is so, however, remains to be seen. Another aspect of the growth of communications technology, and especially satellite communications, is that virtually all parts of the world can know at the same time the course of events elsewhere. Thus social values such as racial or social equality, although expressed differently in different places, could gradually meld into globalized values that might effect the attitudes that political authorities in diverse lands have about the Church and the attitudes that the Church has about itself.

Conclusions

As the Church increases and expands, it encounters a world becoming politically and socially pluralist. This pluralism can create tensions between the Church and various national political policies and social attitudes and aspirations, perhaps posing a dilemma for the Church: should it follow a course of adaptation, as it has on occasion in its more America-centered past, by avoiding confrontation with national laws, or should it rather place its emphasis on maintaining practices and doctrinal consistency worldwide? The dilemma is complicated by the fact that both courses entail certain risks. Too much adaptation can lead to internal pluralism, assimilation, and disintegration; conversely, too much rigidity could invite that loss of dynamism so vital to a growing Church. How to proceed remains a difficult and most delicately balanced question. Clearly the Church must proceed to fulfill its important earthly purpose. Unfortunately, today's choices are not as clearly defined as were Joshua's.[21] It is not a question of whom to serve, but how to serve, of when to stand fast and when to make slight modifications, of when to confront and when to step aside.

Footnotes

1. Several other nineteenth-century American religions did survive well into the twentieth century. Among them are Christian Science, founded by Mary Baker Eddy; Seventh-day

Adventism, founded by Ellen White; and the Jehovah's Witnesses, founded by Charles Taze Russell.

2. The frontier pragmatism and industry of Brigham Young are well known and frequently cited in this connection. Another good, if commonly used, example is the Manifesto, which, to many, combines revelation with a practical realization of an inescapable situation.

3. Two good examples of studies that take this sociological approach are Thomas F. O'Dea, *The Mormons* (Chicago: University of Chicago Press, 1957) and Mark P. Leone, "The Economic Basis for the Evolution of Mormon Religion" in Irving I. Zaretsky and Mark P. Leone, eds., *Religious Movements in Contemporary America* (Princeton, N.J.: Princeton University Press, 1974), pp. 722–66.

4. A few fundamental examples would include the following: (1) the introduction and abolition of polygamy; (2) the substitution of tithing for the united order; (3) the doctrinal importance of the Word of Wisdom; and (4) the continual evolution of Church organization to meet new conditions. Such modifications raise important questions concerning the difference between doctrine, i.e., the revealed word, and convention. This distinction, not always easy to apply, is a central concern in this paper.

5. The following discussion derives largely from Klaus J. Hansen, *Quest for Empire: The Political Kingdom of God and the Council of Fifty in Mormon History* (East Lansing: Michigan State University Press, 1967), perhaps the best scholarly study of Mormon political institutions available to date.

6. Parley P. Pratt, *Key to the Science of Theology,* 10th ed. (Salt Lake City: Deseret Book Co., 1966), p. 76.

7. Both statements may be found in *The Improvement Era* (December 1961), pp. 953 and 954.

8. "Latin America, the Growing Graveyard for Democracies," *New York Times,* 28 March 1976, Sec. 4, p. E1.

9. *Ensign,* (November 1975), pp. 9–10, emphasis in the original.

10. *Improvement Era* (December 1968).

11. The issue for the Church is made even more difficult in this area by the contemporary rise in demands across racial and ethnic boundaries for social equality. The position of the Church on matters of racial and social equality is unambiguous. The Church strongly emphasizes that all mankind is the offspring of the same God and that all individuals are to receive equally of the benefits and blessings appertaining to membership in his Church. The Church did not, however, until mid-1978, extend the priesthood to Blacks of African descent. In some areas (e.g., Brazil, Islamic Middle East) where racial sensitivities are substantially different from other areas of the world where the Church has congregations, difficult political problems could have arisen.

12. See, for example an editorial in the *Church News,* supplement to the *Deseret News* (Salt Lake City, Utah), 18 April 1970, p. 16.

13. In this connection see *Brigham Young University Today,* (March 1977), which contains a series of interviews on the question of population and food supplies.

14. Issued to presidents of stakes, bishops of wards, and presidents of missions, 14 April 1969, and quoted in Robert Kane, Wayne Spencer and Barry Rigby, "Family Planning Attitudes and Practices in a Mormon Community," *Sunstone* 1 (Fall 1976):79; and Lester E. Bush, "Birth Control Among the Mormons: Introduction to an Insistent Question," *Dialogue: a journal of Mormon Thought* 10 (Autumn 1976):27.

15. Address to the Massachusetts Institute of Technology, 28 April 1977, p. 4 of the text.

16. See *The Economist,* 13 March 1976, p. 88.

17. See "The Future Revised," *Wall Street Journal,* 25 March 1976, pp. 1, 21.

18. At a recent United Nations symposium it was recommended that national governments remove restrictions on the availability and use of contraceptives and make them freely available to their citizens. See *The Symposium on Law and Population: Proceedings, Background Papers and Recommendations*, (New York: United Nations Fund for Population Activites, 1975), pp. 284–85.

19. Address to the Massachusetts Institute of Technology, 28 April 1977, p. 32 of the text.

20. See, for example, "Family Planning," pp. 78–84, and "Birth Control," pp. 12–44.

21. Choose ye this day whom ye will serve; but as for me and my house, we will serve the Lord"(Joshua 24:15).

THE CHURCH IN A SECULAR WORLD: FREEDOM, ECONOMIC EFFICIENCY, AND EQUALITY*

J. R. Kearl and Clayne L. Pope

The fostering of full economic freedom lies at the base of our liberties. Only in perpetuating economic freedom can our social, political and religious liberties be preserved.[1]

In the twentieth century, preservation of freedom has been a consistent and recurring concern of the Church. Over the past four decades this concern has often found expression in the addresses and writings of prominent Church leaders. As the Church expands to a worldwide membership, the poignancy of their concern is more and more apparent. Many Mormons now live in lands where constitutional and other freedoms have been collapsing. Under such conditions the Church has sometimes experienced severe strains as it attempts to carry out its mission. Little wonder that freedom has become a central concern. Unfortunately, the trend Church leaders and others concerned about losses of freedom have so often decried—increased governmental involvement in social problems—continues. No doubt many complex reasons for the continuation of this trend exist. Among the most prominent of these is the powerful interplay of social forces and values. A better understanding of these profound social forces and values may allow for the development of an effective strategy to preserve liberty. Hence, in this essay we will describe the interplay of some strong currents within modern societies that seem to have very undesirable consequences for human liberty. Thereafter we will explore a possible remedy.

*We appreciate the comments on earlier drafts given us by Cole Durham, LaMond Tullis, Douglas Tobler, Martin Hickman, and members of the Department of Economics at Brigham Young University.

This essay was not presented at the expanding Church symposia but was prepared especially for this volume.

Secularization and Decentralization

The Industrial Revolution unleashed within Western society a secularization process comprised of three main economic elements. First, economic activity became increasingly rational, and efficiency became an increasingly important criterion by which to judge economic issues; second, the market (voluntary exchange of goods, services, and resources) gradually became the dominant form of economic organization; finally, and most important for our purposes, social equality became and continues to be a driving ethical value and social force within modern society. All these changes have combined to bring more people into conflict with each other over social and economic issues—more people demanding their rights as they see them. These demands for rights (more equitable treatment) are usually connected to measures that redistribute income. Consequently, each country has had to work out its own way of dealing with those conflicts and of deciding how, or by what process, the national income should be divided up or distributed.

This issue may be particularly acute in representative democracies with a strong allegiance to decentralized political power. Here coalitions of voters—with narrow interests but substantial prospective gains to make—use the voting and lobbying processes to effect a redistribution of income. If the prospective losses to other groups are diffuse and relatively insignificant, it may be difficult to form countervailing coalitions. This may be true even, as we shall suggest below, when losses to other groups are substantial. But we shall consider a further problem. Gains accruing to a narrow interest group while the losses are spread over broader groups in the population lead to a particularism we believe to be potentially destructive.

Americans have, of course, had a long and abiding intellectual allegiance to laissez-faire capitalism as well as to decentralized and pluralistic political and legal institutions. By this we mean that it has been America's preference to allow important decisions to be made by other than the central government and also to allow a variety of interests to be involved in the bargaining process (labor unions, professional groups, manufacturer's associations, consumer groups, individuals, and so forth).

This decentralization, combined with the aforementioned economic and social changes, has caused the political and social forces of society that favor more economic equality in America (minorities, consumer groups) to adopt a piecemeal or particularistic approach to income redistribution—an approach that can be contrasted with a general approach. Suppose a society decides to redistribute income to the poor. A piecemeal approach would call for intervention in favor of the poor in particular markets. For example, rent ceilings could be imposed, ceilings on the price of gas and electricity might be established, food prices could be forced down—all through government intervention. Such steps would be focused at helping the poor through lowering the price or improving the quality of goods they purchase.

The market price plays a central role here. Intervention in particular markets is generally based on the assumption that, from some social perspective, the market price is not the appropriate or fair price; hence, the government and other groups attempt to manipulate the price to be something other than that which is market-determined. This particularistic intervention leads to two difficulties: Prices other than market clearing prices lead to inefficient allocations of resources, commodities, and services (unless there are market distortions); prices other than market clearing prices no longer ration resources, commodities, and services among competing claimants. This latter difficulty is particularly threatening to economic freedom: whenever prices fail to ration, an alternative rationing scheme must be instituted. Such schemes usually require an extensive control and enforcement apparatus and, as a consequence, they stimulate the growth of bureaucratic governmental bodies who have the power to control and restrict certain forms of behavior. Thus, piecemeal approaches, requiring intervention in particular markets or segments of the economy (such as transportation, oil, steel) not only reduce economic efficiency but economic freedom as well.

Since the social forces that press for more equal income distribution have become particularly strong and are a major force of our age, not only in America but in all other countries that historically have had some form of capitalist economy, the only effective way to preserve freedom is to adopt general policies that will reduce economic inequality but that will not do as much violence to individual freedom and economic efficiency as do piecemeal approaches to income redistribution. If this line of analysis is correct, it has important implications for the way we Mormons respond socially and politically to twentieth-century society.

Clearly, the distribution of income within a society is an ethical matter which, in democracies, ultimately must be based on a people's values. While we have strong feelings about how income should be distributed, we do not wish this essay to be taken as a polemic on economic justice. Rather, assuming that political liberties, as President McKay stated in the opening quote, derive in part from economic freedom and are therefore a primary objective, we wish to focus on the social forces involved in the income redistribution struggle and upon a strategy for dealing with those forces. Thus our thrust is both analytical and prescriptive: we want to show how the social forces pressing for social and economic equality arose and why they tend to reduce economic freedom and efficiency. But we will also show how those forces can be handled in such a way that their impact upon freedom and economic efficiency can be made less destructive. In addition, after developing the analysis outlined above, we will return to some brief observations about income distribution and social justice.[2]

We will first discuss the attractive characteristics of a capitalistic system: economic freedom and economic efficiency. After considering how freedom and efficiency make capitalism attractive, we will then turn to the elements of the secularization process that generate movements for social equality and that in turn threaten the freedom and efficiency that have made capitalism attractive. Our response to these transformations should follow from an understanding of the secularization process and its relationship to the movement for social equality.

The Attractiveness of Capitalism

Freedom and the Host Society

Church leaders have been deeply concerned about the loss of freedom and the rise of government, trends perceived as dominant in the twentieth century. Authorities such as J. Reuben Clark, Jr., David O. McKay, and Ezra Taft Benson have articulated this concern consistently.

This concern for freedom seems to stem from two Church-related sources, one theological, the other organizational. Theologically, agency and freedom of action are considered essential for human perfection—the goal of our existence. Moreover, coercion and force were part of Lucifer's plan, something to be shunned and avoided if not actively fought. Thus the Church is concerned with the loss of freedom because a loss would constrain individuals and inhibit their development. Similarly, the organization of the Church leads to a preoccupation with freedom. Because the Church is a centrally organized hierarchial unit, freedom from the pressure of a strong central government is necessary if such an organization is to be functional.

No doubt the attractiveness of capitalism within the Church is related to the freedom capitalism engenders. As Noel Reynolds and Dwight Israelsen have noted,[3] we must be concerned about the "host society" in which the Church operates. Capitalism or a market organization of the economy has several characteristics related to freedom that make it an attractive "host" for the Church.[4] For one thing, the freedom associated with a market economy comes from decentralization. A system of competitive markets (where no individual can affect price) disperses power to the point where individuals do not have economic power. Because of this decentralization, individuals in a market economy have a wide range of choice in terms of work and consumption patterns. In one sense this freedom of choice for the individual allows members of the Church in countries governed by such decentralized norms to withdraw from the world and make the atypical choices implied by the gospel.[5]

Another advantage of a decentralized market economy with respect to freedom is the tolerance it has for centralized subunits. The Church is a fairly large and centralized organization. Governments interested in central planning and control usually find such organizations at best an irritant and usually take steps to eliminate what they view as a competitive centralized authority. It is hard to imagine those operating a planned economy looking with favor on the Church welfare program or tolerating a tithing system that centrally collects and disburses funds. Clearly the socio-political power of centralized subunits like the Church would be viewed as inimical to goals and plans of a government intent on central planning and control. This conflict between government and other centralized organizations in a planned economy makes capitalism with its decentralized markets a very attractive host society for the Church. Indeed, we suspect that one source of conflict between the Church and the larger society is rooted in the divergent interests of the Church as it centralizes power and authority and other large institutions (especially government) also striving to centralize power. This necessarily leads the Church to an increasingly vocal opposition to government control.

In the midst of the worldwide growing power of governments in the late 1930s, President J. Reuben Clark articulated this concern:

Reduced to its lowest terms, the great struggle which now rocks the whole earth more and more takes on the character of a struggle of the individual versus the State. Does the individual exist for the benefit of the state, or does the State exist for the benefit of the individual? . . .

This gigantic world-wide struggle more and more takes on the form of a war to the death. We shall do well and wisely so to face and so to enter it. And we must all take part. Indeed, we all are taking part in that struggle, whether we will or not. Upon its final issue, liberty lives or dies.

In the economic field, this earth-wide conflict has taken the form of seizing without compensation from the man who has and giving to the man who has not, of taking from the worker the fruits of his work, and giving to the idler who does no work. It has from its very nature become an economic, uncompensated leveling downward, not upward, of the whole mass. This is the result in every country in which it has been tried. That this result may in one country be reached by confiscatory taxation, and in another by direct seizure, is a mere matter of method. The result is the same. In some countries outright seizure and con-

fiscation are already openly and shamelessly practiced. All is done in the name of the State, as if it were Deity—as if the State, not God, gave all.[6]

Decentralization and Efficiency

Market decentralization is important not simply because it allows people to behave in a variety of ways but because it channels their behavior in an important way. The result is that competitive free markets[7] have the remarkable property of channeling individual pursuit of self-interest into precisely that allocation of commodities and resources that is efficient, where efficiency simply means that the economy, assuming any particular distribution of income, is doing as well as it can. We can judge the efficiency of an economy by asking the following question: Can we make any individual better off (by reorganizing resources) without hurting anyone else? If the answer is yes, the economy is not efficient. This channeling of self-interest through competitive markets to a beneficial end is the essence of Adam Smith's "invisible hand," which he describes in *Wealth of Nations*. In a free market economy, resources are directed, as if by an invisible hand, to their most socially beneficial use. It is not that anyone thinks this self-interested individualistic behavior is of itself socially beneficial but, rather, that free markets channel such behavior into social benefit. Thus decentralization of economic activity such as occurs in free-market capitalism not only yields freedom; it is also socially beneficial because it is economically efficient. No doubt Adam Smith still says it best:

As every individual, therefore, endeavours as much as he can both to employ his capital in the support of domestic industry, and so to direct that industry that its produce may be of the annual revenue of the society as great as he can. He generally, indeed, neither intends to promote the public interest, nor knows how much he is promoting it. . . . He intends only his own security; and by directing that industry in such a manner as its produce is in this, as in many other cases, led by an invisible hand to promote an end which was no part of his intention. Nor is it always the worse for the society that it was no part of it. By pursuing his own interest he frequently promotes that of the society *more effectually than when he really intends to promote it. I have never known much good done by those who affected to trade for the public good. It is an affectation, indeed, not very common among merchants, and very few words need be employed in dissuading them from it.*[8]

Smith's notion of social interest is, in fact, the modern notion of economic efficiency. That is, competitive markets transform the actions of self-interested individuals into an efficient allocation of a nation's resources. There are, of course, some areas in which this "invisible hand" of competitive market capitalism fails. The problems of monopolies, goods consumed in common such as in national defense, and external effects such as the social costs imposed by water or air pollution, are all examples of market failure in the sense of less-than-efficient allocation of resources. Indeed, modern non-Marxian economics (neoclassical economics) has concerned itself with, in part, an analysis of these areas and an investigation of possible remedies as well as a proof of the theorem that competitive markets yield an efficient allocation of resources. However, the premise is always that the remedies ought to ape what the market would do if it were to work perfectly. Using efficiency as a criterion, modern economics has, consequently, provided a powerful argument for free markets.[9]

Market Efficiency and Social Equality

The difficulty, in part, is the economists' criteria for efficiency have almost nothing to say about the distribution of income and therefore about social equality. An efficient allocation is not unique.[10] Any distribution of income, equal or unequal, is compatible with some efficient allocation of resources. Hence, efficiency has little ethical content relative to distributional issues. Thus, for example, a competitive market allocation that resulted in one-individual's having all the society's production with all other members having none would be efficient, just as a completely equal distribution of income is consistent with an efficient allocation of resources. Happily, it is possible, in principle, to have differing distributions of output and consumption and still have efficient allocation. However, it appears that within social organizations, there is, in fact, a tradeoff: different distributional goals must be purchased at the cost of some economic efficiency.[11] It is the *method* of redistribution, not redistribution per se, that causes the tradeoff between more equality and efficiency. That is, if we attempt to accomplish more equality by government control of particular markets, there will be a reduction in economic efficiency. However, if we redistributed income without intervening in individual markets, no market inefficiency would result.

In spite of its failure to answer completely distributional questions, the "invisible hand" argument of Adam Smith about the beneficial collective results from decentralized economic behavior are extremely persuasive because experience has shown that, on the issue of efficiency, economic centralization does *no* better than economic decentralization. (Besides, centralization carries the extra potential risk of undermining the social freedoms that would make a society a good host for subgroups with divergent interests, such as the Church). But it is not decentralization *per se* that yields this socially beneficial result *but decentralization within the market framework.* That is, a decentralized market economy has been shown to have an invisible-hand property relative to efficiency. One cannot infer, however, that all decentralized decisions will also have such a property. Indeed, decentralization of nonmarket decisions (how the national income is to be divided, or whether to prosecute a war or declare a national emergency) may lead to a fallacy of composition where individual pursuit of self-interest leads to collective harm. (A fallacy of composition exists when an argument true for a part is assumed to be true for the whole. For example, if one individual stands up at a sporting event, she might see better, but if all individuals stand they do not have a better view. Indeed, their view, and certainly their comfort, is worse.) We shall argue that income distribution issues are nonmarket in nature and that the decentralization of decisions about them does not result in an invisible-hand type of benefit.

We shall develop this argument by first suggesting that both those interested in economic freedom and those interested in economic efficiency as important properties of a host society have failed to come to grips with secularization as a process rather than the secular as a state of existence. They have, as a consequence, forced one of the products of secularization, the movement for social equality, into a mode—piecemeal approaches to income distribution—that undermines the aforementioned attractive properties of the decentralized market economy.

Secularization and Equality

The Industrial Revolution generated cataclysmic change within Western society and accelerated the process of secularization. Preindustrial man, as molded and idealized by the traditional churches and the Enlightenment, was largely concerned with a well-rounded intellect, religious values, land, and the social ties of community or village. But the Industrial Revolution seemed to create a new idealized image of man—one who was acquisitive, self-interested, thrifty, and completely rational.[12] It took that kind of man, it was thought, to make an industrialized economic order work. Yet the same industrial revolution that created that new image of man also created an economic organization that many observers thought dehumanized him. Consider the following:

All the gains from specialization and industrialization are summed up in the one word, efficiency; it enables us to get more goods, or better; its advantages are instrumental. On the other hand, specialization in itself, is an evil, measured by generally accepted human ideals. It gives us more products, but in its effects on human beings as such it is certainly bad in some respects and in others questionable. In the nature of the case it means a narrowing of the personality; we like to see people of all-around, well-developed powers and capacities. In extreme instances, such as the monotonous work of machine-tending, or repetitive movements at a machine-forced pace, it may be ruinous to health and maddening to the spirit. In this connection it is especially significant that the most important source of gain also involves the most important human cost. The specialization of leadership means that the masses of the people work under conditions which tend to suppress initiative and independence, to develop servility as well as narrowness and in general to dehumanize them.[13]

Reactions to this dehumanization developed on several fronts—religious authorities, Marxists, Utopian socialists—each with widely differing assumptions about the nature of man.[14] Was he secular all along, as Marx and neoclassical economists had argued, and was simply being dehumanized by an exploitative economic system known as capitalism? Or did man by nature more closely approximate the preindustrial ideal, as Christian humanists and Utopian socialists had argued, and was simply becoming secularized by the economic system in which he lives?

As you might imagine, there is yet no agreement as to which of the above two views should prevail. Notwithstanding, do either of them—the assumption by neoclassical economists and Marx that man by nature is secular, or the assumption by Christian humanists and socialists that man, while not secular by nature, has become secularized by the economic system in which he lives—create conflict for the Church at a time when the entire world seems to be getting more secularized? Based on the responses by prominent Mormon leaders, first in the nineteenth and then in the twentieth centuries, we conclude that Mormons have been less concerned about whether man is secular or made so by a secularization process than about societies' responses (especially governmental responses) to the difficulties that either may create. There is a historical ambivalence that seems paradoxical. In the nineteenth century many Mormon leaders were quite critical of capitalism and its values and responded in a way similar to many Christian utopian thinkers. In the twentieth century some spokesmen have rather uncritically embraced modern industrial capitalism. These quite different responses lead us to conclude that the Church must apparently perceive the central threat from the secular world to be not the impact of secularization on individuals but rather the danger to individuals posed by the responses of industrial societies to secularization.

The principal area in which the Church has displayed a deep concern with secularization *per se* is in the area of family disintegration. Clearly the family with internal and external threats to it is the dominant theme of the Church in the seventies. ("Give your children everything. Give them your time.") It also seems clear that family disintegration, though probably exaggerated, is itself a prime result of the same processes of secularization and industrialization that have generated the social tensions that invite governmental intervention in the economy with consequent loss of freedom and efficiency. But, as yet, many Mormons have focused on a symptom (governmental intervention) rather than responding to a cause (secularization and industrialization).

What has been the modern world's response to the secularization brought on by industrial capitalism? We would suggest two general responses. First, societies attempt to facilitate and encourage efficient allocation of resources. Either formal laws or social rules develop around the production and exchange of goods and services. These include contracts and their enforcement, definition and protection of property rights, and ethical norms about honesty and productive effort. On the other hand, and in tension with these developments, societies respond to secularization and the market in ways that attempt to protect individuals from possible adverse effects. In this latter area we argue that the dominant response has been to underwrite a drive for social equality or, more conservatively, to sponsor a drive for less inequality within society. This movement for equality—or less inequality—has included extension of the franchise, equality before the law, and equality of opportunity as embodied in educational reform and passive antidiscrimination laws. Given our earlier discussion of the power of coalitions with narrow interests to use the political process to pursue these interests, the extension of the franchise, although itself a part of the movement for equality, has also facilitated the movement. Moreover, these forms of equality—essentially equality of rights or opportunities—are not independent of less inequality in outcomes. Hence equality of opportunity has appeared to be unattainable[15] because inequality in outcome remains. Thus the policy focus in our time has begun to shift to equality of result with embodiment in direct income transfers and quota-type rectification of past discrimination. This movement for less inequality has largely generated the increase in government intervention that inspires trepidation in Church leaders.

There is logic to the Church's lack of concern with the forces of secularization but its deep concern with society's response to the process. Society's emphasis on social equality as a response to secularization concerns the Church because of the perceived threat to individual freedoms. The Church expects the "world" to become secularized, for that is part of the apocalyptic vision. But the Church does not feel that it can tolerate society's response to the secularization process (restriction of freedom and a concomitant increase in governmental control) because Church members require the freedom to withdraw from the world as that world moves along a secular path to its end. While we shall argue that there is an important consistency to this position, in the twentieth century this consistency may lead Mormons to underestimate the relationship between equality and freedom. This in turn may, in a sort of cruel dilemma, help to destroy freedom—the very thing viewed as important for the Church in a secular world.

It is important to recognize that the policies now followed by the United States government do redistribute income. Unfortunately, these policies are based on interference in particular markets and most certainly interfere with economic efficiency, meaning less for everyone. In addition, growing evidence shows they lead to a diminution of freedom, thereby making modern capitalism less attractive as an economic base for a host society for the Church. Minimum wage laws, price ceilings on particular goods, and business regulation for consumer protection all result from such particular measures to redistribute income. These policies cancel out the invisible hand and thus self-interest cannot be channeled to socially beneficial ends. It is the classic fallacy of composition that can only be thwarted by policies with broader social vision.

To illustrate our point about intervention in particular markets, suppose that the distribution of income in a society were equal. Would there be any pressure to restrict price in a particular market below the market clearing or efficient price? Clearly not. Yet today in all Western democracies with a free market element in the economy, such pressure for low prices to help the poor is evident. Thus, a particularistic approach to income distribution by intervening in various markets is often adopted rather than a general approach of simply transferring income. Ceilings on natural gas and oil prices, rent controls, price controls on food, and usury laws are but a few of the results of these pressures to redistribute income.

The crucial question then is why, given these undesirable side effects, do advocates of income distribution resort to intervention in particular markets? Or, conversely, why do they continue to push for income distribution at all? The answer is that they believe the existing distribution of income violates any possible cannon of justice, and they are therefore prepared to accept some inefficiency and loss of freedom as the price for justice. They choose particular markets because they feel, for example, uncomfortable about the percentage of family income that the poor must spend for certain essential commodities. The problem is, as we have already seen, that such particularism cannot draw upon the model of competitive efficiency, with its invisible but effective hand, to preserve freedom while promoting economic efficiency. Moreover, examination of twentieth-century experience in this area leads one to the conclusion that while, in the pursuit of justice, the particularistic approach to the distribution of income has led to widespread economic inefficiency and some loss of personal freedom, it ironically has done very little to affect a permanent change in the distribution of income.

This, then, is the crux of our current economic dilemma. A grossly uneven distribution of income generates particularistic attempts to redistribute income which, when successful, reduce economic efficiency and liberty. Under these conditions society as a whole would be better off with a more even distribution of income and higher levels of efficiency and more freedom. Furthermore, substantial external effects on freedom and efficiency result from distributional conflict within a society. For example, suppose that John has an income of twenty escudos and Mary has an income of five escudos. The government desires to transfer income and does so by restricting John's access to a particular market. The result is that Mary's income rises to ten escudos while John's income falls to twelve escudos, giving a more equal distribution of income. Obviously, John would be better off if he transferred six escudos to Mary, for they would both have a higher income and more freedom.

There are but two responses to the dilemmas suggested above: completely ignore the distributional issue (which, given the reality of twentieth-century egalitarian social forces, we believe to be unrealistic) or direct the distributional issues to the appropriate general level. (A negative income tax, inheritance, or wealth taxes are examples of general approaches to income redistribution.)[16] Certainly there is no need or justification to continue with present distributional policies.

The almost universal rationalization for the existence of many state activities is the concern for the disadvantaged. Numerous examples could be given, where collectively we recognize the distributional problem and find ourselves willing to pay the price through market distortion. The cruel hoax, at least in the area of income redistribution, is that the benefits almost never accrue directly to the disadvantaged, and the costs of such activities may be extremely high. Hence, there is pressure for even greater particularistic intervention which could be mitigated by a general plan that actually redistributed income to the poor. The appropriate response to the uncomfortable feeling about the share of income that the poor must spend on certain commodities, say heating oil, is not in the oil market but rather in the area of general income redistribution.

Unfortunately, organizations with broad social interests, such as political parties, have not advocated general programs and have allowed special interests to promote particular interventions with the unfortunate consequences we have tried to sketch. Thus, some political leaders attack the nationalization of welfare and urge instead a reliance on the particularism of local agencies as if there were an invisible hand that operated at such levels. But there is none, and refusal to accept a general redistributional scheme has led to forces that threaten to destroy the freedom we all prize.

It would seem to us, therefore, that we Mormons cannot ignore the egalitarian movement, nor can we acquiesce in the current intervention in particular markets. Rather, we must help to channel these strong social forces for greater equality into paths more consistent with those attributes of the larger market system that make it a congenial host economy for the Church. It is our impression that one of Mormonism's problems in the secular world may be a failure to respond to these social forces that may very well, when particularized, undermine the very characteristics of the secular economic world that protect groups such as the Church. Thus, advocacy of freedom without regard for general distributional issues will, we believe, ultimately undermine freedom itself.

An adherence to the principles embodied in the United States Constitution is consistent with what we consider to be the appropriate response. What will avoid the particularism that may prove to be insidious and cancerous is commitment to general income redistribution that is governed by *ex ante* rules that preclude the intervention in particular markets. However, the call for a return to the individualism of the nineteenth century simply validates the fallacy of composition unless society can arrest the egalitarian sentiment. As we have suggested, the latter response is not a practical alternative. This allows only one response consistent with the preservation of a host society congenial to the Church, and that is a strong commitment to general redistribution. To redistribute or not redistribute is not the issue. As we have suggested, as a social system we are heavily involved in redistribution schemes. The issue is the *form* such claims on the social system are allowed to assume. We think the form is a crucial issue. Indeed, it may be the most important issue faced by our social system in general and by the participant groups who find the host society embodied in market capitalism important, if not essential, to their own survival.

A failure to deal appropriately with twentieth-century egalitarian pressures will reduce the Church's opportunity to influence society and will damage almost every other institution with broader social perspective. Insofar as these institutions might have had opportunities to influence an appropriate response to the new social forces but have not, nearly always it has been because they have abandoned distributional issues to people and groups with smaller, particular issues to hammer out. And the piecemeal, specific responses these groups make are undermining both market efficiency and the important characteristic of freedom in the host society. For example, consumer advocacy groups have successfully promoted safety legislation for automobiles, toys, food, and employment. Their motivation has been to transfer power (and income in a real sense) from producers to employees and consumers. Such legislation is in most cases inefficient in that it reduces output and often produces products not desired by consumers. These laws also reduce freedom of employers, coal miners, and consumers. We believe this kind of piecemeal redistribution leads to a trade-off between economic efficiency and equality and, more important, to a trade-off between equality and freedom. In short, social equality goes up; economic efficiency and personal freedom go down.

Mormons who have strongly advocated freedom and the preservation of the host society but who have been much less concerned with equality (of which economic equality is an important element) must, we think, become more concerned with the limits of inequality that a society can bear if the Church is to be effective in defending freedom. It is interesting that in the nineteenth century, Church leaders displayed considerable concern with the issue of economic justice. Orson Pratt, for example, made a passionate plea for economic equality in his essay *On Equality and Oneness of the Saints.*

An inequality in riches lays a foundation for pride, and many other evils. A family who is rich can build comfortable houses, purchase inheritances and fine carriages, clothe themselves in splendid attire, and educate their children in every branch of useful learning; while those who are poor labor and toil from morning until evening to procure a scanty subsistence; their families are coarsely clad, their children are not so highly educated. These opposite circumstances produce distinctions; the rich family does not feel to associate with the same degree of familiarity with the poor as they do with the rich; the sons and daughters of the rich seek for companions among those that are wealthy, the poor feel themselves slighted, and feel envious, because they are not rich. Besides the great inequalities in regard to the actual comforts of life, it produces great inequality in education, in the social circle, in marriage associations, and in almost every other respect. Hence, an inequality in property is the root and foundation of innumerable evils; it tends to division, and to keep asunder the social feelings that should exist among the people of God. It is the great barrier erected by the devil to prevent that unity and oneness which the Gospel requires; it is a principle originated in hell; it is the root of all evil.[17]

Our analysis leads us to suggest that freedom and equality (or less inequality) are not independent. A moral concern for the former requires at least a pragmatic concern for the latter; preservation of market freedom may require nothing less. More specifically, we suggest that the failure to accommodate the egalitarian movement at the appropriate level forces the pressures for less inequality into areas that undermine economic efficiency and market freedom.

We have already expressed our belief that an antiegalitarian policy is no longer viable. It is our judgment that the forces pushing the issue of equality to the fore are important social forces that must be dealt with, not ignored, and that the appropriate response must involve some redistribution of output. One can either view it as appeasing the monster or as the appropriate moral thing to do. We think the polemics of the debate are of little importance. In practice, nations that have consistently refused to recognize the forces for equality have been vulnerable to revolutionary pressures or repressive dictatorships. In both cases freedom is lost. In either case the long-run position of the Church is damaged. If the issue is more equality and more freedom, or inequality and less freedom, we Mormons must support freedom and, therefore, less inequality.

Postscript

In this essay we have shown how twentieth-century social forces are, as a result of the secularization process, undermining the attractiveness of the twin aspects of market capitalism—freedom and economic efficiency—that have made it a congenial host for the Church. We think it unrealistic to assume that the secularization process can be reversed such as to reduce the current trends for social equality—or less inequality. Thus we foresee that societies with market economies, in order to survive at all, will continue to have to respond to those pressures by redistributing income. However, the *form* of this redistribution is important to the Church. We have noted that the particularistic redistribution schemes of the United States and other countries, as a response to egalitarian pressures, have reduced freedom and economic efficiency, thereby reducing the attractiveness of such systems as host societies for the Church.

In order to preserve a modicum of personal freedom and economic efficiency in countries where market economies still exist, thereby salvaging the elements of the host society the Church finds most congenial for its existence, we have argued for general schemes to redistribute income. Yet in our essay we have ignored a very fundamental part of the discussion surrounding inequality, i.e., economic justice. We have ignored it not because it is unimportant but because it is largely a reflection of individual values. Clearly, one can think about economic justice in rigorous analytical terms. There has of late been a revival of just such work as exemplified by Rawls, Nozick, Arrow, and others.[18] But the bottom line of most issues involving economic justice is a question of personal values. Since economists tend to take values as given, we did not want to build a case based on individual preferences for preserving freedom by changing the form of income distribution, since we think there are other important factors involved in the questions of the relationship between the distribution of income and freedom.

However, since economic justice is the root of the question of income distribution, and because it is also a deep moral issue, some comment concerning its relationship to the Church would seem appropriate. If the trend toward pursuit of income redistribution through particular government action continues (and there appears to be every likelihood that it will), we Mormons will probably speak out to warn of the consequences of the loss of freedom due to government intervention in the economy. To people around us, however, our warnings are likely to appear shrill, and to some morally hypocritical if our advocacy of freedom is not coupled with some indication of our feelings about economic justice and the distribution of income.

Douglas F. Tobler, in an essay published in this volume, speaks to the need for us to strike a strong posture toward the dominant intellectual competitor of our day—philosophical Marxism—in order that those seeking a new world view will understand, and be persuaded by, the superiority of the gospel of Jesus Christ over any secular philosophy. Socialism is closely allied with philosophical Marxism. As an ideology it is devoted to the redistribution of income by elimination of private ownership; it is an ideology to which hundreds of millions of people are today attracted. Yet because of socialism's denial of freedoms that the Church views to be essential, we Mormons must define a position on economic justice and the distribution of income if we are to offer a persuasive counter world view, at least as most of humanity is now geared to see it. It is not our intention to propose such a position; that is for others. We would, however, make a few observations.

First, Rawls's concept of the "veil of ignorance" provides an interesting introspective experiment for a person who wishes to clarify his or her thoughts about economic justice. He suggests that we define the limits of the distribution of income in a state where we are totally unaware of our own position in the distribution. Consider oneself in a state of ignorance concerning future income and all characteristics, such as IQ, that might affect one's future income. Now focus on marginal changes in the distribution of income in the particular society in question. Would you favor a less equal or more equal distribution of income if you knew absolutely nothing about the actual outcome? We suspect that most people, if honest, would prefer a more equal outcome.

Second, every government action changes the distribution of income. People see direct transfers such as welfare payments, rent subsidies, and social security. The tendency is to ignore the indirect transfers. Unfortunately, many of the government benefits to the middle and upper classes are indirect, while the transfers to the lower class are direct. Government expenditures on goods and services probably increase the wages of individuals with higher levels of education and skill and reduce the wages of the unskilled. That is, the government buys goods and services that use skilled labor intensively. If one asks the following question: If government were reduced to one-tenth its present level, how would the distribution of income be changed? The answer is ambiguous. We cannot state with any confidence that the poor would be significantly worse off in this situation.

Third, as the Church expands from an American church to a worldwide church, the distribution of income within it becomes more unequal. Per capita income in the United States is almost thirty times the per capita income of the Philippines. It is seven times the per capita income of Mexico. As converts come increasingly from the Pacific or Latin America, the income distribution of the Church will display more inequality. Such inequality may present serious problems in terms of organization and unity, as the comments in this volume by Augusto Lim of the Philippines poignantly illustrate. It will become more difficult to design homogeneous and effective Church programs that are locally financed. It will become more difficult to justify islands of concentrated general expenditure, such as BYU, which benefit relatively few members (drawn from the upper strata of the income distribution). On the other hand, substantial income transfers from the affluent members to poorer members as has already taken place with the impressive building and welfare programs will probably continue. But even there it seems unlikely that these transfers will be sufficient to assuage completely egalitarian tensions within the Church. In the nineteenth century the Church could convert individuals and send them to Zion with quite abundant land and opportunity. We cannot do this now. What is the substitute?

Does the gospel outline a theory of economic justice? It does not appear to do so in any operational manner. The gospel exalts work and condemns idleness, it commends the charitable and cautions those who covet, it condemns the ostentatious consumption of the rich and encourages the Saints to care for the poor; but it does not define the limits of the distribution of income. It is left to each of us to struggle with the dilemma of economic justice and personal freedom.

Footnotes

1. David O. McKay, *Church News,* Supplement to the *Deseret News* (Salt Lake City, Utah), 12 March 1952.

2. The appropriate response to income redistribution elicits a wide variety of responses that reflect, to a considerable extent, individual values. We do not desire to become involved in a discussion of the merits of particular value systems. Rather, we want to focus on the mechanism that generates income redistributional issues and possible strategies implied by this analysis that may be acceptable to individuals with widely differing views about economic justice.

3. Noel B. Reynolds, "Mormonism, Capitalism, and the Rule of Law," September 1975, unpublished manuscript; and L. Dwight Israelsen, "Mormons, the Constitution, and the Host Economy," December 1975, unpublished manuscript.

4. The term *capitalism* has come to have several meanings, including private ownership of productive factors, "class"-determined private ownership of a particular factor, capital and corporate control of capital. We use the term throughout to mean private ownership of all productive factors with free market allocation of those factors.

5. In spite of this argument that capitalism is a better host society than planned societies, it is difficult to find concrete examples that illustrate moral difficulties presented to members of the Church because of limitations on individual decision-making.

6. J. Reuben Clark, Jr., "Constitutional Government: Our Birthright Threatened," *Vital Speeches* 5 (1 January 1939):174–75.

7. The concept of competition as used by economists is very important and often misunderstood. A competitive market exists when no individual buying or selling in that market can appreciably influence price. In such a case, no monopoly power exists.

8. Adam Smith, *Wealth of Nations* (New York: Modern Library, 1937), p. 423; emphasis added.

9. The existence of free markets disperses economic power. When combined with private ownership and the absence of market imperfections suggested earlier (monopoly, externalities) they result in allocative efficiency. Private ownership may be consistent capitalism.

10. See, for example, Hal R. Varian, "Distributive Justice, Welfare Economics, and the Theory of Fairness," *Philosophy and Public Affairs* 4 (Spring 1975):223–47.

11. See, for example, Arthur M. Okun, *Equality and Efficiency* (Washington: The Brookings Institution, 1975).

12. Adam Smith in *The Wealth of Nations* admirably describes *homo economicus.* Smith traces the social benefits of rational self-interested individuals but he is not all that enamored with the individuals themselves. Peter Laslett, *The World We Have Lost* (New York: charles Scribner's Sons, 1971); Karl Polanyi, *The Great Transformation* (Boston: Beacon Press, 1957); and Max Weber, *The Protestant Ethic and the Spirit of Capitalism,* trans. Talcott Parsons (New York: Charles Scribner's Sons, 1958) are but a few of the scholarly works considering the transformation process.

13. Frank H. Knight, *The Economic Organization* (New York: Harper and Row, 1965), p. 21.

14. The utopian socialism that has periodically surfaced in the Christian churches and Western society is probably a reaction to the secularization of life that modern markets are thought to produce. (See, for example, Lewis Mumford, *The Story of Utopia* [New York: The Viking Press, 1962].) But the reaction does not end there. Thus secular economic man has not been considered a threat just to the various Christian notions of the "whole" men defined completely outside the Gospels. Thus, on the basis of their respective perceptions of the "whole" man, both Karl Marx and Robert Owen attack the cancer of capi-

talist secularism. Marx, of course, turns the issue on its head and creates a secular economic gospel defining the "whole" man primarily in terms of his economic role. Marx's concern is not directly with secularization but with industrialization and the alienation of men from themselves and from one another through a particular form of organization of modern production—capitalism—which includes both private and class ownership. (Marx's view is that the secular man is the only kind of man there is.) Alienation results when man, who by nature is productive, is not allowed to benefit from the full results of his efforts in the economic organization he labors in. He is thus dehumanized. Hence, Marx would not view secular man as the culmination of some secularizing process. On the other hand, however, there are others who attack free-market capitalism as a form of organizing production precisely because they do view secularization as a process—an almost inevitable result of the development of the market and private ownership of capital—but a process whose ill effects can be muted by a humanization of the production and exchange processes.

Those who defend market capitalism do not view man as a result of a secularization process. Rather, as we have suggested, modern neoclassical economists view the description of economic man as a description of the basic character of men. The remarkable property of the market is that it channels this self-interest, thrift, acquisitiveness, and rationality into socially beneficial ends. Thus, both Marxian and modern neoclassical economics as developed in the United States and Western Europe place emphasis on what the form of economic organization does, not on the difficulties that may arise as it evolves.

15. Cole Durham suggested to us that the problem is not that equality of opportunity is unattainable but that, when attained, it was not as meaningful as its eighteenth-century advocates assumed it would be.

While this may be true relative to equality before the law, equality of opportunity in the economic sphere and elsewhere in society appears to be unattainable. See, for example, Christopher Jencks et al., *Inequality* (New York: Harper and Row, 1972) for a discussion of the problems with genetics and home environment and "equality of opportunity."

16. The negative income tax is a very attractive program to economists since it appears to accomplish whatever redistribution of income desired while interfering least with freedom and efficiency. The basic principle of the negative income tax is to extend the income tax in the negative as well as the positive direction. To illustrate, assume a family of four with no income, individual exemptions of $1200 per individual and a tax rate of fifty percent. This family has a negative income of $4800 taxed at a rate of fifty percent meaning they will have negative taxes of $2400. They would then be paid $200 per month. If the family were to earn $1200, their income plus exemptions would be $3600 yielding a tax liability of $1800. They would then receive $150 per month in welfare to add to their earnings of $100 per month. Notice that there is an incentive to work since welfare is reduced by a fraction of earnings.

17. Orson Pratt, "The Equality and Oneness of the Saints," in N. B. Lundwall, ed., *Masterful Discourses and Writings of Orson Pratt* (Salt Lake City: By the Editor, n.d.), p. 599.

18. See, for example, John Rawls, *A Theory of Justice* (Cambridge, Mass.: Harvard University Press, 1971); Robert Nozick, *Anarchy, State, and Utopia* (New York: Basic Books, 1974); Lester Thurow, *Generating Inequality* (New York: Basic Books, 1976); Kenneth Arrow, "A Utilitarian Approach to the Concept of Equality in Public Expenditures," *Quarterly Journal of Economics*, vol. 85, no. 3 (August 1971):409–15; and Kenneth Arrow, "Some Ordinalist-Utilitarian Notes on Rawls's Theory of Justice," *The Journal of Philosophy*, vol. 70, no. 9 (May 10, 1973):245–63.

MORMONISM AND THE SECULAR PHILOSOPHIES: COMPETING CREEDS IN THE TWENTIETH CENTURY

Douglas F. Tobler

As The Church of Jesus Christ of Latter-day Saints contemplates the challenges of a more dramatic expansion of its membership and influence into the world in the 1970s and beyond, many Mormons have become more and more aware of the need to understand our fellowmen better so that we can present the gospel message to them more effectively. The Church's geographical expansion into new areas of Europe, Asia, and the Middle East has brought us into contact with a bewildering variety of languages, cultures, and customs, and we perceive more clearly our need to familiarize ourselves with this human cultural diversity. Equally significant, but less universally recognized, is the challenge to understand the changing beliefs and ideologies of our modern world.

Beliefs and ideologies—clusters of ideas that help people interpret reality—have an importance in today's society that can hardly be overemphasized. As Roland Stromberg has observed: "People live in a world of ideas. They think no matter what they are doing, and their thoughts draw upon the store of ideas supplied by the intellectual culture around them."[1] Lord Keynes, no mean practitioner of the art of dealing with ideas, pithily expressed one important way in which ideas influence us: "Madmen in authority," he said, "who hear voices in the air, are distilling their frenzy from some academic scribbler of a few years back."[2]

Individual ideas are important because man's intellectual existence is made up of them. But the human mind must also have a means of sorting out and grouping the swarms of ideas it encounters. The Germans have a good name for this mental and spiritual foundation: *Weltanschauung*, or "world view." It is compiled, among other things, of answers to what Crane Brinton has called, "[Life's] Big Questions—Life, Destiny, Right, Truth, God. . . ."[3] Without answers to these questions, human life loses much of its meaning. Hence, even though the gospel of Jesus Christ is the only philosophical system that contains the whole truth concerning man's relationship with God, as well as insights into the other "big" questions, still every legitimate world view elevates its adherents above an animal existence because it instills in them a concept of virtue and truth and a sense of the destiny and nobility of man.

Notwithstanding the general validity of the foregoing observations on the importance of ideas and value systems, since World War II the intellectual climate of Western civilization has been dominated by both a mood of skepticism and a pervasive movement toward secularization—the loss of concern for God and his work and for the holy and sacred in human life.[4] Today's materialistic, skeptical attitude arose in part out of the profound moral and intellectual trauma Western civilization experienced during World War II. The prewar years had been a time of vigorous ideological activity. In 1939 Max Lerner wrote an article entitled "Ideas are Weapons," expressing very well the popular virulence and power of ideologies in the years just before the war. Lerner quoted a prominent intellectual exile of Hitler's Germany: "You would not understand this perhaps, because you have not experienced it as we have in Germany. [But] there is an important distinction between thought and ideas. Men possess thoughts but ideas possess men."[5] And Lerner himself then observed: "It is the recognition and exploitation of this possessive power of ideas that makes the genius of our age."[6] Perhaps Solomon said it best: "As [a man] thinketh in his heart, so is he" (Prov. 23:7).

After the war, civilization slowly recuperated from the physical and spiritual devastation of that cataclysm. Men everywhere saw in the ruins of once-prosperous nations not only convincing proof of the power of the irrational in man but also a source of profound disillusionment in the radical ideologies which had caused the war and, indeed, in all comprehensive philosophical systems. The resulting mood of suspicion and doubt lasted throughout the 1950s and into the sixties, and is probably one of the underlying causes for the limited success the Church has had in Europe since World War II.

In recent years, however, there has been evidence of renewed interest in comprehensive world views. The gradual passing of the "scarred" generation, coupled with the enormous expansion of both formal and informal education (through means such as television), has produced a youthful society passionately attracted by ideas and ideals, who frantically search for understanding and wholeness in life and who strive to reshape society according to their new-found ideals. Because much of the new ferment is associated with university students, some statistics from Western Europe may give an indication of what is happening. In 1870 there were 14,000 university students in Germany, then considered the most intellectually advanced nation in the world. By 1920 this number had grown to 80,000, out of a population of 52 million. By contrast, in 1970 more than 400,000 students were attending German universities, and a long list of names waited for admission. Similarly, in 1914 France showed a university enrollment of 42,000. This figure doubled by 1939. By 1970 more than 600,000 students were attending French universities, and Britain and Italy showed enrollments of 500,000 and

600,000 respectively. In the United States in 1971 over 800,000 persons graduated from college. It has been estimated that in 1914 probably no more than a thousand persons made up the creative intellectual community in the Western world, whereas by the 1970s this number had grown to at least 1 million.[7]

This new, enlarged generation of Western intellectuals, who play such a vital role in the creation, articulation, and dissemination of ideas that influence the values of our society, and the many more people who study under and with them are generally disillusioned with the skeptical, materialistic, hedonistic philosophy of their elders. Unfortunately, many of them find that their parents' indifference toward religions and metaphysical philosophy has left them no alternative beliefs or explanations. "Perhaps at no other time has wholeness been so difficult," George W. Morgan wrote in *The Human Predicament: Dissolution and Wholeness.* "Our lives, our selves, our ways of being, are subject to dissolution."[8] In his discussion of the causes of disintegration in society, Arnold Toynbee listed "schism of the soul" at the top.[9] Those nineteenth-century thinkers whose ideas still form the basis of what our present society believes—Marx, Ruskin, Emerson, and Nietzsche—"feared the radical dehumanization of man through loss of his 'whole self' to specialized functionalism. This fear has been felt even more keenly in recent times and is a key to much of contemporary thought."[10] Society's enemies have thus become boredom, loneliness, meaninglessness, and emptiness of purpose and soul. Jan Myrdal, the scion of a prominent Swedish socialist intellectual family, bemoaned the humdrum nature of life in the contemporary welfare state;[11] C. A. Johansson, another thoughtful observer living in the same country, has poignantly described how only the joy found in his work and in opportunities for LDS Church service stave off, for him, the meaninglessness (felt by many of his contemporaries)[12] of present-day life in a pallid society.

In my judgment, the renewed interest of today's young people in the big question of life, in *Weltanschauung,* is a golden opportunity for the Church. If we are able, in this time of turmoil and groping, to express our faith in God skillfully and forcefully and to explain our views on the central issues of the day, we can have a great influence in creating a worldwide intellectual climate in which people will respond more readily to the ideas and doctrines presented by our missionaries.

The first step for us in influencing people today who are searching for light and knowledge but who have been attracted to a worldly philosophy such as Marxism is to understand them. The apostle Paul attributed his success in winning converts to his ability to relate well to those he taught: "And unto the Jews I became as a Jew, that I might gain the

Jews; . . . to them that are without law, as without law, . . . that I might gain them. . . . To the weak became I as weak, that I might gain the weak: I am made all things to all men, that I might by all means save some. And this I do for the gospel's sake, that I might be partaker thereof with you" (1 Corinthians 9:20–23).

What this means to us, as Latter-day Saints in a secular world, is that we must thoroughly understand the intellectual climate of our age. We have become aware that society's intellectual perspective is largely determined by what is called the "conventional wisdom," which has been defined as a set of ideas constituting a comprehensive explanation of reality, accepted by the majority of people in a given culture at a given time.[13] What ideas, then, constitute the "conventional wisdom" of our time? What are the historical sources and evolution of those ideas? And what position do we adopt toward those ideas? The better we can answer these questions, the more persuasively we can reply to the disbelief of our age.

The Decline of Traditional Christianity

In the past, we have presumed Christianity to be the foundation of the conventional wisdom; thus, we Mormons have been heavily preoccupied with appealing to other Christians and Christian scholars. This should continue, but we should be aware that the younger generation, in spite of its heightened religious enthusiasm, has shunned traditional Christianity as a creed to live by. The alienation of European intellectuals from Christianity began during the Enlightenment; ever since then, it has been spreading through an ever-increasing segment of Europe's population. The recent emergence of "atheistic theology" is only one example of the kind of theological double-talk not likely to attract many sincere persons seeking for something to believe in. Two other evidences of the impotence of institutional Christianity are the failure of the ecumenical movement to revivify Christianity and the worldwide attempt to make Christianity relevant as a "social gospel," which tries to compete with secular governments and institutions in working for the material betterment of mankind.

Today, the Christianity that most of the world sees and experiences gives only an uncertain sound; few, therefore, prepare themselves for the battle. Some of the reasons for this paralysis in proclaiming a convincing witness were prophetically articulated by Joseph Smith in 1833 and 1834: man, he said, must have a knowledge of God and his attributes, *for without the idea of the existence of the attributes which belong to God, the minds of men could not have power to exercise faith in him so as to lay hold upon eternal life. The God of heaven, understanding most perfectly the constitution of human nature, and the weakness of men, knew what was necessary to be revealed, and what ideas must be planted in their minds in order that they might be enabled to exercise faith in him unto eternal life.*[14]

Protestant and Jewish susceptibility to the dissolving acids of secularism has been well documented, but in our day the Roman Catholic Church has also been attacked by people who question its most basic doctrines. Whether in the years ahead it can withstand the challenges to such doctrines as papal infallibility and clerical celibacy will provide interesting barometers for the likelihood of its continued appeal to a searching, thinking youth.

In any case, little reason exists to doubt Stromberg's assessment that modern Christianity has reached a point of "severe crisis, from which it does not appear that traditional religion will recover," or Malcolm Muggeridge's 1969 opinion (though the timing may be questionable) that: "I personally shall be very surprised if a decade or so from now anything remains of institutional Christianity."[15] A comparable prediction about the future of the Catholic Church was made to me in Vienna in 1974, by a long-time astute observer of Austrian Catholicism.[16]

Similar concerns for the vitality of traditional Christianity in our age and especially in the United States, where the secularization of Christianity has lagged some decades behind, were expressed recently on the Brigham Young University campus by Professor Sidney Ahlstrom. He noted that the Great Puritan epoch in American history has come to an end: Americans are less inclined now than ever before to organize their priorities around the importance of God, Deity, or Providence.[17]

Liberal Humanism—A Substitute?

More powerful than traditional Christianity among scholar-intellectuals and their many followers in the recent past has been the appeal of liberal humanism, an ideology promising men temporal and spiritual freedom through education and democracy. This promise rested on a firm faith in human rationality and scientific insights. The salvation of man, liberal humanists argued, lay in his ability to reason. With reason, man could determine his own true nature and needs, then structure his political, social, and economic institutions in order that his full potential as a human being might be realized. The primary source of this philosophy was the Enlightenment of the eighteenth century, but it reached its optimistic apogee in the scientific discoveries and the political democracy of the nineteenth and early twentieth centuries. Since then, however, liberal humanism has been severely chastened. The inhumanity of two World Wars—especially the terrible genocide of Hitler and Stalin—and the fragility of democracy in supposedly sophisticated, progressive countries have joined with the insights of Nietzsche, Dostoevsky, and Freud to cast doubt upon the rationality of the natural man. These experiences and discoveries have greatly weakened the appeal of liberal humanism.[18] For most intellectuals in our day, the prescient confession of the Italian historian-philosopher, Benedetto Croce, uttered even before the turn of the century, has become only too real:

We no longer believe ... like the Greeks, in happiness of life on earth; we no longer believe, like the Christians, in happiness in an otherworldly life; we no longer believe, like the optimistic philosophers of the last century, in a happy future for the human race.... We no longer believe in anything of that, and what we have alone retained is the consciousness of ourselves, and the need to make that consciousness ever clearer and more evident, *a need for whose satisfaction we turn to science and to art.*[19]

Now even the confidence that science and art could provide keys to life has been shaken and largely abandoned. Moreover, Max Weber's views—that, though reality is dominated by the irrational it can be made comprehensible by human reason—have offered precious little consolation, either in theory or practice.

Today, liberal humanism exists either as an intellectual faith for those who, seeing nothing else to believe in, continue to hope for the best for and from mankind, or they believe in a form so fragmented that it no longer presents a total and complete philosophy for educated men to live by. In one sense, the ideas of sociologist Karl Mannheim served as a bridge for those who, deserting the sinking ship of liberal humanism, sought for something more dynamic, something that could capture the desire to believe and provide the hope for a meaningful future reality. In *Ideology and Utopia,* he pointed out clearly the potential results of the lack of a total, valid *Weltanschauung*:

The complete disappearance of the Utopian element ... would mean that ... human development would take on a totally new character.... We would be faced then with the greatest paradox imaginable, namely, that man, who has achieved the highest degree of rational mastery of existence, left without any ideals, *becomes a mere creature of impulses. Thus ... just at the highest stage of awareness, when history is ceasing to be blind fate, and is becoming more and more man's own creation, with the relinquishment of utopias, man would lose his will to shape history and therewith his ability to understand it.*[20]

Another more recent voice, Professor Carl Degler of Stanford, has indirectly borne witness of the decline of liberal humanism by pointing out how extensively its major manifestation, democracy, is on the defensive around the globe.[21]

Marxist Humanism

Today's subdued, pessimistic liberal humanism has little power to inspire man or to change the world. This means that the liberal democracies of the Western world are left to exist primarily through a kind of economic balancing act of crisis management; they lack the firm underpinnings provided by a strong ideological concept of human dignity. That such an existence may prove tenuous at best is underscored by Henry Kissinger's ominous prediction that within ten years Western Europe could be controlled by Marxists. Already, the Christian Democratic party of Italy is seriously considering a "historic compromise"[22] with the Italian Communist party, a move that would have direct and serious implications for the whole of Europe. And the French Communist party has recently had to free itself from the Soviet shackles in order to pursue its own brand of Marxist humanism. Recent elections in France have demonstrated the popularity of this position.[23]

These evidences of the political vitality of Marxist organizations, even in the more "stable" European countries, do not tell the whole story: for the past several years students in West Germany, the Scandinavian countries, and Britain have received a regular intellectual fare distilled from the ethical and philosophical writings of neo-Marxist scholars such as the Frankfurt School of Horkheimer, Marcuse, Adorno, and Habermas, Jean-Paul Sartre, the writings of Frantz Fanon and George Lukács, and the Marxist humanists surrounding Erich Fromm.[24] These European educational trends are echoed in other parts of the world by the new literature of Marxist and Christian-Marxist reform leaders in Latin America and by those intellectuals who have succeeded in leading the MPLA liberation movement in Angola.[25] Even in the Soviet Union a renewed emphasis has been placed upon the role of Communist ideology in providing goals and motivation for the whole Russian Soviet enterprise and in disciplining dissident Soviet intellectuals. Gerhart Niemeyer has described how the Russian populace literally swims in a sea of propaganda:

Education, from kindergarten up, is shot through and through with ideology until in the last two years about one-half of the program is direct indoctrination. The volume of ideological publications, including the classics, is staggering. Literature, poetry, theater, film, painting, sculpture, all serve ideological purposes, and music is at least prevented from arousing what are considered reactionary emotions. Armed forces are all penetrated by politruks; neighborhoods, student groups, factory sections, collective farms meet weekly for discussions under party supervision. Antitheistic propaganda abounds. The abundance of this kind of evidence establishes a strong prima facie probability that the party has not grown indifferent toward its own ideology. The regime must be called, above all, an ideocracy, the forceful and total imposition of an idea system on a whole people. Since the people, in spite of everything, remain by and large unconvinced, the party's insistence testifies more to its own beliefs than to its worldly wisdom.[26]

Notwithstanding Niemeyer's observation about the Soviet Union, ideological propaganda in Soviet-dominated countries has not been wholly unsuccessful with the populace: the results of an extensive poll taken in Czechoslovakia in 1968 during the Prague Spring show that an incredible 88 percent approved of the "socialist" system.[27]

Despite the horrendous historical track record and the widely publicized criticism of institutional communism for its oppression and real failure to enhance human dignity, an increasing number of younger searching and thinking people around the world are presently turning to Marx for guidance in finding a philosophy of life that to them corresponds to the real world. Marxism, they believe, provides a whole explanation—psychological, economic, social, political, intellectual, and spiritual—for both the successes and abuses of modern industrial society and gives people at the same time something to have faith in, to hope for, and to work for that, in their opinion, would be vastly superior to what they now have and experience. What Sartre had earlier observed, that "Marxism—whatever its objective truth, which is an irrelevancy—is *the* ideology for contemporary man, the only all-inclusive philosophy capable of speaking to his condition"[28] reflects the attitude of much of the new intellectual generation. It tells them why they feel alienated and insecure and provides a credible intellectual explanation for the economic and social inequities that have "enslaved" and "dehumanized" man. At the same time, Marxism's undercurrent of prophetic certitude inspires men to act to help history bring about the longed-for heaven on earth. Arthur Koestler had earlier cast his lot with Marxism for reasons similar to today's generation: "for the intellectual comfort and relief found in escaping from the tragic predicament into a class system of beliefs that left no room for hesitation or doubt."[29]

The Marx that now appeals to the younger generation is not so much the "older," communistic one where the scientific analysis of history or the economic system or even the class struggle dominate the thought, although these still have considerable appeal to intellectuals in more backward countries. Today's generation finds in Marx an explanation of how man has been deprived of his authentic humanity and his wholeness, how he has become alienated from his work and his fellows and from his own nature, how his culture and personality have been fragmented and destroyed by specialization, and how after the Revolution human nature will again be whole, its various fragments reunited into integral selves capable of true art and thought.

Marx had such great confidence in his own ability to construct a comprehensive interpretation of reality that he even felt qualified to replace God and religion with his philosophy of historical materialism. In the introduction to *Contribution to the Critique of Hegel's Philosophy of Right,* which Marx wrote in 1843, he delcared:

The criticism of religion is the premise of all criticism.... The basis of irreligious criticism is this: man makes religion; *religion does not make man. Religion is indeed man's self-consciousness and self-awareness so long as he has not found himself or has lost himself again. But* man is *not an abstract being, squatting outside the world. Man is* the human world, *the state, society. This state, this society, produce religion which is an* inverted world consciousness, *because they are an inverted* world.[30]

Three further quotations from the early Marx capture much of the essence of what today's youth finds captivating:

The criticism of religion ends with the doctrine that man is the supreme being for man. *It ends, therefore, with the* categorical imperative to overthrow all those conditions *in which man is an abased, enslaved, abandoned, contemptible being—conditions which can hardly be better described than in the exclamation of a Frenchman on the occasion of a proposed tax upon dogs: "Wretched dogs! They want to treat you like men!"*[31]

In describing how modern man has become alienated from both himself and his fellowman, Marx pontificated in the *Economic* and *Philosophic Manuscripts of 1844*:

The more man puts into God, the less he retains in himself. The worker puts his life into the object; but now his life no longer belongs to him but to the object. Hence, the greater this activity, the greater is the worker's lack of objects.... The alienation *of the worker in his prod-*

uct means not only that his labour becomes an object, an external *existence, but that it exists* outside him, *independently, as something alien to him, and that it becomes a power of its own confronting him; it means that the life which he has conferred on the object confronts him as something hostile and alien.*[32]

Later he continued:

The positive transcendence of private property as the appropriation of human *life is, therefore, the positive transcendence of all estrangement—that is to say, the return of man from religion, family, state, etc., to his* human, *i.e.,* social *mode of existence. Religious estrangement as such occurs only in the realm of* consciousness, *of man's inner life, but economic estrangement is that of* real life; *its transcendence therefore embraces both aspects. . . . Communism begins from the outset . . . with atheism. . . .*[33]

Finally, Marx triumphantly proclaimed the certainty with which his new order will create the earthly utopia where:

Communism *[to be understood as nineteenth-century Marxism] as the positive transcendence of* private property, *or* human self-estrangement, *and therefore as the* real *appropriation of the* human *essence by and for man; communism therefore as the complete return of man to himself as a* social *(i.e., human) being—a return become conscious, and accomplished within the entire wealth of previous development. This communism, as fully developed naturalism, equals humanism, and as fully-developed humanism equals naturalism, it is the* genuine *resolution of the conflict between man and nature and between man and man—the true resolution of the strife between existence and essence, between objectification and self-confirmation, between freedom and necessity, between the individual and the species. Communism is the riddle of history solved, and it knows itself to be this solution.*[34]

In addition to the over one billion people throughout the world whose daily lives are governed and whose thoughts influenced by one form or another of institutionalized Marxism, a wide spectrum of intellectual movements exists throughout the Western and third worlds (Africa, Asia, and Latin America), which accepts the above-mentioned ideological core of Marxist thought as the new conventional wisdom, or, as Samuel Beer has accurately described it, the newest form of secular religion:

As a whole, the Marxist system is prophecy founded upon vision . . . [It] is especially like religion in the nature of certain basic questions which it attempts to answer. It includes—though not under these names—a theory of how evil came into the world and how it will be eliminated; a vi-

sion of powers which are beyond man's control and inflict suffering upon him, but which carry him onward to a blessed fulfillment, a prophecy of a final paradise where humanity will live in perfect freedom and happiness. It is impossible to understand the deep appeal of the Marxist system unless we consider its powerful effect upon emotions which are essentially religious.[35]

The impact of this Marxist *Weltanschauung* upon the last two generations of scholar-intellectuals and those influenced by them is incalculable, but it is safe to say that no other total philosophy of life, in terms of the relative number of people influenced by it, can presently be considered a serious rival. Roughly, there are at least three groupings deriving their ideology and vision from Marx: Marxist humanists; national communist parties and communist trade unions; and revolutionary Marxists.

The Marxist humanists are highly diverse: disciples of the twentieth-century Marxist interpreters George Lukács; the Frankfurt School of Max Horkheimer, Theodor Adorno, and Herbert Marcuse as well as their successors; Jean-Paul Sartre; Erich Fromm and his followers; the Italian Antonio Gramsci; and the Yugoslav school surrounding Gajo Petrovic and Mihailo Markovic, who view Marxism less as a revolutionary political movement and more as a total philosophy of contemporary man. Marxism provides to all of these an accounting for man's feeling of alienation and loss of freedom in the modern world and at the same time provides some hope and direction in creating something better. For Lukács, as interpreted by R. N. Berki, specifically, Marx's connection of philosophy to the economic and social conditions of the industrial wage-earning proletariat constitutes the head and heart of human emancipation.[36] One must recognize that "the *whole* of human experience is the direct or indirect outcome of man's own social activity."[37] Man, especially proletariat man, must also realize that he, not God, is "the self conscious creator of the Universe"[38] and that it is the role of the intellectual to understand and communicate this insight to his fellowman. Like most Marxist humanists, Lukács believed that new methods and new concepts different from those used in Communist countries must be found to end the "dehumanization" of bourgeois society and the feeling of alienation and lack of self-worth of individual men and women. As formulated by the Yugoslav Marxist, Vranicki,

If our desire is to contribute more fully to human liberation, i.e. to the overcoming of various forms of alienation, then socialism must place its fundamental stress on man and the free personality must be considered a prerequisite to social freedom, in theory and in practice.[39]

For Herbert Marcuse and his disciples, intellectual Marxism is a creed for overcoming the oppression of mass technological society and thereby reclaiming one's individuality.[40] To Fromm and his followers, Marx could be joined with Freud to produce a complete psychosocial[41] explanation of the despair and its causes that countless young intellectuals are experiencing. For example, parents have the greatest influence upon their children, but are really *agents of society.*

The Frankfurt School and other Marxist humanists have attacked the capitalist system "because they say its acquisitiveness has sullied spiritual life. The aim of revolution for them would be not so much to put an end to suffering and exploitation and to liberate productive forces obstructed by capitalism, as to install a higher culture."[42] Similarly, the spiritual father of modern Italian communism, Antonio Gramsci, like Mao Tse-Tung, stressed the cultural goal of Marxism. Gramsci believed that the important revolution is the ideological, not the political one. The sacred task of the party is to educate the proletariat in a new morality that will correspond to a changed social order in which greed, alienation, hypocrisy, and oppression are done away.[43] Intellectuals, Gramsci argued, must put themselves on the same level with the common man if they wish to accomplish this moral and cultural revolution.[44]

The second group, growing in strength and influence, that derives its ideology and vision from Marx and has also appropriated the writings of the Marxist humanists into its thinking, is the national Communist parties and Communist trade unions. Recent events have underscored the power of the 1.7-million-member Communist Party of Italy, which is seriously challenging the ruling Christian Democrats for control of the Italian political system. Party Chief Enrico Berlinguer, speaking in December 1973 to the 135,000-member Communist Youth Organization, called for a "new morality," in which Marxist-indoctrinated youths would become a "last bastion" against the modern barbarism of drugs, the use of force, and the decline of morality.[45] Similarly, in France, the French Communist party's criticism of the "inhuman" policies of the Soviet Union, plus recent regional electoral victories by a communist-socialist front, has underscored the power of reformed Marxist parties in traditionally democratic Western societies. Nor are these mere expressions of traditional French opposition to the status quo; recent studies point out the ideological motivation of those voters.[46]

Even contemporary Britain is heavily influenced by Marxist thinking. In an article entitled, "Who Runs the Unions?" the 19 January 1974 *Economist* noted that while the electoral popularity of the Communist party in Britain has always been very small, its political power is great, because it essentially controls the two largest trade unions—the Transport and General Workers Union, and the Engineers, having together a membership of over three million workers.[47] Nor should we underestimate the power of the Marxist intellectual New Left in Britain. Here are college-age youth led by academicians who, although integrated into a system that absorbs rebels, continue to profess their attachment to Marxism and the human society Marx envisioned.[48]

In addition to Marxist humanism and the growth of national Marxist parties, there is a third influential interpretation of Marxism. Revolutionary Marxism, as articulated by Frantz Fanon and Che Guevara, has had enormous appeal in Latin America, Africa, and Asia, where economic and social conditions are so grim that Marx's promise of utopia immediately kindles active revolutionary activity aimed at bringing about change yesterday.[49] The events of the sixties and seventies around the world are hardly intelligible if one does not take seriously the power Marxism has had in motivating third-world revolutionary leaders to change their societies.

One other group less influential at the present time needs to be considered. Both in Europe and especially in Latin America, attempts to harmonize traditional Christianity and Marxism have been made and will continue in the future. Roger Garaudy, the foremost exponent of this compromise in France, was expelled from the Communist party in 1970. In Italy, both the Christian Democratic party chief, Aminitoe Fanfani, and the Vatican have categorically rejected any possibility of cooperation.[50] However, in Latin America the Archbishop of Recife, Brazil, Dom Helder Pessôa Cámara, has opened dialogue with Marxists. "For Christians it is now clear that we don't have one capitalism and one socialism.... Marxism is not a closed system. Socialism doesn't have to crush people, but can help the human person. Christianity is above ideology."[51]

Implications for Mormons Today

Marxism as a philosophy of life in any of its current varieties which appeal to a searching youthful generation has, I believe, serious implications for the expanding Church of Jesus Christ of Latter-day Saints and special responsibilities for its scholars. As President Dallin H. Oaks observed to the BYU faculty some years ago, in the past some of them seem to have suffered from a slight inferiority complex. They have indulged in a kind of intellectual schizophrenia where intellectual and spiritual lives did not meet. A few may even have found themselves "intellectually" ashamed of the gospel of Christ and therefore both disinclined and paralyzed to project its *Weltanschauung* beyond limited circles. But that day is past. Thomas O'Dea's pessimistic predictions of a decade ago concerning the Church's ability to hold[52] its intellectuals show little likelihood of fulfillment. They are achieving a wholeness of theory and practice that, fortunately, corresponds to responsibilities placed upon them by the expanding Church.

I do not wish to be misunderstood; I am not suggesting a carefully orchestrated symphony of apologies in a variety of disciplines as Fascists and Marxists and even some Christian churches have done. There cannot be a Mormon physics any more than there could be an Aryan one. But gospel principles and the Mormon *Weltanschauung* may, it seems to me, serve as sources of insight and value for a number of disciplines. Thus Mormon scholars can be directly involved in communicating Mormon views on life's big questions—and thereby give answers to people seeking something other than what Marx and his followers or other contemporary secular philosophies provide.

But the power of this message depends on the "wholeness" of the Latter-day Saint scholar. Intellectuals, like other people, will be more likely to listen to another ideology promising hope and an eschatological vision of what human existence can become if they come into contact with a practicing Christian scholar.[53] Thus, the achievement of wholeness in ourselves becomes a key to discharging our intellectual responsibilities.

Central to all the rest of what Mormons might offer is the affirmation of God's existence and of man's relationship to him. Just as Nietzsche propelled the secularization movement forward by ten-league jumps a century ago by pompously declaring the death of God, because there was no evidence that he lived in man, so we can humbly try to reaffirm that existence by the evidence of his life in us.

Both Marx and Nietzsche were correct in identifying the existence of God as the foundation of being and *Weltanschauung*. For as the early Christian church and the medieval mystics taught, man discovers his own self and its worth and also the worth and dignity of his fellowman in the awareness that he is created in God's image.[54] Reality thus becomes much more than the material world about us; it is composed both of matter and spirit. Moreover, the identification of man with God also makes it possible to overcome the true sources of alienation. On all those counts the gospel of Jesus Christ provides answers totally beyond anything in the worldly philosophies so attractive today.

Mormonism also has something to say to those ground down in poverty and subhuman living standards. In addition to giving even the most degenerate souls dignity through their racial lineage with God, it recognizes "that a religion which has not the power to save people temporally and make them prosperous and happy here, cannot be depended upon to save them spiritually, to exalt them in the world to come."[55] Gordon Wagner has again recently called the attention of the Mormon intellectual community to the fact that Mormonism does not view capitalism as the for-all and end-all of present socioeconomic organization, but rather sees in the doctrines of consecration and stewardship the highest law of social justice towards which the Kingdom is striving. That we accept these principles and work toward bringing them about, even slowly, will be important.[56]

On the important question of human alienation, neither Feuerbach's nor Marx's explanations really satisfy. Robert Tucker's analysis here is correct:

[Man's] alienation only becomes in a derivative way an economic fact. Inherently or in itself it is a fact of the life of the self, i.e. a spiritual or, as we say today, psychological fact. It is a sickness of the self growing out of and reflecting a man's confusion of humanity in his own person with deity, his quest to actualize himself as a supra-human absolute being. Alienation is the counterpart of egoism in this sense. It is not, therefore, a general condition of humanity. Man is not born alienated. . . .[57]

Latter-day Saint scholars can also echo Tucker that the real revolution is a moral one within the self. Marx was in error in searching "for a way of transcendence that would entail no moral work of self-liberation on the part of the alienated individual. Magnifying the problem to the proportions of humanity in general, Marx exempted alienated man in particular from all moral responsibility for striving to change himself."[58] Men are primarily alienated from themselves and from their fellowman to the extent that they, through sin, are alienated from God. As Alma said to his son, Corianton, "Wickedness never was happiness" (Alma 41:10).

Thus, Marxism in any and all of its forms has not and cannot produce freedom and peace for either the individual or for society. Hate, violence, and escapism never produce peace. Seeking individuals need to know this. But they must also be given an alternative. Mormonism's *Weltanschauung* does have the power to bring about a moral revolution in individuals. That revolution comes, as Paul said, by "hearing the word" in a cultural language the hearers can understand. That Mormonism may, indeed, be communicated as an alternative *Weltanschauung* for those who, in the earnest quest for a whole philosophy to live by, had earlier embraced Marxism was spontaneously expressed during the course of the secularization session of the symposium. Brother Arthur Henry King explained how as a young man he had been drawn to philosophical Marxism by the same search for ideals that later moved him to accept the restored gospel when he heard it. He had found superficiality in the answers Marxism provided, and so kept up his search. That his search had led him to Marxism is unfortunately typical today, as I have tried to show in this essay. But that he was searching also made him receptive to the gospel when he heard it. Similarly, Brother Seiji Katanuma poignantly retraced his own rather recent spiritual and philosophical hegira that had begun with youthful enthusiasm for the Marxist vision of social justice and had reached maturity and fuller satisfaction in the teachings of Jesus Christ. Undoubtedly there have been others; the story of Elder Louis Bertrand, a nineteenth-century French Latter-day Saint and a contemporary of Marx who, like those after him, found his way to the Church has recently come to light. He was probably the first of what may become a growing stream of those who are learned but "hearken unto the Spirit of God."

Latter-day Saint scholars, therefore, can and must speak to their peers and give them an opportunity to have their lives governed by living faith rather than myth. Then, what Marx hoped to begin and what today's scholar-intellectuals so fervently seek—not just to interpret the world but to change it—can become a reality. Then Brother Katanuma's sincere plea will not go unheeded: "Please don't turn us away."

Footnotes

1. Roland N. Stromberg, *After Everything: Western Intellectual History since 1945* (New York: St. Martin's Press, 1975), preface.

2. Quoted in Robert L. Heilbroner, *The Worldly Philosophers: The Lives, Times, and Ideas of the Great Economic Thinkers,* rev. ed. (New York: Simon and Schuster, 1961), back cover.

3. Crane Brinton, *Ideas and Men: The Story of Western Thought,* 2nd ed. (Englewood Cliffs, N.J.: Prentice-Hall, 1965), p. 6.

4. See Ernst Benz's definition of secularization earlier in this volume.

5. Hermann Kantorowicz, as cited in Max Lerner, *Ideas Are Weapons: The History and Uses of Ideas* (New York: Viking Press, 1939), p. 3.

6. Ibid.

7. *After Everything,* pp. 122–23.

8. George W. Morgan, *The Human Predicament: Dissolution and Wholeness* (Providence: Brown University Press, 1968), ix.

9. Quoted in *After Everything,* p. 217.

10. Ibid.

11. Jan Myrdal, *Confessions of a Disloyal European* (New York: Pantheon Books, 1968).

12. Comments made to the author by Cai-Aage Johansson, April 1975.

13. John Kenneth Galbraith, *The Affluent Society,* 2d ed. rev. (New York and Toronto: Mentor, 1969), pp. 33–42.

14. Joseph Smith, Jr., *A compilation Containing the Lectures on Faith as Delivered at the School of the Prophets at Kirtland, Ohio,* N.B. Lundwall, comp. (Salt Lake City: Bookcraft, n.d.), p. 41.

15. *After Everything,* p. 208.

16. Comments of Dr. Martin Binder to the author, February 1974.

17. Interview with Sidney Ahlstrom in the *BYU Daily Universe,* 1 March 1976.

18. Willson H. Coates and Hayden V. White, *The Ordeal of Liberal Humanism: An Intellectual History of Western Europe,* 2 vols. (New York: McGraw-Hill Book Co., 1970), 2:448–49.

19. Quoted in H. Stuart Hughes, *Consciousness and Society: The Reorientation of European Social Thought, 1890-1930* (New York: Vintage Books, 1961), pp. 428–29.

20. Quoted in ibid., p. 424.

21. Speech given at BYU History Week, 12 February 1976.

22. *Neue Zürcher Zeitung,* 22 December 1975.

23. At the 22nd Party Congress of the PCF (held 4–5 February 1976), party secretary general Georges Marchais "obtained unanimous approval for a decision to drop the ideological concept of 'the dictatorship of the proletariat,' which had meant, in effect, exclusive Communist domination of a government once power was achieved." *Facts on File: Yearbook 1976* 36 (New York: Facts on File, Inc., 1976):119.

24. Some of the more prominent philosophers who share Fromm's basic ideals and beliefs recently contributed essays to a collection edited by him, which was published under the title *Socialist Humanism: An International Symposium* (Garden City, N.Y.: Anchor Books, 1966). Not all the contributors are Marxists, a fact which reflects the broad humanistic appeal of this branch of Marxism. The Marxist contributors to the symposium include Herbert Marcuse, Eugene Kamenka, Adam Schaff, Mihailo Markovic, and Gajo Petrovic.

25. Conversation with Ernest Oates, 23 February 1976.

26. Gerhart Niemeyer, "The Role of Ideology in Communist Systems," *Orbis* 17 (Fall 1973):786.

27. Jaroslaw A. Piekalkiewicz, *Public Opinion Polling in Czechoslovakia, 1968–69: Results and Analysis of Surveys Conducted during the Dubcek Era,* Praeger Special Studies in International Politics and Government (New York: Praeger Publishers, 1972), p. 4.

28. *After Everything,* p. 82. According to one Marxist writer, Raya Dunayevskaya, the "condition" of modern man is extreme alienation of theory and practice. She argues that intellectual and scientific speculation are not interwoven into the fabric of daily life and work; consequently, they create technologies and weapons unsuited to contemporary social and cultural life. She says: "The task that confronts our age, it appears to this writer, is, first, to recognize that there is a movement from practice—from the actual struggles of the day—to theory; and, second, to work out the method whereby the movement *from theory* can meet it. A new relationship of theory to practice, a new appreciation of Subject, of live human beings struggling to reconstruct society, is essential. The challenge of our times is not to science or machines, but to men. The totality of the world crisis demands a new unity of theory and practice, a new relationship of workers and intellectuals. The search for a total philosophy has been disclosed dramatically by the new, third world of underdeveloped countries. But there are also evidences of this search in the struggles for freedom from totalitarian regimes, and in the West. To discern this mass search for a total philosophy it is necessary only to shed the stubborness of all philosophies—the concept of "the backwardness of the masses"—and *listen* to *their* thoughts, as they battle automation, fight for

the end of discrimination, or demand freedom *now*." Raya Dunayevskaya, "Marx's Humanism Today" in *Socialist Humanism*, p. 79.

29. Stromberg, *After Everything*, p. 9.

30. Quoted in Robert C. Tucker, ed., *The Marx-Engels Reader* (New York: W. W. Norton and 1972), p. 11.

31. Ibid., p. 18. In recent years scholars have perceived Marx as more concerned about the dehumanizing forces in society than in the establishment of either authoritarian parties or bloody revolution to bring about improvements in life for the masses.

32. Ibid., p. 58.

33. Ibid., p. 71.

34. Ibid., p. 70.

35. Karl Marx and Friedrich Engels, *The Communist Manifesto*, ed. Samuel H. Beer (New York: Appleton, Century, Crofts, 1955), p. vii.

36. R. N. Berki, "George Lukács in Retorspect: Evolution of the Marxist Thinker," *Problems of Communism* 21 (November-December 1972):53.

37. Ibid., p. 54.

38. Ibid., p. 55.

39. Prediag Vranicki, as cited in Oskar Gruenwald, "Marxist Humanism," *Orbis* 18 (Fall 1974):900.

40. The purpose of Marxist philosophers, according to Marcuse, is to make people aware of the necessity for a cultural revolution. Intellectuals must speak to the "enslaved human beings who must accomplish their own liberation. To develop their conscience and consciousness, to make them aware of what is going on, to prepare the precarious ground for the future alternatives—this is our task: "our" not only as Marxists but as intellectuals, and that means all those who are still free and able to think by themselves and against indoctrination, communist as well as anticommunist." Herbert Marcuse, "Socialist Humanism?", in *Socialist Humanism*, p. 109.

41. In ibid., p. 232.

42. Neil McInnes, *The Western Marxists* (New York: Library Press, 1972), p. 109.

43. Ibid., pp. 88–104.

44. Nigel Todd, "Ideological Superstructure in Gramsci and Mao Tse-Tung," *Journal of the History of Ideas* 35 (January-March 1974):154. Gramsci said: "What a tragedy it would be, if the group of intellectuals who came to the working class, and in whom the working class places its trust, did not feel themselves the same flesh and blood as the most humble, the most backward, the least aware of our workers and peasants! Then all our work would be useless and we should obtain no results" (p. 154).

45. *Neue Zürcher Zeitung*, 22 December 1975.

46. Thomas H. Greene, "The Electorates of Nonruling Communist Parties," *Studies in Comparative Communism* 4 (July-October 1971):68–103. The purpose of this article was to show that support for nonruling communist parties is *not* primarily a reflection of communist voters' economic, social, or psychological alienation from their society. Nor can it be viewed as an expression of incoherent protest against the system by people who see the communist parties as the most militant opponents of constituted authority. Greene states (pp. 90–91): "There is an impressive array of data from several different cultural contexts showing that the great majority of Communist voters share the values and attitudes expressed in the propaganda and behavior of their chosen party. Their opinions on broad political and social questions and on the issues of the day appear to reflect a set of

logically consistent values, values that might best be labelled 'radical-humanist.' After studying all these data, I find it difficult to resist the argument that most Communist voters vote Communist because of what they believe."

47. "Who Runs the Unions?", *The Economist,* 19 January 1974, pp. 62–63.

48. George Watson, "Was the New Left a Success?", *Encounter* 45 (October 1975):13–25. The impact of Marxism on the beliefs of British youth is reflected in the following statement by a young British schoolteacher named Mr. Green, who is a member of the Communist party: "Atheism is one of the basic feelings in my character. Religion gives a false impression of human dignity. It thwarts the destiny of man." To Mr. Green, Marxism allows man "to use to his full stature and to eliminate the barriers which prevent him from doing it in this society." (Quoted in Kenneth Newton, *The Sociology of British Communism,* London: A. Lane, Penguin Press, 1969), pp. 148–9.

49. Che Guevara, "Message to the Tricontinental," in Irving Louis Horowitz, Josue de Castro, and John Gerassi, eds., *Latin American Radicalism: A Documentary Report on Left and Nationalist Movements* (New York: Random House, 1969), pp. 607–20.

50. *Neu Zürcher Zeitung,* 26 May 1975.

51. Joseph A. Page, "From Brazil, An Outraged Cleric Voices a Lonely Protest," *Salt Lake Tribune,* 23 May 1971, p. 4A.

52. Thomas F. O'Dea, *The Mormons* (Chicago: University of Chicago Press, 1957), pp. 222–63. A follow-up article expressing similar concerns appeared in Marvin S. Hill and James B. Allen, eds., *Mormonism and American Culture* (New York: Harper and Row, 1972), pp. 147–67.

53. Recent, unpublished research done for the Church of Jesus Christ of Latter-day Saints' First Council of the Seventy shows that a large number of strong and enduring conversions to the Church result from the observed examples of active Mormon families—of their way of life, their closeness, and their happiness.

54. Ernst Benz, "Der Mensch als Imago Dei," *Eranos-Jahrbuch* 38 (1969):304, 328, 329.

55. Joseph F. Smith, "The Truth About Mormonism," *Out West* 13 (September 1905):242. Quoted in Gordon E. Wagner, "Consecration and Stewardship: A Socially Efficient System of Justice," a working paper presented at the BYU Conference on Economics and the Mormon Culture, Brigham Young University, Provo, Utah, October, 5–7, 1975, p. 48.

56. Gordon E. Wagner, "Consecration and Stewardship."

57. Robert Tucker, "Philosophy and Myth in Karl Marx," in Donald N. Baker and George W. Fasel, eds., *Landmarks in Western Culture: Commentaries and Controversies,* 2 vols. (Englewood Cliffs, N.J.: Prentice-Hall, 1968), 2:315.

58. Ibid., 2:316.

Comments, Elder Neal A. Maxwell

I would like to be brief, as I sense the desire in the group to ask questions of those who presented papers. The excellent point Brother Tobler made about world view is one we must take into account. What fascinates me is that the gospel of Jesus Christ gives us a galactic view of man and his existence; it thus constitutes for man a distinct alternative world view. Given contemporary worldliness, we are a counter-culture. We are a nonviolent counter-culture, but we are a counter-culture.

Our whole assumption is that we change the world by changing individuals. Ours is the original gospel of hope. We also know historically that, while the yield varies, happily the gospel seed grows in many different soils. As it does, it looks to me as though we will see, as we confront secularism, a mix of things happening simultaneously. The Church and its people will be a light on a hill in some respects; we will be known by what we stand for and by what we reject. At the same time, there will be misunderstanding and misrepresentation as the Church expands and as multiple Zions are established all over. And, as the Lord has said, we will pass through great tribulations; but his people will be preserved.

We now have, so far as I am informed, our first Maori member of the Church in the New Zealand Parliament; we have, without help from full-time missionaries in the usual sense, one city in south India with around 120 members. In the Mexico area in the month of February [1976] there were over 3,000 baptisms. The number will probably become 7,000 a month by November. All these things will be happening simultaneously, along with efforts in which individual members of the Church begin to have influence on the secularized society at critical junctures.

Often, and usually through regular social and proper political processes, there will be "Colonel Kanes" raised up to assist us. The yield of new converts will increase as many find that the emptiness of secularism, which has been spoken of so well here, will greatly increase. We will find that secularism will stunt the individual and then complain about his size; whereas the gospel seems ever, to me, to be stretching souls.

We will produce men like a stake president I met a month ago, who just seven years ago was an athiest.

You may all be familiar with the motto Winston Churchill selected for the last volume of his memories of World War II in which he told how the great democracies had won the war and thus were able to resume the follies that so nearly cost them their lives. Happily, the gospel of Jesus Christ gives us a memory; we do not have to reenact human tragedy.

As secularism seems always to be looking beyond the mark, I agree with Brother Tobler that we must articulately put forward the gospel alternative by word and by the eloquence of our example. And we ought to do it so well, on issues such as the institution of the family, that if we are not able to persuade people, then at least we ought to leave them, as the scriptures say, without excuse.

Lastly, what I would add is that I have been given an additional assignment to head a new Church department involved with long-range planning, correlation, and evaluation of Church programs. All our activities are tactical considerations, not doctrinal ones. We do not adjust doctrine in the Kingdom. But one of the challenges we do face is the need for the simplification of our programs; and I hope that the last thing this new department does is create a handbook on simplification. What is fascinating to me is that a couple of years ago I worried greatly about transculturalization. But that was before I met the rising individuals in the Church like Enzio Busche, Rhee Ho Nam, and Charles Didier (who are here), Jacob de Jager, and others.

In his own natural way the Lord is helping us solve the problem of transculturalization. I am still aware that departments at headquarters occasionally err in what they do, but the Lord has always had a solution built in. And it did not require us to produce a handbook on transculturalization because new leaders from many lands are coming naturally into their own in the Church.

So frankly, it seems to me, brothers and sisters, that we are in a situation wherein we seek to change individuals, that we will be blessed as we meet the tactical challenges, but in that process we will have very genuine stress placed upon us. I am grateful to see this symposium focus on this issue, which is very much with us.

Brother Tobler read some early quotes from Karl Marx. I would like to read an early quote from Karl Marx that, on reasonable authority, is valid. Whatever happened to change Marx we do not know, but at one time, as a schoolboy, he wrote this:

Union with Christ imparts an inner elevation, comfort in affliction, tranquil reliance, and a heart which opens itself to everything noble and great—not for the sake of ambition or desire for fame, but for the sake of Christ. Union with Christ produces a joy which the epicurean seeks in vain in a shallow philosophy which the deeper thinker daily pursues in the most hidden depths of knowledge. It is a joy known to the simple and child-like heart. United with Christ, include him with God, a joy which cultivates life and makes it more beautiful[1]

What Marx wrote as a schoolboy obviously had less impact than what he wrote later. But it was much wiser.

Comments, Louis C. Midgley

I must begin by mentioning something in Brother Tobler's excellent paper. He calls the gospel a philosophical system. I am not fond of calling the gospel a philosophical system. Why? Let me explain. Elder Maxwell mentioned that he understands the gospel to be a unique or "distinct alternative world view," and, I would add, it is therefore not merely some human invention called a philosophical system. To label it such might seem to imply that it is merely human and not divine wisdom that we cherish. A theology that is merely man's words about God could be called a philosophical system, but God's words to man ultimately calls into question all such vain philosophy. In the ancient world both Christians and Jews made the radical distinction I am suggesting by identifying man's wisdom with Athens and divine wisdom with Jerusalem. It was the fatal error of medieval theologians to attempt a synthesis of Jerusalem with Athens. We must never make that mistake. There may be nothing necessarily wrong with the pursuit and even love of human wisdom, but the gospel is not, I believe, the fruit of such a merely human activity; to accept the gospel is to accept the divine wisdom symbolized by Jerusalem, and this should not be confused with our own halting efforts we sometimes call philosophy.

The gospel does confront secularized societies, and Brother Tobler has said some very interesting things about that confrontation. In so doing he quoted a very famous passage from Karl Marx. But unfortunately he quit right when he got to the best part. Marx had already indicated that "the criticism of religion is the presupposition of all criticism." And, Marx says, "the criticism of religion is essentially complete."[1] In Germany it is moribound if not dead. More than we Latter-day Saints recognize, outside the Church, especially in highly secularized societies, religion has died. We live in a world where God, especially the belief in God, has died in the hearts of men. There may be some sentimental remembrances at certain times, for example, at birth and death, but as a functioning premise, as anything that explains anything, religion is dead. To me that is not necessarily an evil because the religion that has died is rooted in an apostate theology; it is a corrupt religion that deserves to have died. Listen to what Marx says about it.

> *Religion is the general theory of this world, its encylopedic compendium, its logic in popular form, its spiritual* point d'honneur, *its enthusiasm, its moral sanction, its solemn complement, its universal basis of consolation and justification. It is the realization of the human essence, because the imaginary human essence possesses no true reality. Thus, the struggle against religion is indirectly the struggle against the world whose spiritual aroma is religion.*[2]

Now, of course, I don't buy Marxism, but I do agree that someone needed to say what he said about what had happened to religion in Europe and elsewhere, because it is probably true. The decline of the sectarian religions has not always been an unqualified evil; similarly the influences of some sectarian churches has not always been benign or salutary. The passing of state churches and the theologies of men are hardly events to be mourned, but perhaps celebrated.

Why should we assume that the gospel, our own faith, is necessarily vulnerable to those forces at work in the world that have brought on the decline of religion generally? Consider further Marx's comments: "Religious suffering is at the same time an expression of real suffering and a protest against real suffering. Religion is the sigh of the oppressed creature, the feeling of a heartless world, and the soul of soulless circumstances. It is the opium of the people."[3]

What Marx is describing in this famous passage is a religion that offers *no* genuine hope for the future. But the gospel does offer a hope for the future; we offer it not by having an argument about the psychological use of the term "alienation," nor do we offer hope by engaging in ontological or sociological discussions. Brother Tobler maintained that "man is not born an alien." But I think we are aliens or strangers in this world. Do we really belong to this world? We came here from another world. This is not our home. The Saints have always believed that man in this world is a wanderer in a strange land, a stranger or a sojourner in a dark and dreary waste, a pilgrim or alien.

Mankind now does not seem to have an answer to the great questions. Therefore we have an opportunity to proclaim to them the gospel and show them where we come from and also where we are going beyond the grave. They may think the gospel is fantastic; they may not believe it, for it is quite unlike man's religion. But, at least, our job is to warn and, if possible, teach and, if we can, bring them to the truth. Man comes from another world—his so-called preexistence. This current mortal state of existence is a probation in which his fitness is being tested and he is being prepared, if he is willing, for another, much better world. Our present world is thus a necessary stage or step in a journey that transcends the course of events of profane history—the story of successive generations of mortal men. Our destiny is not tied to what happens in this world in the next fifteen or fifty or hundred years, because, ultimately, the Lord is powerful enough to bring about his own ends, which include the redemption of man from sin and death. I do not think that means we should just give up on the world and go into some kind of holding pattern, unconcerned with genuine efforts to bring about much righteousness. But I am also concerned about Latter-day Saints who feel the need to do the Lord's work for him and who assume that our task is not to preach the gospel of Jesus Christ, but to advance some social or political ideology. Our progress certainly begins prior to and has its end beyond this world. "But our commonwealth is in heaven, and from it we await a Savior, the Lord Jesus Christ, who will change our lowly body to be like his glorious body, by the power which enables him even to subject all things to himself" (Philippians 3:20f., Rev. Standard Version).

Can the Saints involve themselves in the world's politics? Should we not abandon the city of man to its own fate and assume a kind of "holding pattern" while the world disintegrates around us? Some people have felt that way, but I wish to argue that we must have a modest concern for secular politics. Politics has traditionally been considered a search for the commonwealth. As such it includes, at its best, free and open discussions among those seeking attainment of what they consider their own welfare. It is more or less rational activity, a kind of discourse, about ends and means. It should also include, among other things and in addition to a measure of rationality, a humane respect for the other. Obviously we do not find it that way very often. Politics should involve the concept of man's rights as a moral agent. Think of our own passion for the United States Constitution, which the Lord suffered wise men to establish. The founding of the Republic permitted the Church, in its early period, to grow in as protected an atmosphere as possible, one in which we have freedom of conscience and certain other legal protections. Our best efforts should be given to extending the application of those "just and holy principles."

God has not forbidden our participation in the city of man and even encourages us to strive to make our own way as best we can in this world. "But seek the welfare of the city where I have sent you into exile, and pray to the Lord on its behalf, for in its welfare you will find your welfare"(Jeremiah 29:7, Rev. Standard Version). The ends of the secular polity are, in spite of the frequent and considerable moral failures in politics, still valuable after all. We can enter into them to some extent. What worries me, however, is the possibility that we will confuse the gospel with some political ideology or with some partisan matter, and though we may even sometimes be right about it, it may not be worth the cost; it may divert our energies from our highest ends. Having the Church prosper may be far more important than making a stand on a current partisan issue.

What do we do in a world three-quarters of which is dominated by some kind of Marxism and the bulk of the rest heavily influenced by secular humanist ideologies essentially hostile to the gospel? How do we treat this problem? I believe if we are going to preach the gospel in, for example, Eastern Europe and elsewhere and have any genuine possibility of success, we simply must restrain ourselves about some of the things we find wrong, for example, in communism. That is not to ignore what is abhorrent, but it may be worth paying the small price of keeping our mouths shut about some things—at least for the time being. I believe that if we tend well the affairs of the Lord's kingdom, divine providence will settle with communism. Let the Lord take care of that problem in his own way and in his own time; we need not feel a compulsion to rush in to deal with such issues in our own clumsy way.

We serve the Kingdom best by following a policy of modest restraint on political issues. But in the end that policy may fail; we may not be able to avoid trouble with the city of man. I suppose that ultimately we may be faced with the question of obligation; should one obey the city of man or the city of God? And it may be that people who are our enemies, whom the scriptures describe as "filled with darkness," may restrict us.

Is there necessarily a conflict between our loyalty to the Kingdom—to the city of God—and our living in the city of man, wherever it may be? Now these are familiar problems to those who see the city of God their primary citizenship, whose ultimate loyalty is therefore to the kingdom of God and who are often called on the carpet by those who rightly or wrongly fear such primary loyalty. The believer is of course urged by prophetic counsel to give tribute (taxes) to the city of man, to obey its laws (D&C 58:21–22; 134:5–6), to play its game (D&C 63:27). But there is always the possibility of a showdown between the city of man and the people of God. It has happened. Will it happen again? When? Where will we stand if and when it happens? This is not something we want; we do not desire it, nor do we go looking for it. We will try to avoid it at *almost* every cost. If and when it happens, it will have been forced on us from without. The question of one's ultimate loyalty and the possibility of conflicting obligations cannot always be avoided. In the meantime let us follow Paul's admonition: "First of all, then, I urge that supplications, prayers, intercessions, and thanksgivings be made for all men, for kings and all who are in high positions, that we may lead a quiet and peaceable life, godly and respectful in every way" (I Timothy 2:1–3, Rev. Standard Version). I think the scriptures already provide us with a clear measuring rod of how we should act in those emergency situations. I see clear communication on this problem of obedience. You can find it, for example, in the New Testament. We must, of course, choose to "obey God rather than men" (Acts 5:29), but we do not seek an ultimate confrontation. "Whether it be right in the sight of God to listen to you [that is, to some secular authority] rather than to God, you must judge; for we cannot but speak of what we have seen and heard" (Acts 4:19–20, Rev. Standard Version).

I hope we will always be able to obey the injunctions we find in the scriptures. It seems to me we should submit to the abuse of the unknowing—the hardened and the wicked—in order that gentile hearts (and I wish to quote a passage from the Doctrine and Covenants) "may be softened when thy servants shall go out from thy house, O Jehovah, to bear testimony of thy name; that their prejudices [the prejudices of the world] may give way before the truth, and thy people may obtain favor in the sight of all; that all the ends of the earth may know that we, thy servants, have heard thy voice and that thou hast sent us; that from among all these, thy servants ... may gather out the righteous to build a holy city to thy name, as thou hast commanded them" (D&C 109:56–58).

Now, if we can tolerate the manipulating, exploiting evil of the environment in which we live, one from which I personally feel deeply alienated and one that constantly threatens us with its blandishments; if we can restrain the search for power and gain that the Book of Mormon warns us about on practically every page; if we can put up with an economic system without condemning it from the pulpit in rash terms that cause the political system to turn against us and legally restrict us; if we can tolerate all that so that we can still preach the gospel, then I think we may be able in some way to come to terms with preaching the gospel in other environments where perhaps even worse conditions exist. If not, I see little hope for our missionary labors continuing to succeed and flourish in the way President Kimball has urged. We will, then, be faced with frustrations we cannot hope to overcome.

What keeps us on the right track? The prophetic gift and the temple both give us an indication of where we came from and where we are going. The thought was expressed earlier today that we Saints often feel the need for a stake in order to flourish in the Church; a stake is the tent-peg of the tent of Israel as the people of God, under its protective shelter, move through a hostile environment. There is the sense in which we need to refurbish our feelings of being alien in this world. We need to be wiser in our treatment of the darkness that is around us.

One last thought: When the topics like those discussed today are treated, they are frequently dealt with in the vocabulary of contemporary social science. That is not necessarily bad, but it may yield difficulties for the Saints. Let us illustrate my concern. A persistent theme is that a church, if it is to prosper, must engage in something called "social adaptation." The church will fail if it is rigid; it needs to be flexible in political or social matters. Then we are told that the success of the restored Church is found in its adaptability. There are ways in which such observations may be true; if understood in other ways, some serious problems may be encountered. In a contest between the norms of the gospel and those of the world, it would be fatal for the gospel to insist that it must modify to meet the standard set by the world. Words like adaptability, flexibility, rigidity have several meanings and functions in discourse, some of which could get us into serious trouble, especially if we use them to suggest or imply that the doctrines ought to be adapted, modified, or changed in order to avoid our personal discomfort at having the gospel out of line with the world. If we accept that idea, we have signed our death warrant. I abhor that kind of interpretation and wish to go on record against it.

I believe that our problems with the world will be solved only by our believing and acting upon Alma's advice to his son Shiblon: "I would that ye should remember, that as much as ye shall put your trust in God even so much ye shall be delivered out of your trials, and your troubles, and your afflictions, and ye shall be lifted up at the last day" (Alma 38:5). Trust in the Lord seems an unwarranted risk to some, but if we cannot take that step we are unworthy of the title Saint and are not the people of God.

Questions, Answers, and Comments

Question

This question, which I wish to address to Elder Maxwell, has come up in various ways, but not explicitly. During the course of these symposia I have had the feeling that the meetings could not have been held ten years ago because of some of the same kinds of problems that Brother Midgley referred to. Yet, still there are problems. Consider two analogies. If a senate subcommittee were assigned to take care of some problem in the country, it would appropriately conduct hearings to gather information and recommendations. Similar procedures and symposia meetings would also be appropriate for a group of economists at BYU if they were sponsoring a symposium on, say, economic conditions in England. But with the subject matter of the expanding Church, we are in a very awkward situation, especially as academicians at BYU. We do not have the disinterested position economists have as they talk about England. Nor do we have the authoritative position the Senate committee has as it investigates a particular problem. And yet it seems that something good can come from these symposia on the expanding Church, although there are obvious dangers. Do you feel you could comment on this dilemma, and would you recommend some criteria by which one might distinguish what is appropriate for us to examine here in our setting?

Elder Maxwell

The context in which I will respond is that, in my judgment, both the liaison and the mutuality of respect between the Brethren and LDS scholars have never been so good as they are right now. Thus many things occur now that might not have been ventured earlier. That is the general context. Contrary to some predictions, we are not only holding our LDS thinkers, but now they are showing up increasingly in stake presidencies, in mission presidencies, and wherever you point. In such a desirable context it seems to me the only two cautions I would offer would be to continue to do much of what you have already done here, such as making certain you involve an Elder Gordon B. Hinckley so that you would not miss the unusual insight this man and his colleagues have. I think we must involve men like him or Elder Monson, or Brother Busche.

Now my second caution. If I have come to appreciate something else in the last six years more than I did before, it is the degree to which I perhaps had been caught up in academic jargon in my days at the University of Utah. There is a certain pragmatism about the Brethren in terms of their wanting us to say whatever needs saying as simply, directly, and straightforwardly as possible. I am not issuing that caveat just for this symposium, but generally. If we want to draw even closer, our own jargon is sometimes a deterrent.

You are to be commended in what you have done here. Lou [Midgley] just now let me see Noel Reynolds's essay (the first in this volume). I read it and was fascinated by it. There will be some miscues. You cannot venture as much as you are venturing now in these areas and not have an occasional thing happen that we might regret. But the general thrust is just very pleasing to me.

On my little hidden agendum when I became Commissioner roughly six years ago was to do what little I could to draw together those very spiritual resources of the Brethren and the very scholarly resources of the Church. It is very pleasing to see what is happening.

Robert S. Jordan

I really cannot disagree with most of what Lou [Midgley] said. The point here is that the Church lives in a political environment. The early Church [at the time of Christ and the apostles] lived in a political environment. It had to come in contact with a secular authority in one way or another. At certain points it divorced itself from secular authority, appealing to a higher authority; and it took the consequences. At other times it compromised with secular political authority and in some instances even supplanted it and became one itself. The Church in our day has had the same dilemma. What makes the Doctrine and Covenants interesting on this point is that many of the relevations deal with problems that relate to political authority. We cannot escape this reality when we move into the world in a multi-political, multi-polar situation; it simply means, as Brother Maxwell said, that the problem becomes infinitely more complicated. It is not a question of divorcing the fundamental values the Church espouses or those aspects of the doctrine we would regard as eternal. There is a fairly high degree of consensus on what those are, although not completely. The question is one of application—whether or not we are willing as a Church to compromise (and that's not a pejorative word) in favor of one goal at the expense of another. Are we willing, for example, to overlook earlier opinions about communism in order to penetrate communist states to make converts—a very real tactical question. In other words, how do you take these values that are not the fundamental doctrine leading to the world after this one and measure these off against a highly dynamic contemporary world that is politically very complex and that has become increasingly anti-Western—not just Anti-Christian—in which the Church has to project its own form of Christianity. This is the problem I was trying to address here, the dilemma of preaching the political principles of the United States, which was the fundamental bastion and inspiration politically for the Church's beliefs in the world at large.

Arthur Henry King

I first read Marx almost exactly fifty years ago. If it had not been for Marx, I should not yet be in this Church, if at all. I read my Kierkegaard; I read my Nietzsche, but they were engaged in a pseudo-aristocratic withdrawal from the world. Not so Marx, albeit he worked in the British Museum. When he said, "As long as there is a lower class, I am of it," was he saying anything essentially different from what you have written on the Statue of Liberty? I should like Douglas Tobler, whose essay I entirely endorse, and which I think in years to come will be looked back upon as a key essay, to remember the emotive appeal of wanting to raise all suffering humanity as I think the Lord wanted us to do. If we can only remember that men like Solzhenitzyn are, after all, not anti-communists. China and the Soviet Union are profoundly anti-communist. They are not communist states at all.* What I am trying to say, therefore, is this: there has been deep emotive appeal of Marxism to several generations; and I have felt it myself, for I abominated Stalinism, as Marx himself would have abominated it.

But I also saw the grief of so many persons in August-September, 1939, when that awful pact between Stalin and van Ribbentrop was sign-

*Solzenitzyn complains that the USSR is not communist. China and the USSR are tyrannies with multiclass bureaucracies and privileged classes.

ed, and how so much idealism was lost at that time. Suddenly people realized that what they thought was the salvation of mankind was a monstrous tyranny.

Every generation of young people who come out of your country and mine want to help. They want to do, they want to act, they want to engage in social service, they want to help lift the suffering millions, and it seems to me that if we can go to them with the gospel of Christ, knowing that and knowing what lies behind their ideologies, we shall succeed.

Douglas F. Tobler

I wanted to add something that I was not able to get to in my paper. During my travel in Europe in 1974, one of the most interesting conversations I had was with a young man, Dieter Berndt, who was then a member of the Berlin stake presidency and a professor at the Free University of Berlin, a heavily Marxist-influenced institution. He made an observation I think is worth considering. "In the Church," he said, "we have a tendency to damn all insurgent young people who in some cases seem revolutionary or are generally throwing off all kinds of traditions. We see only the negative about them." (The day before, the stake president, to whom he was a counselor, had expressed the view that wild-eyed radicals should be penned up.) "But," Brother Berndt remarked, "I don't believe that. I believe that people are searching. I believe this process is one whereby they are throwing off shackes—the old shackles that have bound them—and they sometimes are doing it very violently; but this is part of the process that is necessary in order that they can be free to accept something else." He concluded by seeing great positive possibilities for the Church for these young people if our attitude is one of understanding rather than condemning out of hand. He was much impressed by their idealism and hoped the Church could communicate a viable alternative idealism to them, for it could take them where they want to go.

Seiji Katanuma

Before joining the Church I was myself a Marxist. Many young generations all over the world had the same ideas as the Marxists because of the contradictions in society. I thought there were contradictions in our society. Japan is so narrow, and there are so many American bases occupying much of the good land; that is why I thought I had to fight contradictions. But ex-Marxists who have reformed their thinking can be brought into the Church. So, please, I have got to stress this point: let's preach the gospel without any suspicion of those young people. That's what I want to say. Thank you.

Question

Since we have some good political scientists here, I want to address myself to the issue of Mormons becoming involved in the political system. It has seemed to be a general feeling in the United States and elsewhere that you get tarnished in politics. There are so many compromises and so many pressures that it is difficult to be honest and maintain gospel ideals if you are a politician. Yet it is precisely in the political arena that one can have great influence. I am wondering, therefore, how you see members of the Church being able to accomplish a good walk in the political system here in the United States as well as in even more difficult situations in Europe where the movement toward socialism, which some Latter-day Saints deplore, is so advanced?

Robert S. Jordan

I can respond on the international side. Your question is the kind that any good member of the Church might want to comment on. My own view is that you cannot escape politics. The Church is as interested in influencing the course of public policy as any other institution, and, when it can, it does. So the question is: who does it and how?

I think members of the Church ought not to turn away from the international side of political affairs. I think there may be a tendency to do so because of the essentially confusing world we live in. We tend to pull back from it and perhaps even make judgments about it. Rather than that, I would encourage members of the Church to become involved in a variety of international economic and political activities and organizations. Without that involvement, we are not going to get the sense of what the true reality of the international scene is. At the same time, if we are to fulfill the world role we feel we should, it is extremely important for us to know about and have a sense for that world. So I would come out in favor of involvement rather than disengagement.

Louis C. Midgley

I think that when we talk about engaging in politics, we often mean running for or holding office. I see the risks there as somewhat the same as entering into business or becoming a professor; you run the risk of subordinating the gospel and its principles to your own narrow ends and ambitions. As you all know, we do not like having scruples get in the way of our ambitions; when they do we rationalize them. I do not know that it is any more a risk to be in politics than in many other activities; it would depend upon the situation and the individual. I think it is possible, even given that risk, for Latter-day Saints to participate in public affairs in such a way as to bring blessings to the city in which we live.

Note to Comments by Neal Maxwell

1. Karl Marx, "Die Vereinigung der Gläubigen mit Christo nach Joh. 15, 1–14, in ihrem Grund und Wesen, in ihrer unbedingten Notwendigkeit und in ihren Wirkungen dargestellt," in *Karl Marx-Friedrich Engels Werke,* Ergänzungsband, *Schriften, Manuskripte, Briefe bis 1844,* Erster Teil (Berlin: Dietz, 1968), pp. 598–601; quotation at p. 601.

Notes to Comments by Louis Midgley

1. Karl Marx, "Towards a Critique of Hegel's 'Philosophy of Right: Introduction,' " in David McLellan, ed., *Karl Marx: Selected Writings* 3d., (Cambridge: Oxford University Press, 1977), p. 63.

2. Ibid., pp. 63ff.

3. Ibid.

EPILOGUE

F. LaMond Tullis

Something fundamental and pervasive is happening to the Church in our time. In part it is our growth, in part its nature—across boundaries of ancestral customs, tradition, race, and nationality as never before—both of which combine to present challenges conquered and others, still unknown and untried, yet before us. Combine this with the threats—and some of the benefits—of secularization, and we have what one observer noted as "a challenge sufficient for ten lifetimes confronting the present membership of the Church." As the world scene becomes more complex, as the gospel impacts throughout the world, as the administrative structure of the Church rises to administer programs and policies worldwide—all these combine to present portents both commendable and ominous, which, in individual Mormon lives, generate those paradoxical sentiments of happiness and frustration, motivation and despair. Few observers today with any insight into religious movements will doubt that something big and important is happening to the Church; few Mormons who have given considered thought to present-day Church events will doubt that in our lifetime they are both invigorating and sobering.

The broad sweep of events seems clear enough: the revitalization of the Church in Europe, its massive growth in Latin America and Asia, the revamping of time-honored procedures to allow for the rapid development of indigenous membership—and all this within the context of fundamental social change throughout the world, wherein difficulties from large-scale secularization and reinforcement of cultural boundaries are increasingly upon us. Yet, as with virtually all phenomena, the more closely we examine and understand them the more we become impressed that they are less simple and no doubt less clear than we had thought. So also is it with the Church in the last days. There is an inescapable conclusion: if we are to be abreast of events, each of us needs to raise his or her level of understanding about them. The "dictates of the spirit" are difficult in an awareness vacuum; the "illumination of the mind" is slow and indirect when no questions are asked. After all, was it not for an answer to a question that the Prophet went to the Sacred Grove? And was it not from his study that he asked the question?

If we can talk about our Church—and we think we can and should—from the vantage of both faith and enlightened observation, we are likely to trace two important consequences. The first is the development of greater awareness and appreciation of the magnitude and complexity of the Mormon experience in its new diverse cultural setting worldwide. There was poignancy in the events surrounding Peter's eventual understanding of the "gentile question" in his day; there is something just as important for us as we attempt to move beyond parochial attachments and to gain a glimpse of the universal in time and space—to approach and touch, where we can, the reality of Mormonism now, and find out how it has been appreciated and encountered in over half the nations of this planet.

The second likely consequence is the development of an inclination for purposeful action, on an individual level, in benefit of the collective spirit of Mormonism. We shall become better brothers and sisters in the Kingdom, and the consequences of that, to both ourselves and generations yet unborn, are incalculable. We have no doubt that the Kingdom will eventually include as much diversity as the phrase "all nations, kindreds, tongues and people" suggests (D&C 42:58). But what will our individual lot be? Kicking hither and yon, demanding molds of character and spirit as parochial as our own minds? Reaching out with the truths of the gospel message in a brotherhood tuned to the galaxy, to the eternities?

Readers of this volume will certainly have developed a greater awareness and appreciation of Mormonism in its new worldwide setting. Many will also have been inclined in varying degrees to some purposeful action. All this inescapably derives from our having been instructed by General Authorities and articulate representatives and members of the Church from Asia, Europe, and Latin America.

We have also had a unique opportunity to interact with Mormon scholars who have demonstrated that bilingualism of faith and scholarship of which Dallin H. Oaks has spoken on many occasions. Having also been in the forefront of ecclesiastical experiences in the Church—serving as bishops, ward and stake leaders, and General Authorities—they are all aware of the occasions when Western rational discourse is insufficient for an adequate understanding of the eternal values associated with the gospel. On the other hand, they also know that we cannot avoid the necessity—indeed, the imperative—to struggle with the world in which we live, to understand it, to make sense out of it, to refine our comprehension of its parts and their interrelationships. The finest compliment I believe can be paid to many of the Church's scholars is that they have in a responsible way been able to bring the two languages of faith and scholarship together. I think it is to their everlasting credit and our everlasting benefit to be associated with them.

We may scan the Mormon experience in the last days as if through the large end of a telescope, viewing the grand sweep of events that transforms nations and peoples, knowing in advance that the outcome—the triumph of the Kingdom—is never in doubt. Or we can turn the telescope around, view in magnification smaller parts of the Mormon reality, and thereby hold them up for closer inspection, not knowing, in any given case, the outcome for particular individuals and groups. The events of this hour, this day, set the scenarios for magnification—the happiness, the heartache, the dilemma. Only a moment's time at the small end of the telescope impresses us that each person's crucial role in the chain of events that links individual lives and feelings about the gospel obliges us to bring all our faculties of mind and spirit to bear on what is happening to us in these latter days.

In the macro view we find agreement and harmony in Mormonism today: the gospel will prevail; the Lord's plan will not be thwarted; the earth will ultimately be renewed to receive its paradisiacal glory. Yet from the other end of the telescope—from the micro view where a close focus may be obtained on the sentiments and values of individuals and groups—differences of opinion exist about the *meaning* of what is seen, or even about *what* is seen. Nevertheless, some of the questions are remarkably persistent and consistent: Is there a gospel culture? How is it distinguished from the Mormon culture of the American West? What aspects of national culture in any land are really compatible—or incompatible—with the expectations of Mormon gospel living? What cultural hangups and confusions thwart (or perhaps in some cases even facilitate) the spreading of the restored gospel to new societies and cultures? Would it be heresy to be an anti-American Mormon? Are processes of secularization making a mockery of our religious practices?

In this book we have looked at selected aspects of the Mormon experience today as if through the small end of the telescope, attempting at the same time to relate our conclusions to the prophetic macro view. It has been an interesting experience; and it has produced diverse responses. Many readers and observers of this book and the symposia from which it derived have been pleased with what has been said. Others were pleased for what was not said. Still others commented: "This is really outstanding and stimulating. Do the General Authorities approve?" Some wondered about the format, others the content, others the handling of the materials—why some really tough questions were not addressed, why more was not said, why it was not said more vigorously, why it was said at all.

The experience differentially produced motivation and skepticism, elation and frustration. Some rejoiced at what they were provoked to think about, others at what they were given an opportunity to ponder. Some desired neither. In microcosm, our experience and the dynamics associated with the symposia and this book have produced many of the emotions about the Church that members at large are experiencing today. Dichotomy exists in contrary sentiments of hope and frustration, motivation, and soberness that is associated with an investigation of heartfelt subjects from the small end of the telescope. It is because our experiences are so diverse, because we feel them so deeply; and we are not yet "of one mind" on these matters.

But we look at our differences as well as our togetherness because all of it is part of our experience. It all vitally affects individual lives, strikes at the heart of the Mormon experience for members in Europe, Latin America, and Asia, and perhaps points the way to higher levels of understanding among Mormons everywhere. While the gospel will prevail, will your family? Mine? Will we, in our individual actions and behavior, benefit the Church or be a liability to it? Proper guides to answers to these questions come by looking from time to time through the small end of the telescope, thereby combining the prophetic with the actual, and the promise with concrete guides to achieve it. Who will say that is not important?

But there is a danger in spending too much time at the small end of the telescope. Elder Gordon B. Hinckley, in his BYU devotional address of 8 April 1976, commented that all our problems of cultural and secular conflict pale when compared to the importance of that which binds us together. That is a worthy subject. And we should not forget it, as might be the case if we spent all our time at the small end of the telescope. While we struggle with our differences, a constant reminder of the prophetic substance that binds us together will help produce a desire, through spirit and understanding, to develop a "circumcision of the heart," a frame of mind that will allow us to bind diverse cultural peoples into the fabric of the Church through willingness not only to tolerate diversity but to respect it. Here, as Elder Hinckley also said in his devotional address, the Spirit of the Lord can overcome differences in cultural and secular points of view among us, because he that teaches by the spirit and he that listens by the spirit can communicate.

He that teaches by the spirit must also know of what he teaches; and he that listens by the spirit must also recognize to what he listens. No one ever said we could absolve ourselves from the obligation to search for the spirit *and* understanding. Again, the events of the Sacred Grove will forever stand as testimony. We return, therefore, to the small end of the telescope, appropriately reminded by Elder Hinckley that in so doing we should remember that large end and look through it frequently.

While the future will not be painless, we may (as we rise, more experienced and less parochial, to the challenges of the twenty-first century) indeed see a part of the promised brotherhood of Jesus Christ meet its prophetic destiny. Should that be our happy lot, we are certain to rejoice with the heavens in having learned at long last to inspire our experiences of reality with a perception of the spiritual and to incarnate the spiritual with a comprehension of reality, of one another, and of what may be if we but learn how to help make the prophetic utterances of the centuries come to pass in our own lifetime.